CONNECTICUT FIREARMS LAW REFERENCE GUIDE

2022

CONNECTICUT FIREARMS LAW REFERENCE GUIDE
2022

Edited by
Harwood W. Loomis

Connecticut Firearms Law Reference Guide 2022

ISBN: 978-1-957418-17-9

Published by:
ELDERSLIE PRESS
172 Peck Hill Road
Woodbridge, Connecticut 06525
United States of America

ACKNOWLEDGEMENTS

The editor wishes to thank former Connecticut Assistant Attorney General Stephen Sarnoski for creating the first editions of this *Guide.* Just the work of researching new legislation and updating both the statutes and the comments and annotations turned out to be considerably more work than originally envisioned. The creation of the first version of this *Guide* and the subsequent updates must have been a Herculean undertaking. Residents of and visitors to Connecticut are indebted to Mr. Sarnoski for his foresight in creating a single source reference document providing access to the myriad of laws and regulations affecting the ownership and use of firearms in the State of Connecticut

PREFACE

The 2022 edition of the *Connecticut Firearms Law Reference Guide* attempts to continue the excellent work begun by Assistant Attorney General Stephen Sarnoski, Office of the Attorney General (Public Safety Department) in cooperation with the Department of Emergency Services and Public Protection Legal Affairs Unit, who generated previous editions of the *Guide* in order to provide a single resource for the most commonly referenced state and federal firearms-related statutes. Mr. Sarnoski retired from State service following the release of the 2015 edition of the *Guide*. Because the State of Connecticut acknowledged that they would not continue to update the Guide following Mr. Sarnoski's retirement, the editor, in recognition of the value of having a single, consolidated reference source for these laws, has undertaken to continue Mr. Sarnoski's excellent work. The current edition has been updated to include changes and additions to Connecticut statutes, as well as (to the best of our ability) changes to relevant Federal statutes and regulations related to the administration of firearms related law which are commonly referred to by police officers and administrators in the course of their duties.

The Connecticut General Statutes are not subject to copyright, nor are the case law citations appended to statutes on the State's web site. However, commentaries from previous editions of the *Connecticut Firearms Law Reference Guide* are work of Stephen Sarnoski, and are used herein by permission of Mr. Sarnoski.

Readers wishing to pursue case law citations regarding any of the statutes reproduced in this *Guide* may research the statute(s) on the State's web site at:

https://www.cga.ct.gov/current/pub/titles.htm

Inquiries concerning this publication, or suggestions for correction of errors or inclusion of additional statutes or regulations should be directed to the following:

Elderslie Press
PO Box 323
Seymour, CT 06483

TABLE OF CONTENTS

Page

PART 1: STATE STATUTES AND REGULATIONS

STATUTES

CONNECTICUT PUBLIC ACTS

CONNECTICUT ADMINISTRATIVE REGULATIONS

PART 2: FEDERAL STATUTES AND REGULATIONS

FEDERAL STATUTES

FEDERAL REGULATIONS

FEDERAL ACTS

CONNECTICUT FIREARMS LAW REFERENCE GUIDE

2022

PART 1: STATE STATUTES AND REGULATIONS

Connecticut General Statutes

Sec. 10-18b. Development of curriculum guides for firearm safety programs.

The State Board of Education, within available appropriations, shall develop guides to aid local and regional boards of education in developing firearm safety programs for students in grades kindergarten to twelve, inclusive, in the public schools. The State Board of Education may consult with the Connecticut Police Chiefs Association when developing such guides. The State Board of Education shall make such guides available to local and regional boards of education.

Sec. 10-18c. Firearm safety programs. Exemption from participation.

(a) Any local or regional board of education may offer firearm safety programs to students in grades kindergarten to twelve, inclusive, in the public schools under its jurisdiction.

(b) No student shall be required by any local or regional board of education to participate in a firearm safety program which may be offered within the public schools. A written notification to the local or regional board by the student's parent or legal guardian shall be sufficient to exempt the student from such program in its entirety or from any portion thereof so specified by the parent or legal guardian.

(c) If a student is exempted from a firearm safety program pursuant to subsection (b) of this section, the local or regional board of education shall provide, during the period of time in which the student would otherwise be participating in such program, an opportunity for other study or academic work.

Sec. 12-412. Exemptions.

Taxes imposed by this chapter shall not apply to the gross receipts from the sale of and the storage, use or other consumption in this state with respect to the following items:

...

(101) **Firearm safety devices.** Sales of and the storage, use or other consumption of firearm safety devices. For purposes of this subdivision, "firearm safety devices" shall include safes, lock boxes, trigger and barrel locks and other items designed to enhance home firearm safety.

Sec. 17a-495. Definitions.

(a) For the purposes of sections 17a-75 to 17a-83, inclusive, and 17a-615 to 17a-618, inclusive, the following terms shall have the following meanings: "Business day" means Monday to Friday, inclusive, except when a legal holiday falls on any such day; "hospital for psychiatric disabilities" means any public or private hospital, retreat, institution, house or place in which any mentally ill person is received or detained as a patient, but shall not include any correctional institution of this state; "mentally ill person" means any person who has a mental or emotional condition which has substantial adverse effects on his or her ability to function and who requires care and treatment, and specifically excludes a person who is an alcohol-dependent person or a drug-dependent person, as defined in section 17a-680; "patient" means any person detained and taken care of as a mentally ill person; "keeper of a hospital for psychiatric disabilities" means any person, body of persons or corporation which has the immediate superintendence, management and control of a hospital for psychiatric disabilities and the patients therein; "support" includes all necessary food, clothing and medicine and all general expenses of maintaining state hospitals for persons with psychiatric disabilities; "indigent person" means any person who has an estate insufficient, in the judgment of the Court of Probate, to provide for his or her support and has no person or persons legally liable who are able to support him or her; "dangerous to himself or herself or others" means there is a substantial risk that physical harm will be inflicted by an individual upon his or her own person or upon another person, and "gravely disabled" means that a person, as a result of mental or emotional impairment, is in danger of serious harm as a result of an inability or failure to provide for his or her own basic human needs such as essential food, clothing, shelter or safety and that hospital treatment is necessary and available and that such person is mentally incapable of determining whether or not to accept such treatment because his judgment is impaired by his psychiatric disabilities. "Respondent" means a person who is alleged to be mentally ill and for whom an application for commitment to a hospital for persons with psychiatric disabilities has been filed; "voluntary patient" means any patient sixteen years of age or older who applies in writing to and is admitted to a hospital for psychiatric disabilities as a mentally ill person or any patient under sixteen years of age whose parent or legal guardian applies in writing to such hospital for admission of such patient; "involuntary patient" means any patient hospitalized pursuant to an order of a judge of the Probate Court after an appropriate hearing or a patient hospitalized for emergency diagnosis, observation or treatment upon certification of a qualified physician.

(b) For the purposes of sections 17a-450 to 17a-484, inclusive, 17a-495 to 17a-528, inclusive, 17a-540 to 17a-550, inclusive, and 17a-560 to 17a-576, inclusive, the following terms shall have the following meanings: "Business day" means Monday to Friday, inclusive, except when a legal holiday falls on any such day; "hospital for persons with psychiatric disabilities" means any public or private hospital, retreat, institution, house or place in which any person with psychiatric disabilities is received or detained as a patient, but shall not include any correctional institution of this state; "patient" means any person detained and taken care of as a person with psychiatric disabilities; "keeper of a hospital for persons with psychiatric disabilities" means any person, body of persons or corporation which has the immediate superintendence, management and control of a hospital for persons with psychiatric disabilities and the patients therein; "support" includes all necessary food, clothing and medicine and all general expenses of maintaining state hospitals for persons with psychiatric disabilities; "indigent person" means any person who has an estate insufficient, in the judgment of the Court of Probate, to provide for his or her support and has no person or persons legally liable who are able to support him or her; "dangerous to himself or herself or others" means there is a substantial risk that physical harm will be inflicted by an individual upon his or her own person or upon another person; "gravely disabled" means that a person, as a result of mental or emotional impairment, is in danger of serious harm as a result of an inability or failure to provide for his or her own basic human needs such as essential food, clothing, shelter or safety and that hospital treatment is necessary and available and that such person is mentally incapable of determining whether or not to accept such treatment because his judgment is impaired by his psychiatric disabilities; "respondent" means a person who is alleged to have psychiatric disabilities and for whom an application for commitment to a hospital for persons with psychiatric disabilities has been filed; "voluntary patient" means any patient sixteen years of age or older who applies in writing to and is admitted to a hospital for persons with psychiatric disabilities as a person with psychiatric disabilities or any patient under sixteen years of age whose parent or legal guardian applies in writing to such hospital for admission of such patient; and "involuntary patient" means any patient hospitalized pursuant to an order of a judge of the Probate Court after an appropriate hearing or a patient hospitalized for emergency diagnosis, observation or treatment upon certification of a qualified physician.

(c) For the purposes of sections 17a-495 to 17a-528, inclusive, "person with psychiatric disabilities" means any person who has a mental or emotional condition which has substantial adverse effects on his or her ability to function and who requires care and treatment, and specifically excludes a person who is an alcohol-dependent person or a drug-dependent person, as defined in section 17a-680.

(d) For the purposes of sections 17a-452 to 17a-454, inclusive, 17a-456, 17a-458 to 17a-464, inclusive, 17a-466 to 17a-469, inclusive, 17a-471, 17a-474, 17a-476 to 17a-484, inclusive, 17a-540 to 17a-550, inclusive, 17a-560 to 17a-576, inclusive, and 17a-615 to 17a-618, inclusive, "person with psychiatric disabilities" means any person who has a mental or emotional condition which has substantial adverse effects on his or her ability to function and who requires care and treatment, and specifically includes a person who is an alcohol-dependent person or a drug-dependent person, as defined in section 17a-680.

Sec. 17a-500. Maintenance and confidentiality of records of cases of persons with psychiatric disabilities. Exchange of information concerning commitment or admission status of firearm permit or certificate applicants and holders.

(a) Each court of probate shall keep a record of the cases relating to persons with psychiatric disabilities coming before it under sections 17a-75 to 17a-83, inclusive, 17a-450 to 17a-484, inclusive, 17a-495 to 17a-528, inclusive, 17a-540 to 17a-550, inclusive, 17a-560 to 17a-576, inclusive, and 17a-615 to 17a-618, inclusive, and the disposition of them. It shall also keep on file the original application and certificate of physicians required by said sections, or a microfilm duplicate of such records in accordance with regulations issued by the Probate Court Administrator. All records maintained in the courts of probate under the provisions of said sections shall be sealed and available only to the respondent or his or her counsel unless the Court of Probate, after hearing held with notice to the respondent, determines such records should be disclosed for cause shown.

(b) The Commissioner of Mental Health and Addiction Services shall, notwithstanding the provisions of subsection (a) of this section, maintain information, in accordance with section 17a-499, on commitment orders by a probate court, and shall maintain information, in accordance with section 17a-506a, on voluntary admissions, and shall provide such information to the Commissioner of Emergency Services and Public Protection in fulfillment of his obligations under sections 29-28 to 29-38, inclusive, and section 53-202d, in such a manner as to report identifying information on the commitment or voluntary admission status, including, but not limited to, name, address, sex, date of birth and date of commitment or admission, for a person who applies for or holds a permit or certificate under said sections 29-28 to 29-38, inclusive, and section 53-202d. The Commissioner of Emergency Services and Public Protection shall maintain as confidential any such information provided to him and shall use such information only for purposes of fulfilling his obligations under sections 29-28 to 29-38, inclusive, and section 53-202d, except that nothing in this section shall prohibit said commissioner from entering such information into evidence at a hearing held in accordance with section 29-32b.

(c) (1) The Commissioner of Mental Health and Addiction Services shall obtain from the Commissioner of Emergency Services and Public Protection the status of any firearm application, permit or certificate under sections 29-28 to 29-38, inclusive, and section 53-202d, of each person who is the subject of an order of commitment as provided in section 17a-499 or is the subject of a voluntary admission as provided in section 17a-506a, in such a manner so as to only receive a report on the firearm application, permit or certificate status of the person with respect to whom the inquiry is made.

(2) The Commissioner of Mental Health and Addiction Services shall report to the Commissioner of Emergency Services and Public Protection any commitment or voluntary admission status and identifying information for any person who is an applicant for or holder of any permit or certificate under said sections 29-28 to 29-38, inclusive, and section 53-202d.

(3) The Commissioner of Mental Health and Addiction Services shall advise the hospital for psychiatric disabilities to which a person has been committed or voluntarily admitted of the status of a firearm application, permit or certificate of such person under sections 29-28 to 29-38, inclusive, and section 53-202d, as reported by the Commissioner of Emergency Services and Public Protection for consideration by such hospital in any psychiatric treatment procedures.

(4) The Commissioner of Mental Health and Addiction Services and a hospital for psychiatric disabilities shall maintain as confidential any information provided to said commissioner or such hospital concerning the status of a firearm application, permit or certificate under sections 29-28 to 29-38, inclusive, and section 53-202d, of any person.

Sec. 22a-74a. Exemption of firing and shooting ranges from criminal and civil liability for noise and noise pollution.

(a) Any owner, operator or user of a firing or shooting range operating on October 1, 1998, shall be exempt from criminal prosecution with respect to noise or noise pollution violations and immune from civil liability with respect to noise or noise pollution resulting from shooting activity on such range provided the range was, at the time of its construction or operational approval by the municipality in which it is located, in compliance with the provisions of this chapter and regulations adopted hereunder.

(b) No standards in a noise control ordinance adopted by any municipality for limiting levels of noise in terms of decibel level which may occur in the outdoor atmosphere shall apply to any firing or shooting range exempted from liability under this section if such standards are inconsistent with the provisions of this chapter or the regulations adopted hereunder.

(c) This section shall not limit the liability of a municipality to evaluate and regulate any increase in noise attributable to a physical expansion of an existing firing or shooting range.

Sec. 29-7h. Firearms evidence databank.

(a) As used in this section:

(1) "Firearms evidence databank" means a computer-based system that scans a test fire and stores an image of such test fire in a manner suitable for retrieval and comparison to other test fires and to other evidence in a case;

(2) "Handgun" means any firearm capable of firing rim-fire or center-fire ammunition and designed or built to be fired with one hand;

(3) "Laboratory" means the Division of Scientific Services forensic science laboratory within the Department of Emergency Services and Public Protection;

(4) "Police department" means the Division of State Police within the Department of Emergency Services and Public Protection or an organized local police department;

(5) "Test fire" means discharged ammunition consisting of a cartridge case or a bullet or a fragment thereof, collected after a handgun is fired and containing sufficient microscopical characteristics to compare to other discharged ammunition or to determine the handgun from which the ammunition was fired.

(b) (1) The Division of Scientific Services shall establish a firearms evidence databank. Test fire evidence submitted to the laboratory or collected from handguns submitted to the laboratory shall be entered into such databank in accordance with specific procedures adopted by the Commissioner of Emergency Services and Public Protection, in the regulations adopted pursuant to subsection (f) of this section.

(2) The firearms evidence databank may be used by laboratory personnel to (A) compare two or more cartridge cases, bullets or other projectiles submitted to the laboratory or produced at the laboratory from a handgun, or (B) upon the request of a police department as part of a criminal case investigation, verify by microscopic examination any resulting match, and shall produce a report stating the results of such a search.

(3) Any image of a cartridge case, bullet or fragment thereof that is not matched by a search of the databank shall be stored in the databank for future searches.

(4) The Division of Scientific Services may permit a firearms section of a police department that complies with all laboratory guidelines and regulations adopted by the commissioner pursuant to subsection (f) of this section regarding the operation of the firearms evidence databank to (A) collect test fires from handguns that come into the custody of the police department, (B) set up a remote terminal to enter test fire images directly into the databank, and (C) search the databank.

(c) (1) Except as provided in subdivision (4) of subsection (b) of this section and subsection (d) of this section, a police department shall submit to the laboratory any handgun that comes into police custody as a result of a criminal investigation, as found property, or for destruction, prior to the return or the destruction of the handgun.

(2) The laboratory shall collect a test fire from each submitted handgun within sixty days of submission. The laboratory shall label the test fire with the handgun manufacturer, type of weapon, serial number, date of the test fire and name of the person collecting the test fire.

(d) (1) A police department shall collect a test fire from every handgun issued by that department to an employee not later than six months after October 1, 2001. On and after October 1, 2001, a police department shall collect a test fire from every handgun to be issued by that department before the handgun is so issued. Any police department may request the assistance of the Division of State Police or the laboratory to collect a test fire.

(2) The police department shall seal the test fire in a tamper-evident manner and label the package with the handgun manufacturer, handgun type, serial number and the name of the person collecting the test fire. The police department shall submit the test fire and two intact cartridges of the same type of ammunition used for the test fire to the laboratory.

(e) The laboratory may share the information in the firearms evidence databank with other law enforcement agencies, both within and outside the state, and may participate in a national firearms evidence databank program.

(f) The commissioner shall adopt regulations, in accordance with the provisions of chapter 54, to carry out the purposes of this section.

Sec. 29-11. State Police Bureau of Identification. Fees. Agreements re fingerprinting. Regulations.

(a) The bureau in the Division of State Police within the Department of Emergency Services and Public Protection known as the State Police Bureau of Identification shall be maintained for the purposes of: (1) Providing an authentic record of each person sixteen years of age or over who is charged with the commission of any crime involving moral turpitude, (2) providing definite information relative to the identity of each person so arrested, (3) providing a record of the final judgment of the court resulting from such arrest, unless such record has been erased pursuant to section 54-142a, and (4) maintaining a central repository of complete criminal history record disposition information. The Commissioner of Emergency Services and Public Protection is directed to maintain the State Police Bureau of Identification, which bureau shall receive, classify and file in an orderly manner all fingerprints, pictures and descriptions, including previous criminal records as far as known of all persons so arrested, and shall classify and file in a like manner all identification material and records received from the government of the United States and from the various state governments and subdivisions thereof, and shall cooperate with such governmental units in the exchange of information relative to criminals. The State Police Bureau of Identification shall accept fingerprints of applicants for admission to the bar of the state and, to the extent permitted by federal law, shall exchange state, multistate and federal criminal history records with the State Bar Examining Committee for purposes of investigation of the qualifications of any applicant for admission as an attorney under section 51-80. The record of all arrests reported to the bureau after March 16, 1976, shall contain information of any disposition within ninety days after the disposition has occurred.

(b) Any cost incurred by the State Police Bureau of Identification in conducting any name search and fingerprinting of applicants for admission to the bar of the state shall be paid from fees collected by the State Bar Examining Committee.

(c) The Commissioner of Emergency Services and Public Protection shall charge the following fees for the service indicated: (1) Name search, thirty-six dollars; (2) fingerprint search, seventy-five dollars; (3) personal record search, seventy-five dollars; (4) letters of good conduct search, seventy-five dollars; (5) bar association search, seventy-five dollars; (6) fingerprinting, fifteen dollars; (7) criminal history record information search, seventy-five dollars. Except as provided in subsection (b) of this section, the provisions of this subsection shall not apply to any federal, state or municipal agency.

(d) The Commissioner of Emergency Services and Public Protection may enter into one or more agreements with independent contractors requiring such contractors to receive and transmit by electronic means fingerprints and demographic information to the State Police Bureau of Identification for the processing of criminal history records checks. The commissioner shall require such contractors to: (1) Collect and remit the fee charged for fingerprinting, as provided in subsection (c) of this section, to the State Police Bureau of Identification, and (2) comply with terms and conditions as the commissioner shall prescribe to protect and ensure the security, privacy, confidentiality and value of the fingerprints and demographic information received and transmitted by such contractors. The commissioner may authorize such contractors to charge a convenience fee, which shall not exceed fifteen dollars, for fingerprinting.

(e) The Commissioner of Emergency Services and Public Protection may adopt regulations, in accordance with the provisions of chapter 54, necessary to implement the provisions of the National Child Protection Act of 1993, the Violent Crime Control and Law Enforcement Act of 1994, the Volunteers for Children Act of 1998, and the National Crime Prevention and Privacy Compact as provided in section 29-164f to provide for national criminal history records checks to determine an employee's or volunteer's suitability and fitness to care for the safety and well-being of children, the elderly and individuals with disabilities.

Sec. 29-27. "Pistol" and "revolver" defined.

The term "pistol" and the term "revolver", as used in sections 29-28 to 29-38 inclusive, mean any firearm having a barrel less than twelve inches in length.

ANNOTATIONS:

State v. Williams, 231 Conn. 235 (1994):

In order to support conviction for criminal possession of "pistol," or "revolver," state is not required to introduce direct numerical evidence of length of barrel of handgun. *See also, State v. Garcia*, 7 Conn. App. 367 (1986).

State v. Allen, 205 Conn. 370 (1987):

State must provide at least some evidence of the length of the barrel of the gun to make out a prima facie case involving a "pistol" or "revolver." *See also, State v. Mcintyre*, 242 Conn. 318 (1997)

State v. Delossantos, 211 Conn. 258 (1989):

The terms "pistol" and "revolver" in Section 29-27, do not incorporate the definition of "firearm" found in Section 53a-3(19) of the Penal Law. This means where Section 29-27 is applicable, a "pistol" or "revolver" does not need to be capable of discharging a shot to meet the statutory definition of a "pistol" or "revolver," as would be necessary under Section 53a-3(19) of the Penal Law.

Sec. 29-28. Permit for sale at retail of pistol or revolver. Permit to carry pistol or revolver. Confidentiality of name and address of permit holder. Permits for out-of-state residents.

(a) No person who sells ten or more pistols or revolvers in a calendar year or is a federally licensed firearm dealer shall advertise, sell, deliver, or offer or expose for sale or delivery, or have in such person's possession with intent to sell or deliver, any pistol or revolver at retail without having a permit therefor issued as provided in this subsection. The chief of police or, where there is no chief of police, the warden of the borough or the first selectman of the town, as the case may be, may, upon the application of any person, issue a permit in such form as may be prescribed by the Commissioner of Emergency Services and Public Protection for the sale at retail of pistols and revolvers within the jurisdiction of the authority issuing such permit. No permit for the sale at retail of any pistol or revolver shall be issued unless the applicant holds a valid eligibility certificate for a pistol or revolver issued pursuant to section 29-36f or a valid state permit to carry a pistol or revolver issued pursuant to subsection (b) of this section and the applicant submits documentation sufficient to establish that local zoning requirements have been met for the location where the sale is to take place, except that any person selling or exchanging a pistol or revolver for the enhancement of a personal collection or for a hobby or who sells all or part of such person's personal collection of pistols or revolvers shall not be required to submit such documentation for the location where the sale or exchange is to take place.

(b) Upon the application of any person having a bona fide permanent residence within the jurisdiction of any such authority, such chief of police, warden or selectman may issue a temporary state permit to such person to carry a pistol or revolver within the state, provided such authority shall find that such applicant intends to make no use of any pistol or revolver which such applicant may be permitted to carry under such permit other than a lawful use and that such person is a suitable person to receive such permit. No state or temporary state permit to carry a pistol or revolver shall be issued under this subsection if the applicant (1) has failed to successfully complete a course approved by the Commissioner of Emergency Services and Public Protection in the safety and use of pistols and revolvers including, but not limited to, a safety or training course in the use of pistols and revolvers available to the public offered by a law enforcement agency, a private or public educational institution or a firearms training school, utilizing instructors certified by the National Rifle Association or the Department of Energy and Environmental Protection and a safety or training course in the use of pistols or revolvers conducted by an instructor certified by the state or the National Rifle Association, (2) has been convicted of (A) a felony, or (B) [on or after October 1, 1994,] a misdemeanor violation of section 21a-279 on or after October 1, 2015, or (C) a misdemeanor violation of section 53a-58, 53a-61, 53a-61a, 53a-62, 53a-63, 53a-96, 53a-175, 53a-176, 53a-178 or 53a-181d during the preceding twenty years, (3) has been convicted as delinquent for the commission of a serious juvenile offense, as defined in section 46b-120, (4) has been discharged from custody within the preceding twenty years after having been found not guilty of a crime by reason of mental disease or defect pursuant to section 53a-13, (5) (A) has been confined in a hospital for persons with psychiatric disabilities, as defined in section 17a-495, within the preceding sixty months by order of a probate court, or (B) has been voluntarily admitted on or after October 1, 2013, to a hospital for persons with psychiatric disabilities, as defined in section 17a-495, within the preceding six months for care and treatment of a psychiatric disability and not solely for being an alcohol-dependent person or a drug-dependent person as those terms are defined in section 17a-680, (6) is subject to a restraining or protective order issued by a court in a case involving the use, attempted use or threatened use of physical force against another person, including an ex parte order issued pursuant to section 46b-15 or 46b-16a, (7) is subject to a firearms seizure order issued prior to June 1, 2022, pursuant to [subsection (d) of] section 29-38c after notice and hearing, or a risk protection order or risk protection investigation order issued on or after June 1, 2022, pursuant to section 29-38c, as amended by this act, (8) is prohibited from shipping, transporting, possessing or receiving a firearm pursuant to 18 USC 922(g)(4), (9) is an alien illegally or unlawfully in the United States, or (10) is less than twenty-one years of age. Nothing in this section shall require any person who holds a valid permit to carry a pistol or revolver on October 1, 1994, to participate in any additional training in the safety and use of pistols and revolvers. No person may apply for a temporary state permit to carry a pistol or revolver more than once within any twelve-month period, and no temporary state permit to carry a pistol or revolver shall be issued to any person who has applied for such permit more than once within the preceding twelve months. Any person who applies for a temporary state permit to carry a pistol or revolver shall indicate in writing on the application, under penalty of false statement in such manner as the issuing authority prescribes, that such person has not applied for a temporary state permit to carry a pistol or revolver within the past twelve months. Upon issuance of a temporary state permit to carry a pistol or revolver to the applicant, the local authority shall forward the original application to the commissioner. Not later than sixty days after receiving a temporary state permit, an applicant shall appear at a location designated by the commissioner to receive the state permit. The commissioner may then issue, to any holder of any temporary state permit, a state permit to carry a pistol or revolver within the state. issuance of the state permit, the commissioner shall make available to the permit holder a copy of the law regarding the permit holder's responsibility to report the loss or theft of a firearm and the penalties associated with the failure to comply with such law. Upon issuance of the state permit, the commissioner shall forward a record of such permit to the local authority issuing the temporary state permit. The commissioner shall retain records of all applications, whether approved or denied. The copy of the state permit delivered to the permittee shall be laminated and shall contain a full-face photograph of such permittee. A person holding a state permit issued pursuant to this subsection shall notify the issuing authority within two business days of any change of such person's address. The notification shall include the old address and the new address of such person.

(c) No issuing authority may require any sworn member of the Department of Emergency Services and Public Protection or an organized local police department to furnish such sworn member's residence address in a permit application. The issuing authority shall allow each such sworn member who has a permit to carry a pistol or revolver issued by such authority to revise such member's application to include a business or post office address in lieu of the residence address. The issuing authority shall notify each such member of the right to revise such application.

(d) Notwithstanding the provisions of sections 1-210 and 1-211, the name and address of a person issued a permit to sell at retail pistols and revolvers pursuant to subsection (a) of this section or a state or a temporary state permit to carry a pistol or revolver pursuant to subsection (b) of this section, or a local permit to carry pistols and revolvers issued by local authorities prior to October 1, 2001, shall be confidential and shall not be disclosed, except (1) such information may be disclosed to law enforcement officials acting in the performance of their duties, including, but not limited to, employees of the United States Probation Office acting in the performance of their duties, and parole officers within the Department of Correction acting in the performance of their duties, (2) the issuing authority may disclose such information to the extent necessary to comply with a request made pursuant to section 29-33, 29-37a or 29-38m for verification that such state or temporary state permit is still valid and has not been suspended or revoked, and the local authority may disclose such information to the extent necessary to comply with a request made pursuant to section 29-33, 29-37a or 29-38m for verification that a local permit is still valid and has not been suspended or revoked, and (3) such information may be disclosed to the Commissioner of Mental Health and Addiction Services to carry out the provisions of subsection (c) of section 17a-500.

(e) The issuance of any permit to carry a pistol or revolver does not thereby authorize the possession or carrying of a pistol or revolver in any premises where the possession or carrying of a pistol or revolver is otherwise prohibited by law or is prohibited by the person who owns or exercises control over such premises.

(f) Any bona fide resident of the United States having no bona fide permanent residence within the juris0diction of any local authority in the state, but who has a permit or license to carry a pistol or revolver issued by the authority of another state or subdivision of the United States, may apply directly to the Commissioner of Emergency Services and Public Protection for a permit to carry a pistol or revolver in this state. All provisions of subsections (b), (c), (d) and (e) of this section shall apply to applications for a permit received by the commissioner under this subsection.

ANNOTATIONS:

State v. Eliglio, 172 Conn. 21, 372 A.2d 141 (1976):

The State has the burden of proof in showing that an individual did not have a proper pistol permit when charging an individual with any form of unlawful possession of a pistol.

Dwyer v. Farrell, 193 Conn. 7, 475 A.2d 257 (1984):

State statutes, including Section 29-28, preempt local ordinances seeking to regulate the same class of activity when the local ordinance is in conflict with the state statute, or when the local ordinance substantially frustrates the legislative intent for the state statute. This means a municipality cannot restrict the sale of pistols, or the permitting process, in any way that would frustrate the current statutory scheme of Section 29-28.

Superintendent of Police of the City of Bridgeport v. Freedom of Information Commission, 222 Conn. 621, 609 A.2d 998 (1992):

Municipal permits for the carrying of pistols and revolvers are not exempted from disclosure under the Freedom of Information Act. The City of Bridgeport tried to claim that pistol permits were "similar" files, compared to medical and personnel files, and exempt under Section 1-210(b)(2) of the Connecticut General Statutes, but the court rejected the claim.

State v. Brunson, 36 Conn. App. 576, 651 A.2d 1335 (1995):

The State does not need to prove that a defendant does not have a pistol permit in any jurisdiction as an element of a crime, the State need only show that the defendant did not have a pistol permit, and therefore the right to carry, within the jurisdiction in which the defendant is charged.

Storace v. Mariano, 35 Conn. Supp. 28, 391 A.2d 1347 (1978):

In overturning the BFPE's finding that Storace was not a suitable person based on lack of factual support, the court stated that the term "suitable" person has a legally fixed meaning which should be construed in light of the fundamental purposes of the statute regulating the activity.

Final Decision, Petition for Declaratory Ruling of, inter alia, the Board of Firearms Permit Examiners by Jack Goldberg, (January 14, 2010):

Nothing in the statute authorizes an issuing authority to add to the requirements of the statute or to the form prescribed by the Commissioner of Public Safety at the time a person submits an application for a permit to carry pistols and revolvers. ... Refusal to submit additional material with the initial application, such as letters of reference, does not, ipso facto, render the applicant unsuitable. ... If the issue of applicant's suitability arises during the investigation, and the issuing authority seeks further specific information, failure to provide such information may, by itself, be sufficient to deem an applicant unsuitable. However, such a determination must be made on a case by case basis.

Commissioner, Dept. Of Public Safety v. Bd. Of Firearms Permit Examiners, 2010 Conn. Super. LEXIS 1750, 2010 WL 3039575 (Superior Court, J.J. New Britain) (July 13, 2010), reversed on other grounds, Commissioner of Public Safety v. Bd. Of Firearms Permit Examiners, 129 Conn. App. 414, 21 A.3d 847 (2011):

The "other than lawful use" test gives the Commissioner of the Connecticut Department of Public Safety the important authority to deny a permit when he becomes aware of conduct that is relevant to handgun possession but did not result in a conviction or even an arrest. The Commissioner has the authority to deny, and thus to revoke, a permit when he finds that the applicant intends to make a use of any pistol or revolver which such applicant may be permitted to carry under such permit other than a lawful use, regardless of whether the Commissioner could nonetheless deem the applicant a suitable person.

Commissioner of Public Safety v. Bd. Of Firearms Permit Examiners, 129 Conn. App. 414, 21 A.3d. 847 (2011):

The words "suitable person" have a definite meaning in Connecticut law, and their use in the act furnishes a standard by which the agency must be guided. A person is suitable who, by reason of his character, his reputation in the community, his previous conduct as a licensee, is shown to be suited or adapted to the orderly conduct of a business which the law regards as so dangerous to public welfare that its transaction by any other than a carefully selected person duly licensed is made a criminal offense. It is patent that the adaptability of any person to such a business depends upon facts and circumstances that may be indicated but cannot be fully defined by law, whose probative force will differ in different cases, and must in each case depend largely upon the sound judgment of the selecting tribunal. Specifically in the context of a firearms permit, Conn. Gen. Stat. §§ 29-28 through 29-38 clearly indicate a legislative intent to protect the safety of the general public from individuals whose conduct has shown them to be lacking the essential character or temperament necessary to be entrusted with a weapon.

Kibbie v. Danaher, Docket No. 10-278-R (Board of Firearms Permit Examiners) (October 31, 2011):

On appeal to the Board of Firearms Permit Examiners, revocation of appellant's permit to carry pistols or revolvers in Connecticut was affirmed where he engaged in an ongoing dispute with his neighbor, displayed confrontational, antagonistic and aberrant behavior, had a history of minor criminal convictions for Breach of Peace and Harassment, stored weapons in an unsafe manner within his home and failed to convince the Board that he could conform himself to the ordinary requirements of the law if he were permitted to go at large while armed.

Kuck v. Danaher, 822 F.Supp.2d 109 (D.Conn. 2011):

Discretionary "suitability" requirement under Connecticut statute governing issuance of permits to carry pistol or revolver in public was substantially related to state's compelling interest in protecting public from persons who could pose a danger if entrusted with firearm, and therefore state public safety officials did not violate permittee's Second Amendment right to bear arms by revoking his pistol permit based upon determination, under statute, that he was not "suitable" to hold permit in light of his arrest for breach of the peace; statute could not set forth every possible circumstance in which person could pose unacceptable danger to public if entrusted with firearm, suitability requirement did not give officials unbridled discretion in permit decisions, and permittee's arrest provided reasonable basis for revocation pending further determination of his suitability to hold permit.

Kristoffersen v. Bradford, Docket No. 11-29-R (Board of Firearms Permit Examiners) (January 6, 2012):

On appeal to the Board of Firearms Permit Examiners, revocation of the appellant's permit to carry pistols or revolvers in the State of Connecticut was affirmed where he confronted a jogger on a trail in a state park, and became involved in a verbal altercation regarding the jogger's failure to have his dogs on a leash while running, drew his gun out of fear of the dogs even though they were not acting aggressively, and was subsequently arrested for reckless endangerment and carrying a handgun on state property.

Deblasi v. Dortenzio, Docket No. 12-253-D (Board of Firearms Permit Examiners) (September 14, 2012):

Appeal from denial of temporary permit to carry pistols or revolvers by Chief of Police Town of Wallingford, upheld where appellant stood convicted of Criminal Mischief in the Second Degree, Falsely Reporting an Incident, Breach of Peace in the Second Degree, and Speeding within the five year period preceding his application. Testimony at hearing further established that appellant wrongfully impersonated a police officer, requiring the Board to give paramount consideration to the protection of the public safety and deny a pistol permit to an individual who lacks the essential character or temperament necessary to be trusted with a weapon.

Peruta v. Freedom of Information Commission, 157 Conn. App. 684 (2015):

Freedom of Information Commission properly construed public safety statute when it concluded that the intention of the legislature was to exempt from disclosure under Freedom of Information Act the names and addresses of persons who had applied for but had not yet received permits to carry revolvers or pistols.

Commentary

The Final Decision, Petition for Declaratory Ruling of, inter alia, the Board of Firearms Permit Examiners by Jack Goldberg, (January 14, 2010) contains an excellent summary of the substantive and procedural requirements and limitations surrounding the submission and consideration of an application for a permit to carry a pistol or revolver in the State of Connecticut. The Final Decision of the Board of Firearms Permit Examiners set forth therein constitutes a quick, but valuable, reference for anyone who intends to submit such an application, who is considering such an application on behalf of an issuing authority, or who intends to appear before the Board of Firearms Permit Examiners during the course of an appeal.

Sec. 29-28a. Application for permit. Notice of decision to applicant.

(a) Requests for temporary state permits under section 29-28 shall be submitted to the chief of police, or, where there is no chief of police, to the warden of the borough or the first selectman of the town, as the case may be, on application forms prescribed by the Commissioner of Emergency Services and Public Protection. Upon written request by any person for a temporary state permit not on a prescribed application form, or upon request by any person for such application form, the local authority shall supply such forms. When any such request is made in person at the office of the local authority, the local authority shall supply such application form immediately. When any such request is made in any other manner, the local authority shall supply such application form not later than one week after receiving such request. If such application form is not supplied within the time limits required by this section, the request therefore shall constitute a sufficient application. If any local authority fails to supply an application form upon the request of any person, such person may request an application form from the Commissioner of Emergency Services and Public Protection or any barracks of the Division of State Police, and the time limits and procedures set forth in this section for handling request for such forms shall be applicable.

(b) The local authority shall, not later than eight weeks after a sufficient application for a temporary state permit has been made, inform the applicant that such applicant's request for a temporary state permit has been approved or denied. The local authority shall forward a copy of the application indicating approval or denial of the temporary state permit to the Commissioner of Emergency Services and Public Protection. If the local authority has denied the application for a temporary state permit, no state permit may be issued. The commissioner shall, not later than eight weeks after receiving an application indicating approval from the local authority, inform the applicant in writing that the applicant's application for a state permit has been approved or denied, or that the results of the national criminal history records check have not been received. If grounds for denial become known after a temporary state permit has been obtained, the temporary state permit shall be immediately revoked pursuant to section 29-32.

ANNOTATIONS:

Ambrogio v. Bd. Of Firearms Permit Examiners, 42 Conn. Supp. 157, 607 A.2d 460 (Conn. Super. 1992):

Appeal was taken from order of board of firearms permit examiners which directed that handgun permit be issued. The Superior Court, Judicial District of Hartford, New

Britain, demayo, J., held that statutory provision that police chief shall make finding on application for gun permit within eight weeks is directory, not mandatory, and police chief may await results of FBI fingerprint check.

Dwyer v. Farrell, 193 Conn. 7, 13, 475 A.2d. 257 (1984):

General Statutes §§ 29-28 through 29-38 clearly indicate a legislative intent to protect the safety of the general public from individuals whose conduct has shown them to be lacking the essential character or temperament necessary to be entrusted with a weapon.

Appeal of Smith, 65 Conn. 135, 138, 31 A. 529 (1894):

The word "suitable" as descriptive of an applicant for license under the statute, is insusceptible of any legal definition that wholly excludes the personal views of the tribunal authorized to determine the suitability of the applicant. A person is "suitable" who by reason of his character--his reputation in the community, his previous conduct as a licensee--is shown to be suited or adapted to the orderly conduct of a business which the law regards as so dangerous to public welfare that its transaction by any other than a carefully selected person duly licensed is made a criminal offense. It is patent that the adaptability of any person to such a business depends upon facts and circumstances that may be indicated but cannot be fully defined by law, whose probative force will differ in different cases, and must in each case depend largely upon the sound judgment of the selecting tribunal.

Connecticut Board of Firearms Permit Examiners v. Narowski, Docket No. CV12-6028868 (Superior Court, J.D. Hartford) (February 3, 2012):

Order for Writ of Mandamus directing the Police Chief for the Town of Derby, Connecticut, absent evidence of unsuitability, to issue a permit to carry pistols or revolvers to aggrieved applicant following police chief's failure to carry out the order of the Board. Costs adjudged against the Town of Derby in the amount of $51.79.

Commentary

The statute does not contain any definition of the phrase "suitable person." Nor have the appellate courts precisely defined the phrase "suitable person" under the firearms statutes. Instead, they have held only generally that the purpose of the firearms permit statutes is to determine whether the applicant lacks "the essential character or temperament necessary to be entrusted with a weapon. Thus, while an applicant's improper use of a firearm is undoubtedly a factor to consider in the permit process, neither the legislature nor the appellate courts have made it a disqualifying factor as a matter of law. As a result, the revocation of a permit to carry firearms will focus on all of the facts and circumstances relevant to the question of whether a specific individual presents a danger to the public if allowed to publicly carry a firearm in the future. For additional details concerning the decisional process associated with determining who is a suitable person to carry a pistol or revolver in the State of Connecticut, the reader should refer to the Final Decision, Petition for Declaratory Ruling of, inter alia, the Board of Firearms Permit Examiners by Jack Goldberg, (January 14, 2010), a complete copy of which has been appended to this publication at Appendix B.

Sec. 29-29. Information concerning criminal records of applicants for permits.

(a) No temporary state permit for carrying any pistol or revolver shall be issued under the provisions of section 29-28 unless the applicant for such permit gives to the local authority, upon its request, full information concerning the applicant's criminal record. The local authority shall require the applicant to submit to state and national criminal history records checks. The local authority shall take a full description of such applicant and make an investigation concerning the applicant's suitability to carry any such weapons.

(b) The local authority shall take the fingerprints of such applicant or conduct any other method of positive identification required by the State Police Bureau of Identification or the Federal Bureau of Investigation, unless the local authority determines that the fingerprints of such applicant have been previously taken and the applicant's identity established, and such applicant presents identification that the local authority verifies as valid. The local authority shall record the date the fingerprints were taken in the applicant's file and, within five business days of such date, shall forward such fingerprints or other positive identifying information to the State Police Bureau of Identification which shall conduct criminal history records checks in accordance with section 29-17a.

(c) The local authority may, in its discretion, issue a temporary state permit before a national criminal history records check relative to such applicant's record has been received. Upon receipt of the results of such national criminal history records check, the commissioner shall send a copy of the results of such national criminal history records check to the local authority, which shall inform the applicant and render a decision on the application within one week of the receipt of such results. If such results have not been received within eight weeks after a sufficient application for a permit has been made, the local authority shall inform the applicant of such delay, in writing. No temporary state permit shall be issued if the local authority has reason to believe the applicant has ever been convicted of a felony, or that any other condition exists for which the issuance of a permit for possession of a pistol or revolver is prohibited under state or federal law.

(d) The commissioner may investigate any applicant for a state permit and shall investigate each applicant for renewal of a state permit to ensure that such applicant is eligible under state law for such permit or for renewal of such permit.

(e) No state permit may be issued unless either the local authority or the commissioner has received the results of the national criminal history records check.

ANNOTATIONS:

Baker v. Bd. Of Firearms Permit Examiners, 39 Conn. Supp. 202, 474 A.2d 115 (Conn. Super. 1984):

When an individual has their pistol permit revoked for a felony conviction, and they challenge the revocation, the board of Examiners must afford them a hearing, even when the basis of revocation is not discretionary.

Attorney General's Opinion No. 85-11(1985):

This section prohibits the issuance of a permit to a person who has been convicted of a felony and the post-conviction re-classification of the crime to a misdemeanor by the Legislature does not affect the statutory prohibition. 1985 Conn. Op. Atty. Gen. 37

Godbout v. Formica, Case No.12-356-D (Board of Firearms Permit Examiners) (December 18, 2012):

The applicant's failure to submit proof of the completion of the course in pistol safety prescribed by Conn. Gen. Stat. §29-28(b) is sufficient, by itself, to justify denial of his application for a permit to carry a pistol or revolver in the State of Connecticut. In addition, the appellant's intentional refusal to present a sufficient application; i.e., refusal to provide fingerprints; refusal to provide employment history; falsely answering the question concerning military service; and refusing to furnish a Form DD-214 [Certificate of Release or Discharge from Active Duty] constituted sufficient evidence of his unsuitability to carry a pistol or revolver in the State of Connecticut so as to find that the issuing authority's denial based on suitability was for just and proper cause.

Haughton v. Ackley, Case No. 13-054-D (Board of Firearms Permit Examiners) (January 24, 2013):

Appeal from denial of application for temporary permit to carry pistols or revolvers in the State of Connecticut by the Chief of Police, City of New London dismissed where applicant admitted to three previous arrests for possession, sale or transfer of illegal drugs, including both marijuana and crack cocaine, one of which resulted in a misdemeanor conviction, the others having been dismissed following successful completion of pre-trial diversionary programs.

Sec. 29-30. Fees for pistol and revolver permits. Expiration and renewal of permits. (a) The fee for each permit originally issued under the provisions of subsection (a) of section 29-28 for the sale at retail of pistols and revolvers shall be two hundred dollars and for each renewal of such permit two hundred dollars. The fee for each state permit originally issued under the provisions of subsection (b) of section 29-28 for the carrying of pistols and revolvers shall be one hundred forty dollars plus sufficient funds as required to be transmitted to the Federal Bureau of Investigation to cover the cost of a national criminal history records check. The local authority shall forward sufficient funds for the national criminal history records check to the commissioner no later than five business days after receipt by the local authority of the application for the temporary state permit. Seventy dollars shall be retained by the local authority. Upon approval by the local authority of the application for a temporary state permit, seventy dollars shall be sent to the commissioner. The fee to renew each state permit originally issued under the provisions of subsection (b) of section 29-28 shall be seventy dollars. Upon deposit of such fees in the General Fund, ten dollars of each fee shall be credited within thirty days to the appropriation for the Department of Emergency Services and Public Protection to a separate nonlapsing account for the purposes of the issuance of permits under subsections (a) and (b) of section 29-28.

(b) A local permit originally issued before October 1, 2001, whether for the sale at retail of pistols and revolvers or for the carrying of pistols and revolvers, shall expire five years after the date it becomes effective and each renewal of such permit shall expire five years after the expiration date of the permit being renewed. On and after October 1, 2001, no local permit for the carrying of pistols and revolvers shall be renewed.

(c) A state permit originally issued under the provisions of section 29-28 for the carrying of pistols and revolvers shall expire five years after the date such permit becomes effective and each renewal of such permit shall expire five years after the expiration date of the state permit being renewed and such renewal shall not be contingent on the renewal or issuance of a local permit. A temporary state permit issued for the carrying of pistols and revolvers shall expire sixty days after the date it becomes effective, and may not be renewed.

(d) The renewal fee required pursuant to subsection (a) of this section shall apply for each renewal which is requested not earlier than thirty-one days before, and not later than thirty-one days after, the expiration date of the state permit being renewed.

(e) No fee or portion of any fee paid under the provisions of this section for issuance or renewal of a state permit shall be refundable except if such permit for which the fee or portion was paid was not issued or renewed. The portion of the fee expended on the national criminal history records check for any such permit that was not issued or renewed shall not be refunded.

(f) The issuing authority shall send a notice of the expiration of a state permit to carry a pistol or revolver, issued pursuant to section 29-28, to the holder of such permit, by first class mail, not less than ninety days before such expiration, and shall enclose with such notice a form for the renewal of said state permit. The holder of such permit may mail the form for renewal to the issuing authority and the issuing authority shall accept such form as a valid application for renewal, provided the holder (1) completed the form according to instructions provided by the Department of Emergency Services and Public Protection, (2) enclosed the appropriate fee to renew, in accordance with subsection (a) of this section, (3) enclosed a copy of proof of citizenship or legal residency of the holder, (4) enclosed a photograph of the holder that is either notarized or date stamped, and (5) is otherwise eligible for such permit pursuant to section 29-28. A state permit to carry a pistol or revolver, issued pursuant to section 29-28, shall be valid for a period of ninety days after the expiration date, except this provision shall not apply to any state permit to carry a pistol or revolver which has been revoked or for which revocation is pending, pursuant to section 29-32.

Sec. 29-31. Display of permit to sell. Record of sales.

No sale of any pistol or revolver shall be made except in the room, store or place described in the permit for the sale of pistols and revolvers, and such permit or a copy thereof certified by the authority issuing the same shall be exposed to view within the room, store or place where pistols or revolvers are sold or offered or exposed for sale. No sale or delivery of any pistol or revolver shall be made unless the purchaser or person to whom the same is to be delivered is personally known to the vendor of such pistol or revolver or the person making delivery thereof or unless the person making such purchase or to whom delivery thereof is to be made provides evidence of his or her identity. The vendor of any pistol or revolver shall keep a record of each pistol or revolver sold in a book kept for that purpose, which record shall be in such form as is prescribed by 27 CFR 478.125. The vendor of any pistol or revolver shall make such record available for inspection upon the request of any sworn member of an organized local police department or the Division of State Police within the Department of Emergency Services and Public Protection or any investigator assigned to the statewide firearms trafficking task force established under section 29-38e.

Sec. 29-32. Revocation of permit. Notification. Confiscation. Penalty for failure to surrender permit. Reinstatement of permit.

(a) For the purposes of this section, "conviction" means the entry of a judgment of conviction by any court of competent jurisdiction.

(b) Any state permit or temporary state permit for the carrying of any pistol or revolver may be revoked by the Commissioner of Emergency Services and Public Protection for cause and shall be revoked by said commissioner upon conviction of the holder of such permit of a felony or of any misdemeanor specified in subsection (b) of section 29-28 or upon the occurrence of any event which would have disqualified the holder from being issued the state permit or temporary state permit pursuant to subsection (b) of section 29-28. Upon the revocation of any state permit or temporary state permit, the person whose state permit or temporary state permit is revoked shall be notified in writing and such state permit or temporary state permit shall be forthwith delivered to the commissioner. Any law enforcement authority shall confiscate and immediately forward to the commissioner any state permit or temporary state permit that is illegally possessed by any person. The commissioner may revoke the state permit or temporary state permit based upon the commissioner's own investigation or upon the request of any law enforcement agency. Any person who fails to surrender any permit within five days of notification in writing of revocation thereof shall be guilty of a class A misdemeanor.

(c) Any local permit for the carrying of a pistol or revolver issued prior to October 1, 2001, may be revoked by the authority issuing the same for cause, and shall be revoked by the authority issuing the same upon conviction of the holder of such permit of a felony or of any misdemeanor specified in subsection (b) of section 29-28 or upon the occurrence of any event which would have disqualified the holder from being issued such local permit. Upon the revocation of any local permit, the person whose local permit is revoked shall be notified in writing and such permit shall be forthwith delivered to the authority issuing the same. Upon the revocation of any local permit, the authority issuing the same shall forthwith notify the commissioner. Upon the revocation of any permit issued by the commissioner, the commissioner shall forthwith notify any local authority which the records of the commissioner show as having issued a currently valid local permit to the holder of the permit revoked by the commissioner. Any person who fails to surrender such permit within five days of notification in writing or revocation thereof shall be guilty of a class A misdemeanor.

(d) If a state permit or temporary state permit for the carrying of any pistol or revolver is revoked because the person holding such permit is subject to an ex parte order issued pursuant to section 46b-15 or 46b-16a, upon expiration of such order, such person may notify the Department of Emergency Services and Public Protection that such order has expired. Upon verification of such expiration and provided such person is not otherwise disqualified from holding such permit pursuant to subsection (b) of section 29-28, the department shall reinstate such permit.

ANNOTATIONS:

Appeal of Hopson, 65 Conn. 140, 31 A. 531 (1894):

... the fitness of the man to the legal requirement must of necessity in each case be determined, in view of the statutory regulations, by the licensing authority in the exercise of its best judgment.

Taylor v. Kirschner, 243 Conn. 250, 702 A.2d 138 (1997):

Revocation of permit to carry a pistol based upon permittee's conviction for marijuana possession was required, despite the fact that conviction occurred prior to effective date of act making revocation a consequence of possession, because legislative history revealed legislature's clear intent that the act be applied retrospectively. Any person convicted of disqualifying offense is subject to revocation of permit to carry a pistol without regard to when convictions occurred.

Rabbitt v. Leonard, 36 Conn. Supp. 108, 413 A.2d 489 (1979):

Statutory scheme permitting revocation of pistol permit for cause and providing notice of revocation and opportunity for de novo post revocation hearing was adequate to meet requirements of procedural due process, and thus former pistol permit holder, whose pistol permit had been summarily revoked, was not entitled to writ of mandamus ordering reinstatement of the permit and hearing prior to any future revocation. It is not mandatory that a permittee receive notice and hearing before revocation of the permit becomes effective; he may take action for reversal after the revocation.

Thomson v. Board. Of Firearms Permit Examiners, No. NNH950369628, 1996 Conn. Super. LEXIS 70 (1996):

The police department and the board are not limited to revoking gun permits only of those who are actually convicted of crimes, including crimes involving possession or use of firearms. Rather, they may look more broadly to the suitability of a permit holder.

Kristoffersen v. Bradford, Case No. 11-29 R (Board of Firearms Permit Examiners) (January 6, 2012):

On appeal to the Board of Firearms Permit Examiners, revocation of the appellant's permit to carry pistols or revolvers in the State of Connecticut was affirmed where he confronted a jogger on a trail in a state park, and became involved in a verbal altercation regarding the jogger's failure to have his dogs on a leash while running, drew his gun out of fear of the dogs even though they were not acting aggressively, and was subsequently arrested for reckless endangerment and carrying a handgun on state property.

Sec. 29-32b. Board of Firearms Permit Examiners. Appeals to board. Hearings.

(a) There is established a Board of Firearms Permit Examiners, within the Office of Governmental Accountability established under section 1-300, to be comprised of nine members, eight of whom shall be appointed by the Governor to serve during the Governor's term and until such members' successors are appointed and qualify, and one of whom shall be a retired judge of the Superior Court appointed by the Chief Court Administrator. With the exception of two public members, the members appointed by the Governor shall be appointed from nominees of the Commissioner of Emergency Services and Public Protection, the Commissioner of Mental Health and Addiction Services, the Connecticut State Association of Chiefs of Police, the Commissioner of Energy and Environmental Protection, The Connecticut State Rifle and Revolver Association, Inc., and Ye Connecticut Gun Guild, Inc., and each of said organizations shall be entitled to representation on the board. At least one member of the board appointed by the Governor shall be a lawyer licensed to practice in this state who shall act as chairman of the board during the hearing of appeals brought under this section.

(b) Any person aggrieved by any refusal to issue or renew a permit or certificate under the provisions of section 29-28, 29-36f, 29-37p or 29-38n, or by any limitation or revocation of a permit or certificate issued under any of said sections, or by a refusal or failure of any issuing authority to furnish an application as provided in section 29-28a, may, within ninety days after receipt of notice of such refusal, limitation or revocation, or refusal or failure to supply an application as provided in section 29-28a, and without prejudice to any other course of action open to such person in law or in equity, appeal to the board. On such appeal the board shall inquire into and determine the facts, de novo, and unless it finds that such a refusal, limitation or revocation, or such refusal or failure to supply an application, as the case may be, would be for just and proper cause, it shall order such permit or certificate to be issued, renewed or restored, or the limitation removed or modified, as the case may be. If the refusal was for failure to document compliance with local zoning requirements, under subsection (a) of section 29-28, the board shall not issue a permit.

(c) Any person aggrieved by the action of an issuing authority may file with the board a clear and concise statement of the facts on which such person relies for relief, and shall state the relief sought by the appellant. The receipt by the board of the appellant's statement shall initiate the appeals process, and no appeal may be rejected for mere lack of formality. The board shall, not later than ten days after receipt of the appeal, set a time and place at which the appeal shall be heard. The board, while such appeal is pending, may request such additional information from the appellant and from the issuing authority as it deems reasonably necessary to conduct a fair and impartial hearing, and shall require of the issuing authority from whose decision or action the appeal is being sought a written statement setting forth the reasons for such failure, refusal, revocation or limitation. The failure, absent good cause shown, or refusal of the issuing authority to furnish such written statement, or to supply the appellant with an application, at least ten days prior to the hearing shall be cause for the board to grant the relief sought, forthwith and without further hearing. If the issuing authority shows good cause for its failure to furnish such written statement, the board shall continue the matter to the next scheduled meeting of the board, provided the issuing authority shall be allowed only one such continuance.

(d) The board shall hold hearings at such times and places as it in its discretion reasonably determines to be required, but not less than once every ninety days, and shall give reasonable notice of the time and place of the hearing to the appellant and to the issuing authority. The board shall have the power to compel attendance at its sessions.

(e) All appeals hearings shall be conducted in an informal manner, but otherwise according to the rules of evidence, and all witnesses shall be sworn by the chairman. The board shall cause a verbatim transcript of the hearing to be kept in such manner as it may determine, and shall furnish such transcript to any party appealing its decision as hereinafter set forth. The statements of witnesses made under oath shall be privileged. Decisions of the board shall be by majority vote and shall be communicated in writing to the appellant and to the issuing authority within twenty days after the rendering of the decision. If any issuing authority neglects or refuses to comply with a decision of the board within ten days after notice of the board's decision has been given to such issuing authority, the board shall apply to the superior court for a writ of mandamus to enforce the board's decision.

(f) Any person aggrieved by the decision of the board may appeal therefrom in accordance with the provisions of section 4-183.

(g) The board shall serve without compensation, but its members shall be entitled to reasonable subsistence and travel allowances in the performance of their duties.

ANNOTATIONS:

Commissioner of Public Safety v. Board of Firearms Permit Examiners, ex rel mcwhorter, 129 Conn. App. 414, 21 A.3d 847 (2011):

It is apparent that the commissioner of public safety has the statutory authority unilaterally to deny or revoke a permit without giving the aggrieved party the benefit of a hearing. Conn. Gen. Stat. §§ 29-28(b) and 29-32(b). The opportunity for a hearing, subject to procedural safeguards, arises only if the aggrieved party timely appeals to the board, whose sole purpose is to hear such appeals. See General Statutes § 29-32b. It is, therefore, logical that § 29-32b directs the board to find facts de novo, given that a hearing in which aggrieved parties may present evidence and argument was not available to the issuing authority when it denied or revoked a firearms permit. It also follows logically that the legislature intended for the board to be able to draw its own conclusions as to whether the denial or revocation of a permit would be for just and proper cause from this more developed record. Therefore, § 29-32b(b) plainly and unambiguously does not limit the board to a deferential review of the judgment of the issuing authority.

Kuck v. Danaher, 600 F.3d 159 (2d Cir. 2010):

Applicants to renew their permits to carry a firearm under Connecticut law are entitled to basic due process protections, including a meaningful opportunity to be heard after a denial or revocation.

Rabbitt v. Leonard, 36 Conn. Supp. 108, 413 A.2d 489 (1979):

Statutory scheme permitting revocation of pistol permit for cause and providing notice of revocation and opportunity for de novo post-revocation hearing was adequate to meet requirements of procedural due process, and thus former pistol permit holder, whose pistol permit had been summarily revoked, was not entitled to writ of mandamus ordering reinstatement of the permit and hearing prior to any future revocation. It is not mandatory that a permittee receive notice and hearing before revocation of the permit becomes effective; he may take action for reversal after the revocation.

Baker v. Bd. Of Firearms Permit Examiners, 39 Conn. Supp. 202, 474 A.2d 115 (1984):

Where plaintiff who was holder of two duly issued gun permits, was informed by letter of chief of police of city that city permit was revoked as result of determination of his unsuitability to have pistol permit and by letter from state police commissioner, that his arrest and recent conviction for crime classified as felony necessitated revocation of state permit, Board of Firearms Permit Examiners was required, both under statute establishing Board, and under contested case provision of Administrative Procedure Act, to afford plaintiff opportunity to come before it for review of revocation decisions.

Basilicato v. State, 46 Conn. Supp. 550, 760 A.2d 155 (1999):

The plaintiff indicated that he was treated for mental and emotional problems in his pistol permit application to the Town of West Haven. The permit officer requested that the plaintiff provide a letter from his counselor, detailing that the plaintiff was fit to carry a pistol. The plaintiff failed to provide the requested letter and chief of police refused to issue a permit. The plaintiff appealed to the Board of Examiners and the Board denied the plaintiff's request on the grounds that the plaintiff's mental or emotional state is an important consideration in determining suitability to carry a pistol. The court upheld the ruling, observing that the determination of the Board as to the plaintiff's suitability to possess a permit is subject to great deference.

Storace v. Mariano, 35 Conn. Supp. 28, 391 A.2d 1347 (1978):

The plaintiff had his permit revoked by the defendant, Chief of Police for the Town of Naugatuck. The plaintiff appealed the revocation to the Board of Firearms Permit

Examiners. The Board failed to secure a hearing on the appeal within the ten days required by statute, and instead the hearing took place a year after the revocation. The court held that the Board should have given the plaintiff the relief sought, reinstatement of the permit, because of the failure to provide a hearing within the ten day statutory requirement. Also, the revocation was overturned because it was found to be for personal reasons, and there was no factual support for the conclusion that the plaintiff was not suitable to carry.

Town of Farmington v. Bd. Of Firearms Permit Examiners, No. CV 95-0550258S, 1996 Conn. Super. LEXIS 503 1996 WL 106842 (Conn. Super. 1996):

In finding that the board failed to make a fact based determination of suitability when the local authority failed to properly process an application, the court stated that the board is required to receive evidence and make a finding with respect to an appellant's suitability prior to ordering the issuance of a permit.

Hanson v. Bd. Of Firearms Permit Examiners, No. 960392053, 1997 Conn. Super. LEXIS 1312 (Conn. Super. 1997):

In remanding a case involving, at worst evidence of an individual's immaturity by engaging in prankish behavior that was not shown to involve misuse of a firearm or any tendency toward reckless or violent behavior of any kind, armed or unarmed, the court found the board's decision of unsuitability was not reasonably supported by facts.

Frosceno v. Bd. Of Firearms Permit Examiners, No. CV970571959, 1998 Conn. Super. LEXIS 637, 1998 WL 128792 (Conn. Super. 1998):

In sustaining an appeal to a case previously remanded to the BOFPE, the court found that the board had improperly made a finding of unsuitability where an individual had been convicted of 4th degree larceny and thereby had only violated the high degree of trust placed in a security officer. The record contained no evidence that a gun was involved in the incident or that there was any threat of injury to any person. A general finding of a lack of credibility is clearly not enough. The board's bare finding that the plaintiff violated the high degree of trust of a security officer does not establish him as a danger to the public if he is allowed to carry a gun outside his home.

Saviske v. Corradino, Chairman Bd. Of Firearms Permit Examiners, No. CV106006014S, 2011 Conn. Super. LEXIS 1396, 2011 WL 2536461 (Superior Court, J.D. New Britain) (June 1, 2011):

Under Conn. Gen. Stat. § 29-32b(c) and Board of Firearms Permit Examiners regulation § 29-32b-7, the Board of Firearms Permit Examiners' secretary has the right to make a thorough inquiry of the facts of the appeal. Thus the board regulations envision that the plaintiff should make available hospital records and expert opinions that bear on his appeal. Indeed, the board is entitled to such records to determine if a specific disqualification applies to a plaintiff. Section § 29-32(b) refers to Reg. § 29-28(b)(5), under which disqualification is required if a permittee has been confined in a hospital for persons with psychiatric disabilities within the preceding twelve months by order of a probate court.

Commentary

The Final Decision, Petition for Declaratory Ruling of, inter alia, the Board of Firearms Permit Examiners by Jack Goldberg, (January 14, 2010) contains an excellent summary of the substantive and procedural requirements and limitations surrounding the submission and consideration of an application for a permit to carry a pistol or revolver in the State of Connecticut. The Final Decision of the Board of Firearms Permit Examiners set forth therein constitutes a quick, but valuable, reference for anyone who intends to submit such an application, who is considering such an application on behalf of an issuing authority, or who intends to appear before the Board of Firearms Permit Examiners during the course of an appeal. To assist the reader in understanding the applicable legal principles, the referenced Final Decision has been reproduced in full at Appendix B to this publication.

Sec. 29-33. Sale, delivery or transfer of pistols and revolvers. Procedure. Penalty.

(a) No person, firm or corporation shall sell, deliver or otherwise transfer any pistol or revolver to any person who is prohibited from possessing a pistol or revolver as provided in section 53a-217c.

(b) On and after October 1, 1995, no person may purchase or receive any pistol or revolver unless such person holds a valid permit to carry a pistol or revolver issued pursuant to subsection (b) of section 29-28, a valid permit to sell at retail a pistol or revolver issued pursuant to subsection (a) of section 29-28 or a valid eligibility certificate for a pistol or revolver issued pursuant to section 29-36f or is a federal marshal, parole officer or peace officer.

(c) No person, firm or corporation shall sell, deliver or otherwise transfer any pistol or revolver except upon written application on a form prescribed and furnished by the Commissioner of Emergency Services and Public Protection. Such person, firm or corporation shall insure that all questions on the application are answered properly prior to releasing the pistol or revolver and shall retain the application, which shall be attached to the federal sale or transfer document, for at least twenty years or until such vendor goes out of business. Such application shall be available for inspection during normal business hours by law enforcement officials. No sale, delivery or other transfer of any pistol or revolver shall be made unless the person making the purchase or to whom the same is delivered or transferred is personally known to the person selling such pistol or revolver or making delivery or transfer thereof or provides evidence of his identity in the form of a motor vehicle operator's license, identity card issued pursuant to section 1-1h or valid passport. No sale, delivery or other transfer of any pistol or revolver shall be made until the person, firm or corporation making such transfer obtains an authorization number from the Commissioner of Emergency Services and Public Protection. Said commissioner shall perform the national instant criminal background check and make a reasonable effort to determine whether there is any reason that would prohibit such applicant from possessing a pistol or revolver as provided in section 53a-217c. If the commissioner determines the existence of such a reason, the commissioner shall deny the sale and no pistol or revolver shall be sold, delivered or otherwise transferred by such person, firm or corporation to such applicant.

(d) No person, firm or corporation shall sell, deliver or otherwise transfer any pistol or revolver, other than at wholesale, unless such pistol or revolver is equipped with a reusable trigger lock, gun lock or gun locking device appropriate for such pistol or revolver, which lock or device shall be constructed of material sufficiently strong to prevent it from being easily disabled and have a locking mechanism accessible by key or by electronic or other mechanical accessory specific to such lock or device to prevent unauthorized removal. No pistol or revolver shall be loaded or contain therein any gunpowder or other explosive or any bullet, ball or shell when such pistol or revolver is sold, delivered or otherwise transferred.

Sec. 29-35. Carrying of pistol or revolver without permit prohibited. Exceptions.

(a) No person shall carry any pistol or revolver upon his or her person, except when such person is within the dwelling house or place of business of such person, without a permit to carry the same issued as provided in section 29-28. The provisions of this subsection shall not apply to the carrying of any pistol or revolver by any parole officer or peace officer of this state, or any Department of Motor Vehicles inspector appointed under section 14-8 and certified pursuant to section 7-294d, or parole officer or peace officer of any other state while engaged in the pursuit of official duties, or federal marshal or federal law enforcement agent, or to any member of the armed forces of the United States, as defined in section 27-103, or of the state, as defined in section 27-2, when on duty or going to or from duty, or to any member of any military organization when on parade or when going to or from any place of assembly, or to the transportation of pistols or revolvers as merchandise, or to any person transporting any pistol or revolver while contained in the package in which it was originally wrapped at the time of sale and while transporting the same from the place of sale to the purchaser's residence or place of business, or to any person removing such person's household goods or effects from one place to another, or to any person while transporting any such pistol or revolver from such person's place of residence or business to a place or individual where or by whom such pistol or revolver is to be repaired or while returning to such person's place of residence or business after the same has been repaired, or to any person transporting a pistol or revolver in or through the state for the purpose of taking part in competitions, taking part in formal pistol or revolver training, repairing such pistol or revolver or attending any meeting or exhibition of an organized collectors' group if such person is a bona fide resident of the United States and is permitted to possess and carry a pistol or revolver in the state or subdivision of the United States in which such person resides, or to any person transporting a pistol or revolver to and from a testing range at the request of the issuing authority, or to any person transporting an antique pistol or revolver, as defined in section 29-33. For the purposes of this subsection, "formal pistol or revolver training" means pistol or revolver training at a locally approved or permitted firing range or training facility, and "transporting a pistol or revolver" means transporting a pistol or revolver that is unloaded and, if such pistol or revolver is being transported in a motor vehicle, is not readily accessible or directly accessible from the passenger compartment of the vehicle or, if such pistol or revolver is being transported in a motor vehicle that does not have a compartment separate from the passenger compartment, such pistol or revolver shall be contained in a locked container other than the glove compartment or console. Nothing in this section shall be construed to prohibit the carrying of a pistol or revolver during formal pistol or revolver training or repair.

(b) The holder of a permit issued pursuant to section 29–28, as amended by this act, shall carry such permit upon one's person while carrying such pistol or revolver. Such holder shall present his or her permit upon the request of a law enforcement officer who has reasonable suspicion of a crime for purposes of verification of the validity of the permit or identification of the holder, provided such holder is carrying a pistol or revolver that is observed by such law enforcement officer.

ANNOTATIONS:

State v. Tinsley, 181 Conn. 388, 435 A.2d 1002 (1980):

In prosecution for carrying pistol without permit wherein evidence established essential elements of crime, and defendant offered no evidence to put exceptions to statute in issue, burden was not upon State to disprove every listed exception in statute; therefore, conviction after State offered no evidence to disprove statutory exceptions did not violate defendant's rights.

State v. Bailey, 209 Conn. 322, 551 A.2d 1206 (1988):

Self-defense is a justification for the *use* of force but not for possession of firearm. Therefore, an individual that justifiably uses a pistol in self-defense can still be convicted of unlawful possession of a pistol without a permit, in violation of Section 29-35.

State v. Ortiz, 15 Conn. App. 749, 546 A.2d 338 (1988):

A defendant can be charged and convicted of both criminal possession of a firearm and carrying a pistol without a permit. Convictions on both charges do not constitute a violation of federal constitutional double jeopardy protections.

State v. L'Minggio, 71 Conn. App. 656, 672, 803 A.2d 408 (2002):

Carrying and possession are different concepts and § 29-35 (a) is designed to prohibit the carrying of a pistol without a permit and not the possession of one.

State v. Hopes, 26 Conn. App. 367, 374, 602 A.2d 23, *cert. Denied,* 221 Conn. 915, 603 A.2d 405 (1992):

The term “carry” with Section 29-35 does not require asportation of the pistol to satisfy the statute. No proof that the pistol was actually moved or transported by the defendant is necessary to support a conviction of “carrying” a pistol without a permit. The court recognized “carry” as meaning “to bear upon one’s person,” or to have “within the defendant's control or dominion in a public area.”

State v. Brunson, 36 Conn. App. 576, 651 A.2d 1335 (1995):

The State does not need to prove that a defendant does not have a pistol permit in any jurisdiction as an element of a crime, the State need only show that the defendant did not have a pistol permit, and therefore the right to carry, within the jurisdiction in which the defendant is charged.

State v. Bradley, 39 Conn. App. 82, 663 A.2d 1100, *cert. Denied,* 232 Conn. 920, 656 A.2d 669 (1995):

To obtain conviction for carrying pistol without permit, prosecution need prove only that accused carried pistol while outside dwelling or place of business and that he did not have permit to do so; however, operability of weapon is not an element of crime.

State v. Vickers, 260 Conn. 219, 796 A.2d 502 (2002):

Defendant, who was carrying firearm while at his workplace, had fair warning that his conduct was proscribed by statute providing that no person shall carry any pistol upon his person, except when such person is within his dwelling house or place of business, without a permit to carry the same, and thus, defendant was not deprived of his right to due process; court construed phrase “place of business” as meaning that in which one had possessory or proprietary interest, and this construction was neither unexpected nor indefensible and, therefore, was binding upon the defendant.

State v. Lutters, 270 Conn. 198, 853 A.2d 434 (2004):

Taxicab, in which taxicab driver had a proprietary interest, did not fall within the “place of business” exception to the offense of carrying a pistol without a permit; sister statute expressly prohibits a person from transporting, without a permit, a pistol or revolver in a motor vehicle.

Gonzalez v. Village of West Milwaukee, No. 09-CV-0384, 2010 U.S. Dist. LEXIS 46281 (E.D. Wis. 2010):

> Conduct is "otherwise disorderly" if it is similar to the types of conduct enumerated in the statute in that it has a tendency to disrupt good order . . . . "[I]t is the combination of conduct and circumstances that is crucial in applying the statute to a particular situation." . . . . Convictions under such proscription typically involve conduct that is inappropriate because of the circumstances involved. *Id.* At 672-73. . . . No reasonable person would dispute that walking into a retail store openly carrying a firearm is highly disruptive conduct which is virtually certain to create a disturbance. This is so because when employees and shoppers in retail stores see a person carrying a lethal weapon, they are likely to be frightened and possibly even panicky. Many employees and shoppers are likely to think that the person with the gun is either deranged or about to commit a felony or both. Further, it is almost certain that someone will call the police. And when police respond to a "man with a gun" call, they have no idea what the armed individual's intentions are. The volatility inherent in such a situation could easily lead to someone being seriously injured or killed. . . . Plaintiff's conduct caused store employees to become frightened and to notify their managers. The managers also became frightened and called the police, who immediately responded. The responding officers clearly had reason to believe that the combination of plaintiff's conduct and the circumstances in which it was committed "tended to provoke a disturbance" and constituted disorderly conduct.

Commentary

The Connecticut statute permitting the carrying of firearms does not specifically address whether or not a pistol or revolver, carried upon the person in a public place, may be carried openly or must be concealed. Accordingly, the mere carrying of a properly permitted firearm openly in a public place does not explicitly violate Conn. Gen. Stat. § 29-35. However, depending upon the totality of the facts and circumstances, an individual carrying a properly permitted firearm openly in a public place may violate other criminal statutes, for example, Disorderly Conduct (Conn. Gen. Stat. § 53a-182), Breach of Peace (Conn. Gen. Stat. § 181), or Threatening in the Second Degree (Conn. Gen. Stat. § 53a-62). The use of mature judgment and sound discretion is required where an individual wishes to carry a properly permitted pistol or revolver in a public place, whether concealed or otherwise.

Sec. 29-36. Alteration of firearm identification mark, number or name.

(a) No person shall remove, deface, alter or obliterate the name of any maker or model or any maker's number, unique serial number or other mark of identification on any firearm as defined in section 53a-3. The possession of any firearm upon which any identifying mark, number or name has been removed, defaced, altered or obliterated shall be prima facie evidence that the person owning or in possession of such firearm has removed, defaced, altered or obliterated the same.

(b) Any person who violates any provision of this section shall be guilty of a class C felony for which two years of the sentence imposed may not be suspended or reduced by the court, and five thousand dollars of the fine imposed may not be remitted or reduced by the court unless the court states on the record its reasons for remitting or reducing such fine, and any firearm found in the possession of any person in violation of said provision shall be forfeited.

ANNOTATIONS:

State v. Turner, 62 Conn. App. 376, 771 A.2d 206 (2001):

Statute making possession of any pistol or revolver with obliterated identification mark prima facie evidence that person possessing pistol or revolver has altered, removed or obliterated the mark did not create unconstitutional presumption.

Sec. 29-36a. Manufacture of a firearm. Acquisition of unique serial number or other mark of identification. Exceptions. Penalty.

(a) No person shall complete the manufacture of a firearm without subsequently (1) obtaining a unique serial number or other mark of identification from the Department of Emergency Services and Public Protection pursuant to subsection (b) of this section, and (2) engraving upon or permanently affixing to the firearm such serial number or other mark in a manner that conforms with the requirements imposed on licensed importers and licensed manufacturers of firearms pursuant to 18 USC 923(i), as amended from time to time, and any regulation adopted thereunder.

(b) Not later than thirty days after a person completes the manufacture of a firearm or ninety days after the Department of Emergency Services and Public Protection provides notice in accordance with section 29-36b that the system to distribute a unique serial number or other mark of identification pursuant to this section is operational, whichever date is later, such person shall notify the department of such manufacture and provide any identifying information to the department concerning the firearm and the owner of such firearm, in a manner prescribed by the Commissioner of Emergency Services and Public Protection. Upon receiving a properly submitted request for a unique serial number or other mark of identification from a person who completes manufacture of a firearm, the department shall determine if such person is prohibited from purchasing a firearm and if not, shall issue to such person a unique serial number or other mark of identification immediately and in no instance more than three business days after the department receives such request. Issuance of a unique serial number or other mark of identification pursuant to this subsection shall not be evidence that the firearm is otherwise lawfully possessed.

(c) The provisions of subsections (a) and (b) of this section shall not apply to the manufacture of a firearm manufactured using an unfinished frame or lower receiver on which a serial number or other mark has been engraved or permanently affixed pursuant to subsection (c) of section 53-206j.

(d) No person shall transfer to another person any firearm manufactured in violation of this section.

(e) The provisions of this section shall not apply to (1) the manufacture of firearms by a federally licensed firearm manufacturer, (2) (A) any antique firearm, as defined in 18 USC 921, as amended from time to time, or (B) any firearm manufactured prior to the effective date of this section, provided such firearm is otherwise lawfully possessed, or (3) delivery or transfer of a firearm to a law enforcement agency.

(f) No person shall facilitate, aid or abet the manufacture of a firearm (1) by a person or for a person who is otherwise prohibited by law from purchasing or possessing a firearm, or (2) that a person is otherwise prohibited by law from purchasing or possessing.

(g) If the court finds that a violation of this section is not of a serious nature and that the person charged with such violation (1) will probably not offend in the future, (2) has not previously been convicted of a violation of this section, and (3) has not previously had a prosecution under this section suspended pursuant to this subsection, the court may order suspension of prosecution. The court shall not order suspension of prosecution unless the accused person has acknowledged that he or she understands the consequences of the suspension of prosecution. Any person for whom prosecution is suspended shall agree to the tolling of any statute of limitations with respect to such violation and to a waiver of his or her right to a speedy trial. Such person shall appear in court and shall be released to the custody of the Court Support Services Division for such period, not exceeding two years, and under such conditions as the court shall order. If the person refuses to accept, or, having accepted, violates such conditions, the court shall terminate the suspension of prosecution and the case shall be brought to trial. If such person satisfactorily completes such person's period of probation, he or she may apply for dismissal of the charges against such person and the court, on finding such satisfactory completion, shall dismiss such charges. If the person does not apply for dismissal of the charges against such person after satisfactorily completing such person's period of probation, the court, upon receipt of a report submitted by the Court Support Services Division that the person satisfactorily completed such person's period of probation, may on its own motion make a finding of such satisfactory completion and dismiss such charges. Upon dismissal, all records of such charges shall be erased pursuant to section 54-142a. An order of the court denying a motion to dismiss the charges against a person who has completed such person's period of probation or terminating the participation of a defendant in such program shall be a final judgment for purposes of appeal.

(h) Any person who violates any provision of this section shall be guilty of a class C felony for which two years of the sentence imposed may not be suspended or reduced by the court, and five thousand dollars of the fine imposed may not be remitted or reduced by the court unless the court states on the record its reasons for remitting or reducing such fine, and any firearm found in the possession of any person in violation of any provision of this section shall be forfeited.

(i) For purposes of this section, "manufacture" means to fabricate or construct a firearm including the initial assembly, "firearm" means firearm, as defined in section 53a-3 and "law enforcement agency" means law enforcement agency, as defined in section 29-1i.

Sec. 29-36b. Distribution of unique serial number or other mark of identification for firearms.

Not later than October 1, 2019, the Department of Emergency Services and Public Protection, in consultation with the federal Bureau of Alcohol, Tobacco, Firearms and Explosives as needed, shall develop and maintain a system to distribute a unique serial number or other mark of identification to any person requesting such number or mark pursuant to section 29-36a or 53-206j, and provide written notification that such system is operational by: (1) Posting the notification on the department's Internet web site, and (2) providing the notification electronically to federally licensed firearm dealers. The department shall maintain identifying information of the person requesting the number or mark and of the firearm or unfinished frame or lower receiver for which each such number or mark is requested.

Sec. 29-36f. Eligibility certificate for pistol or revolver.

(a) Any person who is twenty-one years of age or older may apply to the Commissioner of Emergency Services and Public Protection for an eligibility certificate for a pistol or revolver.

(b) The Commissioner of Emergency Services and Public Protection shall issue an eligibility certificate unless said commissioner finds that the applicant: (1) Has failed to successfully complete a course approved by the Commissioner of Emergency Services and Public Protection in the safety and use of pistols and revolvers including, but not limited to, a safety or training course in the use of pistols and revolvers available to the public offered by a law enforcement agency, a private or public educational institution or a firearms training school, utilizing instructors certified by the National Rifle Association or the Department of Energy and Environmental Protection and a safety or training course in the use of pistols or revolvers conducted by an instructor certified by the state or the National Rifle Association; (2) has been convicted of (A) a felony, (B) a misdemeanor violation of section 21a-279 on or after October 1, 2015, or (C) a misdemeanor violation of section 53a-58, 53a-61, 53a-61a, 53a-62, 53a-63, 53a-96, 53a-175, 53a-176, 53a-178 or 53a-181d during the preceding twenty years; (3) has been convicted as delinquent for the commission of a serious juvenile offense, as defined in section 46b-120; (4) has been discharged from custody within the preceding twenty years after having been found not guilty of a crime by reason of mental disease or defect pursuant to section 53a-13; (5) (A) has been confined in a hospital for persons with psychiatric disabilities, as defined in section 17a-495, within the preceding sixty months by order of a probate court; or (B) has been voluntarily admitted on or after October 1, 2013, to a hospital for persons with psychiatric disabilities, as defined in section 17a-495, within the preceding six months for care and treatment of a psychiatric disability and not solely for being an alcohol-dependent person or a drug-dependent person as those terms are defined in section 17a-680; (6) is subject to a restraining or protective order issued by a court in a case involving the use, attempted use or threatened use of physical force against another person, including an ex parte order issued pursuant to section 46b-15 or section 46b-16a; (7) is subject to a firearms seizure order issued prior to June 1, 2022, pursuant to section 29-38c after notice and hearing, or a risk protection order or risk protection investigative order issued on or after June 1, 2022, pursuant to section 29-38c; (8) is prohibited from shipping, transporting, possessing or receiving a firearm pursuant to 18 USC 922(g)(4); or (9) is an alien illegally or unlawfully in the United States.

Sec. 29-36g. Application for eligibility certificate. Criminal history records check. Deadline for approval or denial of application. Form of certificate. Change of address. Confidentiality of name and address of certificate holder. Scope of certificate.

(a) Requests for eligibility certificates under section 29-36f shall be submitted to the Commissioner of Emergency Services and Public Protection on application forms prescribed by the commissioner. No eligibility certificate for a pistol or revolver shall be issued under the provisions of said section unless the applicant for such certificate gives to the Commissioner of Emergency Services and Public Protection, upon the commissioner's request, full information concerning the applicant's criminal record and relevant information concerning the applicant's mental health history. The commissioner shall require each applicant to submit to state and national criminal history records checks. The commissioner shall take a full description of such applicant. The commissioner shall take the fingerprints of such applicant or conduct any other method of positive identification required by the State Police Bureau of Identification or the Federal Bureau of Investigation. The commissioner shall record the date the fingerprints were taken in the applicant's file and shall conduct criminal history records checks in accordance with section 29-17a. The commissioner shall, within sixty days of receipt of the national criminal history records check from the Federal Bureau of Investigation, either approve the application and issue the eligibility certificate or deny the application and notify the applicant of the reason for such denial in writing.

(b) (1) With respect to any application for an eligibility certificate filed with the Commissioner of Emergency Services and Public Protection on or before July 1, 1995, the commissioner shall, not later than October 1, 1995, (A) approve the application and issue the eligibility certificate, (B) issue a temporary eligibility certificate, or (C) deny the application and notify the applicant of the reason for such denial in writing.

(2) With respect to any application for an eligibility certificate filed with the Commissioner of Emergency Services and Public Protection after July 1, 1995, the commissioner shall, within ninety days, (A) approve the application and issue the eligibility certificate, (B) issue a temporary eligibility certificate, or (C) deny the application and notify the applicant of the reason for such denial in writing.

(3) A temporary certificate issued under this subsection shall be valid until such time as the commissioner either approves or denies the application.

(c) An eligibility certificate for a pistol or revolver shall be of such form and content as the commissioner may prescribe, shall be signed by the certificate holder and shall contain an identification number, the name, address, place and date of birth, height, weight and eye color of the certificate holder and a full-face photograph of the certificate holder.

(d) A person holding an eligibility certificate issued by the commissioner shall notify the commissioner within two business days of any change of his address. The notification shall include his old address and his new address.

(e) Notwithstanding the provisions of sections 1-210 and 1-211, the name and address of a person issued an eligibility certificate for a pistol or revolver under the provisions of section 29-36f shall be confidential and shall not be disclosed, except (1) such information may be disclosed to law enforcement officials acting in the performance of their duties, including, but not limited to, employees of the United States Probation Office acting in the performance of their duties, and parole officers within the Department of Correction acting in performance of their duties, (2) the Commissioner of Emergency Services and Public Protection may disclose such information to the extent necessary to comply with a request made pursuant to section 29-33, 29-37a or 29-38m for verification that such certificate is still valid and has not been suspended or revoked, and (3) such information may be disclosed to the Commissioner of Mental Health and Addiction Services to carry out the provisions of subsection (c) of section 17a-500.

(f) An eligibility certificate for a pistol or revolver shall not authorize the holder thereof to carry a pistol or revolver upon his person in circumstances for which a permit to carry a pistol or revolver issued pursuant to subsection (b) of section 29-28 is required under section 29-35.

Commentary

Unlike permits to carry pistols or revolvers issued pursuant to Conn. Gen. Stat. § 29-28, applications for an eligibility certificate for pistols or revolvers cannot be denied on the basis of the applicant's overall "suitability." The grounds for denial of a certificate of eligibility for pistol or revolver are set forth in Conn. Gen. Stat. § 29-36f and, upon proper application and receipt of the results of the criminal history records check mandated by Conn. Gen. Stat. § 29-36g, are exclusive. Persons aggrieved by a denial of a certificate of eligibility for pistol or revolver may appeal such action to the Board of Firearms Permit Examiners in accordance with the provisions of Conn. Gen. Stat. § 29-32b above.

Sec. 29-36h. Fee for eligibility certificate. Expiration and renewal of eligibility certificate.

(a) The fee for each eligibility certificate for a pistol or revolver originally issued under the provisions of section 29-36f shall be thirty-five dollars and for each renewal thereof thirty-five dollars, which fees shall be paid to the Commissioner of Emergency Services and Public Protection. Upon deposit of such fees in the General Fund, the fees shall be credited to the appropriation to the Department of Emergency Services and Public Protection to a separate nonlapsing account for the purposes of the issuance of eligibility certificates under said section.

(b) An eligibility certificate originally issued under the provisions of section 29-36f, shall expire five years after the date it becomes effective and each renewal thereof shall expire five years after the expiration date on the certificate being renewed.

(c) The renewal fee shall apply for each renewal which is requested not earlier than thirty-one days before, and not later than thirty-one days after, the expiration date of the certificate being renewed.

(d) No fee or portion thereof paid under the provisions of this section for issuance or renewal of an eligibility certificate shall be refundable except if the eligibility certificate for which the fee or portion thereof was paid was not issued or renewed.

(e) The Commissioner of Emergency Services and Public Protection shall send a notice of the expiration of an eligibility certificate issued pursuant to section 29-36f, to the holder of such certificate, by first class mail, at the address of such person as shown by the records of the commissioner, not less than ninety days before such expiration, and shall enclose therein a form for the renewal of said certificate. An eligibility certificate issued pursuant to said section, shall be valid for a period of ninety days from the expiration date, except this provision shall not apply to any certificate which has been revoked or for which revocation is pending, pursuant to section 29-36i.

Sec. 29-36i. Revocation of eligibility certificate. Reinstatement.

(a) Any eligibility certificate for a pistol or revolver shall be revoked by the Commissioner of Emergency Services and Public Protection upon the occurrence of any event which would have disqualified the holder from being issued the certificate pursuant to section 29-36f.

(b) Upon the revocation of any eligibility certificate, the person whose eligibility certificate is revoked shall be notified in writing and such certificate shall be forthwith delivered to the Commissioner of Emergency Services and Public Protection. Any person who fails to surrender such certificate within five days of notification in writing of revocation thereof shall be guilty of a class A misdemeanor.

(c) If an eligibility certificate for a pistol or revolver is revoked because the person holding such certificate is subject to an ex parte order issued pursuant to section 46b-15 or 46b-16a, upon expiration of such order, such person may notify the Department of Emergency Services and Public Protection that such order has expired. Upon verification of such expiration and provided such person is not otherwise disqualified from holding such certificate pursuant to section 29-36f, the department shall reinstate such certificate.

Commentary

Unlike permits to carry pistols or revolvers issued pursuant to Conn. Gen. Stat. § 29-28, applications for an eligibility certificate for pistols or revolvers cannot be revoked on the basis of the applicant's overall "suitability." The grounds for revocation of a certificate of eligibility for pistol or revolver are set forth in Conn. Gen. Stat. § 29-36f and are exclusive. Persons aggrieved by a revocation of a certificate of eligibility for pistol or revolver may appeal such action to the Board of Firearms Permit Examiners in accordance with the provisions of Conn. Gen. Stat. § 29-32b above.

Sec. 29-36k. Transfer, delivery or surrender of firearms by persons ineligible to possess firearms or ammunition. Destruction of firearms. Penalty.

(a) Except as provided in subsection (b) of this section, not later than two business days after the occurrence of any event that makes a person ineligible to possess a pistol or revolver or other firearm or ammunition, such person shall (1) transfer in accordance with section 29-33 all pistols and revolvers which such person then possesses to any person eligible to possess a pistol or revolver and transfer in accordance with any applicable state and federal laws all other firearms to any person eligible to possess such other firearms by obtaining an authorization number for the sale or transfer of the firearm from the Commissioner of Emergency Services and Public Protection, and submit a sale or transfer of firearms form to said commissioner within two business days, or (2) deliver or surrender such pistols and revolvers and other firearms and ammunition to the Commissioner of Emergency Services and Public Protection, provided a local police department may accept such pistols, revolvers, and other firearms and ammunition on behalf of said commissioner, or (3) transfer such ammunition to any person eligible to possess such ammunition. The commissioner and a local police department shall exercise due care in the receipt and holding of such pistols and revolvers and other firearms or ammunition.

(b) Immediately, but in no event more than twenty-four hours after notice has been provided to a person subject to a restraining or protective order or a foreign order of protection, such person shall (1) transfer any pistol, revolver or other firearm or ammunition which such person then possesses to a federally licensed firearms dealer pursuant to the sale of the pistol, revolver or other firearm or ammunition to the federally licensed firearms dealer, or (2) deliver or surrender such pistols and revolvers and other firearms and ammunition to the Commissioner of Emergency Services and Public Protection, provided a local police department may accept such pistols, revolvers, other firearms and ammunition on behalf of said commissioner. For the purposes of this section, a "person subject to a restraining or protective order or a foreign order of protection" means a person who knows that such person is subject to (A) a restraining or protective order of a court of this state that has been issued against such person, after notice has been provided to such person, in a case involving the use, attempted use or threatened use of physical force against another person, or (B) a foreign order of protection, as defined in section 46b-15a, that has been issued against such person in a case involving the use, attempted use or threatened use of physical force against another person.

(c) (1) A person subject to a restraining order or protective order or a foreign order of protection or an order of protection issued under section 46b-16a, who has delivered or surrendered any pistol, revolver, or other firearm or ammunition to the Commissioner of Emergency Services and Public Protection or a local police department, may request the return of such pistol, revolver, or other firearm or ammunition, upon (A) the expiration of the restraining order or protective order or a foreign order of protection or an order of protection issued under section 46b-16a, or (B) the issuance of a subsequent court order that rescinds the restraining order or protective order or a foreign order of protection or an order of protection issued under section 46b-16a.

(2) When making such request, the person described in subdivision (1) of this subsection shall provide notification of (A) the expiration of the restraining order or protective order or a foreign order of protection or an order of protection issued under section 46b-16a, or (B) the issuance of a subsequent court order that rescinds the restraining order or protective order or a foreign order of protection or an order of protection issued under section 46b-16a, to the Commissioner of Emergency Services and Public Protection or a local police department.

(3) Not later than five business days after the date on which a person has made a request pursuant to subdivision (1) of this subsection, the commissioner or a local police department shall review the request and make available for retrieval any pistol, revolver, or other firearm or ammunition to such person provided the commissioner or a local police department confirms: (A) (i) The expiration of the restraining order or protective order or a foreign order of protection or an order of protection issued under section 46b-16a, or (ii) the issuance of a subsequent court order that rescinds the restraining order or protective order or a foreign order of protection or an order of protection issued under section 46b-16a, (B) that such person is not otherwise disqualified from possessing such pistol, revolver, or other firearm or ammunition, and (C) that such person was legally entitled to possess such pistol, revolver, or other firearm or ammunition at the time of delivery or surrender to the commissioner or a local police department.

(d) Such person, or such person's legal representative, may, at any time up to one year after such delivery or surrender, transfer such pistols and revolvers in accordance with the provisions of section 29-33 to any person eligible to possess a pistol or revolver and transfer

or protective order or a foreign order of protection, as defined in section 29-36k, transfers such pistol or revolver or other firearm, or delivers or surrenders such pistol or revolver or other firearm, pursuant to arrangements made with an organized local police department or the Division of State Police in advance of such transfer, delivery or surrender.

(b) The Commissioner of Emergency Services and Public Protection, in conjunction with the Chief State's Attorney and the Connecticut Police Chiefs Association, shall update the protocol developed pursuant to subsection (a) of this section to reflect the provisions of sections 29-7h, 29-28, 29-28a, 29-29, 29-30, 29-32 and 29-35, subsections (b) and (h) of section 46b-15, subsections (c) and (d) of section 46b-38c and sections 53-202a, 53-202*l*, 53-202m and 53a-217 and shall include in such protocol specific instructions for the transfer, delivery or surrender of pistols and revolvers and other firearms and ammunition when the assistance of more than one law enforcement agency is necessary to effect the requirements of section 29-36k.

Sec. 29-37. Penalties.

(a) Any person violating any provision of section 29-28 or 29-31 shall be guilty of a class E felony, and any pistol or revolver found in the possession of any person in violation of any of said provisions shall be forfeited.

(b) Any person violating any provision of subsection (a) of section 29-35 shall be guilty of a class D felony, and, in the absence of any mitigating circumstances as determined by the court, one year of the sentence imposed may not be suspended or reduced by the court. The court shall specifically state the mitigating circumstances, or the absence thereof, in writing for the record. Any pistol or revolver found in the possession of any person in violation of any provision of subsection (a) of section 29-35 shall be forfeited.

(c) Any person violating any provision of subsection (b) of section 29-35 shall have committed an infraction and shall be fined thirty-five dollars.

Sec. 29-37a. Sale or delivery or transfer of long guns. Procedure. Penalty.

(a) For the purposes of this section, "long gun" means a firearm, as defined in section 53a-3, other than a pistol or revolver.

(b) (1) Except as provided in subdivision (2) of this subsection, no person, firm or corporation may sell, deliver or otherwise transfer, at retail, any long gun to any person under eighteen years of age.

(2) No person, firm or corporation may sell, deliver or otherwise transfer, at retail, any semi-automatic centerfire rifle that has or accepts a magazine with a capacity exceeding five rounds to any person under twenty-one years of age. The provisions of this subdivision shall not apply to the sale, delivery or transfer of such a rifle to any person who is a member or employee of an organized local police department, the Department of Emergency Services and Public Protection or the Department of Correction or a member of the military or naval forces of this state or of the United States for use in the discharge of their duties.

(c) On and after April 1, 2014, no person may purchase or receive any long gun unless such person holds a valid long gun eligibility certificate issued pursuant to section 29-37p, a valid permit to carry a pistol or revolver issued pursuant to subsection (b) of section 29-

28, a valid permit to sell at retail a pistol or revolver issued pursuant to subsection (a) of section 29-28 or a valid eligibility certificate for a pistol or revolver issued pursuant to section 29-36f.

(d) No person, firm or corporation may sell, deliver or otherwise transfer, at retail, any long gun to any person unless such person makes application on a form prescribed and furnished by the Commissioner of Emergency Services and Public Protection, which shall be attached by the transferor to the federal sale or transfer document and filed and retained by the transferor for at least twenty years or until such transferor goes out of business. Such application shall be available for inspection during normal business hours by law enforcement officials. No such sale, delivery or other transfer of any long gun shall be made until the person, firm or corporation making such sale, delivery or transfer has ensured that such application has been completed properly and has obtained an authorization number from the Commissioner of Emergency Services and Public Protection for such sale, delivery or transfer. The Department of Emergency Services and Public Protection shall make every effort, including performing the national instant criminal background check, to determine if the applicant is eligible to receive such long gun. If it is determined that the applicant is ineligible to receive such long gun, the Commissioner of Emergency Services and Public Protection shall immediately notify the person, firm or corporation to whom such application was made and no such long gun shall be sold, delivered or otherwise transferred to such applicant by such person, firm or corporation. When any long gun is delivered in connection with any sale or purchase, such long gun shall be enclosed in a package, the paper or wrapping of which shall be securely fastened, and no such long gun when delivered on any sale or purchase shall be loaded or contain any gunpowder or other explosive or any bullet, ball or shell. Upon the sale, delivery or other transfer of the long gun, the transferee shall sign in triplicate a receipt for such long gun, which shall contain the name, address and date and place of birth of such transferee, the date of such sale, delivery or transfer and the caliber, make, model and manufacturer's number and a general description thereof. Not later than twenty-four hours after such sale, delivery or transfer, the transferor shall send by first class mail or electronically transfer one receipt to the Commissioner of Emergency Services and Public Protection and one receipt to the chief of police or, where there is no chief of police, the warden of the borough or the first selectman, of the town in which the transferee resides, and shall retain one receipt, together with the original application, for at least five years.

(e) No sale, delivery or other transfer of any long gun shall be made by a person who is not a federally licensed firearm manufacturer, importer or dealer to a person who is not a federally licensed firearm manufacturer, importer or dealer unless:

(1) The prospective transferor and prospective transferee comply with the provisions of subsection (d) of this section and the prospective transferor has obtained an authorization number from the Commissioner of Emergency Services and Public Protection for such sale, delivery or transfer; or

(2) The prospective transferor or prospective transferee requests a federally licensed firearm dealer to contact the Department of Emergency Services and Public Protection on behalf of such prospective transferor or prospective transferee and the federally licensed firearm dealer has obtained an authorization number from the Commissioner of Emergency Services and Public Protection for such sale, delivery or transfer.

(f) (1) On and after January 1, 2014, for purposes of a transfer pursuant to subdivision (2) of subsection (e) of this section, a prospective transferor or prospective transferee may request a federally licensed firearm dealer to contact the Department of Emergency Services and Public Protection to obtain an authorization number for such sale, delivery or transfer. If a federally licensed firearm dealer consents to contact the department on behalf of the prospective transferor or prospective transferee, the prospective transferor or prospective transferee shall provide to such dealer the name, sex, race, date of birth and state of residence of the prospective transferee and, if necessary to verify the identity of the prospective transferee, may provide a unique numeric identifier including, but not limited to, a Social Security number, and additional identifiers including, but not limited to, height, weight, eye and hair color, and place of birth. The prospective transferee shall present to the dealer such prospective transferee's valid long gun eligibility certificate issued pursuant to section 29-37p, valid permit to carry a pistol or revolver issued pursuant to subsection (b) of section 29-28, valid permit to sell at retail a pistol or revolver issued pursuant to subsection (a) of section 29-28 or valid eligibility certificate for a pistol or revolver issued pursuant to section 29-36f. The dealer may charge a fee for contacting the department on behalf of the prospective transferor or prospective transferee.

(2) The Department of Emergency Services and Public Protection shall make every effort, including performing the national instant criminal background check, to determine if the prospective transferee is eligible to receive such long gun. The Commissioner of Emergency Services and Public Protection shall immediately notify the dealer of the department's determination and the dealer shall immediately notify the prospective transferor or prospective transferee of such determination. If the department determines the prospective transferee is ineligible to receive such long gun, no long gun shall be sold, delivered or otherwise transferred by the prospective transferor to the prospective transferee. If the department determines the prospective transferee is eligible to receive such long gun and provides an authorization number for such sale, delivery or transfer, the prospective transferor may proceed to sell, deliver or otherwise transfer the long gun to the prospective transferee.

(3) Upon the sale, delivery or other transfer of the long gun, the transferor or transferee shall complete a form, prescribed by the Commissioner of Emergency Services and Public Protection, that contains the name and address of the transferor, the name and address of the transferee, the date and place of birth of such transferee, the firearm permit or certificate number of the transferee, the firearm permit or certificate number of the transferor, if any, the date of such sale, delivery or transfer, the caliber, make, model and manufacturer's number and a general description of such long gun and the authorization number provided by the department. Not later than twenty-four hours after such sale, delivery or transfer, the transferor shall send by first class mail or electronically transfer one copy of such form to the Commissioner of Emergency Services and Public Protection and one copy to the chief of police or, where there is no chief of police, the warden of the borough or the first selectman, of the town in which the transferee resides, and shall retain one copy, for at least five years.

(g) Prior to April 1, 2014, no sale, delivery or other transfer of any long gun shall be made until the expiration of two weeks from the date of the application, except that such waiting period shall not apply to any federal marshal, parole officer or peace officer, or to the sale, delivery or other transfer of (1) any long gun to a holder of a valid state permit to carry a pistol or revolver issued under the provisions of section 29-28, a valid eligibility certificate issued under the provisions of section 29-36f, or a valid long gun eligibility certificate issued under the provisions of section 29-37p, (2) any long gun to an active member of the armed forces of the United States or of any reserve component thereof, (3) any long gun to a holder of a valid hunting license issued pursuant to chapter 490,1 or (4) antique firearms. For the purposes of this subsection, "antique firearm" means any firearm which was manufactured in or before 1898 and any replica of such firearm, provided such replica is not designed or redesigned for using rimfire or conventional centerfire fixed ammunition except rimfire or conventional centerfire fixed ammunition which is no longer manufactured in the United States and not readily available in the ordinary channel of commercial trade.

(h) The provisions of subsections (c) to (g), inclusive of this section shall not apply to the sale, delivery or transfer of (1) long guns to (A) the Department of Emergency Services and Public Protection, police departments, the Department of Correction, the Division of Criminal Justice, the Department of Motor Vehicles, the Department of Energy and Environmental Protection or the military or naval forces of this state or of the United States, (B) a sworn and duly certified member of an organized police department, the Division of State Police within the Department of Emergency Services and Public Protection or the Department of Correction, a chief inspector or inspector in the Division of Criminal Justice, a salaried inspector of motor vehicles designated by the Commissioner of Motor Vehicles, a conservation officer or special conservation officer appointed by the Commissioner of Energy and Environmental Protection pursuant to section 26-5, or a constable who is certified by the Police Officer Standards and Training Council and appointed by the chief executive authority of a town, city or borough to perform criminal law enforcement duties, pursuant to a letter on the letterhead of such department, division, commissioner or authority authorizing the purchase and stating that the sworn member, inspector, officer or constable will use the long gun in the discharge of official duties, and that a records check indicates that the sworn member, inspector, officer or constable has not been convicted of a crime of family violence, for use by such sworn member, inspector, officer or constable in the discharge of such sworn member's, inspector's, officer's or constable's official duties or when off duty, (C) a member of the military or naval forces of this state or of the United States, or (D) a nuclear facility licensed by the United States Nuclear Regulatory Commission for the purpose of providing security services at such facility, or any contractor or subcontractor of such facility for the purpose of providing security services at such facility; (2) long guns to or between federally licensed firearm manufacturers, importers or dealers; (3) curios or relics, as defined in 27 CFR 478.11, to or between federally licensed firearm collectors; or (4) antique firearms, as defined in subsection (g) of this section.

(i) If the court finds that a violation of this section is not of a serious nature and that the person charged with such violation (1) will probably not offend in the future, (2) has not previously been convicted of a violation of this section, and (3) has not previously had a prosecution under this section suspended pursuant to this subsection, it may order suspension of prosecution. The court shall not order suspension of prosecution unless the accused person has acknowledged that he understands the consequences of the suspension of prosecution. Any person for whom prosecution is suspended shall agree to the tolling of any statute of limitations with respect to such violation and to a waiver of his right to a speedy trial. Such person shall appear in court and shall be released to the custody of the Court Support Services Division for such period, not exceeding two years, and under such conditions as the court shall order. If the person refuses to accept, or, having accepted, violates such conditions, the court shall terminate the suspension of prosecution and the case shall be brought to trial. If such person satisfactorily completes his period of probation, he may apply for dismissal of the charges against him and the court, on finding such satisfactory completion, shall dismiss such charges. If the person does not apply for dismissal of the charges against him after satisfactorily completing his period of probation, the court, upon receipt of a report submitted by the Court Support Services Division that the person satisfactorily completed his period of probation, may on its own motion make a finding of such satisfactory completion and dismiss such charges. Upon dismissal, all records of such charges shall be erased pursuant to section 54-142a. An order of the court denying a motion to dismiss the charges against a person who has completed his period of probation or terminating the participation of a defendant in such program shall be a final judgment for purposes of appeal.

(j) Any person who violates any provision of this section shall be guilty of a class D felony, except that any person who sells, delivers or otherwise transfers a long gun in violation of the provisions of this section, knowing that such long gun is stolen or that the manufacturer's number or other mark of identification on such long gun has been altered, removed or obliterated, shall be guilty of a class B felony, and any long gun found in the possession of any person in violation of any provision of this section shall be forfeited.

Sec. 29-37b. Retail dealer to equip pistols and revolvers with gun locking device and provide written warning at time of sale. Penalty.

(a) Each person, firm or corporation which engages in the retail sale of any pistol or revolver, at the time of sale of any such pistol or revolver, shall (1) equip such pistol or revolver with a reusable trigger lock, gun lock or gun locking device appropriate for such firearm, which lock or device shall be constructed of material sufficiently strong to prevent it from being easily disabled and have a locking mechanism accessible by key or by electronic or other mechanical accessory specific to such lock or device to prevent unauthorized removal, and (2) provide to the purchaser thereof a written warning which shall state in block letters not less than one inch in height "UNLAWFUL STORAGE OF A LOADED FIREARM MAY RESULT IN IMPRISONMENT OR FINE."

(b) Each such person, firm or corporation shall conspicuously post and at all times display the warning specified in subsection (a) of this section in block letters not less than three inches in height.

(c) Any person, firm or corporation which violates any provision of this section shall be fined not less than five hundred dollars for each violation.

Sec. 29-37d. Firearms dealer to install burglar alarm system on premises of its establishment. Exceptions.

(a) On and after July 1, 1993, each business organization which engages in the retail sale of firearms, as defined in section 53a-3, as a regular course of trade or business, shall have a burglar alarm system installed on the premises of its establishment in which ten or more firearms are stored and kept for sale. Such alarm system shall be directly connected to the local police department or monitored by a central station and shall activate upon unauthorized entry or interruption to such system. For the purposes of this section, "business organization" means a sole proprietorship, partnership, firm, corporation or other form of business or legal entity. The provisions of this section shall not apply to any person who (1) sells or exchanges a firearm for the enhancement of a personal collection or as a hobby, (2) sells all or part of a personal collection of firearms, or (3) sells firearms from his own residence and keeps for sale not more than ten firearms.

(b) The Commissioner of Emergency Services and Public Protection may, after notice and opportunity for a hearing, impose a civil penalty of not more than one hundred dollars for a violation of this section. Each violation shall be a separate and distinct offense and, in case of a continuing violation, each day's continuance thereof shall be deemed a separate and distinct offense, provided the civil penalty may not exceed four thousand nine hundred dollars in the aggregate for a continuing violation.

(c) The commissioner may adopt regulations, in accordance with the provisions of chapter 54, to implement the provisions of this section.

Sec. 29-37e. False statement or information in connection with the sale or transfer of firearm other than pistol or revolver prohibited.

(a) No person shall make any false statement or give any false information connected with any purchase, sale, delivery or other transfer of any firearm other than a pistol or revolver. Any person violating any provision of this subsection shall be guilty of a class D felony.

(b) Any firearm found in the possession of any person in violation of this section shall be forfeited.

Sec. 29-37f. Qualifications of retail store employees who sell firearms.

No person, firm or corporation that engages in the retail sale of goods, where the principal part of such trade or business is the retail sale of goods other than firearms, shall employ a person to sell firearms in a retail store unless such person (1) is at least eighteen years of age, (2) has submitted to state and national criminal history records checks and such checks indicate that such person has not been convicted of a felony or a violation specified in subdivision (2) of subsection (b) of section 29-36f, and (3) has successfully completed a course or testing approved by the Commissioner of Emergency Services and Public Protection in firearms safety and statutory procedures relating to the sale of firearms. The sale of firearms by such person, firm or corporation shall be accomplished only by an employee qualified pursuant to this section. Any employer who employs a person to sell firearms in violation of the provisions of this section shall be liable for a civil penalty of not more than ten thousand dollars per day for each violation. The Attorney General shall institute a civil action to recover such penalty.

Sec. 29-37g. Gun show requirements.

(a) For the purposes of this section, (1) "gun show" means any event (A) at which fifty or more firearms are offered or exhibited for sale, transfer or exchange to the public and (B) at which two or more persons are exhibiting one or more firearms for sale, transfer or exchange to the public; and (2) "gun show promoter" means any person who organizes, plans, promotes or operates a gun show.

(b) Not later than thirty days before commencement of a gun show, the gun show promoter shall notify the Commissioner of Emergency Services and Public Protection and the chief of police or, where there is not chief of police, the warden of the borough or the chief executive officer of the town in which the gun show is to take place of the date, time, duration and location of the gun show.

(c) No person, firm or corporation shall sell, deliver or otherwise transfer a firearm at a gun show until such person, firm or corporation has complied with the provisions of section 29-36*l*.

Sec. 29-37i. (Formerly Sec. 29-37c). Responsibilities re storage of loaded firearms.

No person shall store or keep any firearm, as defined in section 53a-3, on any premises under such person's control if such person knows or reasonably should know that (1) a minor is likely to gain access to the firearm without the permission of the parent or guardian of the minor, (2) a resident of the premises is ineligible to possess a firearm under state or federal law, (3) a resident of the premises is subject to a risk protection order issued pursuant to section 29-38c, or (4) a resident of the premises poses a risk of imminent personal injury to himself or herself or to another person, unless such person (A) keeps the firearm in a securely locked box or other container or in a manner which a reasonable person would believe to be secure, or (B) carries the firearm on his or her person or within such close proximity thereto that such person can readily retrieve and use the firearm as if such person carried the firearm on his or her person. For the purposes of this section, "minor" means any person under the age of eighteen years.

ANNOTATIONS:

State v. Wilchinski, 242 Conn. 211, 700 A.2d 1 (1997):

> For purposes of Conn. Gen. Stat. §29-37i(1), "locked" modifies both "container" and "box" for the keeping of firearms. The legislative history of § 29-37i further indicates that, although no specific storage method is required, some physical impediment to access is mandatory... The most appropriate and efficient means to achieve the goal of restricting access to a loaded firearm depends on facts uniquely within the knowledge of the individual gun owner. The most obvious variables include the ages of children in the household, the physical layout of the home, and the availability of locked safes or closets. A high shelf in a closet may be a secure location when the only child in the household is a toddler, but when older children are present in the home, it may be necessary to use trigger locks and a locked container..."§ 29-37i defines a standard of care for the storage of loaded firearms and § 53a-217a punishes the criminally negligent violation of that standard of care."

Sec. 29-37j. Purchase of firearm with intent to transfer to person prohibited from purchasing or receiving a firearm. Assistance from person prohibited from purchasing or receiving a firearm. Penalties.

(a) Any person who purchases a firearm, as defined in section 53a-3, pursuant to section 29-33 or 29-37a with the intent to transfer such firearm to any other person who the transferor knows or has reason to believe is prohibited from purchasing or otherwise receiving such a firearm pursuant to section 29-33 or 29-37a shall be guilty of a class C felony for which two years of the sentence imposed may not be suspended or reduced by the court, and five thousand dollars of the fine imposed may not be remitted or reduced by the court unless the court states on the record its reasons for remitting or reducing such fine.

(b) Any person prohibited from purchasing or otherwise receiving or possessing a firearm and who solicits, employs or assists any person in violating the provisions of subsection (a) of this section shall be guilty of a class D felony for which one year of the sentence imposed may not be suspended or reduced by the court, and three thousand dollars of the fine imposed may not be remitted or reduced by the court unless the court states on the record its reasons for remitting or reducing such fine, except that if such person who is prohibited from purchasing or otherwise receiving or possessing a firearm obtains a firearm pursuant to a violation of subsection (a) of this section, such person shall be guilty of a class C felony for which two years of the sentence imposed may not be suspended or reduced by the court, and five thousand dollars of the fine imposed may not be remitted or reduced by the court unless the court states on the record its reasons for remitting or reducing such fine. Each transfer shall constitute a separate offense.

(c) Any person convicted of violating the provisions of subsection (a) or (b) of this section and who was convicted of a felony within the prior five-year period shall be guilty of a class B felony for which three years of the sentence imposed may not be suspended or reduced by the court, and ten thousand dollars of the fine imposed may not be remitted or reduced by the court unless the court states on the record its reasons for remitting or reducing such fine.

Sec. 29-37p. Long gun eligibility certificate. Disqualifiers.

(a) Any person who is eighteen years of age or older may apply to the Commissioner of Emergency Services and Public Protection for a long gun eligibility certificate.

(b) The Commissioner of Emergency Services and Public Protection shall issue a long gun eligibility certificate unless said commissioner finds that the applicant: (1) Has failed to successfully complete a course approved by the Commissioner of Emergency Services and Public Protection in the safety and use of firearms including, but not limited to, a safety or training course in the use of firearms available to the public offered by a law enforcement agency, a private or public educational institution or a firearms training school, utilizing instructors certified by the National Rifle Association or the Department of Energy and Environmental Protection and a safety or training course in the use of firearms conducted by an instructor certified by the state or the National Rifle Association; (2) has been convicted of (A) a felony, (B) a misdemeanor violation of section 21a-279 on or after October 1, 2015, or (C) a misdemeanor violation of section 53a-58, 53a-61, 53a-61a, 53a-62, 53a-63, 53a-96, 53a-175, 53a-176, 53a-178 or 53a-181d during the preceding twenty years; (3) has been convicted as delinquent for the commission of a serious juvenile offense, as defined in section 46b-120; (4) has been discharged from custody within the preceding twenty years after having been found not guilty of a crime by reason of mental disease or defect pursuant to section 53a-13; (5) has been confined in a hospital for persons with psychiatric disabilities, as defined in section 17a-495, within the preceding sixty months by order of a probate court; (6) has been voluntarily admitted to a hospital for persons with psychiatric disabilities, as defined in section 17a-495, within the preceding six months for care and treatment of a psychiatric disability and not solely for being an alcohol-dependent person or a drug-dependent person as those terms are defined in section 17a-680; (7) is subject to a restraining or protective order issued by a court in a case involving the use, attempted use or threatened use of physical force against another person, including an ex parte order issued pursuant to section 46b-15 or 46b-16a; (8) is subject to a firearms seizure order issued prior to June 1, 2022, pursuant to section 29-38c after notice and hearing, or a risk protection order or risk protection investigation order issued on or after June 1, 2022, pursuant to section 29-38c; (9) is prohibited from shipping, transporting, possessing or receiving a firearm pursuant to 18 USC 922(g)(4); or (10) is an alien illegally or unlawfully in the United States.

Commentary

Unlike permits to carry pistols or revolvers issued pursuant to Conn. Gen. Stat. § 29-28, applications for a long gun eligibility certificate cannot be denied on the basis of the applicant's overall "suitability." The grounds for denial of a long gun eligibility certificate are set forth in Conn. Gen. Stat. § 29-37p and, upon proper application and receipt of the results of the criminal history records check mandated by Conn. Gen. Stat. § 29-37q, are exclusive. Persons aggrieved by a denial of a long gun eligibility certificate may appeal such action to the Board of Firearms Permit Examiners in accordance with the provisions of Conn. Gen. Stat. § 29-32b above.

Sec. 29-37q. Long gun eligibility certificate. Application. Form and content. Confidentiality.

(a) Requests for long gun eligibility certificates under section 29-37p shall be submitted to the Commissioner of Emergency Services and Public Protection on application forms prescribed by the commissioner. No long gun eligibility certificate shall be issued under the provisions of section 29-37p unless the applicant for such certificate gives to the Commissioner of Emergency Services and Public Protection, upon the commissioner's request, full information concerning the applicant's criminal record and relevant information concerning the applicant's mental health history. The commissioner shall require each applicant to submit to state and national criminal history records checks in accordance with section 29-17a. The commissioner shall take a full description of such applicant. The commissioner shall take the fingerprints of such applicant or conduct any other method of positive identification required by the State Police Bureau of Identification or the Federal Bureau of Investigation. The commissioner shall record the date the fingerprints were taken in the applicant's file and shall conduct criminal history records checks in accordance with section 29-17a. The commissioner shall, not later than sixty days after receipt of the national criminal history records check from the Federal Bureau of Investigation, either approve the application and issue the long gun eligibility certificate or deny the application and notify the applicant of the reason for such denial in writing.

(b) A long gun eligibility certificate shall be of such form and content as the commissioner may prescribe, shall be signed by the certificate holder and shall contain an identification number, the name, address, place and date of birth, height, weight and eye color of the certificate holder and a full-face photograph of the certificate holder.

(c) A person holding a long gun eligibility certificate issued by the commissioner shall notify the commissioner not later than two business days after any change of such person's address. The notification shall include both the old address and the new address of such person.

(d) Notwithstanding the provisions of sections 1-210 and 1-211, the name and address of a person issued a long gun eligibility certificate under the provisions of section 29-37p shall be confidential and shall not be disclosed, except (1) such information may be disclosed to law enforcement officials acting in the performance of their duties, including, but not limited to, employees of the United States Probation Office acting in the performance of their duties and parole officers within the Department of Correction acting within the performance of their duties, (2) the Commissioner of Emergency Services and Public Protection may disclose such information to the extent necessary to comply with a request made pursuant to section 29-37a or 29-38m for verification that such certificate is still valid and has not been suspended or revoked, and (3) such information may be disclosed to the Commissioner of Mental Health and Addiction Services to carry out the provisions of subsection (c) of section 17a-500.

Sec. 29-37r. Long gun eligibility certificate. Fees. Expiration and renewal.

(a) The fee for each long gun eligibility certificate originally issued under the provisions of section 29-37p shall be thirty-five dollars and for each renewal thereof thirty-five dollars, which fees shall be paid to the Commissioner of Emergency Services and Public Protection. Upon deposit of such fees in the General Fund, the fees shall be credited to the appropriation to the Department of Emergency Services and Public Protection to a separate nonlapsing account for the purposes of the issuance of long gun eligibility certificates under said section.

(b) A long gun eligibility certificate originally issued under the provisions of section 29-37p shall expire five years after the date it becomes effective and each renewal thereof shall expire five years after the expiration date of the certificate being renewed.

(c) The renewal fee shall apply for each renewal that is requested not earlier than thirty-one days before, and not later than thirty-one days after, the expiration date of the certificate being renewed.

(d) No fee or portion thereof paid under the provisions of this section for issuance or renewal of a long gun eligibility certificate shall be refundable except if the certificate for which the fee or portion thereof was paid was not issued or renewed.

(e) The Commissioner of Emergency Services and Public Protection shall send a notice of the expiration of a long gun eligibility certificate issued pursuant to section 29-37p to the holder of such certificate, by first class mail, at the address of such person as shown by the records of the commissioner, not less than ninety days before such expiration, and shall enclose therein a form for the renewal of such certificate. A long gun eligibility certificate issued pursuant to said section shall be valid for a period of ninety days from the expiration date, except this provision shall not apply to any certificate which has been revoked or for which revocation is pending, pursuant to section 29-37s.

Sec. 29-37s. Long gun eligibility certificate. Revocation. Reinstatement.

(a) A long gun eligibility certificate shall be revoked by the Commissioner of Emergency Services and Public Protection upon the occurrence of any event which would have disqualified the holder from being issued the certificate pursuant to section 29-37p.

(b) Upon the revocation of any long gun eligibility certificate, the person whose certificate is revoked shall be notified, in writing, and such certificate shall be forthwith delivered to the Commissioner of Emergency Services and Public Protection. Any person who fails to surrender such certificate within five days of notification, in writing, of revocation thereof shall be guilty of a class A misdemeanor.

(c) If a long gun eligibility certificate is revoked because the person holding such certificate is subject to an ex parte order issued pursuant to section 46b-15 or 46b-16a, upon expiration of such order, such person may notify the Department of Emergency Services and Public Protection that such order has expired. Upon verification of such expiration and provided such person is not otherwise disqualified from holding such certificate pursuant to section 29-37p, the department shall reinstate such certificate.

Commentary

Unlike permits to carry pistols or revolvers issued pursuant to Conn. Gen. Stat. § 29-28, applications for a long gun eligibility certificate cannot be revoked on the basis of the applicant's overall "suitability." The grounds for revocation of a long gun eligibility certificate are set forth in Conn. Gen. Stat. § 29-37s and, upon proper application and receipt of the results of the criminal history records check mandated by Conn. Gen. Stat. § 29-37q, are exclusive. Persons aggrieved by a denial of a long gun eligibility certificate may appeal such action to the Board of Firearms Permit Examiners in accordance with the provisions of Conn. Gen. Stat. § 29-32b above

Sec. 29-38. Weapons in vehicles. Penalty. Exceptions.

(a) Any person who knowingly has, in any vehicle owned, operated or occupied by such person, any weapon, any pistol or revolver for which a proper permit has not been issued as provided in section 29-28 or any machine gun which has not been registered as required by section 53-202, shall be guilty of a class D felony, and the presence of any such weapon, pistol or revolver, or machine gun in any vehicle shall be prima facie evidence of a violation of this section by the owner, operator and each occupant thereof. The word "weapon", as used in this section, means any BB. gun, any blackjack, any metal or brass knuckles, any police baton or nightstick, any dirk knife or switch knife, any knife having an automatic spring release device by which a blade is released from the handle, having a blade of over one and one-half inches in length, any stiletto, any knife the edged portion of the blade of which is four inches or more in length, any martial arts weapon or electronic defense weapon, as defined in section 53a-3, or any other dangerous or deadly weapon or instrument.

(b) The provisions of this section shall not apply to: (1) Any officer charged with the preservation of the public peace while engaged in the pursuit of such officer's official duties; (2) any security guard having a baton or nightstick in a vehicle while engaged in the pursuit of such guard's official duties; (3) any person enrolled in and currently attending a martial arts school, with official verification of such enrollment and attendance, or any certified martial arts instructor, having any such martial arts weapon in a vehicle while traveling to or from such school or to or from an authorized event or competition; (4) any person having a BB. gun in a vehicle provided such weapon is unloaded and stored in the trunk of such vehicle or in a locked container other than the glove compartment or console; (5) any person having a knife, the edged portion of the blade of which is four inches or more in length, in a vehicle if such person is (A) any member of the armed forces of the United States, as defined in section 27-103, or any reserve component thereof, or of the armed forces of the state, as defined in section 27-2, when on duty or going to or from duty, (B) any member of any military organization when on parade or when going to or from any place of assembly, (C) any person while transporting such knife as merchandise or for display at an authorized gun or knife show, (D) any person while lawfully removing such person's household goods or effects from one place to another, or from one residence to another, (E) any person while actually and peaceably engaged in carrying any such knife from such person's place of abode or business to a place or person where or by whom such knife is to be repaired, or while actually and peaceably returning to such person's place of abode or business with such knife after the same has been repaired, (F) any person holding a valid hunting, fishing or trapping license issued pursuant to chapter 490 or any saltwater fisherman while having such knife in a vehicle for lawful hunting, fishing or trapping activities, or (G) any person participating in an authorized historic reenactment; or (6) any person having an electronic defense weapon, as defined in section 53a-3, in a vehicle, who is twenty-one years of age or older and possesses a permit or certificate issued under the provisions of section 29-28, 29-36f, 29-37p 0r 29-38n; or (7) any person having a dirk knife or police baton in a vehicle while lawfully moving such person's household goods or effects from one place to another, or from one residence to another.

Sec. 29-38b. Determination of commitment status of person who applies for or seeks renewal of firearm permit or certificate. Report on status of application.

(a) The Commissioner of Emergency Services and Public Protection, in fulfilling his obligations under sections 29-28 to 29-38, inclusive, and section 53-202d, shall verify that any person who, on or after October 1, 1998, applies for or seeks renewal of a permit to sell at retail a pistol or revolver, a permit to carry a pistol or revolver, an eligibility certificate for a pistol or revolver or a certificate of possession for an assault weapon, or who, on or after July 1, 2013, applies for or seeks renewal of a long gun eligibility certificate, has not been confined in a hospital for persons with psychiatric disabilities, as defined in section 17a-495, within the preceding sixty months by order of a probate court or has not been voluntarily admitted to a hospital for persons with psychiatric disabilities, as defined in section 17a-495, within the preceding six months for care and treatment of a psychiatric disability and not solely for being an alcohol-dependent person or a drug-dependent person as those terms are defined in section 17a-680, by making an inquiry to the Department of Mental Health and Addiction Services in such a manner so as to only receive a report on the commitment or admission status of the person with respect to whom the inquiry is made including identifying information in accordance with the provisions of subsection (b) of section 17a-500.

(b) If the Commissioner of Emergency Services and Public Protection determines pursuant to subsection (a) of this section that a person has been confined in a hospital for persons with psychiatric disabilities, as defined in section 17a-495, within the preceding sixty months by order of a probate court or has been voluntarily admitted to a hospital for persons with psychiatric disabilities, as defined in section 17a-495, within the preceding six months for care and treatment of a psychiatric disability and not solely for being an alcohol-dependent person or a drug-dependent person as those terms are defined in section 17a-680, said commissioner shall report the status of such person's application for or renewal of a permit to sell at retail a pistol or revolver, a permit to carry a pistol or revolver, an eligibility certificate for a pistol or revolver, a certificate of possession for an assault weapon or a long gun eligibility certificate to the Commissioner of Mental Health and Addiction Services for the purpose of fulfilling his responsibilities under subsection (c) of section 17a-500.

Section 29-38c. Seizure of firearms of person posing risk of imminent personal injury to self or others.

(a) Upon complaint on oath by any state's attorney or assistant state's attorney or by any two police officers, to any judge of the Superior Court, that such state's attorney, assistant state's attorney or police officers have probable cause to believe that a person poses a risk of imminent personal injury to himself or herself or to another person, the judge may issue a risk protection order prohibiting such person from acquiring or possessing a firearm or other deadly weapon or ammunition. As part of or following the issuance of such order, if there is probable cause to believe that (1) such person possesses one or more firearms or other deadly weapons, and (2) such firearm or firearms or other deadly weapon or deadly weapons are within or upon any place, thing or person, such judge shall issue a warrant commanding a police officer to enter into or upon such place or thing, search the same or the person and take into such officer's custody any and all firearms and other deadly weapons and ammunition. Such state's attorney, assistant state's attorney or police officers may not make such complaint unless such state's attorney, assistant state's attorney or police officers have conducted an independent investigation and determined that such probable cause exists. Upon the issuance of any such order and warrant, if applicable, the judge shall order the clerk of the court to give notice to the Commissioner of Emergency Services and Public Protection of the issuance of such order and warrant, if applicable.

(b) (1) Any family or household member or medical professional who has a good faith belief that a person poses a risk of imminent personal injury to himself or herself or to another person may make an application for a risk protection order investigation with the clerk of the court for any geographical area. The application and accompanying affidavit shall be made under oath and indicate: (A) The factual basis for the applicant's belief that such person poses a risk of imminent personal injury to himself or herself or to another person; (B) whether such person holds a permit under subsection (b) of section 29-28, as amended by this act, or an eligibility certificate issued under section 29-36f, as amended by this act, 29-37p, as amended by this act, or 29-38n or currently possesses one or more firearms or other deadly weapons or ammunition, if known; and (C) where any such firearm or other deadly weapon or ammunition is located, if known.

(2) Upon receipt of an application and affidavit pursuant to this subsection, if the court finds that there is a good faith belief that a person poses a risk of imminent personal injury to himself or herself or to another person, the court shall order a risk protection order investigation to determine if the person who is the subject of the application poses a risk

of imminent personal injury to himself or herself or to another person. Upon issuance by the court of an order for investigation, the court shall: (A) Give notice to the Commissioner of Emergency Services and Public Protection of the issuance of the order for a risk protection order investigation; and (B) immediately give notice of the order and transmit the order and the application and affidavit on which the order is based to the law enforcement agency for the town in which the subject of the investigation resides. The court shall immediately enter into the National Instant Criminal Background Check System (NICS) a record indicating that the person who is the subject of the investigation is ineligible to purchase or otherwise receive a firearm.

(3) Upon receipt of an investigation order, the law enforcement agency shall immediately investigate whether the subject of the investigation poses a risk of imminent personal injury to himself or herself or to another person. If the law enforcement agency determines that there is probable cause to believe that the subject of the investigation poses a risk of imminent personal injury to himself or herself or to another person, such law enforcement agency shall seek a risk protection order, and when applicable, a warrant pursuant to subsection (a) of this section not later than twenty-four hours after receiving the investigation order, or, if the law enforcement agency needs additional time to complete the investigation, as soon thereafter as is practicable. If the law enforcement agency determines that there is no probable cause to believe that the subject of the investigation poses a risk of imminent personal injury to himself or herself or to another person, the law enforcement agency shall notify the court, the applicant, and the Commissioner of Emergency Services and Public Protection of such determination, in writing, not later than forty-eight hours after receiving the investigation order, if practicable, or, if the law enforcement agency needs additional time to complete the risk warrant investigation, as soon thereafter as is practicable. Upon receiving such notification that there was not a finding of probable cause, the court shall immediately remove or cancel any record entered into the National Instant Criminal Background Check System associated with such investigation for which there was no finding of probable cause.

(c) A risk protection order and warrant, if applicable, issued under subsection (a) of this section, may issue only on affidavit sworn to by the complainant or complainants before the judge and establishing the grounds for issuing the order and warrant, if applicable, which shall be part of the court file. In determining whether there is probable cause for a risk protection order and warrant, if applicable, under subsection (a) of this section, the judge shall consider: (1) Recent threats or acts of violence by such person directed toward other persons; (2) recent threats or acts of violence by such person directed toward himself or herself; and (3) recent acts of cruelty to animals as provided in subsection (b) of section 53-247 by such person. In evaluating whether such recent threats or acts of violence constitute probable cause to believe that such person poses a risk of imminent personal injury to himself or herself or to others, the judge may consider other factors including, but not limited to (A) the reckless use, display or brandishing of a firearm or other deadly weapon by such person, (B) a history of the use, attempted use or threatened use of physical force by such person against other persons, (C) prior involuntary confinement of such person in a hospital for persons with psychiatric disabilities, and (D) the illegal use of controlled substances or abuse of alcohol by such person. In the case of a complaint made under subsection (a) of this section, if the judge is satisfied that the grounds for the complaint exist or that there is probable cause to believe that such grounds exist, such judge shall issue a risk protection order and warrant, if applicable, naming or describing the person, and, in the case of the issuance of a warrant, the place or thing to be searched. If the requisite circumstances are met, the judge shall issue a risk protection order regardless of whether the person is already ineligible to possess a firearm. The warrant shall be directed to any police officer of a regularly organized police department or any state police officer. The order and warrant, if applicable, shall state the grounds or probable cause for issuance and, in the case of a warrant, the warrant shall command the officer to search within a reasonable time the person, place or thing named for any and all firearms and other deadly weapons and ammunition. A copy of the order and warrant, if applicable, shall be given to the person named in the order together with a notice informing the person that such person has the right to a hearing under this section, the telephone number for the court clerk who can inform the person of the date and time of such hearing and the right to be represented by counsel at such hearing.

(d) (1) In the case of a warrant, the municipal or state police agency that executed the warrant shall file a copy of the application for the warrant and all affidavits upon which the warrant is based with the clerk of the court for the geographical area within which the search was conducted and with the state's attorney's office for such judicial district no later than the next business day following the execution of the warrant. Prior to the execution and return of the warrant, the clerk of the court shall not disclose any information pertaining to the application for the warrant or any affidavits upon which the warrant is based. The warrant shall be executed and returned with reasonable promptness consistent with due process of law and shall be accompanied by a written inventory of all firearms and other deadly weapons and ammunition seized.

(2) In the case of a risk protection order, not later than the next business day following the service of the order, the municipal or state police agency that served the order shall file with the court of the geographical area in the location in which the subject of the order resides a copy of the order and transmit to the state's attorney's office for such judicial district a return of service stating the date and time that the order was served. Prior to the service and return of the order, the clerk of court shall not disclose any information pertaining to the application for the order or any affidavits upon which the order is based to any person outside the Judicial Branch, the municipal or state police agency that served the order, or the state's attorney's office for the judicial district within which the order was served. The order shall be served and returned with reasonable promptness consistent with due process of law.

(e) Not later than fourteen days after the service of a risk protection order or execution of a warrant under this section, the court for the geographical area where the person named in the order or warrant resides shall hold a hearing to determine whether the risk protection order should continue to apply and whether the firearm or firearms or other deadly weapon or deadly weapons and any ammunition seized should be returned to the person named in the warrant or should continue to be held by the state. At such hearing the state shall have the burden of proving all material facts by clear and convincing evidence. If, after such hearing, the court finds by clear and convincing evidence that the person poses a risk of imminent personal injury to himself or herself or to another person, the court may order that the risk protection order continue to apply and that the firearm or firearms or other deadly weapon or deadly weapons and any ammunition seized pursuant to the warrant issued under subsection (a) of this section continue to be held by the state until such time that the court shall terminate such order pursuant to subsection (f) of this section and order the firearm or firearms or other deadly weapon or deadly weapons and any ammunition seized to be returned as soon as practicable to the person named in the warrant, provided such person is otherwise legally able to possess such firearm or firearms or other deadly weapon or deadly weapons and ammunition. If the court finds that the state has failed to prove by clear and convincing evidence that the petitioner poses a risk of imminent personal injury to himself or herself or to another person, the court shall terminate such order and warrant, if applicable, and order the firearm or firearms or other deadly weapon or deadly weapons and any ammunition seized to be returned as soon as is practicable to the person named in the warrant, provided such person is otherwise legally able to possess such firearm or firearms or other deadly weapon or deadly weapons and ammunition. If the court finds that the person poses a risk of imminent personal injury to himself or herself or to another person, the court shall give notice to the Department of Mental Health and Addiction Services which may take such action pursuant to chapter 319i as the department deems appropriate.

(f) A risk protection order, and warrant, if applicable, shall continue to apply and the firearm or firearms or other deadly weapon or deadly weapons and any ammunition held pursuant to subsection (e) of this section shall continue to be held by the state until such time that the person named in the order and warrant, if applicable, successfully petitions the court to terminate such order and warrant, if applicable. The person named in the order may first petition the court of the geographical area where the proceeding was originally conducted for a hearing to terminate such order, and warrant if applicable, at least one hundred eighty days after the hearing held pursuant to subsection (e) of this section. Upon the filing of such petition, the court shall (1) provide to the petitioner a hearing date that is on the twenty-eighth day following the filing of such petition or the business day nearest to such day if such twenty-eighth day is not a business day, (2) notify the Division of Criminal Justice of the filing of such petition, and (3) direct the law enforcement agency for the town in which the petitioner resides to determine, not later than fourteen days after the filing of such petition, whether there is probable cause to believe that the petitioner poses a risk of imminent personal injury to himself or herself or to another person. No finding of probable cause may be found solely because the petitioner is subject to an existing risk protection order or warrant. If the law enforcement agency finds no probable cause, the agency shall so notify the court which shall cancel the hearing and terminate the order and warrant, if applicable. If the law enforcement agency finds probable cause, the agency shall notify the court of such finding and the hearing shall proceed as scheduled. At such hearing the state shall have the burden of proving all material facts by clear and convincing evidence. If the court, following such hearing, finds by clear and convincing evidence that the petitioner poses a risk of imminent personal injury to himself or herself or to another person, the order and warrant, if applicable, shall remain in effect. If the court finds that the state has failed to prove by clear and convincing evidence that the petitioner poses a risk of imminent personal injury to himself or herself or to another person, the court shall terminate such order and warrant, if applicable. Any person whose petition is denied may file a subsequent petition in accordance with the provisions of this subsection at least one hundred eighty days after the date on which the court denied the previous petition.

(g) The court shall immediately upon termination of a risk protection order pursuant to this section remove or cancel any record entered into the National Instant Criminal Background Check System associated with such order.

(h) Any person whose firearm or firearms and ammunition have been ordered seized pursuant to subsection (e) of this section, or such person's legal representative, may transfer such firearm or firearms and ammunition in accordance with the provisions of section 29-33 or other applicable state or federal law, to a federally licensed firearm dealer. Upon notification in writing by such person, or such person's legal representative, and the dealer, the head of the state agency holding such seized firearm or firearms and ammunition shall within ten days deliver such firearm or firearms and ammunition to the dealer.

(i) Notwithstanding the provisions of section 29-36k, the Commissioner of Emergency Services and Public Protection holding any firearm or firearms or other deadly weapon or deadly weapons and any ammunition seized pursuant to a warrant issued under this section, or any local police department holding on behalf of said commissioner any such firearm or firearms or other deadly weapon or deadly weapons or ammunition, shall not destroy any such firearm or other deadly weapon or ammunition until at least one year has passed since date of the termination of a warrant under subsection (e) of this section.

(j) For the purposes of this section, (1) “ammunition” means a loaded cartridge, consisting of a primed case, propellant or projectile, designed for use in any firearm, (2) "family or household member" means (A) a person eighteen years of age or older who is a: (i) Spouse, (ii) parent, (iii) child, (iv) sibling, (v) grandparent, (vi) grandchild, (vii) step-parent, (viii) step-child, (ix) step-sibling, (x) mother or father-in-law, (xi) son or daughter-in-law, or (xii) brother or sister-in-law of the person who is the subject of an application pursuant to subsection (b) of this section; (B) a person residing with the person who is the subject of the application; (C) a person who has a child in common with the person who is the subject of the application; (D) a person who is dating or an intimate partner of the person who is the subject of the application; or (E) a person who is the legal guardian or former legal guardian of the person who is the subject of the application, (3) "medical professional" means any person who has examined the person who is the subject of the application and who is (A) a physician or physician assistant licensed under chapter 370, (B) an advanced practice registered nurse licensed under chapter 378, (C) a psychologist licensed under chapter 383, or (D) a clinical social worker licensed under chapter 383b, and (4) "deadly weapon" means a deadly weapon, as defined in section 53a-3.

ANNOTATIONS:

In Re Addie May Nesbitt, 124 Conn. App. 400; 5 A.3d 518, cert. Denied, 299 Conn. 917; 10 A.3d 1051 (2010):

> Statutory definition of "'possess'" is set forth in *General Statutes § 53a-3 (2)*: "'Possess' means to have physical possession or otherwise to exercise dominion or control over tangible property . . . ." Respondent "possessed" the firearms in the present case even though they were in the evidence room in the Litchfield barracks. Respondent had a possessory interest in the weapons because she owned them, and, in the absence of the warrant, could have gone to the Litchfield barracks to reclaim the weapons upon her release from the hospital.

In Re Nardelli-Firearms Safety Hearing, 50 Conn. Supp. 246, 918 A.2d 1081 (2007):

In ordering the return of seized firearms, the court found that although the state arguably had raised significant concerns regarding an individual's mental health and possible paranoia, the state had failed provide clear and convincing evidence that an individual posed a risk of imminent personal injury to himself or other individual with firearms where, among other things, an individual had always called the police when he felt threatened, and had no criminal record or record of reckless firearms use or misuse.

State v. Avery, 1999 Conn. Super. LEXIS 3231 (Conn. Super. 1999):

In ordering the return of firearms seized pursuant to Conn. Gen. Stat. §29-38(c), the court found that the warrant lacked legal sufficiency since it did not contain a factual representation sufficient for the court to support a finding that "no reasonable alternative" is available before a warrant may be considered by a judge. Among other things, the court found that police had not asked the individual to voluntarily surrender his weapons to police or others when the individual was being held in custody and did not have immediate access to the firearms.

Sec. 29-38d. Interstate transportation of firearms through state.

(a) The provisions of sections 29-35 and 29-38 shall not apply to the interstate transportation of firearms through this state in accordance with 18 USC 926A and 927, as amended from time to time, by any person who is not otherwise prohibited from shipping, transporting, receiving or possessing a firearm. Such person may transport a firearm for any lawful purpose from any place where such person may lawfully possess and carry such firearm through this state to any other place where such person may lawfully possess and carry such firearm provided such transportation is in accordance with subsection (b) of this section.

(b) During the transportation of a firearm through this state as authorized in subsection (a) of this section, such firearm shall be unloaded and neither such firearm nor any ammunition being transported shall be readily accessible or directly accessible from the passenger compartment of this vehicle. If the vehicle does not have a compartment separate from the passenger compartment, such firearm shall be unloaded and such firearm and any ammunition being transported shall be contained in a locked container other than the glove compartment or console.

(c) No person who is transporting a firearm through this state in accordance with this section may use or carry such firearm or sell, deliver or otherwise transfer such firearm while in this state.

Sec. 29-38e. Statewide firearms trafficking task force. Composition. Duties.

(a) There shall be within the Division of State Police, within the Department of Emergency Services and Public Protection, a statewide firearms trafficking task force for the effective cooperative enforcement of the laws of this state concerning the distribution and possession of firearms.

(b) The task force shall be comprised of municipal and state law enforcement officers and may include federal law enforcement officers. Such task force shall be authorized to conduct any investigation authorized by this section at any place within the state as may be deemed necessary.

(c) The task force may request and may receive from any federal, state or local agency, corporation and assistance in the performance of its duties, including the temporary assignment of personnel which may be necessary to carry out the performance of its functions.

(d) The task force may enter into mutual assistance and cooperation agreements with other states pertaining to firearms law enforcement matters extending across state boundaries, and may consult and exchange information and personnel with agencies of other states with reference to firearms law enforcement problems of mutual concern.

(e) The Commissioner of Emergency Services and Public Protection may appoint a commanding officer and such other personnel as the commissioner deems necessary for the duties of the task force, within available appropriations.

(f) The task force shall: (1) Review the problem of illegal trafficking in firearms and its effects, including its effects on the public, and implement solutions to address the problem; (2) identify persons illegally trafficking in firearms and focus resources to prosecute such persons; (3) track firearms which were sold or distributed illegally and implement solutions to remove such firearms from persons illegally in possession of them; and (4) coordinate its activities with other law enforcement agencies within and without the state.

Sec. 29-38f. Statewide firearms trafficking task force policy board. Composition. Duties.

(a) There shall be a State-Wide Firearms Trafficking Task Force Policy Board within the Division of State Police, within the Department of Emergency Services and Public Protection, for administrative purposes only, consisting of the Commissioner of Emergency Services and Public Protection, the Chief State's Attorney, the agent in Connecticut in charge of the federal Bureau of Alcohol, Tobacco and Firearms, the president of the Connecticut Police Chiefs Association and five chiefs of police designated by said association, each to serve for a term of one year, provided one such chief of police shall be from a municipality with a population of one hundred thousand or more.

(b) The policy board shall direct the formulation of policies and operating procedures of the task force.

(c) The policy board may apply for and administer any federal, state, local or private appropriations or grant funds made available for the operation of the task force.

(d) The receipts from the sale of seized firearms and ammunition pursuant to section 54-36e shall be deposited in the General Fund and credited to a separate, nonlapsing forfeit firearms account which shall be established by the Comptroller. All moneys in the account are deemed to be appropriated and shall be expended for the purposes established in section 29-38e.

Sec. 29-38g. Storing or keeping pistol or revolver in unattended motor vehicle. Prohibited. Exceptions. Penalty.

(a)(1) No person shall store or keep any pistol or revolver in any motor vehicle that is unattended unless such pistol or revolver is in the trunk, a locked safe or locked glove box.

(2) For purposes of this subsection, (A) a motor vehicle is unattended if no person who is at least twenty-one years of age and who is the owner or operator or a passenger of such motor vehicle is inside the motor vehicle or is within close enough proximity to the motor vehicle to prevent unauthorized access to the motor vehicle, (B) "pistol" and "revolver" mean pistol and revolver, each as defined in section 29-27, (C) "motor vehicle" means a motor vehicle, as defined in section 14-1, and (D) "trunk" means (i) the fully enclosed and locked main storage or luggage compartment of a motor vehicle that is not accessible from the passenger compartment, or (ii) a locked toolbox or utility box attached to the bed of a pickup truck, as defined in section 14-1. "Trunk" does not include the rear of a pickup truck, except as otherwise provided, or of a hatchback, station-wagon-type automobile or sport utility vehicle or any compartment that has a window.

(b) The provisions of subsection (a) of this section shall not apply to any pistol or revolver issued or possessed by: (1) The Department of Emergency Services and Public Protection, police departments, the Department of Correction, the Division of Criminal Justice, the Department of Motor Vehicles, the Department of Energy and Environmental Protection, the Department of Revenue Services or the military or naval forces of this state or of the United States, (2) a sworn member of a law enforcement unit, as defined in section 7-294a, including, but not limited to, the Department of Correction or the Division of State Police within the Department of Emergency Services and Public Protection, a chief inspector or inspector in the Division of Criminal Justice, a salaried inspector of motor vehicles designated by the Commissioner of Motor Vehicles, a conservation officer or special conservation officer appointed by the Commissioner of Energy and Environmental Protection pursuant to section 26-5 or a constable who is certified by the Police Officer Standards and Training Council and appointed by the chief executive authority of a town, city or borough to perform criminal law enforcement duties, for use by such sworn member, inspector, officer or constable in the discharge of such sworn member's, inspector's, officer's or constable's official duties or when off duty, (3) a member of the military or naval forces of this state or of the United States, or (4) a nuclear facility licensed by the United States Nuclear Regulatory Commission for the purpose of providing security services at such facility, or any contractor or subcontractor of such facility for the purpose of providing security services at such facility, provided such pistol or revolver issued or possessed by any such agency, department, municipality, organization, force or entity or person described in subdivisions (1) to (4), inclusive, of this subsection, is being kept or stored in accordance with such issuing or possessing agency, department, municipality, organization, force or entity or person's policy concerning safe keeping or storage of a pistol or revolver in a motor vehicle.

(c) The court may order suspension of prosecution if the court finds that a violation of this section is not of a serious nature and that the person charged with such violation (1) (A) will probably not offend in the future, (B) has not previously been convicted of a violation of this section, and (C) has not previously had a prosecution under this section suspended pursuant to this subsection, or (2) was charged with such violation because of facts or circumstances accurately reported by such person to an organized local police department concerning a lost or stolen firearm in accordance with the provisions of section 53-202g. The court shall not order suspension of prosecution unless the accused person has acknowledged that he or she understands the consequences of the suspension of prosecution. Any person for whom prosecution is suspended shall agree to the tolling of any statute of limitations with respect to such violation and to a waiver of his or her right to a speedy trial. Such person shall appear in court and shall be released to the custody of the Court Support Services Division for such period, not exceeding two years, and under such conditions as the court shall order. If the person refuses to accept, or, having accepted, violates such conditions, the court shall terminate the suspension of prosecution and the case shall be brought to trial. If such person satisfactorily completes such person's period of probation, he or she may apply for dismissal of the charges against such person and the court, on finding such satisfactory completion, shall dismiss such charges. If the person does not apply for dismissal of the charges against such person after satisfactorily completing such person's period of probation, the court, upon receipt of a report submitted by the Court Support Services Division that the person satisfactorily completed such person's period of probation, may on its own motion make a finding of such satisfactory completion and dismiss such charges. Upon dismissal, all records of such charges shall be erased pursuant to section 54-142a. An order of the court denying a motion to dismiss the charges against a person who has completed such person's period of probation or terminating the participation of a defendant in such program shall be a final judgment for purposes of appeal.

(d) Any person who violates any provision of subsection (a) of this section shall be guilty of a class A misdemeanor for a first offense and a class D felony for any subsequent offense.

Sec. 29-38m. Sale of ammunition or ammunition magazine.

(a) For the purposes of this section and sections 29-38n to 29-38p, inclusive, “ammunition” means a loaded cartridge, consisting of a primed case, propellant or projectile, designed for use in any firearm, “firearm” has the meaning provided in section 53a-3, and “magazine” means any firearm magazine, belt, drum, feed strip or similar device that accepts ammunition.

(b) No person, firm or corporation shall sell ammunition or an ammunition magazine to any person under eighteen years of age.

(c) On and after October 1, 2013, no person, firm or corporation shall sell ammunition or an ammunition magazine to any person unless such person holds a valid permit to carry a pistol or revolver issued pursuant to subsection (b) of section 29-28, a valid permit to sell at retail a pistol or revolver issued pursuant to subsection (a) of section 29-28, a valid eligibility certificate for a pistol or revolver issued pursuant to section 29-36f or a valid long gun eligibility certificate issued pursuant to section 29-37p and presents to the transferor such permit or certificate, or unless such person holds a valid ammunition certificate issued pursuant to section 29-38n and presents to the transferor such certificate and such person's motor vehicle operator's license, passport or other valid form of identification issued by the federal government or a state or municipal government that contains such person's date of birth and photograph.

(d) The provisions of subsection (c) of this section shall not apply to the sale of ammunition to (1) the Department of Emergency Services and Public Protection, police departments, the Department of Correction, the Division of Criminal Justice, the Department of Motor Vehicles, the Department of Energy and Environmental Protection or the military or naval forces of this state or of the United States; (2) a sworn and duly certified member of an organized police department, the Division of State Police within the Department of Emergency Services and Public Protection or the Department of Correction, a chief inspector or inspector in the Division of Criminal Justice, a salaried inspector of motor vehicles designated by the Commissioner of Motor Vehicles, a conservation officer or special conservation officer appointed by the Commissioner of Energy and Environmental Protection pursuant to section 26-5, or a constable who is certified by the Police Officer Standards and Training Council and appointed by the chief executive authority of a town, city or borough to perform criminal law enforcement duties, for use by such sworn member, inspector, officer or constable in the discharge of such sworn member's, inspector's, officer's or constable's official duties or when off duty; (3) a member of the military or naval forces of this state or of the United States; (4) a nuclear facility licensed by the United States Nuclear Regulatory Commission for the purpose of providing security services at such facility, or any contractor or subcontractor of such facility for the purpose of providing security services at such facility; or (5) a federally licensed firearm manufacturer, importer, dealer or collector.

(e) Any person who violates any provision of this section shall be guilty of a class D felony.

Sec. 29-38n. Ammunition certificate. Issuance. Form and content. Confidentiality.

(a) Any person who is eighteen years of age or older may request the Commissioner of Emergency Services and Public Protection to (1) conduct a state criminal history records check of such person, in accordance with the provisions of section 29-17a, using such person's name and date of birth only, and (2) issue an ammunition certificate to such person in accordance with the provisions of this section.

(b) After conducting the state criminal history records check of such person, the commissioner shall issue an ammunition certificate to such person unless the commissioner determines, based on a review of the results of such criminal history records check, that such person would be ineligible to be issued a long gun eligibility certificate under section 29-37p, except that a conviction of a violation specified in subparagraph (B) of subdivision (2) of subsection (b) of section 29-37p shall cause such person to be ineligible for an ammunition certificate only if such conviction was for a violation committed on or after July 1, 2013.

(c) Such ammunition certificate shall be of such form as the commissioner may prescribe, contain an identification number and the name, address and date of birth of the certificate holder and be signed by the certificate holder.

(d) A person holding an ammunition certificate issued by the commissioner shall notify the commissioner not later than two business days after any change of such person's address. The notification shall include both the old address and the new address of such person.

(e) Notwithstanding the provisions of sections 1-210 and 1-211, the name and address of a person issued an ammunition certificate under this section shall be confidential and shall not be disclosed, except (1) such information may be disclosed to law enforcement officials acting in the performance of their duties, including, but not limited to, employees of the United States Probation Office acting in the performance of their duties and parole officers within the Department of Correction acting in the performance of their duties, (2) the Commissioner of Emergency Services and Public Protection may disclose such information to the extent necessary to comply with a request made pursuant to section 29-38m for verification that such certificate is still valid and has not been suspended or revoked, and (3) such information may be disclosed to the Commissioner of Mental Health and Addiction Services to carry out the provisions of subsection (c) of section 17a-500.

Commentary

Unlike permits to carry pistols or revolvers issued pursuant to Conn. Gen. Stat. § 29-28, applications for an ammunition certificate cannot be denied on the basis of the applicant's overall "suitability." The grounds for denial of an ammunition certificate are set forth in Conn. Gen. Stat. § 29-38n and, upon proper application and receipt of the results of the criminal history records check mandated by Conn. Gen. Stat. § 29-38n, and verification that the applicant is not otherwise ineligible to be issued a long gun eligibility certificate under section 29-37p, are exclusive. Persons aggrieved by a denial of an ammunition certificate may appeal such action to the Board of Firearms Permit Examiners in accordance with the provisions of Conn. Gen. Stat. § 29-32b above.

Sec. 29-38o. Ammunition certificate. Fees. Expiration and renewal.

(a) The fee for each ammunition certificate originally issued under the provisions of this section shall be thirty-five dollars and for each renewal thereof thirty-five dollars, which fees shall be paid to the Commissioner of Emergency Services and Public Protection and shall be in addition to the fee paid pursuant to subsection (b) of section 29-17a for conducting the national criminal history records check. Upon deposit of such fees in the General Fund, the fees shall be credited to the appropriation to the Department of Emergency Services and Public Protection to a separate nonlapsing account for the purposes of the issuance of ammunition certificates under section 29-38n.

(b) An ammunition certificate originally issued under the provisions of section 29-38n shall expire five years after the date it becomes effective and each renewal thereof shall expire five years after the expiration date of the certificate being renewed.

(c) The renewal fee shall apply for each renewal that is requested not earlier than thirty-one days before, and not later than thirty-one days after, the expiration date of the certificate being renewed.

(d) No fee or portion thereof paid under the provisions of this section for issuance or renewal of an ammunition certificate shall be refundable except if the certificate for which the fee or portion thereof was paid was not issued or renewed.

(e) An ammunition certificate issued pursuant to section 29-38n shall be valid for a period of ninety days from the expiration date, except this provision shall not apply to any certificate which has been revoked or for which revocation is pending, pursuant to section 29-38p.

Sec. 29-38p. Ammunition certificate. Revocation. Reinstatement.

(a) An ammunition certificate shall be revoked by the Commissioner of Emergency Services and Public Protection upon the occurrence of any event which would have disqualified the holder from being issued the certificate pursuant to section 29-38n.

(b) Upon the revocation of any ammunition certificate, the person whose certificate is revoked shall be notified, in writing, and such certificate shall be forthwith delivered to the Commissioner of Emergency Services and Public Protection. Any person who fails to surrender such certificate within five days of notification, in writing, of revocation thereof shall be guilty of a class A misdemeanor.

(c) If an ammunition certificate is revoked because the person holding such certificate is subject to an ex parte order issued pursuant to section 46b-15 or 46b-16a, upon expiration of such order, such person may notify the Department of Emergency Services and Public Protection that such order has expired. Upon verification of such expiration and provided such person is not otherwise disqualified from holding such certificate pursuant to section 29-38n the department shall reinstate such certificate.

Commentary

Unlike permits to carry pistols or revolvers issued pursuant to Conn. Gen. Stat. § 29-28, applications for an ammunition certificate cannot be revoked on the basis of the applicant's overall "suitability." The grounds for revocation of an ammunition certificate are set forth in Conn. Gen. Stat. § 29-38p and, upon proper application and receipt of the results of the criminal history records check mandated by Conn. Gen. Stat. § 29-38n, and verification that the applicant is not otherwise ineligible to be issued a long gun eligibility certificate under section 29-37p, are exclusive. Persons aggrieved by revocation of an ammunition certificate may appeal such action to the Board of Firearms Permit Examiners in accordance with the provisions of Conn. Gen. Stat. § 29-32b above.

Sec. 29-152m. Permit to carry firearm required. Training required. Regulations.

(a) No professional bondsman licensed under chapter 533, surety bail bond agent licensed under chapter 700f or bail enforcement agent licensed under sections 29-152f to 29-152i, inclusive, shall carry a pistol, revolver or other firearm while engaging in the business of a professional bondsman, surety bail bond agent or bail enforcement agent, as the case may be, or while traveling to or from such business unless such bondsman or agent obtains a special permit from the Commissioner of Emergency Services and Public Protection in accordance with the provisions of subsection (b) of this section. The permit required under this section shall be in addition to the permit requirement imposed under section 29-28.

(b) The Commissioner of Emergency Services and Public Protection may grant to any professional bondsman licensed under chapter 533, surety bail bond agent licensed under chapter 700f or bail enforcement agent licensed under sections 29-152f to 29-152i, inclusive, a permit to carry a pistol or revolver or other firearm while engaging in the business of professional bondsman, surety bail bond agent or bail enforcement agent, as the case may be, or while traveling to or from such business, provided that such bondsman or agent has proven to the satisfaction of the commissioner that such bondsman or agent has successfully completed a course, approved by the commissioner, of training in the safety and use of firearms. The commissioner shall adopt regulations in accordance with the provisions of chapter 54 concerning the approval of schools, institutions or organizations offering such courses, requirements for instructors and the required number of hours and content of such courses.

(c) An application for a permit pursuant to this section shall be made on forms provided by the commissioner and shall be accompanied by a fee of sixty-two dollars. Such permit shall have an expiration date that coincides with that of the state permit to carry a pistol or revolver issued pursuant to section 29-28.

(d) A permit issued pursuant to this section shall be renewable every five years with a renewal fee of sixty-two dollars. Each holder of a permit issued pursuant to this section shall successfully complete an annual firearms safety refresher course approved by the commissioner as a condition of such renewal. The commissioner shall send, by first class mail, a notice of expiration of the bail enforcement agent firearms permit issued pursuant to this section, together with a notice of expiration of the permit to carry a pistol or revolver issued pursuant to section 29-28, in one combined form. The commissioner shall send such combined notice to the holder of the permits not later than ninety days before the date of the expiration of both permits, and shall enclose a form for renewal of the permits. A bail enforcement agent firearms permit issued pursuant to this section shall be valid for a period of ninety days after the expiration date, except this provision shall not apply if the permit to carry a pistol or revolver has been revoked or revocation is pending pursuant to section 29-32, in which case the bail enforcement agent firearms permit shall also be revoked.

(e) The commissioner shall adopt regulations in accordance with the provisions of chapter 54 concerning the approval of schools, institutions or organizations offering firearms safety courses, the requirements for instructors and the required number of hours and content of such courses.

Sec. 29-161z. Permit to carry firearms required. Firearm safety course. Regulations. Instructor approval. Penalty. License, permit or approval suspension or revocation. Appeal.

(a) No employee of a licensed security service and no employee hired by a firm or corporation to perform work as a security officer may carry a pistol, revolver or other firearm while on duty or directly en route to or from such employment unless such employee obtains a special permit from the Commissioner of Emergency Services and Public Protection in accordance with the provisions of subsection (b) of this section. No licensed security service and no firm or corporation may permit any employee to carry a pistol, revolver or other firearm while on duty or directly en route to or from such employment unless it obtains proof that such employee has obtained such permit from the commissioner. The permit required under this section shall be in addition to the permit requirement imposed under section 29-28.

(b) The Commissioner of Emergency Services and Public Protection may grant to any suitable employee of a licensed security service, or to an employee hired by a firm or corporation to perform work as a uniformed or nonuniformed security officer, a special permit to carry a pistol or revolver or other firearm while actually on duty on the premises of the employer, or, while directly en route to or from such employment, provided that such employee has proven to the satisfaction of the commissioner that such employee has successfully completed a course, approved by the commissioner, of training in the safety and use of firearms. The commissioner may grant to such employee a temporary permit pending issuance of the permit, provided such employee has submitted an application and successfully completed such training course immediately following employment. All armed security officers shall complete such safety course and yearly complete a refresher safety course approved by the commissioner. The commissioner shall adopt regulations in accordance with the provisions of chapter 54 [FN1] concerning the approval of schools, institutions or organizations offering such courses, requirements for instructors and the required number of hours and content of such courses.

(c) Application for a special permit shall be made on forms provided by the commissioner and shall be accompanied by a sixty-two-dollar fee. Such permit shall have the same expiration date as the pistol permit issued under subsection (b) of section 29-28 and may be renewed for additional five-year periods.

Sec. 45a-99. Jurisdiction to grant change of name. Exceptions. Requirements re offenders required to register with Commissioner of Emergency Services and Public Protection. Commissioner's standing to challenge change of name.

(a) The courts of probate shall have concurrent jurisdiction with the Superior Court, as provided in section 52-11, to grant a change of name, except a change of name granted in accordance with subsection (a) of section 46b-63, except that no court of probate may issue an order or otherwise allow for the change of name of a person who is required to register with the Commissioner of Emergency Services and Public Protection as a sexual offender or as an offender convicted of committing a crime with a deadly weapon unless such person complies with the requirements of subdivision (1) of subsection (b) of this section.

(b) (1) Any person who is required to register with the Commissioner of Emergency Services and Public Protection as a sexual offender or as an offender convicted of committing a crime with a deadly weapon who files an application with the Court of Probate for a change of name shall (A) prior to filing such application, notify the Commissioner of Emergency Services and Public Protection, on such form as the commissioner may prescribe, that the person intends to file an application for a change of name, indicating the change of name sought, and (B) include with such application a sworn statement that such change of name is not being sought for the purpose of avoiding the legal consequences of a criminal conviction, including, but not limited to, a criminal conviction that requires such person to register as a sexual offender or as an offender convicted of committing a crime with a deadly weapon.

(2) The Commissioner of Emergency Services and Public Protection shall have standing to challenge such person's application for a change of name in the court of probate where such change of name is sought. The commissioner shall challenge the change of name through the Attorney General. The court of probate may deny such person's application for a change of name if the court finds, by a preponderance of the evidence, that the person is applying for such change of name for the purpose of avoiding the legal consequences of a criminal conviction.

(c) Whenever the court, pursuant to this section, orders a change of name of a person, the court shall notify the Commissioner of Emergency Services and Public Protection of the issuance of such order if the court finds that such person is listed in the registry established and maintained pursuant to section 54-257 or in the registry established and maintained pursuant to section 54-280.

Sec. 45a-100. Power to grant relief from federal firearms disability.

(a) Any person having a federal firearms disability under 18 USC 922(d)(4) and 18 USC 922(g)(4), as a result of an adjudication or commitment rendered in this state, may petition the probate court for the district in which such person resides for relief from the federal firearms disability that resulted from such adjudication or commitment.

(b) The petitioner shall submit to the Probate Court, together with the petition and the releases required by subsection (d) of this section, information in support of the petition, including, but not limited to:

(1) Certified copies of medical records detailing the petitioner's psychiatric history where applicable, including records pertaining to the specific adjudication or commitment that is the subject of the petition;

(2) Certified copies of medical records from all of the petitioner's current treatment providers, if the petitioner is receiving treatment;

(3) A certified copy of all criminal history information maintained on file by the State Police Bureau of Identification and the Federal Bureau of Investigation pertaining to the petitioner or a copy of the response from said bureaus indicating that there is no criminal history information on file;

(4) Evidence of the petitioner's reputation, which may include notarized letters of reference from current and past employers, family members or personal friends, affidavits from the petitioner or other character evidence; and

(5) Any further information or documents specifically requested by the court, which documents shall be certified copies of original documents.

(c) The petitioner shall cause a copy of the petition and all supporting documents submitted to the Probate Court pursuant to subsection (b) of this section to be delivered to the Commissioner of Emergency Services and Public Protection and shall certify to the Probate Court that such delivery has been made.

(d) The petitioner shall provide for the release of all of the petitioner's records that may relate to the petition, including, but not limited to, health, mental health, military, immigration, juvenile court, civil court and criminal records, on forms prescribed by the Probate Court Administrator. The releases shall authorize the Commissioner of Emergency Services and Public Protection to obtain any of such records for use at the Probate Court hearing or in any appeal from the decision of the Probate Court.

(e) The petitioner shall ensure that all required information accompanies the petition at the time it is submitted to the court. Unless specifically requested by the court, information provided after receipt of the petition by the court shall not be considered. Information specifically requested by the court must be received by the court no later than fifteen days after the date of the request in order for the information to be considered. The court may extend such time period for good cause shown. Failure to provide the requested information within such time period may result in a denial of the petition.

(f) Upon the filing of the petition, the Probate Court shall set a date, time and place for a hearing and shall give notice of such hearing to (1) the petitioner, (2) the Commissioner of Emergency Services and Public Protection, (3) the court that rendered the adjudication or commitment, (4) the conservator appointed for the petitioner, if any, and (5) any other person determined by the court to have an interest in the matter.

(g) The court shall cause a recording of the testimony given at such hearing to be made. Such recording shall be transcribed only in the event of an appeal from the decision rendered by the Probate Court under this section. A copy of such transcript shall be furnished without charge to any appellant whom the Probate Court finds is unable to pay for such copy. The cost of such transcript shall be paid from funds appropriated to the Judicial Department.

(h) The petitioner shall have the burden of establishing by clear and convincing evidence that (1) the petitioner is not likely to act in a manner that is dangerous to public safety, and (2) granting relief from the federal firearms disability is not contrary to the public interest. The Commissioner of Emergency Services and Public Protection and any other person determined by the court to have an interest in the matter may present any and all relevant information at the Probate Court hearing and in any appeal to the Superior Court.

(i) In determining whether to grant relief under this section, the court shall consider the following:

(1) The circumstances regarding the firearms disability imposed by 18 USC 922(d)(4) and 18 USC 922(g)(4);

(2) The petitioner's record, which shall include, at a minimum, the petitioner's mental health records and criminal history records, if any;

(3) The petitioner's reputation, which the petitioner must demonstrate through character witness statements, testimony or other character evidence; and

(4) Any other relevant information provided by the petitioner, the Commissioner of Emergency Services and Public Protection or any other person determined by the court to have an interest in the matter.

(j) The court shall grant relief under this section if it finds by clear and convincing evidence that: (1) The petitioner will not be likely to act in a manner dangerous to public safety, and (2) granting the relief will not be contrary to the public interest. The court shall include in its decision the specific findings of fact on which it bases its decision.

(k) Notwithstanding the provisions of subsection (j) of this section, the court shall not grant relief under this section if it finds that the petitioner is otherwise prohibited from possessing a firearm pursuant to section 53a-217.

(l) The petitioner or the Commissioner of Emergency Services and Public Protection may appeal the final decision of the Probate Court to the Superior Court in accordance with the provisions of section 45a-186. Notwithstanding any other provision of the general statutes, any review of the decision of the Probate Court by the Superior Court shall be de novo.

(m) Enforcement of any decision of the Probate Court granting relief pursuant to the petition shall be stayed until the period in which to take an appeal under section 45a-186 has expired or, if an appeal is taken, until the final decision of the court. If the court grants the relief and no appeal is taken or an appeal is taken and the decision is upheld, the court granting relief shall notify the Commissioner of Emergency Services and Public Protection of that decision.

(n) As soon as practicable after receiving notice of the decision of the court granting relief, the Commissioner of Emergency Services and Public Protection shall (1) coordinate the removal or cancellation of the record in the National Instant Criminal Background Check System (NICS), and (2) notify the Attorney General of the United States that the basis of the record no longer applies.

(o) All proceedings in the Probate Court under the provisions of this section shall be closed to the public and all records of the proceedings shall be confidential and not subject to disclosure except to the petitioner or his or her counsel and the Commissioner of Emergency Services and Public Protection, unless the Probate Court, after notice to the parties and a hearing, determines that such records should be disclosed for good cause shown.

Sec. 46b-15. Relief from physical abuse, stalking or pattern of threatening by family or household member. Application. Court orders. Duration. Service of application, affidavit, any ex parte order and notice of hearing. Copies. Expedited hearing for violation of order. Other remedies.

(a) (1) The office of the Chief Court Administrator shall revise and simplify the process for filing an application for relief under section 46b-15. The office of the Chief Court Administrator shall ensure that any person seeking to file an application for relief is provided with a one-page, plain language explanation of how to apply for relief under section 46b-15.

(2) The office of the Chief Court Administrator shall develop and make available to the public educational materials concerning the [warrant process] risk protection order and warrant processes set forth in section 29-38c, as amended by this act, relating to a person who poses a risk of imminent personal injury to himself or herself or to [other individuals.] another person. The office of the Chief Court Administrator shall develop and make available to the public in hard copy and electronically on the Internet web site of the Judicial Branch a form to enable a family or household member or medical professional, each as defined in section 29-38c, as amended by this act, to apply to have a risk protection order investigation ordered and a one-page, plain language explanation of how to apply for such order. The form shall contain questions designed to solicit information significant to a determination. The public educational materials and form shall prominently advise the applicant that a risk protection order or warrant may be sought through and with the assistance of a municipal or state police agency or a state's attorney's office, and of the benefits of doing so.

(b) The application form shall allow the applicant, at the applicant's option, to indicate whether the respondent holds a permit to carry a pistol or revolver, an eligibility certificate for a pistol or revolver, a long gun eligibility certificate or an ammunition certificate or possesses one or more firearms or ammunition. The application shall be accompanied by an affidavit made under oath which includes a brief statement of the conditions from which relief is sought. Upon receipt of the application the court shall order that a hearing on the application be held not later than fourteen days from the date of the order except that, if the application indicates that the respondent holds a permit to carry a pistol or revolver, an eligibility certificate for a pistol or revolver, a long gun eligibility certificate or an ammunition certificate or possesses one or more firearms or ammunition, and the court orders an ex parte order, the court shall order that a hearing be held on the application not later than seven days from the date on which the ex parte order is issued. The court, in its discretion, may make such orders as it deems appropriate for the protection of the applicant and such dependent children or other persons as the court sees fit. In making such orders ex parte, the court, in its discretion, may consider relevant court records if the records are available to the public from a clerk of the Superior Court or on the Judicial Branch's Internet web site. In addition, at the time of the hearing, the court, in its discretion, may also consider a report prepared by the family services unit of the Judicial Branch that may include, as available: Any existing or prior orders of protection obtained from the protection order registry; information on any pending criminal case or past criminal case in which the respondent was convicted of a violent crime; any outstanding arrest warrant for the respondent; and the respondent's level of risk based on a risk assessment tool utilized by the Court Support Services Division. The report may also include information pertaining to any pending or disposed family matters case involving the applicant and respondent. Any report provided by the Court Support Services Division to the court shall also be provided to the applicant and respondent. Such orders may include temporary child custody or visitation rights, and such relief may include, but is not limited to, an order enjoining the respondent from (1) imposing any restraint upon the person or liberty of the applicant; (2) threatening, harassing, assaulting, molesting, sexually assaulting or attacking the applicant; or (3) entering the family dwelling or the dwelling of the applicant. Such order may include provisions necessary to protect any animal owned or kept by the applicant including, but not limited to, an order enjoining the respondent from injuring or threatening to injure such animal. If an applicant alleges an immediate and present physical danger to the applicant, the court may issue an ex parte order granting such relief as it deems appropriate. If a postponement of a hearing on the application is requested by either party and granted, the ex parte order shall not be continued except upon agreement of the parties or by order of the court for good cause shown. If a hearing on the application is scheduled or an ex parte order is granted and the court is closed on the scheduled hearing date, the hearing shall be held on the next day the court is open and any such ex parte order shall remain in effect until the date of such hearing. If the applicant is under eighteen years of age, a parent, guardian or responsible adult who brings the application as next friend of the applicant may not speak on the applicant's behalf at such hearing unless there is good cause shown as to why the applicant is unable to speak on his or her own behalf, except that nothing in this subsection shall preclude such parent, guardian or responsible adult from testifying as a witness at such hearing. As used in this subsection, "violent crime" includes: (A) An incident resulting in physical harm, bodily injury or assault; (B) an act of threatened violence that constitutes fear of imminent physical harm, bodily injury or assault, including, but not limited to, stalking or a pattern of threatening; (C) verbal abuse or argument if there is a present danger and likelihood that physical violence will occur; and (D) cruelty to animals as set forth in section 53-247.

(c) If the court issues an ex parte order pursuant to subsection (b) of this section and service has not been made on the respondent in conformance with subsection (h) of this section, upon request of the applicant, the court shall, based on the information contained in the original application, extend any ex parte order for an additional period not to exceed fourteen days from the originally scheduled hearing date. The clerk shall prepare a new order of hearing and notice containing the new hearing date, which shall be served upon the respondent in accordance with the provisions of subsection (h) of this section.

(d) Any ex parte restraining order entered under subsection (b) of this section in which the applicant and respondent are spouses, or persons who have a dependent child or children in common and who live together, may include, if no order exists, and if necessary to maintain the safety and basic needs of the applicant or the dependent child or children in common of the applicant and respondent, in addition to any orders authorized under subsection (b) of this section, any of the following: (1) An order prohibiting the respondent from (A) taking any action that could result in the termination of any necessary utility services or necessary services related to the family dwelling or the dwelling of the applicant, (B) taking any action that could result in the cancellation, change of coverage or change of beneficiary of any health, automobile or homeowners insurance policy to the detriment of the applicant or the dependent child or children in common of the applicant and respondent, or (C) transferring, encumbering, concealing or disposing of specified property owned or leased by the applicant; or (2) an order providing the applicant with temporary possession of an automobile, checkbook, documentation of health, automobile or homeowners insurance, a document needed for purposes of proving identity, a key or other necessary specified personal effects.

(e) At the hearing on any application under this section, if the court grants relief pursuant to subsection (b) of this section and the applicant and respondent are spouses, or persons who have a dependent child or children in common and who live together, and if necessary to maintain the safety and basic needs of the applicant or the dependent child or children in common of the applicant and respondent, any orders entered by the court may include, in addition to the orders authorized under subsection (b) of this section, any of the following: (1) An order prohibiting the respondent from (A) taking any action that could result in the termination of any necessary utility services or services related to the family dwelling or the dwelling of the applicant, (B) taking any action that could result in the cancellation, change of coverage or change of beneficiary of any health, automobile or homeowners insurance policy to the detriment of the applicant or the dependent child or children in common of the applicant and respondent, or (C) transferring, encumbering, concealing or disposing of specified property owned or leased by the applicant; (2) an order providing the applicant with temporary possession of an automobile, checkbook, documentation of health, automobile or homeowners insurance, a document needed for purposes of proving identity, a key or other necessary specified personal effects; or (3) an order that the respondent: (A) Make rent or mortgage payments on the family dwelling or the dwelling of the applicant and the dependent child or children in common of the applicant and respondent, (B) maintain utility services or other necessary services related to the family dwelling or the dwelling of the applicant and the dependent child or children in common of the applicant and respondent, (C) maintain all existing health, automobile or homeowners insurance coverage without change in coverage or beneficiary designation, or (D) provide financial support for the benefit of any dependent child or children in common of the applicant and the respondent, provided the respondent has a legal duty to support such child or children and the ability to pay. The court shall not enter any order of financial support without sufficient evidence as to the ability to pay, including, but not limited to, financial affidavits. If at the hearing no order is entered under this subsection or subsection (d) of this section, no such order may be entered thereafter pursuant to this section. Any order entered pursuant to this subsection shall not be subject to modification and shall expire one hundred twenty days after the date of issuance or upon issuance of a superseding order, whichever occurs first. Any amounts not paid or collected under this subsection or subsection (d) of this section may be preserved and collectible in an action for dissolution of marriage, custody, paternity or support.

(f) Every order of the court made in accordance with this section shall contain the following language: (1) "This order may be extended by the court beyond one year. In accordance with section 53a-107 of the Connecticut general statutes, entering or remaining in a building or any other premises in violation of this order constitutes criminal trespass in the first degree. This is a criminal offense punishable by a term of imprisonment of not more than one year, a fine of not more than two thousand dollars or both."; and (2) "In accordance with section 53a-223b of the Connecticut general statutes, any violation of subparagraph (A) or (B) of subdivision (2) of subsection (a) of section 53a-223b constitutes criminal violation of a restraining order which is punishable by a term of imprisonment of not more than five years, a fine of not more than five thousand dollars, or both. Additionally, any violation of subparagraph (C) or (D) of subdivision (2) of subsection (a) of section 53a-223b constitutes criminal violation of a restraining order which is punishable by a term of imprisonment of not more than ten years, a fine of not more than ten thousand dollars, or both.".

(g) No order of the court shall exceed one year, except that an order may be extended by the court upon motion of the applicant for such additional time as the court deems necessary. If the respondent has not appeared upon the initial application, service of a motion to extend an order may be made by first-class mail directed to the respondent at the respondent's last-known address.

(h) (1) The applicant shall cause notice of the hearing pursuant to subsection (b) of this section and a copy of the application and the applicant's affidavit and of any ex parte order issued pursuant to subsection (b) of this section to be served on the respondent not less than three days before the hearing. The cost of such service shall be paid for by the Judicial Branch.

(2) When (A) an application indicates that a respondent holds a permit to carry a pistol or revolver, an eligibility certificate for a pistol or revolver, a long gun eligibility certificate or an ammunition certificate or possesses one or more firearms or ammunition, and (B) the court has issued an ex parte order pursuant to this section, the proper officer responsible for executing service shall, whenever possible, provide in-hand service and, prior to serving such order, shall (i) provide notice to the law enforcement agency for the town in which the respondent will be served concerning when and where the service will take place, and

(ii) send, or cause to be sent by facsimile or other means, a copy of the application, the applicant's affidavit, the ex parte order and the notice of hearing to such law enforcement agency, and (iii) request that a police officer from the law enforcement agency for the town in which the respondent will be served be present when service is executed by the proper officer. Upon receiving a request from a proper officer under the provisions of this subdivision, the law enforcement agency for the town in which the respondent will be served may designate a police officer to be present when service is executed by the proper officer.

(3) Upon the granting of an ex parte order, the clerk of the court shall provide two copies of the order to the applicant. Upon the granting of an order after notice and hearing, the clerk of the court shall provide two copies of the order to the applicant and a copy to the respondent. Every order of the court made in accordance with this section after notice and hearing shall be accompanied by a notification that is consistent with the full faith and credit provisions set forth in 18 USC 2265(a), as amended from time to time. Immediately after making service on the respondent, the proper officer shall (A) send or cause to be sent, by facsimile or other means, a copy of the application, or the information contained in such application, stating the date and time the respondent was served, to the law enforcement agency or agencies for the town in which the applicant resides, the town in which the applicant is employed and the town in which the respondent resides, and (B) as soon as possible, but not later than two hours after the time that service is executed, input into the Judicial Branch's Internet-based service tracking system the date, time and method of service. If, prior to the date of the scheduled hearing, service has not been executed, the proper officer shall input into such service tracking system that service was unsuccessful. The clerk of the court shall send, by facsimile or other means, a copy of any ex parte order and of any order after notice and hearing, or the information contained in any such order, to the law enforcement agency or agencies for the town in which the applicant resides, the town in which the applicant is employed and the town in which the respondent resides, within forty-eight hours of the issuance of such order. If the victim, or victim's minor child protected by such order, is enrolled in a public or private elementary or secondary school, including a technical education and career school, or an institution of higher education, as defined in section 10a-55, the clerk of the court shall, upon the request of the victim, send, by facsimile or other means, a copy of such ex parte order or of any order after notice and hearing, or the information contained in any such order, to such school or institution of higher education, the president of any institution of higher education at which the victim, or victim's minor child protected by such order, is enrolled and the special police force established pursuant to section 10a-156b, if any, at the institution of higher education at which the victim, or victim's minor child protected by such order, is enrolled, if the victim provides the clerk with the name and address of such school or institution of higher education.

(i) A caretaker who is providing shelter in his or her residence to a person sixty years or older shall not be enjoined from the full use and enjoyment of his or her home and property. The Superior Court may make any other appropriate order under the provisions of this section.

(j) When a motion for contempt is filed for violation of a restraining order, there shall be an expedited hearing. Such hearing shall be held within five court days of service of the motion on the respondent, provided service on the respondent is made not less than twenty-four hours before the hearing. If the court finds the respondent in contempt for violation of an order, the court may impose such sanctions as the court deems appropriate.

(k) An action under this section shall not preclude the applicant from seeking any other civil or criminal relief.

(l) For purposes of this section, "police officer" means a state police officer or a sworn member of a municipal police department and "law enforcement agency" means the Division of State Police within the Department of Emergency Services and Public Protection or any municipal police department.

Sec. 46b-38a. Family violence prevention and response: Definitions.

For the purposes of sections 46b-38a to 46b-38f, inclusive:

(1) "Family violence" means an incident resulting in physical harm, bodily injury or assault, or an act of threatened violence that constitutes fear of imminent physical harm, bodily injury or assault, including, but not limited to, stalking or a pattern of threatening, between family or household members. Verbal abuse or argument shall not constitute family violence unless there is present danger and the likelihood that physical violence will occur.

(2) "Family or household member" means any of the following persons, regardless of the age of such person: (A) Spouses or former spouses; (B) parents or their children; (C) persons related by blood or marriage; (D) persons other than those persons described in subparagraph (C) of this subdivision presently residing together or who have resided together; (E) persons who have a child in common regardless of whether they are or have been married or have lived together at any time; and (F) persons in, or who have recently been in, a dating relationship.

(3) "Family violence crime" means a crime as defined in section 53a-24, other than a delinquent act as defined in section 46b-120, which, in addition to its other elements, contains as an element thereof an act of family violence to a family or household member. "Family violence crime" does not include acts by parents or guardians disciplining minor children unless such acts constitute abuse.

Sec. 46b-38b. Investigation of family violence crime by peace officer. Arrest. Assistance to victim. Guidelines. Education and training program. Compliance with model law enforcement policy on family violence. Assistance and protocols for victims whose immigration status is questionable.

(a) Whenever a peace officer determines upon speedy information that a family violence crime has been committed within such officer's jurisdiction, such officer shall arrest the person or persons suspected of its commission and charge such person or persons with the appropriate crime. The decision to arrest and charge shall not (1) be dependent on the specific consent of the victim, (2) consider the relationship of the parties, or (3) be based solely on a request by the victim. Whenever a peace officer determines that a family violence crime has been committed, such officer may seize any firearm or electronic defense weapon, as defined in section 53a-3, or ammunition at the location where the crime is alleged to have been committed that is in the possession of any person arrested for the commission of such crime or suspected of its commission or that is in plain view. Not later than seven days after any such seizure, the law enforcement agency shall return such firearm, electronic defense weapon or ammunition in its original condition to the rightful owner thereof unless such person is ineligible to possess such firearm, electronic defense weapon or ammunition or unless otherwise ordered by the court.

Commentary

This statute is not re-printed in its entirety. Refer to C.G.S. 46b-38b for subsections (b) through (g) for a complete understanding of the provisions of this statute as they relate to the investigations and reporting of family violence incidents.

Sec. 46b-38c. Family violence response and intervention units. Local units. Duties and functions. Protective orders. Electronic monitoring pilot program. Pretrial family violence education program; fees. Training program.

(a) There shall be family violence response and intervention units in the Connecticut judicial system to respond to cases involving family violence. The units shall be coordinated and governed by formal agreement between the Chief State's Attorney and the Judicial Department.

...

(c) Each such local family violence intervention unit shall: (1) Accept referrals of family violence cases from a judge or prosecutor, (2) prepare written or oral reports on each case for the court by the next court date to be presented at any time during the court session on that date, (3) provide or arrange for services to victims and offenders, (4) administer contracts to carry out such services, and (5) establish centralized reporting procedures. All information provided to a family relations counselor, family relations counselor trainee or family services supervisor employed by the Judicial Department in a local family violence intervention unit shall be used solely for the purposes of preparation of the report and the protective order forms for each case and recommendation of services and shall otherwise be confidential and retained in the files of such unit and not be subject to subpoena or other court process for use in any other proceeding or for any other purpose, except that a family relations counselor, family relations counselor trainee or family services supervisor employed by the Judicial Department:

(A) Shall disclose to the court and the prosecuting authority for appropriate action information that the victim has indicated that the defendant holds a permit to carry a pistol or revolver, possesses one or more firearms or possesses ammunition;

(B) Shall disclose to an employee of the Department of Children and Families information that indicates that a defendant poses a danger or threat to a child or a custodial parent of the child;

...

(E) May disclose to a law enforcement agency information that indicates that a defendant poses a danger or threat to another person;

Commentary

This statute is not re-printed in its entirety. Refer to C.G.S. 46b-38c for a complete understanding of the provisions of this statute as they relate to the investigation and reporting of family violence incidents.

Sec. 52-11. Complaints for change of name. Exceptions re offenders required to register with Commissioner of Emergency Services and Public Protection. Commissioner's standing to challenge change of name.

(a) The superior court in each judicial district shall have jurisdiction of complaints praying for a change of name, brought by any person residing in the judicial district, and may change the name of the complainant, who shall thereafter be known by the name prescribed by said court in its decree, except that no superior court may issue an order or otherwise allow for the change of name of a person who is required to register with the Commissioner of Emergency Services and Public Protection as a sexual offender or as an offender convicted of committing a crime with a deadly weapon unless such person complies with the requirements of subdivision (1) of subsection (b) of this section.

(b) (1) Any person who is required to register with the Commissioner of Emergency Services and Public Protection as a sexual offender or as an offender convicted of committing a crime with a deadly weapon who files an application with the Superior Court for a change of name shall (A) prior to filing such application, notify the Commissioner of Emergency Services and Public Protection, on such form as the commissioner may prescribe, that the person intends to file an application for a change of name, indicating the change of name sought, and (B) include with such application a sworn statement that such change of name is not being sought for the purpose of avoiding the legal consequences of a criminal conviction, including, but not limited to, a criminal conviction that requires such person to register as a sexual offender or as an offender convicted of committing a crime with a deadly weapon.

(2) The Commissioner of Emergency Services and Public Protection shall have standing to challenge such person's application for a change of name in the superior court where such change of name is sought. The commissioner shall challenge the change of name through the Attorney General. The superior court may deny such person's application for a change of name if the court finds, by a preponderance of the evidence, that the person is applying for such change of name for the purpose of avoiding the legal consequences of a criminal conviction.

(c) Whenever the court, pursuant to this section, orders a change of name of a person, the clerk of the court shall notify the Commissioner of Emergency Services and Public Protection of the issuance of such order if the clerk finds that such person is listed in the registry established and maintained pursuant to section 54-257 or in the registry established and maintained pursuant to section 54-280.

Sec. 52-571f. Strict liability of person who illegally transfers a firearm.

Any person who sells, delivers or otherwise transfers a firearm, as defined in section 53a-3, to a person knowing that such other person is prohibited from possessing such firearm shall be strictly liable for damages for the injury or death of another person resulting from the use of such firearm by any person.

Sec. 52-571g. Strict liability of person who fails to securely store a loaded firearm.

Any person whose act or omission constitutes a violation of section 29-37i shall be strictly liable for damages when a minor or, a resident of the premises who is ineligible to possess a firearm under state or federal law or who poses a risk of imminent personal injury to himself or herself or to other individuals, obtains a firearm, as defined in section 53a-3, and causes the injury or death of such minor, resident or any other person. For the purposes of this section, "minor" means any person under the age of eighteen years.

Sec. 53-202. Machine guns.

(a) As used in this section:

(1) "Machine gun" shall apply to and include a weapon of any description, loaded or unloaded, which shoots, is designed to shoot or can be readily restored to shoot automatically more than one projectile, without manual reloading, by a single function of the trigger, and shall also include any part or combination of parts designed for use in converting a weapon into a machine gun and any combination of parts from which a machine gun can be assembled if such parts are in the possession of or under the control of a person. (2) "Crime of violence" shall apply to and include any of the following-named crimes or an attempt to commit any of the same: Murder, manslaughter, kidnapping, sexual assault and sexual assault with a firearm, assault in the first or second degree, robbery, burglary, larceny and riot in the first degree. (3) "Projectile" means any size bullet that when affixed to any cartridge case may be propelled through the bore of a machine gun.

(b) Any person who possesses or uses a machine gun in the perpetration or attempted perpetration of a crime of violence shall be imprisoned not less than ten years nor more than twenty years.

(c) Any person who (1) possesses or uses a machine gun for an offensive or aggressive purpose, or (2) notwithstanding the provisions of subdivision (3) of subsection (h) of this section, transfers, sells or gives a machine gun to a person under sixteen years of age, including the temporary transfer of a machine gun to such person for use in target shooting or on a firing or shooting range or for any other purpose, shall be fined not more than one thousand dollars or imprisoned not less than five years nor more than ten years or be both fined and imprisoned.

(d) The possession or use of a machine gun shall be presumed to be for an offensive or aggressive purpose: (1) When the machine gun is on premises not owned or rented, for bona fide permanent residence or business occupancy, by the person in whose possession the machine gun was found; or (2) when in the possession of, or used by, an unnaturalized foreign-born person, or a person who has been convicted of a crime of violence in any state or federal court of record of the United States of America, its territories or insular possessions; or (3) when the machine gun is of the kind described in subsection (g) hereof and has not been registered as therein required; or (4) when empty or loaded projectiles of any caliber which have been or are susceptible of use in the machine gun are found in the immediate vicinity thereof.

(e) The presence of a machine gun in any room, boat or vehicle shall be presumptive evidence of the possession or use of a machine gun by each person occupying such room, boat or vehicle.

(f) Each manufacturer shall keep a register of all machine guns manufactured or handled by the manufacturer. Such register shall show the model and serial number, the date of manufacture, sale, loan, gift, delivery or receipt, of each machine gun, the name, address and occupation of the person to whom the machine gun was sold, loaned, given or delivered, or from whom it was received and the purpose for which it was acquired by the person to whom the machine gun was sold, loaned, given or delivered. Upon demand, any manufacturer shall permit any marshal or police officer to inspect such manufacturer's entire stock of machine guns, and parts and supplies thereof, and shall produce the register, herein required, for inspection. Any person who violates any provision of this subsection shall be fined not more than two thousand dollars.

(g) Each machine gun in this state adapted to use projectiles of any caliber shall be registered in the office of the Commissioner of Emergency Services and Public Protection within twenty-four hours after its acquisition and, thereafter, annually, on July first. Blanks for registration shall be prepared by said commissioner and furnished upon application. To comply with this subsection, the application as filed shall show the model and serial number of the gun, the name, address and occupation of the person in possession, and from whom and the purpose for which the gun was acquired. The registration data shall not be subject to inspection by the public. Any person who fails to register any gun as required hereby shall be presumed to possess the same for an offensive or aggressive purpose. The provisions of this subsection shall not apply to any machine gun which has been registered under the provisions of subsection (f) and which is still in the actual possession of the manufacturer.

(h) No provision of this section shall apply to: (1) The manufacture of machine guns for sale or transfer to the United States government, to any state, territory or possession of the United States or to any political subdivision thereof or to the District of Columbia; (2) the possession of a machine gun rendered inoperable by welding of all critical functioning parts and possessed as a curiosity, ornament or keepsake; or (3) a machine gun acquired, transferred or possessed in accordance with the National Firearms Act, as amended, provided such machine gun shall be subject to the provisions of subsection (g) of this section.

Sec. 53-202a. Assault weapons: Definition (Revised as of June 18, 2013).

As used in this section and sections 53-202b to 53-202k, inclusive:

(1) "Assault weapon" means:

(A) (i) Any selective-fire firearm capable of fully automatic, semiautomatic or burst fire at the option of the user or any of the following specified semiautomatic firearms: Algimec Agmi; Armalite AR-180; Australian Automatic Arms SAP Pistol; Auto-Ordnance Thompson type; Avtomat Kalashnikov AK-47 type; Barrett Light-Fifty model 82A1; Beretta AR-70; Bushmaster Auto Rifle and Auto Pistol; Calico models M-900, M-950 and 100-P; Chartered Industries of Singapore SR-88; Colt AR-15 and Sporter; Daewoo K-1, K-2, Max-1 and Max-2; Encom MK-IV, MP-9 and MP-45; Fabrique Nationale FN/FAL,

FN/LAR, or FN/FNC; FAMAS MAS 223; Feather AT-9 and Mini-AT; Federal XC-900 and XC-450; Franchi SPAS-12 and LAW-12; Galil AR and ARM; Goncz High-Tech Carbine and High-Tech Long Pistol; Heckler & Koch HK-91, HK-93, HK-94 and SP-89; Holmes MP-83; MAC-10, MAC-11 and MAC-11 Carbine type; Intratec TEC-9 and Scorpion; Iver Johnson Enforcer model 3000; Ruger Mini-14/5F folding stock model only; Scarab Skorpion; SIG 57 AMT and 500 series; Spectre Auto Carbine and Auto Pistol; Springfield Armory BM59, SAR-48 and G-3; Sterling MK-6 and MK-7; Steyr AUG; Street Sweeper and Striker 12 revolving cylinder shotguns; USAS-12; UZI Carbine, Mini-Carbine and Pistol; Weaver Arms Nighthawk; Wilkinson "Linda" Pistol;

(ii) A part or combination of parts designed or intended to convert a firearm into an assault weapon, as defined in subparagraph (A)(i) of this subdivision, or any combination of parts from which an assault weapon, as defined in subparagraph (A)(i) of this subdivision, may be rapidly assembled if those parts are in the possession or under the control of the same person;

(B) Any of the following specified semiautomatic centerfire rifles, or copies or duplicates thereof with the capability of any such rifles, that were in production prior to or on April 4, 2013:

(i) AK-47; (ii) AK-74; (iii) AKM; (iv) AKS-74U; (v) ARM; (vi) MAADI AK47; (vii) MAK90; (viii) MISR; (ix) NHM90 and NHM91; (x) Norinco 56, 56S, 84S and 86S; (xi) Poly Technologies AKS and AK47; (xii) SA 85; (xiii) SA 93; (xiv) VEPR; (xv) WASR-10; (xvi) WUM; (xvii) Rock River Arms LAR-47; (xviii) Vector Arms AK-47; (xix) AR-10; (xx) AR-15; (xxi) Bushmaster Carbon 15, Bushmaster XM15, Bushmaster ACR Rifles, Bushmaster MOE Rifles; (xxii) Colt Match Target Rifles; (xxiii) Armalite M15; (xxiv) Olympic Arms AR-15, A1, CAR, PCR, K3B, K30R, K16, K48, K8 and K9 Rifles; (xxv) DPMS Tactical Rifles; (xxvi) Smith and Wesson M&P15 Rifles; (xxvii) Rock River Arms LAR-15; (xxviii) Doublestar AR Rifles; (xxix) Barrett REC7; (13-3) Beretta Storm; (13-3i) Calico Liberty 50, 50 Tactical, 100, 100 Tactical, I, I Tactical, II and II Tactical Rifles; (13-3ii) Hi-Point Carbine Rifles; (13-3iii) HK-PSG-1; (13-3iv) Kel-Tec Sub-2000, SU Rifles, and RFB; (13-3v) Remington Tactical Rifle Model 7615; (13-3vi) SAR-8, SAR-4800 and SR9; (13-3vii) SLG 95; (13-3viii) SLR 95 or 96; (13-3ix) TNW M230 and M2HB; (xl) Vector Arms UZI; (xli) Galil and Galil Sporter; (xlii) Daewoo AR 100 and AR 110C; (xliii) Fabrique Nationale/FN 308 Match and L1A1 Sporter; (xliv) HK USC; (xlv) IZHMASH Saiga AK; (xlvi) SIG Sauer 551-A1, 556, 516, 716 and M400 Rifles; (xlvii) Valmet M62S, M71S and M78S; (xlviii) Wilkinson Arms Linda Carbine; and (xlix) Barrett M107A1;

(C) Any of the following specified semiautomatic pistols, or copies or duplicates thereof with the capability of any such pistols, that were in production prior to or on April 4, 2013: (i) Centurion 39 AK; (ii) Draco AK-47; (iii) HCR AK-47; (iv) IO Inc. Hellpup AK-47; (v) Mini-Draco AK-47; (vi) Yugo Krebs Krink; (vii) American Spirit AR-15; (viii) Bushmaster Carbon 15; (ix) Doublestar Corporation AR; (x) DPMS AR-15; (xi) Olympic Arms AR-15; (xii) Rock River Arms LAR 15; (xiii) Calico Liberty III and III Tactical Pistols; (xiv) Masterpiece Arms MPA Pistols and Velocity Arms VMA Pistols; (xv) Intratec TEC-DC9 and AB-10; (xvi) Colefire Magnum; (xvii) German Sport 522 PK and Chiappa Firearms Mfour-22; (xviii) DSA SA58 PKP FAL; (xix) I.O. Inc. PPS-43C; (xx)

Kel-Tec PLR-16 Pistol; (xxi) Sig Sauer P516 and P556 Pistols; and (xxii) Thompson TA5 Pistols;

(D) Any of the following semiautomatic shotguns, or copies or duplicates thereof with the capability of any such shotguns, that were in production prior to or on April 4, 2013: All IZHMASH Saiga 12 Shotguns;

(E) Any semiautomatic firearm regardless of whether such firearm is listed in subparagraphs (A) to (D), inclusive, of this subdivision, and regardless of the date such firearm was produced, that meets the following criteria:

(i) A semiautomatic, centerfire rifle that has an ability to accept a detachable magazine and has at least one of the following:

(I) A folding or telescoping stock;

(II) Any grip of the weapon, including a pistol grip, a thumbhole stock, or any other stock, the use of which would allow an individual to grip the weapon, resulting in any finger on the trigger hand in addition to the trigger finger being directly below any portion of the action of the weapon when firing;

(III) A forward pistol grip;

(IV) A flash suppressor; or

(V) A grenade launcher or flare launcher; or

(ii) A semiautomatic, centerfire rifle that has a fixed magazine with the ability to accept more than ten rounds; or

(iii) A semiautomatic, centerfire rifle that has an overall length of less than thirty inches; or

(iv) A semiautomatic pistol that has an ability to accept a detachable magazine and has at least one of the following:

(I) An ability to accept a detachable ammunition magazine that attaches at some location outside of the pistol grip;

(II) A threaded barrel capable of accepting a flash suppressor, forward pistol grip or silencer;

(III) A shroud that is attached to, or partially or completely encircles, the barrel and that permits the shooter to fire the firearm without being burned, except a slide that encloses the barrel; or

(IV) A second hand grip; or

(v) A semiautomatic pistol with a fixed magazine that has the ability to accept more than ten rounds; or

(vi) A semiautomatic shotgun that has both of the following:

(I) A folding or telescoping stock; and

(II) Any grip of the weapon, including a pistol grip, a thumbhole stock, or any other stock, the use of which would allow an individual to grip the weapon, resulting in any finger on the trigger hand in addition to the trigger finger being directly below any portion of the action of the weapon when firing; or (vii) A semiautomatic shotgun that has the ability to accept a detachable magazine; or

(viii) A shotgun with a revolving cylinder; or

(ix) Any semiautomatic firearm that meets the criteria set forth in subdivision (3) or (4) of subsection (a) of section 53-202a of the general statutes, revision of 1958, revised to January 1, 2013; or

(F) A part or combination of parts designed or intended to convert a firearm into an assault weapon, as defined in any provision of subparagraphs (B) to (E), inclusive, of this subdivision, or any combination of parts from which an assault weapon, as defined in any provision of subparagraphs (B) to (E), inclusive, of this subdivision, may be assembled if those parts are in the possession or under the control of the same person;

(2) "Assault weapon" does not include (A) any firearm modified to render it permanently inoperable, or (B) a part or any combination of parts of an assault weapon, that are not assembled as an assault weapon, when in the possession of a licensed gun dealer, as defined in subsection (f) of section 53-202f, or a gunsmith who is in the licensed gun dealer's employ, for the purposes of servicing or repairing lawfully possessed assault weapons under sections 53-202a to 53-202k, inclusive;

(3) "Action of the weapon" means the part of the firearm that loads, fires and ejects a cartridge, which part includes, but is not limited to, the upper and lower receiver, charging handle, forward assist, magazine release and shell deflector;

(4) "Detachable magazine" means an ammunition feeding device that can be removed without disassembling the firearm action;

(5) "Firearm" means a firearm, as defined in section 53a-3;

(6) "Forward pistol grip" means any feature capable of functioning as a grip that can be held by the nontrigger hand;

(7) "Lawfully possesses" means, with respect to an assault weapon described in any provision of subparagraphs (B) to (F), inclusive, of this subdivision, (A) actual possession that is lawful under sections 53-202b to 53-202k, (B) constructive possession pursuant to a lawful purchase transacted prior to or on April 4, 2013, regardless of whether the assault weapon was delivered to the purchaser prior to or on April 4, 2013, which lawful purchase is evidenced by a writing sufficient to indicate that (i) a contract for sale was made between the parties prior to or on April 4, 2013, for the purchase of the assault weapon, or (ii) full or partial payment for the assault weapon was made by the purchaser to the seller of the assault weapon prior to or on April 4, 2013, or (C) actual possession under subparagraph (A) of this subdivision, or constructive possession under subparagraph (B) of this subdivision, as evidenced by a written statement made under penalty of false statement on such form as the Commissioner of Emergency Services and Public Protection prescribes;

(8) "Pistol grip" means a grip or similar feature that can function as a grip for the trigger hand; and

(9) "Second hand grip" means a grip or similar feature that can function as a grip that is additional to the trigger hand grip.

ANNOTATIONS:

Benjamin v. Bailey, 234 Conn. 455, 662 A.2d 1226 (1995):

Statutes banning assault weapons did not violate the right to bear arms recognized by the Conn. Const. Art. I §15; Use of the modifier "type" in Conn. Gen. Stat. §53-202a did not create a vagueness issue because "AK 47 type", MAC 10, MAC 11, and MAC 11 Carbine type", and "Auto-Ordinance Thompson type" were sufficiently clear as to the firearms listed to satisfy due process.

State v. Kalman, 93 Conn. App. 129, 887 A. 2d 950 (2006):

> During the trial the court received testimony that in analyzing whether a particular weapon is an "AK-47 type," the state police determine whether it looks like an AK-47, works like an AK-47 and whether the parts can be interchanged with other AK-47 weapons. The court found that utilization of that test was a valid way to determine whether the particular weapon was of the "type" prohibited by the statute.

Sec. 53-202b. Sale or transfer of assault weapon prohibited. Exemptions. Olympic pistols. Regulations. Class C felony.

(a) (1) Any person who, within this state, distributes, transports or imports into the state, keeps for sale, or offers or exposes for sale, or who gives any assault weapon, except as provided by sections 53-202a to 53-202k, inclusive, shall be guilty of a class C felony and shall be sentenced to a term of imprisonment of which two years may not be suspended or reduced by the court.

(2) Any person who transfers, sells or gives any assault weapon to a person under eighteen years of age in violation of subdivision (1) of this subsection shall be sentenced to a term of imprisonment of six years, which shall not be suspended or reduced by the court and shall be in addition and consecutive to the term of imprisonment imposed under subdivision (1) of this subsection.

(b) The provisions of subsection (a) of this section shall not apply to:

(1) The sale of assault weapons to: (A) The Department of Emergency Services and Public Protection, police departments, the Department of Correction, the Division of Criminal Justice, the Department of Motor Vehicles, the Department of Energy and Environmental Protection or the military or naval forces of this state or of the United States; (B) a sworn and duly certified member of an organized police department, the Division of State Police within the Department of Emergency Services and Public Protection or the Department of Correction, a chief inspector or inspector in the Division of Criminal Justice, a salaried inspector of motor vehicles designated by the Commissioner of Motor Vehicles, a conservation officer or special conservation officer appointed by the Commissioner of Energy and Environmental Protection pursuant to section 26-5, or a constable who is certified by the Police Officer Standards and Training Council and appointed by the chief executive authority of a town, city or borough to perform criminal law enforcement duties, pursuant to a letter on the letterhead of such department, division, commissioner or authority authorizing the purchase and stating that the sworn member, inspector, officer or constable will use the assault weapon in the discharge of official duties, and that a records check indicates that the sworn member, inspector, officer or constable has not been convicted of a crime of family violence, for use by such sworn member, inspector, officer or constable in the discharge of such sworn member's, inspector's, officer's or constable's official duties or when off duty, (C) a member of the military or naval forces of this state or of the United States, or (D) a nuclear facility licensed by the United States Nuclear Regulatory Commission for the purpose of providing security services at such facility, or any contractor or subcontractor of such facility for the purpose of providing security services at such facility;

(2) A person who is the executor or administrator of an estate that includes an assault weapon for which a certificate of possession has been issued under section 53-202d which

is disposed of as authorized by the Probate Court, if the disposition is otherwise permitted by sections 53-202a to 53-202k, inclusive;

(3) The transfer of an assault weapon for which a certificate of possession has been issued under section 53-202d, by bequest or intestate succession, or, upon the death of a testator or settlor: (A) To a trust, or (B) from a trust to a beneficiary who is eligible to possess the assault weapon;

(4) The sale of a semiautomatic pistol that is defined as an assault weapon in any provision of subparagraphs (B) to (F), inclusive, of subdivision (1) of section 53-202a that the Commissioner of Emergency Services and Public Protection designates as being designed expressly for use in target shooting events at the Olympic games sponsored by the International Olympic Committee pursuant to regulations adopted under this subdivision, and for which the purchaser signs a form prescribed by the commissioner and provided by the seller that indicates that the pistol will be used by the purchaser primarily for target shooting practice and events. The Commissioner of Emergency Services and Public Protection shall adopt regulations, in accordance with chapter 54, to designate semiautomatic pistols that are defined as assault weapons in any provision of subparagraphs (B) to (F), inclusive, of subdivision (1) of section 53-202a that may be sold pursuant to this subdivision, provided the use of such pistols is sanctioned by the International Olympic Committee and USA Shooting, or any subsequent corresponding governing board for international shooting competition in the United States.

Sec. 53-202c. Possession of assault weapon prohibited. Exemptions. Class D felony.

(a) Except as provided in section 53-202e, any person who, within this state, possesses an assault weapon, except as provided in sections 53-202a to 53-202k, inclusive, and 53-202o, shall be guilty of a class D felony and shall be sentenced to a term of imprisonment of which one year may not be suspended or reduced by the court, except that a first-time violation of this subsection shall be a class A misdemeanor if (1) the person presents proof that such person lawfully possessed the assault weapon (A) prior to October 1, 1993, with respect to an assault weapon described in subparagraph (A) of subdivision (1) of section 53-202a, or (B) on April 4, 2013, under the provisions of sections 53-202a to 53-202k, inclusive, in effect on January 1, 2013, with respect to an assault weapon described in any provision of subparagraphs (B) to (F), inclusive, of subdivision (1) of section 53-202a, and (2) the person has otherwise possessed the assault weapon in compliance with subsection (f) of section 53-202d.

(b) The provisions of subsection (a) of this section shall not apply to the possession of assault weapons by: (1) The Department of Emergency Services and Public Protection, police departments, the Department of Correction, the Division of Criminal Justice, the Department of Motor Vehicles, the Department of Energy and Environmental Protection or the military or naval forces of this state or of the United States, (2) a sworn and duly certified member of an organized police department, the Division of State Police within the Department of Emergency Services and Public Protection or the Department of Correction, a chief inspector or inspector in the Division of Criminal Justice, a salaried inspector of motor vehicles designated by the Commissioner of Motor Vehicles, a conservation officer or special conservation officer appointed by the Commissioner of Energy and Environmental Protection pursuant to section 26-5, or a constable who is certified by the Police Officer Standards and Training Council and appointed by the chief executive authority of a town, city or borough to perform criminal law enforcement duties, for use by such sworn member, inspector, officer or constable in the discharge of such sworn member's, inspector's, officer's or constable's official duties or when off duty, (3) a member of the military or naval forces of this state or of the United States, or (4) a nuclear facility licensed by the United States Nuclear Regulatory Commission for the purpose of providing security services at such facility, or any contractor or subcontractor of such facility for the purpose of providing security services at such facility.

(c) The provisions of subsection (a) of this section shall not apply to the possession of an assault weapon described in subparagraph (A) of subdivision (1) of section 53-202a by any person prior to July 1, 1994, if all of the following are applicable:

(1) The person is eligible under sections 53-202a to 53-202k, inclusive, to apply for a certificate of possession for the assault weapon by July 1, 1994;

(2) The person lawfully possessed the assault weapon prior to October 1, 1993; and

(3) The person is otherwise in compliance with sections 53-202a to 53-202k, inclusive.

(d) The provisions of subsection (a) of this section shall not apply to the possession of an assault weapon described in any provision of subparagraphs (B) to (F), inclusive, of subdivision (1) of section 53-202a by any person prior to April 5, 2013, if all of the following are applicable:

(1) The person is eligible under sections 53-202a to 53-202k, inclusive, to apply for a certificate of possession for the assault weapon by January 1, 2014;

(2) The person lawfully possessed the assault weapon on April 4, 2013, under the provisions of sections 53-202a to 53-202k, inclusive, in effect on January 1, 2013; and

(3) The person is otherwise in compliance with sections 53-202a to 53-202k, inclusive.

(e) The provisions of subsection (a) of this section shall not apply to a person who is the executor or administrator of an estate that includes an assault weapon, or the trustee of a trust that includes an assault weapon, for which a certificate of possession has been issued under section 53-202d if the assault weapon is possessed at a place set forth in subdivision (1) of subsection (f) of section 53-202d or as authorized by the Probate Court.

(f) The provisions of subsection (a) of this section shall not apply to the possession of a semiautomatic pistol that is defined as an assault weapon in any provision of subparagraphs (B) to (F), inclusive, of subdivision (1) of section 53-202a that the Commissioner of Emergency Services and Public Protection designates as being designed expressly for use in target shooting events at the Olympic games sponsored by the International Olympic Committee pursuant to regulations adopted under subdivision (4) of subsection (b) of section 53-202b that is (1) possessed and transported in accordance with subsection (f) of section 53-202d, or (2) possessed at or transported to or from a collegiate, Olympic or target pistol shooting competition in this state which is sponsored by, conducted under the auspices of, or approved by a law enforcement agency or a nationally or state recognized entity that fosters proficiency in, or promotes education about, firearms, provided such pistol is transported in the manner prescribed in subsection (a) of section 53-202f.

Sec. 53-202d. Certificate of possession of assault weapon. Certificate of transfer of assault weapon to gun dealer. Circumstances where possession of assault weapon authorized.

(a) (1) (A) Except as provided in subparagraph (B) of this subdivision, any person who lawfully possesses an assault weapon, as defined in subparagraph (A) of subdivision (1) of section 53-202a, prior to October 1, 1993, shall apply by October 1, 1994, or, if such person is a member of the military or naval forces of this state or of the United States and is unable to apply by October 1, 1994, because such member is or was on official duty outside of this state, shall apply within ninety days of returning to the state to the Department of Emergency Services and Public Protection, for a certificate of possession with respect to such assault weapon.

(B) No person who lawfully possesses an assault weapon pursuant to subdivision (1), (2) or (4) of subsection (b) of section 53-202c shall be required to obtain a certificate of possession pursuant to this subdivision with respect to an assault weapon used for official duties, except that any person described in subdivision (2) of subsection (b) of section 53-202c who purchases an assault weapon, as defined in subparagraph (A) of subdivision (1) of section 53-202a, for use in the discharge of official duties who retires or is otherwise separated from service shall apply within ninety days of such retirement or separation from service to the Department of Emergency Services and Public Protection for a certificate of possession with respect to such assault weapon.

(2) (A) Except as provided in subparagraph (B) of this subdivision, any person who lawfully possesses an assault weapon, as defined in any provision of subparagraphs (B) to (F), inclusive, of subdivision (1) of section 53-202a, on April 4, 2013, under the provisions of sections 53-202a to 53-202k, inclusive, in effect on January 1, 2013, or any person who regains possession of an assault weapon as defined in any provision of said subparagraphs pursuant to subsection (e) of section 53-202f, or any person who lawfully purchases a firearm on or after April 4, 2013, but prior to June 18, 2013, that meets the criteria set forth in subdivision (3) or (4) of subsection (a) of section 53-202a of the general statutes, revision of 1958, revised to January 1, 2013, shall apply by January 1, 2014, or, if such person is a member of the military or naval forces of this state or of the United States and is unable to apply by January 1, 2014, because such member is or was on official duty outside of this state, shall apply within ninety days of returning to the state to the Department of Emergency Services and Public Protection for a certificate of possession with respect to such assault weapon. Any person who lawfully purchases a semiautomatic pistol that is defined as an assault weapon in any provision of subparagraphs (B) to (F), inclusive, of subdivision (1) of section 53-202a that the Commissioner of Emergency Services and Public Protection designates as being designed expressly for use in target shooting events at the Olympic games sponsored by the International Olympic Committee pursuant to regulations adopted under subdivision (4) of subsection (b) of section 53-202b shall apply within ninety days of such purchase to the Department of Emergency Services and Public Protection for a certificate of possession with respect to such assault weapon.

(B) No person who lawfully possesses an assault weapon pursuant to subdivision (1), (2) or (4) of subsection (b) of section 53-202c shall be required to obtain a certificate of possession pursuant to this subdivision with respect to an assault weapon used for official duties, except that any person described in subdivision (2) of subsection (b) of section 53-202c who purchases an assault weapon, as defined in any provision of subparagraphs (B) to (F), inclusive, of subdivision (1) of section 53-202a for use in the discharge of official duties who retires or is otherwise separated from service shall apply within ninety days of such retirement or separation from service to the Department of Emergency Services and Public Protection for a certificate of possession with respect to such assault weapon.

(3) Any person who obtained a certificate of possession for an assault weapon, as defined in subparagraph (A) of subdivision (1) of section 53-202a, prior to April 5, 2013, that is defined as an assault weapon pursuant to any provision of subparagraphs (B) to (F), inclusive, of subdivision (1) of section 53-202a shall be deemed to have obtained a certificate of possession for such assault weapon for the purposes of sections 53-202a to 53-202k, inclusive, and shall not be required to obtain a subsequent certificate of possession for such assault weapon.

(4) The certificate of possession shall contain a description of the firearm that identifies it uniquely, including all identification marks, the full name, address, date of birth and thumbprint of the owner, and any other information as the department may deem appropriate.

(5) The department shall adopt regulations, in accordance with the provisions of chapter 54, to establish procedures with respect to the application for and issuance of certificates of possession pursuant to this section. Notwithstanding the provisions of sections 1-210 and 1-211, the name and address of a person issued a certificate of possession shall be confidential and shall not be disclosed, except such records may be disclosed to (A) law enforcement agencies and employees of the United States Probation Office acting in the performance of their duties and parole officers within the Department of Correction acting in the performance of their duties, and (B) the Commissioner of Mental Health and Addiction Services to carry out the provisions of subsection (c) of section 17a-500.

(b) (1) No assault weapon, as defined in subparagraph (A) of subdivision (1) of section 53-202a, possessed pursuant to a certificate of possession issued under this section may be sold or transferred on or after January 1, 1994, to any person within this state other than to a licensed gun dealer, as defined in subsection (f) of section 53-202f, or as provided in section 53-202e, or by bequest or intestate succession, or, upon the death of a testator or settlor: (A) To a trust, or (B) from a trust to a beneficiary who is eligible to possess the assault weapon.

(2) No assault weapon, as defined in any provision of subparagraphs (B) to (F), inclusive, of subdivision (1) of section 53-202a, possessed pursuant to a certificate of possession issued under this section may be sold or transferred on or after April 5, 2013, to any person within this state other than to a licensed gun dealer, as defined in subsection (f) of section 53-202f, or as provided in section 53-202e, or by bequest or intestate succession, or, upon the death of a testator or settlor: (A) To a trust, or (B) from a trust to a beneficiary who is eligible to possess the assault weapon.

(c) Any person who obtains title to an assault weapon for which a certificate of possession has been issued under this section by bequest or intestate succession shall, within ninety days of obtaining title, apply to the Department of Emergency Services and Public Protection for a certificate of possession as provided in subsection (a) of this section, render the assault weapon permanently inoperable, sell the assault weapon to a licensed gun dealer or remove the assault weapon from the state.

(d) Any person who moves into the state in lawful possession of an assault weapon, shall, within ninety days, either render the assault weapon permanently inoperable, sell the assault weapon to a licensed gun dealer or remove the assault weapon from this state, except that any person who is a member of the military or naval forces of this state or of the United States, is in lawful possession of an assault weapon and has been transferred into the state after October 1, 1994, may, within ninety days of arriving in the state, apply to the Department of Emergency Services and Public Protection for a certificate of possession with respect to such assault weapon.

(e) If an owner of an assault weapon sells or transfers the assault weapon to a licensed gun dealer, such dealer shall, at the time of delivery of the assault weapon, execute a certificate of transfer and cause the certificate of transfer to be mailed or delivered to the Commissioner of Emergency Services and Public Protection. The certificate of transfer shall contain: (1) The date of sale or transfer; (2) the name and address of the seller or transferor and the licensed gun dealer, their Social Security numbers or motor vehicle operator license numbers, if applicable; (3) the licensed gun dealer's federal firearms license number and seller's permit number; (4) a description of the assault weapon, including the caliber of the assault weapon and its make, model and serial number; and (5) any other information the commissioner prescribes. The licensed gun dealer shall present such dealer's motor vehicle operator's license or Social Security card, federal firearms license and seller's permit to the seller or transferor for inspection at the time of purchase or transfer. The Commissioner of Emergency Services and Public Protection shall maintain a file of all certificates of transfer at the commissioner's central office.

(f) Any person who has been issued a certificate of possession for an assault weapon under this section may possess the assault weapon only under the following conditions:

(1) At that person's residence, place of business or other property owned by that person, or on property owned by another person with the owner's express permission;

(2) While on the premises of a target range of a public or private club or organization organized for the purpose of practicing shooting at targets;

(3) While on a target range which holds a regulatory or business license for the purpose of practicing shooting at that target range;

(4) While on the premises of a licensed shooting club;

(5) While attending any exhibition, display or educational project which is about firearms and which is sponsored by, conducted under the auspices of, or approved by a law enforcement agency or a nationally or state recognized entity that fosters proficiency in, or promotes education about, firearms;

(6) While transporting the assault weapon between any of the places set forth in this subsection, or to any licensed gun dealer, as defined in subsection (f) of section 53-202f, for servicing or repair pursuant to subsection (c) of section 53-202f, provided the assault weapon is transported as required by section 53-202f;

(7) With respect to a nonresident of this state, while transporting a semiautomatic pistol that is defined as an assault weapon in any provision of subparagraphs (B) to (F), inclusive, of subdivision (1) of section 53-202a that the Commissioner of Emergency Services and

Public Protection designates as being designed expressly for use in target shooting events at the Olympic games sponsored by the International Olympic Committee pursuant to regulations adopted under subdivision (4) of subsection (b) of section 53-202b, into or through this state in order to attend any exhibition, display or educational project described in subdivision (5) of this subsection, or to participate in a collegiate, Olympic or target pistol shooting competition in this state which is sponsored by, conducted under the auspices of, or approved by a law enforcement agency or a nationally or state recognized entity that fosters proficiency in, or promotes education about, firearms, provided (A) such pistol is transported into or through this state not more than forty-eight hours prior to or after such exhibition, display, project or competition, (B) such pistol is unloaded and carried in a locked carrying case and the ammunition for such pistol is carried in a separate locked container, (C) such nonresident has not been convicted of a felony in this state or of an offense in another state that would constitute a felony if committed in this state, and (D) such nonresident has in his or her possession a pistol permit or firearms registration card if such permit or card is required for possession of such pistol under the laws of his or her state of residence.

Sec. 53-202e. Relinquishment of assault weapon to law enforcement agency.

Any individual may arrange in advance to relinquish an assault weapon to a police department or the Department of Emergency Services and Public Protection. The assault weapon shall be transported in accordance with the provisions of section 53-202f.

Commentary

The provisions of Section 53-202e do not provide a person who arranges to relinquish an assault weapon to a police department or to the Department of Emergency Services and Public Protection with immunity from prosecution for possession of an illegally possessed assault weapon.

Sec. 53-202f. Transportation and transfer of assault weapon. Authorized actions of gun dealer, manufacturer, pawnbroker or consignment shop operator.

(a) While transporting an assault weapon between any of the places set forth in subdivisions (1) to (6), inclusive, of subsection (f) of section 53-202d, no person shall carry a loaded assault weapon concealed from public view or knowingly have, in any motor vehicle owned, operated or occupied by such person (1) a loaded assault weapon, or (2) an unloaded assault weapon unless such weapon is kept in the trunk of such vehicle or in a case or other container which is inaccessible to the operator of such vehicle or any passenger in such vehicle. The provisions of this subsection shall not apply to a member, inspector, officer or constable that possesses an assault weapon pursuant to subdivision (2) of subsection (b) of section 53-202c. Any person who violates the provisions of this subsection shall be guilty of a class E felony.

(b) Any licensed gun dealer, as defined in subsection (f) of this section, who lawfully possesses an assault weapon pursuant to section 53-202d, in addition to the uses allowed in section 53-202d, may transport the assault weapon between dealers or out of the state, display the assault weapon at any gun show licensed by a state or local governmental entity or sell the assault weapon to a resident outside the state. Any transporting of the assault weapon allowed by this subsection must be done as required by subsection (a) of this section.

(c) (1) Any licensed gun dealer, as defined in subsection (f) of this section, or a federally-licensed firearm manufacturer may take possession of any assault weapon for the purposes of servicing or repair from any person to whom has been issued a certificate of possession for such weapon pursuant to sections 53-202a to 53-202k, inclusive. (2) Any licensed gun dealer may transfer possession of any assault weapon received pursuant to subdivision (1) of this subsection to a gunsmith for purposes of accomplishing service or repair of the same. Such transfers are permissible only to the following persons:

(A) A gunsmith who is in the licensed gun dealer's employ; or

(B) A gunsmith with whom the dealer has contracted for gunsmithing services, provided the gunsmith receiving the assault weapon holds a dealer's license issued pursuant to Chapter 44, commencing with Section 921, of Title 18 of the United States Code and the regulations issued pursuant thereto.

(d) Not later than December 31, 2013, any person who lawfully possessed an assault weapon described in any provision of subparagraphs (B) to (F), inclusive, of subdivision (1) of section 53-202a on April 4, 2013, which was lawful under the provisions of sections 53-202a to 53-202k, inclusive, in effect on January 1, 2013, may transfer possession of the assault weapon to a licensed gun dealer within or outside of this state for sale outside of this state, and may transport the assault weapon to such dealer for the purpose of making such transfer, without obtaining a certificate of possession under section 53-202d.

(e) Not later than October 1, 2013, any licensed gun dealer, pawnbroker licensed under section 21-40, or consignment shop operator, as defined in section 21-39a, may transfer possession of an assault weapon to any person who (1) legally possessed the assault weapon prior to or on April 4, 2013, (2) placed the assault weapon in the possession of such dealer, pawnbroker or operator prior to or on April 4, 2013, pursuant to an agreement between such person and such dealer, pawnbroker or operator for the sale of the assault weapon to a third person, and (3) is eligible to possess a firearm on the date of such transfer.

(f) The term "licensed gun dealer", as used in sections 53-202a to 53-202k, inclusive, means a person who has a federal firearms license and a permit to sell firearms pursuant to section 29-28.

Sec. 53-202g. Report of loss or theft of assault weapon or other firearm. Penalty.

(a) Any person who lawfully possesses an assault weapon under sections 53-202a to 53-202k, inclusive, or a firearm, as defined in section 53a-3, that is lost or stolen from such person shall report the loss or theft to the organized local police department for the town in which the loss or theft occurred or, if such town does not have an organized local police department, to the state police troop having jurisdiction for such town within seventy-two hours of when such person discovered or should have discovered the loss or theft. Such department or troop shall forthwith forward a copy of such report to the Commissioner of Emergency Services and Public Protection. The provisions of this subsection shall not apply to the loss or theft of an antique firearm as defined in section 29-37a.

(b) Any person who fails to make a report required by subsection (a) of this section within the prescribed time period shall commit an infraction and be fined not more than ninety dollars for a first offense and be guilty of a class C felony for any subsequent offense, except that, if such person intentionally fails to make such report within the prescribed time period, such person shall be guilty of a class B felony. Any person who violates subsection (a) of this section for the first offense shall not lose such person's right to hold or obtain any firearm permit under the general statutes.

Commentary

The purpose of this statute is to encourage those individuals who discover that they have lost or misplaced a firearm to report this fact promptly to the authorities. A permit to carry a firearm cannot be revoked for failure to report the loss or theft of a firearm if the failure to report such loss or theft is a first offense. However, if an individual is convicted of a felony for intentionally failing to report the loss or theft of a firearm, that individual's permit to carry a firearm must be revoked on the basis of that felony conviction under both state and federal law. Although not specifically addressed by the statute, an individual who properly reports the loss or theft of a firearm should not be subjected to revocation of his/her permit to carry a firearm on that basis alone, absent additional circumstances evidencing a continuing danger to public safety.

Sec. 53-202h. Temporary transfer or possession of assault weapon for transport to out-of-state event.

The provisions of subsection (a) of section 53-202b and subsection (a) of section 53-202c shall not apply to the temporary transfer or possession of an assault weapon, for which a certificate of possession has been issued pursuant to section 53-202d, for purposes of transporting such weapon to and from any shooting competition or exhibition, display or educational project which is about firearms and which is sponsored by, conducted under the auspices of, or approved by a law enforcement agency or a nationally or state recognized entity that fosters proficiency in, or promotes education about, firearms, which competition, exhibition, display or educational project is held outside this state.

Sec. 53-202i. Circumstances in which manufacture, transportation or temporary transfer of assault weapons not prohibited.

Nothing in sections 53-202a to 53-202k, inclusive, shall be construed to prohibit a federally-licensed firearm manufacturer engaged in the business of manufacturing assault weapons in this state from (1) manufacturing or transporting assault weapons in this state for sale within this state in accordance with subdivision (1) of subsection (b) of section 53-202b or for sale outside this state, or (2) transporting and temporarily transferring assault weapons to and from a third party for the sole purpose of permitting the third party to perform a function in the manufacturing production process.

Sec. 53-202j. Commission of class A, B or C felony with an assault weapon: Eight-year nonsuspendable sentence.

Any person who commits a class A, B or C felony and in the commission of such felony uses, or is armed with and threatens the use of, or displays, or represents by his words or conduct that he possesses an assault weapon, as defined in section 53-202a, shall be imprisoned for a term of eight years, which shall not be suspended or reduced and shall be in addition and consecutive to any term of imprisonment imposed for conviction of such felony.

Sec. 53-202k. Commission of a class A, B or C felony with a firearm: Five-year nonsuspendable sentence.

Any person who commits a class A, B or C felony and in the commission of such felony uses, or is armed with and threatens the use of, or displays, or represents by his words or conduct that he possesses any firearm, as defined in section 53a-3, except an assault weapon, as defined in section 53-202a, shall be imprisoned for a term of five years, which shall not be suspended or reduced and shall be in addition and consecutive to any term of imprisonment imposed for conviction of such felony.

ANNOTATIONS:

State v. Grant, 294 Conn. 151, 161-62, 982 A.2d 169 (2009):

For purposes of General Statutes § 53-202k, a BB gun does not fall outside the definitional purview of § 53a-3(19), which defines the term firearm, merely because it operates without gunpowder.

Sec. 53-202l. Armor piercing and incendiary .50 caliber ammunition: Definition. Sale or transfer prohibited. Class D Felony.

(a) For the purposes of this section:

(1) "Armor piercing bullet" means (A) any .50 caliber bullet that (i) is designed for the purpose of, (ii) is held out by the manufacturer or distributor as, or (iii) is generally recognized as having a specialized capability to penetrate armor or bulletproof glass, including, but not limited to, such bullets commonly designated as "M2 Armor-Piercing" or "AP", "M8 Armor-Piercing Incendiary" or "API", "M20 Armor-Piercing Incendiary Tracer" or "APIT", "M903 Caliber .50 Saboted Light Armor Penetrator" or "SLAP", or "M962 Saboted Light Armor Penetrator Tracer" or "SLAPT", or (B) any bullet that can be fired from a pistol or revolver that (i) has projectiles or projectile cores constructed entirely, excluding the presence of traces of other substances, from tungsten alloys, steel, iron, brass, bronze, beryllium copper or depleted uranium, or (ii) is fully jacketed with a jacket weight of more than twenty-five per cent of the total weight of the projectile, is larger than .22 caliber and is designed and intended for use in a firearm, and (iii) does not have projectiles whose cores are composed of soft materials such as lead or lead alloys, zinc or zinc alloys, frangible projectiles designed primarily for sporting purposes, or any other projectiles or projectile cores that the Attorney General of the United States finds to be primarily intended to be used for sporting purposes or industrial purposes or that otherwise does not constitute "armor piercing ammunition" as defined in federal law. "Armor piercing bullet" does not include a shotgun shell.

(2) "Incendiary .50 caliber bullet" means any .50 caliber bullet that (A) is designed for the purpose of, (B) is held out by the manufacturer or distributor as, or (C) is generally recognized as having a specialized capability to ignite upon impact, including, but not limited to, such bullets commonly designated as "M1 Incendiary", "M23 Incendiary", "M8

Armor-Piercing Incendiary" or "API", or "M20 Armor-Piercing Incendiary Tracer" or "APIT".

(b) Any person who knowingly distributes, transports or imports into the state, keeps for sale or offers or exposes for sale or gives to any person any ammunition that is an armor piercing bullet or an incendiary .50 caliber bullet shall be guilty of a class D felony, except that a first-time violation of this subsection shall be a class A misdemeanor.

(c) Any person who knowingly transports or carries a firearm with an armor piercing bullet or incendiary .50 caliber bullet loaded shall be guilty of a class D felony.

(d) The provisions of subsections (b) and (c) of this section shall not apply to the following:

(1) The sale of such ammunition to the Department of Emergency Services and Public Protection, police departments, the Department of Correction or the military or naval forces of this state or of the United States for use in the discharge of their official duties;

(2) A sworn and duly certified member of the Department of Emergency Services and Public Protection or a police department when transporting or carrying a firearm with an armor piercing bullet or incendiary .50 caliber bullet loaded;

(3) A person who is the executor or administrator of an estate that includes such ammunition that is disposed of as authorized by the Probate Court; or

(4) The transfer of such ammunition by bequest or intestate succession, or, upon the death of a testator or settlor: (A) To a trust, or (B) from a trust to a beneficiary who is eligible to possess such ammunition.

(e) If the court finds that a violation of this section is not of a serious nature and that the person charged with such violation (1) will probably not offend in the future, (2) has not previously been convicted of a violation of this section, and (3) has not previously had a prosecution under this section suspended pursuant to this subsection, it may order suspension of prosecution in accordance with the provisions of subsection (h) of section 29-33.

Sec. 53-202m. Circumstances when assault weapons exempt from limitations on transfers and registration requirements.

Notwithstanding any provision of the general statutes, sections 53-202a to 53-202*l*, inclusive, shall not be construed to limit the transfer or require the registration of an assault weapon as defined in subdivision (3) or (4) of subsection (a) of section 53-202a of the general statutes, revision of 1958, revised to January 1, 2013, provided such firearm was legally manufactured prior to September 13, 1994.

Commentary

On October 11, 2013, then Commissioner Reuben Bradford of the Department of Emergency Services and Public Protection published a letter which opined that Section 11 of Public Act 13-220 was enacted to clarify that it was the intent of the legislature to exclude assault weapons manufactured before September 13, 1994 from transfer restrictions and registration requirements. The plain language of the Public Act, codified above, does not support this expansive interpretation of the law. Rather, the statute provides that only those assault weapons adjudged as such pursuant to the provisions of subdivision (3) or (4) of subsection (a) of section 53-202a of the general statutes, revision of 1958, revised to January 1, 2013, provided such firearm was legally manufactured prior to September 13, 1994, are exempted from transfer restrictions and registration requirements. Assault weapons enumerated as such in subdivision (1) of section 53-202a of the general statutes, revision of 1958, revised to January 1, 2013, remain subject to these restrictions and requirements regardless of the date of their manufacture.

Sec. 53-202n. Possession of specified assault weapon permitted under certain circumstances. Notice requirement.

(a) For the purpose of subsection (a) of section 53-202c, this section and section 53-202o, "specified assault weapon" means any type of the following firearms: Auto-Ordnance Thompson type, Avtomat Kalashnikov AK-47 type, or MAC-10, MAC-11 and MAC-11 Carbine type.

(b) The provisions of subsection (a) of section 53-202c shall not apply to any person who (1) in good faith purchased or otherwise obtained title to a specified assault weapon on or after October 1, 1993, and prior to May 8, 2002, in compliance with any state and federal laws concerning the purchase or transfer of firearms, (2) is not otherwise disqualified or prohibited from possessing such specified assault weapon, and (3) has notified the Department of Emergency Services and Public Protection in accordance with subsection (c) of this section prior to October 1, 2003, that he or she possesses such specified assault weapon.

(c) A person complies with the notice requirement of subdivision (3) of subsection (b) of this section if such person provides the Department of Emergency Services and Public Protection with: (1) A copy of the proof of purchase for such specified assault weapon, and (2) one of the following: (A) A copy of state form DPS-3 with respect to such specified assault weapon, (B) a copy of federal ATF form 4473 with respect to such specified assault weapon, or (C) a sworn affidavit from such person that such specified assault weapon was purchased in compliance with any state and federal laws concerning the purchase or transfer of firearms; except that, if such person does not have a copy of the proof of purchase for such specified assault weapon, such person may satisfy the requirement of subdivision (1) of this subsection, by not later than January 1, 2003, providing such information as the department may require on a form prescribed by the department together with a sworn affidavit from such person that such specified assault weapon was purchased in compliance with any state and federal laws concerning the purchase or transfer of firearms.

(d) Any person who is a member of the military or naval forces of this state or of the United States and is unable to meet the notice requirements of subdivision (3) of subsection (b) and of subsection (c) of this section by October 1, 2003, because such person is or was on official duty outside this state, may file such notice within ninety days of returning to the state.

(e) As proof that a person has complied with the notice requirement of this section that such notice has been received by the Department of Emergency Services and Public Protection, the department shall issue a certificate of possession for such specified assault weapon. Such certificate shall contain a description of the firearm that identifies it uniquely, including all identification marks, and the full name, address and date of birth of the owner.

> **Commentary**
>
> *The provisions of Section 53-202n are properly viewed as creating a special exception to the requirements pertaining to the possession and registration of Auto-Ordnance Thompson type, Avtomat Kalashnikov AK-47 type, or MAC-10, MAC-11 and MAC-11 Carbine type assault weapons set forth in the statutes, independent of that created by Section 53-202m.*

Sec. 53-202o. Affirmative defense in prosecution of possession of specified assault weapon.

(a) In any prosecution for a violation of section 53-202c based on the possession by the defendant of a specified assault weapon, it shall be an affirmative defense that the defendant (1) in good faith purchased or otherwise obtained title to such specified assault weapon on or after October 1, 1993, and prior to May 8, 2002, in compliance with any state and federal laws concerning the purchase or transfer of firearms, (2) is not otherwise disqualified or prohibited from possessing such specified assault weapon, and (3) has possessed such specified assault weapon in compliance with subsection (f) of section 53-202d.

(b) In any such prosecution, if such defendant proves such affirmative defense by a preponderance of the evidence, the specified assault weapon shall be returned to such defendant upon such defendant notifying the Department of Emergency Services and Public Protection in accordance with subdivision (3) of subsection (b) and of subsection (c) of section 53-202n and obtaining a certificate of possession, provided such notification is made not later than October 1, 2003.

Sec. 53-202w. Large capacity magazines. Definitions. Sale, transfer or possession prohibited. Exceptions.

(a) As used in this section and section 53-202x:

(1) "Large capacity magazine" means any firearm magazine, belt, drum, feed strip or similar device that has the capacity of, or can be readily restored or converted to accept, more than ten rounds of ammunition, but does not include: (A) A feeding device that has been permanently altered so that it cannot accommodate more than ten rounds of ammunition, (B) a .22 caliber tube ammunition feeding device, (C) a tubular magazine that is contained in a lever-action firearm, or (D) a magazine that is permanently inoperable;

(2) "Lawfully possesses", with respect to a large capacity magazine, means that a person has (A) actual and lawful possession of the large capacity magazine, (B) constructive possession of the large capacity magazine pursuant to a lawful purchase of a firearm that contains a large capacity magazine that was transacted prior to or on April 4, 2013, regardless of whether the firearm was delivered to the purchaser prior to or on April 4, 2013, which lawful purchase is evidenced by a writing sufficient to indicate that (i) a contract for sale was made between the parties prior to or on April 4, 2013, for the purchase of the firearm, or (ii) full or partial payment for the firearm was made by the purchaser to the seller of the firearm prior to or on April 4, 2013, or (C) actual possession under

subparagraph (A) of this subdivision, or constructive possession under subparagraph (B) of this subdivision, as evidenced by a written statement made under penalty of false statement on such form as the Commissioner of Emergency Services and Public Protection prescribes; and

(3) "Licensed gun dealer" means a person who has a federal firearms license and a permit to sell firearms pursuant to section 29-28.

(b) Except as provided in this section, on and after April 5, 2013, any person who, within this state, distributes, imports into this state, keeps for sale, offers or exposes for sale, or purchases a large capacity magazine shall be guilty of a class D felony. On and after April 5, 2013, any person who, within this state, transfers a large capacity magazine, except as provided in subsection (f) of this section, shall be guilty of a class D felony.

(c) Except as provided in this section and section 53-202x: (1) Any person who possesses a large capacity magazine on or after January 1, 2014, that was obtained prior to April 5, 2013, shall commit an infraction and be fined not more than ninety dollars for a first offense and shall be guilty of a class D felony for any subsequent offense, and (2) any person who possesses a large capacity magazine on or after January 1, 2014, that was obtained on or after April 5, 2013, shall be guilty of a class D felony.

(d) A large capacity magazine may be possessed, purchased or imported by:

(1) The Department of Emergency Services and Public Protection, police departments, the Department of Correction, the Division of Criminal Justice, the Department of Motor Vehicles, the Department of Energy and Environmental Protection or the military or naval forces of this state or of the United States;

(2) A sworn and duly certified member of an organized police department, the Division of State Police within the Department of Emergency Services and Public Protection or the Department of Correction, a chief inspector or inspector in the Division of Criminal Justice, a salaried inspector of motor vehicles designated by the Commissioner of Motor Vehicles, a conservation officer or special conservation officer appointed by the Commissioner of Energy and Environmental Protection pursuant to section 26-5, or a constable who is certified by the Police Officer Standards and Training Council and appointed by the chief executive authority of a town, city or borough to perform criminal law enforcement duties, for use by such sworn member, inspector, officer or constable in the discharge of such sworn member's, inspector's, officer's or constable's official duties or when off duty;

(3) A member of the military or naval forces of this state or of the United States;

(4) A nuclear facility licensed by the United States Nuclear Regulatory Commission for the purpose of providing security services at such facility, or any contractor or subcontractor of such facility for the purpose of providing security services at such facility;

(5) Any person who is sworn and acts as a policeman on behalf of an armored car service pursuant to section 29-20 in the discharge of such person's official duties; or

(6) Any person, firm or corporation engaged in the business of manufacturing large capacity magazines in this state that manufactures, purchases, tests or transports large capacity magazines in this state for sale within this state to persons specified in subdivisions (1) to (5), inclusive, of this subsection or for sale outside this state, or a

federally-licensed firearm manufacturer engaged in the business of manufacturing firearms or large capacity magazines in this state that manufactures, purchases, tests or transports firearms or large capacity magazines in this state for sale within this state to persons specified in subdivisions (1) to (5), inclusive, of this subsection or for sale outside this state.

(e) A large capacity magazine may be possessed by:

(1) A licensed gun dealer;

(2) A gunsmith who is in a licensed gun dealer's employ, who possesses such large capacity magazine for the purpose of servicing or repairing a lawfully possessed large capacity magazine;

(3) A person, firm, corporation or federally-licensed firearm manufacturer described in subdivision (6) of subsection (d) of this section that possesses a large capacity magazine that is lawfully possessed by another person for the purpose of servicing or repairing the large capacity magazine;

(4) Any person who has declared possession of the magazine pursuant to section 53-202x; or

(5) Any person who is the executor or administrator of an estate that includes a large capacity magazine, or the trustee of a trust that includes a large capacity magazine, the possession of which has been declared to the Department of Emergency Services and Public Protection pursuant to section 53-202x, which is disposed of as authorized by the Probate Court, if the disposition is otherwise permitted by this section and section 53-202x.

(f) Subsection (b) of this section shall not prohibit:

(1) The transfer of a large capacity magazine, the possession of which has been declared to the Department of Emergency Services and Public Protection pursuant to section 53-202x, by bequest or intestate succession, or, upon the death of a testator or settlor: (A) To a trust, or (B) from a trust to a beneficiary;

(2) The transfer of a large capacity magazine to a police department or the Department of Emergency Services and Public Protection;

(3) The transfer of a large capacity magazine to a licensed gun dealer in accordance with section 53-202x; or

(4) The transfer of a large capacity magazine prior to October 1, 2013, from a licensed gun dealer, pawnbroker licensed under section 21-40, or consignment shop operator, as defined in section 21-39a, to any person who (A) possessed the large capacity magazine prior to or on April 4, 2013, (B) placed a firearm that such person legally possessed, with the large capacity magazine included or attached, in the possession of such dealer, pawnbroker or operator prior to or on April 4, 2013, pursuant to an agreement between such person and such dealer, pawnbroker or operator for the sale of the firearm to a third person, and (C) is eligible to possess the firearm on the date of such transfer.

(g) If the court finds that a violation of this section is not of a serious nature and that the person charged with such violation (1) will probably not offend in the future, (2) has not previously been convicted of a violation of this section, and (3) has not previously had a prosecution under this section suspended pursuant to this subsection, it may order suspension of prosecution in accordance with the provisions of subsection (h) of section 29-33.

Sec. 53-202x. Declaration of possession of large capacity magazine. Regulations.

(a)(1) Except as provided in subdivision (2) of this subsection, any person who lawfully possesses a large capacity magazine prior to January 1, 2014, shall apply by January 1, 2014, or, if such person is a member of the military or naval forces of this state or of the United States and is unable to apply by January 1, 2014, because such member is or was on official duty outside of this state, shall apply within ninety days of returning to the state to the Department of Emergency Services and Public Protection to declare possession of such magazine. Such application shall be made on such form or in such manner as the Commissioner of Emergency Services and Public Protection prescribes.

(2) No person who lawfully possesses a large capacity magazine pursuant to subdivision (1), (2), (4) or (5) of subsection (d) of section 53-202w shall be required to declare possession of a large capacity magazine pursuant to this section with respect to a large capacity magazine used for official duties, except that any such person who retires or is otherwise separated from service who possesses a large capacity magazine that was purchased or obtained by such person for official use before such person retired or separated from service shall declare possession of the large capacity magazine within ninety days of such retirement or separation from service to the Department of Emergency Services and Public Protection. No person that lawfully possesses a large capacity magazine pursuant to subdivision (6) of subsection (d) of section 53-202w shall be required to declare possession of such large capacity magazine.

(b) In addition to the application form prescribed under subsection (a) of this section, the department shall design or amend the application forms for a certificate of possession for an assault weapon under section 53-202d or for a permit to carry a pistol or revolver under section 29-28a, a long gun eligibility certificate under section 29-37p, an eligibility certificate for a pistol or revolver under section 29-36f or any renewal of such permit or certificate to permit an applicant to declare possession of a large capacity magazine pursuant to this section upon the same application.

(c) The department may adopt regulations, in accordance with the provisions of chapter 54, to establish procedures with respect to applications under this section. Notwithstanding the provisions of sections 1-210 and 1-211, the name and address of a person who has declared possession of a large capacity magazine shall be confidential and shall not be disclosed, except such records may be disclosed to (1) law enforcement agencies and employees of the United States Probation Office acting in the performance of their duties and parole officers within the Department of Correction acting in the performance of their duties, and (2) the Commissioner of Mental Health and Addiction Services to carry out the provisions of subsection (c) of section 17a-500.

(d) Any person who moves into the state in lawful possession of a large capacity magazine shall, within ninety days, either render the large capacity magazine permanently inoperable, sell the large capacity magazine to a licensed gun dealer or remove the large capacity magazine from this state, except that any person who is a member of the military or naval forces of this state or of the United States, is in lawful possession of a large capacity magazine and has been transferred into the state after January 1, 2014, may, within ninety days of arriving in the state, apply to the Department of Emergency Services and Public Protection to declare possession of such large capacity magazine.

(e) (1) If an owner of a large capacity magazine transfers the large capacity magazine to a licensed gun dealer, such dealer shall, at the time of delivery of the large capacity magazine, execute a certificate of transfer. For any transfer prior to January 1, 2014, the dealer shall provide to the Commissioner of Emergency Services and Public Protection monthly reports, on such form as the commissioner prescribes, regarding the number of transfers that the dealer has accepted. For any transfer on or after January 1, 2014, the dealer shall cause the certificate of transfer to be mailed or delivered to the Commissioner of Emergency Services and Public Protection. The certificate of transfer shall contain: (A) The date of sale or transfer; (B) the name and address of the seller or transferor and the licensed gun dealer, and their Social Security numbers or motor vehicle operator license numbers, if applicable; (C) the licensed gun dealer's federal firearms license number; and (D) a description of the large capacity magazine.

(2) The licensed gun dealer shall present such dealer's federal firearms license and seller's permit to the seller or transferor for inspection at the time of purchase or transfer.

(3) The Commissioner of Emergency Services and Public Protection shall maintain a file of all certificates of transfer at the commissioner's central office.

(f) Any person who declared possession of a large capacity magazine under this section may possess the large capacity magazine only under the following conditions:

(1) At that person's residence;

(2) At that person's place of business or other property owned by that person, provided such large capacity magazine contains not more than ten bullets;

(3) While on the premises of a target range of a public or private club or organization organized for the purpose of practicing shooting at targets;

(4) While on a target range which holds a regulatory or business license for the purpose of practicing shooting at that target range;

(5) While on the premises of a licensed shooting club;

(6) While transporting the large capacity magazine between any of the places set forth in this subsection, or to any licensed gun dealer, provided (A) such large capacity magazine contains not more than ten bullets, and (B) the large capacity magazine is transported in the manner required for an assault weapon under subdivision (2) of subsection (a) of section 53-202f; or

(7) Pursuant to a valid permit to carry a pistol or revolver, provided such large capacity magazine (A) is within a pistol or revolver that was lawfully possessed by the person prior to April 5, 2013, (B) does not extend more than one inch below the bottom of the pistol grip, and (C) contains not more than ten bullets.

(g) Any person who violates the provisions of subsection (f) of this section shall be guilty of a class C misdemeanor.

Sec. 53-202aa. Firearms trafficking: Class C or B felony.

(a) A person is guilty of firearms trafficking if such person, knowingly and intentionally, directly or indirectly, causes one or more firearms that such person owns, is in possession of or is in control of to come into the possession of or control of another person who such person knows or has reason to believe is prohibited from owning or possessing any firearm under state or federal law.

(b) (1) Any person who violates any provision of this section shall be guilty of a class C felony if such person, on or after October 1, 2007, but prior to October 1, 2013, sells, delivers or otherwise transfers five or fewer firearms, and a class B felony if such person, on or after October 1, 2007, but prior to October 1, 2013, sells, delivers or otherwise transfers more than five firearms. (2) Any person who violates any provision of this section on or after October 1, 2013, shall be guilty of a class B felony for which three years of the sentence imposed may not be suspended or reduced by the court, and ten thousand dollars of the fine imposed may not be remitted or reduced by the court unless the court states on the record its reasons for remitting or reducing such fine.

(c) For the purposes of this section, "firearm" means "firearm" as defined in section 53a-3, but does not include a rifle or shotgun or an antique firearm as defined in section 29-37a.

Sec. 53-203. Unlawful discharge of firearms.

Any person who intentionally, negligently or carelessly discharges any firearm in such a manner as to be likely to cause bodily injury or death to persons or domestic animals, or the wanton destruction of property shall be guilty of a class C misdemeanor.

Sec. 53-204. Hunting or discharging firearm from public highway.

Any person who hunts or discharges any firearm from any public highway shall be fined not more than one hundred dollars. This section shall not apply to any law or conservation enforcement officer in the performance of his duty. Enforcement officers of the Department of Environmental Protection are empowered to arrest for the violation of the provisions of this section.

Sec. 53-205. Loaded shotguns, rifles and muzzleloaders in vehicles and snowmobiles.

(a) No person shall carry or possess in any vehicle or snowmobile any shotgun or rifle or muzzleloader of any gauge or caliber while such shotgun or rifle or muzzleloader contains in the barrel, chamber or magazine any loaded shell or cartridge capable of being discharged or when such muzzleloader has a percussion cap in place or when the powder pan of the flint lock contains powder. Muzzleloader as used in this section means a rifle or shotgun, incapable of firing a self-contained cartridge and which may be loaded at the muzzle end.

(b) The enforcement officers of the Department of Environmental Protection are empowered to enforce this section.

(c) The provisions of this section shall not apply to members of the military departments of the government or state while on duty or while traveling to or from assignments, or to enforcement officers, security guards or other persons employed to protect public or private property while in the performance of such duties.

(d) Any person who violates any provision of this section shall be guilty of a class D misdemeanor.

Sec. 53-206. Carrying of Dangerous Weapons Prohibited.

(a) Any person who carries upon his or her person any BB. gun, blackjack, metal or brass knuckles, or any dirk knife, or any switch knife, or any knife having an automatic spring release device by which a blade is released from the handle, having a blade of over one and one-half inches in length, or stiletto, or any knife the edged portion of the blade of which is four inches or more in length, any police baton or nightstick, or any martial arts weapon or electronic defense weapon, as defined in section 53a-3, as amended by this act, or any other dangerous or deadly weapon or instrument, shall be guilty of a class E felony. Whenever any person is found guilty of a violation of this section, any weapon or other instrument within the provisions of this section, found upon the body of such person, shall be forfeited to the municipality wherein such person was apprehended, notwithstanding any failure of the judgment of conviction to expressly impose such forfeiture.

(b) The provisions of this section shall not apply to (1) any officer charged with the preservation of the public peace while engaged in the pursuit of such officer's official duties; (2) the carrying of a baton or nightstick by a security guard while engaged in the pursuit of such guard's official duties; (3) the carrying of a knife, the edged portion of the blade of which is four inches or more in length, by (A) any member of the armed forces of the United States, as defined in section 27-103, or any reserve component thereof, or of the armed forces of the state, as defined in section 27-2, when on duty or going to or from duty, (B) any member of any military organization when on parade or when going to or from any place of assembly, (C) any person while transporting such knife as merchandise or for display at an authorized gun or knife show, (D) any person who is found with any such knife concealed upon one's person while lawfully removing such person's household goods or effects from one place to another, or from one residence to another, (E) any person while actually and peaceably engaged in carrying any such knife from such person's place of abode or business to a place or person where or by whom such knife is to be repaired, or while actually and peaceably returning to such person's place of abode or business with such knife after the same has been repaired, (F) any person holding a valid hunting, fishing or trapping license issued pursuant to chapter 490 or any saltwater fisherman carrying such knife for lawful hunting, fishing or trapping activities, or (G) any person while participating in an authorized historic reenactment; (4) the carrying by any person enrolled in or currently attending, or an instructor at, a martial arts school of a martial arts weapon while in a class or at an authorized event or competition or while transporting such weapon to or from such class, event or competition; (5) the carrying of a BB. gun by any person taking part in a supervised event or competition of the Boy Scouts of America or the Girl Scouts of America or in any other authorized event or competition while taking part in such event or competition or while transporting such weapon to or from such event or competition; (6) the carrying of an electronic defense weapon, as defined in section 53a-3, as amended by this act, by any person who is twenty-one years of age or older and possesses a permit or certificate issued under the provisions of section 29-28, 29-36f, 29-37p or 29-38n; and

[(6)] (7) the carrying of a BB. gun by any person upon such person's own property or the property of another person provided such other person has authorized the carrying of such weapon on such property, and the transporting of such weapon to or from such property.

ANNOTATIONS:

State v. Holloway, 11 Conn. App. 665, 528 A.2d 1176 (1987):
The definition of a dangerous instrument found in Section 53a-2 applies to Section 53-206.

State v. Prat, 66 Conn. App. 91, 784 A.2d 367 (2001):
Convictions for assault in first degree and carrying a dangerous instrument, both of which resulted from defendant's act of striking victim with baseball bat, did not constitute multiple punishments for the same offense in violation of the double jeopardy clause; each statute required proof of an element that was not found in the other.

State v. Ramos, 271 Conn. 785, 860 A.2d 249 (2004):
In prosecution for carrying a dangerous weapon, a defendant is entitled to instruction on self-defense when the defendant's use of a knife that is less than four inches long makes the knife a dangerous instrument.

State v. Campbell, 300 Conn. 368; 13 A.3d 661 (2011):
Implicit exception to statute, which prohibited carrying dangerous weapons, for carrying of a knife in one's residence or place of abode, did not apply to defendant who was carrying switchblade knife in common hallway of college dormitory in which he was a resident; exception only applied to long knives.

State v. Sealy, 208 Conn. 689, 546 A.2d 271 (1988):
Stairway and landing where defendant was carrying knife outside of his apartment were common hallway, rather than part of his residence or abode which was only apartment on third floor, and, thus, defendant was carrying dangerous weapon; although he had principal use of third floor landing and stairway, other persons had right to use that area.

Sec. 53-206b. Unlawful training in the use of firearms, explosive or incendiary devices or techniques capable of causing injury. Class C felony.

(a) as used in this section:

(1) "Civil disorder" means a public disturbance involving acts of violence by a group of three or more persons which causes an immediate danger of or results in damage to the property of or injury to any other person.

(2) "Explosive or incendiary device" means (A) dynamite and all other forms of high explosives, (B) any explosive bomb, grenade, missile or similar device, and (C) any incendiary bomb or grenade, fire bomb or similar device, including any device which (i) consists of or includes a breakable container which contains a flammable liquid or compound and a wick composed of any material which, when ignited, is capable if igniting such flammable liquid or compound, and (ii) can be carried or thrown by an individual.

(3) "Firearm" means a firearm as defined in section 53a-3.

(b) No person shall (1) teach or demonstrate to any person the use, application or making of any firearm, explosive or incendiary device, or technique capable of causing injury or death to a person, knowing or intending that such firearm, explosive, incendiary device or technique will be unlawfully employed for use in, or in furtherance of, a civil disorder; or (2) assemble with one or more persons for the purpose of training with, practicing with or being instructed in the use of any firearm, explosive or incendiary device, or technique capable of causing injury or death to a person, intending to employ unlawfully such firearm, explosive, incendiary device or technique for use in, or in furtherance of, a civil disorder.

(c) Any person who violates any provision of this section shall be guilty of a class C felony.

(d) Nothing in this section shall make unlawful any act of any peace officer, as defined in section 53a-3, performed in the lawful discharge of his duties.

Sec. 53-206c. Sale, carrying and brandishing of facsimile firearms prohibited. Class B misdemeanor.

(a) For the purposes of this section:

(1) "Facsimile of a firearm" means (A) any nonfunctional imitation of an original firearm which was manufactured, designed and produced since 1898, or (B) any nonfunctional representation of a firearm other than an imitation of an original firearm, provided such representation could reasonably be perceived to be a real firearm. Such term does not include any look-a-like, nonfiring, collector replica of an antique firearm developed prior to 1898, or traditional BB. Or pellet-firing air gun that expels a metallic or paint-contained projectile through the force of air pressure.

(2) "Firearm" means firearm as defined in Section 53a-3.

(b) No person shall give, offer for sale or sell any facsimile of a firearm. The provisions of this subsection shall not apply to any facsimile of a firearm, which, because of its distinct color, exaggerated size or other design feature, cannot reasonably be perceived to be a real firearm.

(c) Except in self-defense, no person shall carry, draw, exhibit or brandish a facsimile of a firearm or simulate a firearm in a threatening manner, with intent to frighten, vex or harass another person.

(d) No person shall draw, exhibit or brandish a facsimile of a firearm or simulate a firearm in the presence of a peace officer, firefighter, emergency medical technician or paramedic engaged in the performance of his duties knowing or having reason to know that such peace officer, firefighter, emergency medical technician or paramedic is engaged in the performance of his duties, with intent to impede such person in the performance of such duties.

(e) Any person who violates any provision of this section shall be guilty of a class B misdemeanor.

Sec. 53-206d. Carrying of firearm while under the influence of intoxicating liquor or drug prohibited.

(a)(1) No person shall carry a pistol, revolver, machine gun, shotgun, rifle or other firearm, which is loaded and from which a shot may be discharged, upon his person (A) while under the influence of intoxicating liquor or any drug, or both, or (B) while the ratio of alcohol in the blood of such person is eight-hundredths of one per cent or more of alcohol, by weight.

(2) Any person who violates any provision of this subsection shall be guilty of a class B misdemeanor.

(b) (1) No person shall engage in hunting while under the influence of intoxicating liquor or any drug, or both. A person shall be deemed under the influence when at the time of the alleged offense the person (A) is under the influence of intoxicating liquor or any drug, or both, or (B) has an elevated blood alcohol content. For the purposes of this subdivision, "elevated blood alcohol content" means (i) a ratio of alcohol in the blood of such person that is eight-hundredths of one per cent or more of alcohol, by weight, or (ii) if such person is under twenty-one years of age, a ratio of alcohol in the blood of such person that is two-hundredths of one per cent or more of alcohol, by weight.

(2) Any person who violates any provision of this subsection shall be guilty of a class A misdemeanor.

(3) Enforcement officers of the Department of Energy and Environmental Protection are empowered to arrest for a violation of the provisions of this subsection.

Sec. 53-206f. Failure of parent or guardian to halt illegal possession of firearm by minor child.

Any parent or guardian of a minor child who, knowing that such child possesses a firearm, as defined in section 53a-3, and is ineligible to possess such firearm, fails to make reasonable efforts to halt such possession shall be guilty of (1) a class A misdemeanor, or (2) if such child causes the injury or death of another person with such firearm, a class D felony.

Sec. 53-206g. Sale, possession, use or manufacture of bump stocks or other rates of fire enhancement prohibited. Class D felony or Class D misdemeanor.

(a) Except as provided in subsection (e) of this section, no person, other than a licensed firearms manufacturer under 18 USC 923(i) fulfilling a military contract, may sell, offer to sell, otherwise transfer or offer to transfer, purchase, possess, use or manufacture any rate of fire enhancement.

(b) Except as provided in subsection (d) of this section, a person who violates any provision of subsection (a) of this section shall be guilty of a class D felony.

(c) For purposes of this section, "firearm" means firearm as defined in section 53a-3, and "rate of fire enhancement" means any device, component, part, combination of parts, attachment or accessory that: (1) Uses energy from the recoil of a firearm to generate a reciprocating action that causes repeated function of the trigger, including, but not limited to, a bump stock; (2) repeatedly pulls the trigger of a firearm through the use of a crank, lever or other part, including, but not limited to, a trigger crank; or (3) causes a semiautomatic firearm to fire more than one round per operation of the trigger, where the trigger pull and reset constitute a single operation of the trigger, including, but not limited to, a binary trigger system.

(d) Except as provided in subsection (e) of this section, any person who holds a valid permit to carry a pistol or revolver issued pursuant to subsection (b) of section 29-28, a valid eligibility certificate for a pistol or revolver issued pursuant to section 29-36f, a valid long gun eligibility certificate issued pursuant to section 29-37p or an ammunition certificate issued or renewed pursuant to section 29-38n or section 29-38o and possesses a rate of fire enhancement prior to July 1, 2019, shall be guilty of a class D misdemeanor for a first offense and shall be guilty of a class D felony for any subsequent offense.

(e) (1) (A) Except as provided in subparagraph (B) of this subdivision, any person who moves into the state in lawful possession of a rate of fire enhancement shall, within ninety days, render the rate of fire enhancement permanently inoperable, remove the rate of fire enhancement from this state, or surrender the rate of fire enhancement to the Department of Emergency Services and Public Protection for destruction and, during such ninety-day period, shall not be subject to the penalties in subsection (b) or (d) of this section.

(B) Any such person who sells or offers to sell or otherwise transfers or offers to transfer, except as permitted by subparagraph (A) of this subdivision, or uses such rate of fire enhancement during such ninety-day period, shall be subject to the penalties in subsection (b) or (d) of this section, as applicable.

(2) (A) Except as provided in subparagraph (B) of this subdivision, any military personnel stationed or otherwise residing in this state who is deployed from this state on October 1, 2018, or is under deployment from this state on said date, and who was in lawful possession of a rate of firearm enhancement on September 30, 2018, shall, within ninety days of returning to this state from deployment, render the rate of fire enhancement permanently inoperable, remove the rate of fire enhancement from this state or surrender the rate of fire enhancement to the Department of Emergency Services and Public Protection for destruction.

(B) Except as provided in subparagraph (A) of this subdivision, any such military personnel who sells or offers to sell or otherwise transfers or offers to transfer, except as permitted by subparagraph (A) of this subdivision, or uses such rate of fire enhancement during such ninety-day period, shall be subject to the penalties in subsection (b) or (d) of this section, as applicable.

(f) If the court finds that a violation of this section is not of a serious nature and that the person charged with such violation (1) will probably not offend in the future, (2) has not previously been convicted of a violation of this section, and (3) has not previously had a prosecution under this section suspended pursuant to this subsection, it may order suspension of prosecution in accordance with the provisions of subsection (h) of section 29-33.

Sec. 53-206h. Bump stocks or other rates of fire enhancement prohibition. Notice.

(a) Not later than thirty days after May 31, 2018, the Commissioner of Emergency Services and Public Protection shall, within available appropriations, provide written notification of the provisions of section 53-206g by: (1) Posting the notification on the department's Internet web site, and (2) providing the notification electronically to federally licensed firearm dealers.

(b) Commencing thirty days after May 31, 2018, but prior to July 1, 2023, the commissioner shall include a written notification of the provisions of section 53-206g with: (1) (A) A permit to carry a pistol or revolver issued pursuant to subsection (b) of section 29-28, (B) an eligibility certificate for a pistol or revolver issued pursuant to section 29-36f, (C) a long gun eligibility certificate issued pursuant to section 29-37p, and (D) an ammunition certificate issued or renewed pursuant to section 29-38n or section 29-38o; and (2) a notice of expiration mailed to a holder of such permit or certificate pursuant to (A) subsection (f) of section 29-30, (B) subsection (e) of section 29-36h, or (C) subsection (e) of section 29-37r.

Sec. 53-206i. Manufacture of firearm from polymer plastic without detectable security exemplar. Prohibited. Penalty.

(a) No person shall manufacture any firearm from polymer plastic that, after removal of grips, stocks and magazines, is not as detectible as the security exemplar, by walk-through metal detectors calibrated and operated to detect the security exemplar.

(b) If the court finds that a violation of this section is not of a serious nature and that the person charged with such violation (1) will probably not offend in the future, (2) has not previously been convicted of a violation of this section, and (3) has not previously had a prosecution under this section suspended pursuant to this subsection, the court may order suspension of prosecution. The court shall not order suspension of prosecution unless the accused person has acknowledged that he or she understands the consequences of the suspension of prosecution. Any person for whom prosecution is suspended shall agree to the tolling of any statute of limitations with respect to such violation and to a waiver of his or her right to a speedy trial. Such person shall appear in court and shall be released to the custody of the Court Support Services Division for such period, not exceeding two years, and under such conditions as the court shall order. If the person refuses to accept, or, having accepted, violates such conditions, the court shall terminate the suspension of prosecution and the case shall be brought to trial. If such person satisfactorily completes such person's period of probation, he or she may apply for dismissal of the charges against such person and the court, on finding such satisfactory completion, shall dismiss such charges. If the person does not apply for dismissal of the charges against such person after satisfactorily completing such person's period of probation, the court, upon receipt of a report submitted by the Court Support Services Division that the person satisfactorily completed such person's period of probation, may on its own motion make a finding of such satisfactory completion and dismiss such charges. Upon dismissal, all records of such charges shall be erased pursuant to section 54-142a. An order of the court denying a motion to dismiss the charges against a person who has completed such person's period of probation or terminating the participation of a defendant in such program shall be a final judgment for purposes of appeal.

(c) Any person who violates any provision of this section shall be guilty of a class C felony for which two years of the sentence imposed may not be suspended or reduced by the court, and five thousand dollars of the fine imposed may not be remitted or reduced by the court unless the court states on the record its reasons for remitting or reducing such fine, and any firearm found in the possession of any person in violation of any provision of this section shall be forfeited.

(d) For purposes of this section, "firearm" means firearm, as defined in section 53a-3, but does not include the frame or receiver of any such weapon and "security exemplar" means "security exemplar" as defined in 18 USC 922(p), as amended from time to time, and any regulation adopted thereunder.

Sec. 53-206j. Sale, delivery or transfer of unfinished frame or lower receiver. Prohibited. Exceptions. Penalty.

(a) No person shall purchase or receive or sell, deliver or otherwise transfer an unfinished frame or lower receiver, except as provided in: (1) Subsections (b) and (c) of this section; or (2) subsection (d) of this section; or (3) subsection (e) of this section.

(b) The procedures for the purchase or receipt or sale, delivery or other transfer of an unfinished frame or lower receiver shall be the same procedures as apply to the purchase or receipt or sale, delivery or other transfer of a pistol or revolver under subsections (b) to (e), inclusive, of section 29-33, provided such purchase or receipt or sale, delivery or other transfer of an unfinished frame or lower receiver is in accordance with the provisions of subsection (c) of this section.

(c) (1) No person shall sell, deliver or otherwise transfer an unfinished frame or lower receiver pursuant to subsection (b) of this section that does not have a unique serial number or other mark of identification, obtained pursuant to: (A) The serial numbering program of the federal Bureau of Alcohol, Tobacco, Firearms and Explosives, or (B) subdivisions (2) and (3) of this subsection.

(2) A person may obtain a unique serial number or other mark of identification for an unfinished frame or lower receiver by providing to the Department of Emergency Services and Public Protection any identifying information concerning the unfinished frame or lower receiver and the owner of such unfinished frame or lower receiver, in a manner prescribed by the Commissioner of Emergency Services and Public Protection. Upon receiving a properly submitted request for a unique serial number or other mark of identification for an unfinished frame or lower receiver, the Department of Emergency Services and Public Protection shall determine if such person is prohibited from purchasing a firearm, and if not, shall issue to such person a unique serial number or other mark of identification immediately and in no instance more than (A) three business days after the Department of Emergency Services and Public Protection receives such request, or (B) ten business days after the system to distribute a unique serial number or other mark of identification pursuant to section 29-36b is operational, whichever date is later.

(3) Such unique serial number or other mark of identification shall be engraved upon or permanently affixed to the unfinished frame or lower receiver in a manner that conforms with the requirements imposed on licensed importers and licensed manufacturers of firearms pursuant to 18 USC 923(i), as amended from time to time, and any regulation adopted thereunder.

(d) The provisions of subsections (a) to (c), inclusive, of this section shall not apply to the sale, delivery or transfer of any unfinished frame or lower receiver between (1) a federally licensed firearm manufacturer and a federally licensed firearm dealer, (2) a federally licensed firearm importer and a federally licensed firearm dealer, or (3) federally licensed firearm dealers.

(e) Any person may arrange in advance to deliver and transfer an unfinished frame or lower receiver to a police department or the Department of Emergency Services and Public Protection.

(f) On and after October 1, 2019, no person shall possess an unfinished frame or lower receiver unless such person is eligible to purchase a firearm under state and federal law.

(g) If the court finds that a violation of this section is not of a serious nature and that the person charged with such violation (1) will probably not offend in the future, (2) has not previously been convicted of a violation of this section, and (3) has not previously had a prosecution under this section suspended pursuant to this subsection, the court may order suspension of prosecution. The court shall not order suspension of prosecution unless the accused person has acknowledged that he or she understands the consequences of the suspension of prosecution. Any person for whom prosecution is suspended shall agree to the tolling of any statute of limitations with respect to such violation and to a waiver of his or her right to a speedy trial. Such person shall appear in court and shall be released to the custody of the Court Support Services Division for such period, not exceeding two years, and under such conditions as the court shall order. If the person refuses to accept, or, having accepted, violates such conditions, the court shall terminate the suspension of prosecution and the case shall be brought to trial. If such person satisfactorily completes such person's period of probation, he or she may apply for dismissal of the charges against such person and the court, on finding such satisfactory completion, shall dismiss such charges. If the person does not apply for dismissal of the charges against such person after satisfactorily completing such person's period of probation, the court, upon receipt of a report submitted by the Court Support Services Division that the person satisfactorily completed such person's period of probation, may on its own motion make a finding of such satisfactory completion and dismiss such charges. Upon dismissal, all records of such charges shall be erased pursuant to section 54-142a. An order of the court denying a motion to dismiss the charges against a person who has completed such person's period of probation or terminating the participation of a defendant in such program shall be a final judgment for purposes of appeal.

(h) Any person who violates any provision of this section shall be guilty of a class C felony for which two years of the sentence imposed may not be suspended or reduced by the court, and five thousand dollars of the fine imposed may not be remitted or reduced by the court unless the court states on the record its reasons for remitting or reducing such fine, except that any person who sells, delivers or otherwise transfers an unfinished frame or lower receiver in violation of the provisions of this section knowing that such unfinished frame or lower receiver is stolen or that the manufacturer's number or other mark of identification on such unfinished frame or lower receiver has been altered, removed or obliterated, shall be guilty of a class B felony for which three years of the sentence imposed may not be suspended or reduced by the court, and ten thousand dollars of the fine imposed may not be remitted or reduced by the court unless the court states on the record its reasons for remitting or reducing such fine, and any unfinished frame or lower receiver found in the possession of any person in violation of any provision of this section shall be forfeited.

(i) For purposes of this section, “unfinished frame or lower receiver” means a blank, casting or machined body intended to be turned into the frame or lower receiver of a firearm, as defined in section 53a-3, with additional machining, and which has been formed or machined to the point where most major machining operations have been completed to turn the blank, casting or machined body into a frame or lower receiver of a firearm, even if the fire-control cavity area of such blank, casting or machined body is still completely solid and unmachined. An “unfinished frame or lower receiver” is not a firearm, as defined in 18 USC 921(a), as amended from time to time.

Sec. 53a-3. Definitions.

Except where different meanings are expressly specified, the following terms have the following meanings when used in this title:

(2) "Possess" means to have physical possession or otherwise to exercise dominion or control over tangible property;

(6) "Deadly weapon" means any weapon, whether loaded or unloaded, from which a shot may be discharged, or a switchblade knife, gravity knife, billy, blackjack, bludgeon, or metal knuckles. The definition of "deadly weapon" in this subdivision shall be deemed not to apply to section 29-38 or 53-206;

(7) "Dangerous instrument" means any instrument, article or substance which, under the circumstances in which it is used or attempted or threatened to be used, is capable of causing death or serious physical injury, and includes a "vehicle" as that term is defined in this section and includes a dog that has been commanded to attack, except a dog owned by a law enforcement agency of the state or any political subdivision thereof or of the federal government when such dog is in the performance of its duties under the direct supervision, care and control of an assigned law enforcement officer;

(15) "Machine gun" means a weapon of any description, irrespective of size, by whatever name known, loaded or unloaded, from which a number of shots or bullets may be rapidly or automatically discharged from a magazine with one continuous pull of the trigger and includes a submachine gun;

(16) "Rifle" means a weapon designed or redesigned, made or remade, and intended to be fired from the shoulder and designed or redesigned and made or remade to use the energy of the explosive in a fixed metallic cartridge to fire only a single projectile through a rifled bore for each single pull of the trigger;

(17) "Shotgun" means a weapon designed or redesigned, made or remade, and intended to be fired from the shoulder and designed or redesigned and made or remade to use the energy of the explosive in a fixed shotgun shell to fire through a smooth bore either a number of ball shot or a single projectile for each single pull of the trigger;

(18) "Pistol" or "revolver" means any firearm having a barrel less than twelve inches;

(19) "Firearm" means any sawed-off shotgun, machine gun, rifle, shotgun, pistol, revolver or other weapon, whether loaded or unloaded from which a shot may be discharged;

(20) "Electronic defense weapon" means a weapon which by electronic impulse or current is capable of immobilizing a person temporarily, including a stun gun or other conductive energy device;

(21) "Martial arts weapon" means a nunchaku, kama, kasari-fundo, octagon sai, tonfa or chinese star;

Commentary

This statute is not re-printed in its entirety. Refer to C.G.S. 53a-3 for a complete understanding of the definitions applicable to the provisions of the state penal code.

The definition of "Electronic defense weapon" was revised by Public Act 21-31 to remove the clause "but is not capable of inflicting death or serious physical injury" from the definition.

Sec. 53a-8. Criminal liability for acts of another.

(a) A person, acting with the mental state required for commission of an offense, who solicits, requests, commands, importunes or intentionally aids another person to engage in conduct which constitutes an offense shall be criminally liable for such conduct and may be prosecuted and punished as if he were the principal offender.

(b) A person who sells, delivers or provides any firearm, as defined in subdivision (19) of section 53a-3, to another person to engage in conduct which constitutes an offense knowing or under circumstances in which he should know that such other person intends to use such firearm in such conduct shall be criminally liable for such conduct and shall be prosecuted and punished as if he were the principal offender.

Sec. 53a-16a. Affirmative defense in certain situations involving firearms; exceptions.

In any prosecution for an offense under section 53a-55a, 53a-56a, 53a-60a, 53a-92a, 53a-94a, 53a-102a or 53a-103a, it shall be an affirmative defense that the pistol, revolver, rifle, shotgun, machine gun or other firearm was not a weapon from which a shot could be discharged, but it shall not be an affirmative defense to any prosecution under section 53a-55, 53a-56, 53a-60, 53a-92, 53a-94, 53a-102 or 53a-103.

Sec. 53a-16b. Affirmative defense of coparticipant to offense with firearm.

In any prosecution of an offense under section 53a-55a, 53a-56a, 53a-60a, 53a-92a, 53a-94a, 53a-102a or 53a-103a in which the defendant was not the only participant, it shall be an affirmative defense that the defendant: (1) Was not armed with a pistol, revolver, machine gun, shotgun, rifle or other firearm, and (2) had no reasonable ground to believe that any other participant was armed with such a weapon.

Sec. 53a-61aa. Threatening in the first degree: Class D or class C felony.

(a) A person is guilty of threatening in the first degree when such person (1) (A) threatens to commit any crime involving the use of a hazardous substance with the intent to terrorize another person, to cause evacuation of a building, place of assembly or facility of public transportation or otherwise to cause serious public inconvenience, or (B) threatens to commit such crime in reckless disregard of the risk of causing such terror, evacuation or inconvenience; (2) (A) threatens to commit any crime of violence with the intent to cause evacuation of a building, place of assembly or facility of public transportation or otherwise to cause serious public inconvenience, or (B) threatens to commit such crime in reckless disregard of the risk of causing such evacuation or inconvenience; (3) commits threatening in the second degree as provided in section 53a-62, and in the commission of such offense such person uses or is armed with and threatens the use of or displays or represents by such person's words or conduct that such person possesses a pistol, revolver, shotgun, rifle, machine gun or other firearm; or (4) violates subdivision (1) or (2) of this subsection with the intent to cause an evacuation of a building or the grounds of a (A) house of religious worship, (B) religiously-affiliated community center, (C) public or nonpublic preschool, school or institution of higher education, or (D) day care center, as defined in section 19a-87g, during operational, preschool, school or instructional hours or when a building or the grounds of such house of worship, community center, preschool, school, institution or day care center are being used for the provision of religious or community services, or house of worship, community center, preschool, school, institution or day care center-sponsored activities. No person shall be found guilty of threatening in the first degree under subdivision (3) of this subsection and threatening in the second degree upon the same transaction but such person may be charged and prosecuted for both such offenses upon the same information.

(b) For the purposes of this section, “hazardous substance” means any physical, chemical, biological or radiological substance or matter which, because of its quantity, concentration or physical, chemical or infectious characteristics, may cause or significantly contribute to an increase in mortality or an increase in serious irreversible or incapacitating reversible illness, or pose a substantial present or potential hazard to human health and “religiously-affiliated community center” means real property used for the provision of recreational, social or educational services that is owned or leased by a nonprofit organization that holds such property out as being affiliated with an organized religion.

(c) Threatening in the first degree is a class D felony, except that a violation of subdivision (4) of subsection (a) of this section is a class C felony.

Sec. 53a-211. Possession of a sawed-off shotgun or silencer: Class D felony.

(a) A person is guilty of possession of a sawed-off shotgun or a silencer when he owns, controls or possesses any sawed-off shotgun that has a barrel of less than eighteen inches or an overall length of less than twenty-six inches or when he owns, controls or possesses any silencer designed to muffle the noise of a firearm during discharge.

(b) The provisions of this section shall not apply to person, firms, corporations or museums licensed or otherwise permitted by federal or state law to possess, control or own a sawed-off shotguns or silencers.

(c) Possession of a sawed-off shotgun or a silencer is a class D felony.

Sec. 53a-212. Stealing a firearm: Class C felony.

(a) A person is guilty of stealing a firearm when, with intent to deprive another person of such other person's firearm or to appropriate the firearm to such person or a third party, such person wrongfully takes, obtains or withholds a firearm, as defined in subdivision (19) of section 53a-3.

(b) Stealing a firearm is a class C felony for which two years of the sentence imposed may not be suspended or reduced by the court, and five thousand dollars of the fine imposed may not be remitted or reduced by the court unless the court states on the record its reasons for remitting or reducing such fine.

Sec. 53a-216. Criminal use of firearm or electronic defense weapon: Class D felony.

(a) A person is guilty of criminal use of a firearm or electronic defense weapon when he commits any class A, B or C or unclassified felony as defined in section 53a-25 and in the commission of such felony he uses or threatens the use of a pistol, revolver, machine gun, shotgun, rifle or other firearm or electronic defense weapon. No person shall be convicted of criminal use of a firearm or electronic defense weapon and the underlying felony upon the same transaction but such person may be charged and prosecuted for both such offenses upon the same information.

(b) Criminal use of a firearm or electronic defense weapon is a class D felony for which five years of the sentence imposed may not be suspended or reduced by the court.

Sec. 53a-217. Criminal possession of a firearm, ammunition or electronic defense weapon: Class C felony.

(a) A person is guilty of criminal possession of a firearm, ammunition or an electronic defense weapon when such person possesses a firearm, ammunition or an electronic defense weapon and (1) has been convicted of (A) a felony committed prior to, on or after October 1, 2013, (B) a misdemeanor violation of section 21a-279 on or after October 1, 2015, or (C) a misdemeanor violation of section 53a-58, 53a-61, 53a-61a, 53a-62, 53a-63, 53a-96, 53a-175, 53a-176, 53a-178 or 53a-181d committed on or after October 1, 2013, and during the preceding twenty years (2) has been convicted as delinquent for the commission of a serious juvenile offense, as defined in section 46b-120, (3) has been discharged from custody within the preceding twenty years after having been found not guilty of a crime by reason of mental disease or defect pursuant to section 53a-13, (4) knows that such person is subject to (A) a restraining or protective order of a court of this state that has been issued against such person, after notice has been provided to such person, in a case involving the use, attempted use or threatened use of physical force against another person, or (B) a foreign order of protection, as defined in section 46b-15a, that has been issued against such person in a case involving the use, attempted use or threatened use of physical force against another person, (5) (A) has been confined on or after October 1, 2013, in a hospital for persons with psychiatric disabilities, as defined in section 17a-495, within the preceding sixty months by order of a probate court, or with respect to any person who holds a valid permit or certificate that was issued or renewed under the provisions of section 29-28 or 29-36f in effect prior to October 1, 2013, such person has been confined in such hospital within the preceding twelve months, or (B) has been voluntarily admitted on or after October 1, 2013, to a hospital for persons with psychiatric disabilities, as defined in section 17a-495, within the preceding six months for care and treatment of a psychiatric disability, unless the person (i) was voluntarily admitted solely for being an alcohol-dependent person or a drug-dependent person as those terms are defined in section 17a-680, or (ii) is a police officer who was voluntarily admitted and had his or her firearm, ammunition or electronic defense weapon used in the performance of the police officer's official duties returned in accordance with section 7-291d, (6) knows that such person is subject to a firearms seizure order issued prior to June 1, 2022, pursuant to [subsection (d) of] section 29-38c after notice and an opportunity to be heard has been provided to such person, or a risk protection order or risk protection investigation order issued on or after June 1, 2022, pursuant to section 29-38c, as amended by this act, or (7) is prohibited from shipping, transporting, possessing or receiving a firearm pursuant to 18 USC 922(g)(4). For the purposes of this section, "convicted" means having a judgment of conviction entered by a court of competent jurisdiction, "ammunition" means a loaded cartridge, consisting of a primed case, propellant or projectile, designed for use in any firearm, and a motor vehicle violation for which a sentence to a term of imprisonment of more than one year may be imposed shall be deemed an unclassified felony.

(b) Criminal possession of a firearm, ammunition or an electronic defense weapon is a class C felony, for which two years of the sentence imposed may not be suspended or reduced by the court, and five thousand dollars of the fine imposed may not be remitted or reduced by the court unless the court states on the record its reasons for remitting or reducing such fine.

ANNOTATIONS:

State v. Knight, 266 Conn. 658, 835 A.2d 47 (2003):

> The Penal Code defines the word "possess," as it applies to § 53a-217, as "to have physical possession or otherwise to exercise dominion or control over tangible property ...."

Sec. 53a-217a. Criminally negligent storage of a firearm: Class D felony.

(a) A person is guilty of criminally negligent storage of a firearm when such person violates the provisions of section 29-37i and a minor or, a resident of the premises who is ineligible to possess a firearm under state or federal law or who poses a risk of imminent personal injury to himself or herself or to other individuals, obtains the firearm and causes the injury or death of such minor, resident or any other person. For the purposes of this section, "minor" means any person under the age of eighteen years.

(b) The provisions of this section shall not apply if the minor obtains the firearm as a result of an unlawful entry to any premises by any person.

(c) Criminally negligent storage of a firearm is a class D felony.

ANNOTATIONS:

State v. Wilchinski, 242 Conn. 211, 700 A.2d 1 (1997):

> "The text and legislative history of § 53a-217a clearly indicate that gun owners must use age appropriate physical impediments to prevent children from gaining access to and misusing guns. The statute therefore has a core meaning that is sufficiently clear to satisfy the due process requirements of the state and federal constitutions."

Sec. 53a-217b. Possession of a weapon on school grounds: Class D felony.

(a) A person is guilty of possession of a weapon on school grounds when, knowing that such person is not licensed or privileged to do so, such person possesses a firearm or deadly weapon, as defined in section 53a-3, (1) in or on the real property comprising a public or private elementary or secondary school, or (2) at a school-sponsored activity as defined in subsection (h) of section 10-233a.

(b) The provisions of subsection (a) of this section shall not apply to the otherwise lawful possession of a firearm (1) by a person for use in a program approved by school officials in or on such school property or at such school-sponsored activity, (2) by a person in accordance with an agreement entered into between school officials and such person or such person's employer, (3) by a peace officer, as defined in subdivision (9) of section 53a-3, while engaged in the performance of such peace officer's official duties, or (4) by a person while traversing such school property for the purpose of gaining access to public or private lands open to hunting or for other lawful purposes, provided such firearm is not loaded and the entry on such school property is permitted by the local or regional board of education.

(c) Possession of a weapon on school grounds is a class D felony.

Sec. 53a-217c. Criminal possession of a pistol or revolver: Class C felony.

(a) A person is guilty of criminal possession of a pistol or revolver when such person possesses a pistol or revolver, as defined in section 29-27, and (1) has been convicted of (A) a felony committed prior to, on or after October 1, 2013, (B) a misdemeanor violation of section 21a-279 committed on or after October 1, 2015, or (C) a misdemeanor violation of section 53a-58, 53a-61, 53a-61a, 53a-62, 53a-63, 53a-96, 53a-175, 53a-176, 53a-178 or 53a-181d committed within the preceding twenty years, (2) has been convicted as delinquent for the commission of a serious juvenile offense, as defined in section 46b-120, (3) has been discharged from custody within the preceding twenty years after having been found not guilty of a crime by reason of mental disease or defect pursuant to section 53a-13, (4) (A) has been confined prior to October 1, 2013, in a hospital for persons with psychiatric disabilities, as defined in section 17a-495, within the preceding twelve months by order of a probate court, or has been confined on or after October 1, 2013, in a hospital for persons with psychiatric disabilities, as defined in section 17a-495, within the preceding sixty months by order of a probate court, or, with respect to any person who holds a valid permit or certificate that was issued or renewed under the provisions of section 29-28 or 29-36f in effect prior to October 1, 2013, such person has been confined in such hospital within the preceding twelve months, or (B) has been voluntarily admitted on or after October 1, 2013, to a hospital for persons with psychiatric disabilities, as defined in section 17a-495, within the preceding six months for care and treatment of a psychiatric disability and not solely for being an alcohol-dependent person or a drug-dependent person as those terms are defined in section 17a-680, (5) knows that such person is subject to (A) a restraining or protective order of a court of this state that has been issued against such person, after notice has been provided to such person, in a case involving the use, attempted use or threatened use of physical force against another person, or (B) a foreign order of protection, as defined in section 46b-15a, that has been issued against such person in a case involving the use, attempted use or threatened use of physical force against another person,

(6) knows that such person is subject to a firearms seizure order issued prior to June 1, 2022, pursuant to section 29-38c after notice and an opportunity to be heard has been provided to such person, or a risk protection order or risk protection investigation order issued on or after June 1, 2022, pursuant to section 28-38c, (7) is prohibited from shipping, transporting, possessing or receiving a firearm pursuant to 18 USC 922(g)(4), or (8) is an alien illegally or unlawfully in the United States. For the purposes of this section, "convicted" means having a judgment of conviction entered by a court of competent jurisdiction.

(b) Criminal possession of a pistol or revolver is a class C felony, for which two years of the sentence imposed may not be suspended or reduced by the court, and five thousand dollars of the fine imposed may not be remitted or reduced by the court unless the court states on the record its reasons for remitting or reducing such fine.

Sec. 53a-217d. Criminal possession of body armor: Class A misdemeanor.

(a) A person is guilty of criminal possession of body armor when he possesses body armor and has been (1) convicted of a capitol felony, a class A felony, except a conviction under section 53a-196a, a class B felony, except a conviction under section 53a-86, 53a-122 or 53a-196b, a class C felony, except a conviction under section 53a-87, 53a-152 or 53a-153 or a class D felony under sections 53a-60 to 53a-60c, inclusive, 53a-72a, 53a-72b, 53a-95, 53a-103, 53a-103a, 53a-114, 53a-136 or 53a-216, or (2) convicted as delinquent for the commission of a serious juvenile offense, as defined in section 46b-120.

(b) For the purposes of this section, "body armor" means any material designed to be worn on the body and to provide bullet penetration resistance and "convicted" means having a judgment of conviction entered by a court of competent jurisdiction.

(c) Criminal possession of body armor is a class A misdemeanor.

Sec. 54-36e. Firearms to be turned over to state police. Sale at public auction.

(a) Except as provided in sections 26-85 and 26-90, firearms and ammunition, adjudged by the court to be contraband pursuant to subsection (c) of section 54-36a, or adjudicated a nuisance pursuant to section 54-33g, shall be turned over to the Bureau of Identification of the Connecticut Division of State Police within the Department of Emergency Services and Public Protection for destruction or appropriate use or disposal by sale at public auction.

(b) Firearms and ammunition turned over to the state police pursuant to subsection (a) of this section which are not destroyed or retained for appropriate use shall be sold at public auctions, conducted by the Commissioner of Administrative Services or said commissioner's designee. Pistols and revolvers, as defined in section 53a-3, which are antiques, as defined in section 29-33, or curios or relics, as defined in the Code of Federal Regulations, Title 27, Chapter 1, Part 178, or modern pistols and revolvers which have a current retail value of one hundred dollars or more may be sold at such public auctions, provided such pistols and revolvers shall be sold only to persons who have a valid permit to sell a pistol or revolver, or a valid permit to carry a pistol or revolver, issued pursuant to section 29-28. Rifles and shotguns, as defined in section 53a-3, shall be sold only to persons qualified under federal law to purchase such rifles and shotguns and who have a valid long gun eligibility certificate issued pursuant to section 29-37p. The proceeds of any such sale shall be paid to the State Treasurer and deposited by the State Treasurer in the forfeit firearms account within the General Fund.

Sec. 54-36n. Identification and tracing of seized and recovered firearms and ammunition.

(a) Whenever a law enforcement agency seizes a firearm in connection with a criminal arrest or pursuant to a search warrant without an arrest or otherwise recovers a firearm, such agency shall forthwith take all appropriate steps to identify and trace the history of such firearm.

(b) In complying with the provisions of subsection (a) of this section, a law enforcement agency shall use the National Tracing Center of the Federal Bureau of Alcohol, Tobacco and Firearms. Such law enforcement agency shall immediately transmit the National Tracing Center, by facsimile or by entering such information on the Connecticut On-Line Law Enforcement Communication Teleprocessing (COLLECT) System when said system becomes available for transmitting such information directly to the National Tracing Center, all information necessary to comply with the provisions of subsection (a) of this section.

(c) The Department of Emergency Services and Public Protection shall take appropriate action to allow the COLLECT System to be used by law enforcement agencies in complying with the provisions of this section.

(d) Whenever a firearm is identified and is determined to have been stolen, the law enforcement agency shall return such firearm, and any ammunition seized or recovered with such firearm that is determined to be stolen, to the rightful owner thereof, provided such owner is not prohibited from possessing such firearm or ammunition and such agency does not need to retain such firearm or ammunition as evidence in a criminal prosecution.

Sec. 54-280. Definitions. Registry of offenders convicted of offense committed with a deadly weapon. Suspension of registration. Registration information. Notification protocol. Confidentiality.

(a) For the purposes of this section and sections 45a-99, 52-11, 54-280a and 54-280b:

(1) "Commissioner" means the Commissioner of Emergency Services and Public Protection;

(2) "Convicted" means that a person has a judgment entered in this state against such person by a court upon a plea of guilty, a plea of nolo contendere or a finding of guilty by a jury or the court notwithstanding any pending appeal or habeas corpus proceeding arising from such judgment;

(3) "Deadly weapon" means a deadly weapon, as defined in section 53a-3;

(4) "Department" means the Department of Emergency Services and Public Protection;

(5) "Identifying factors" means fingerprints, a photographic image, and a description of any other identifying characteristics as may be required by the Commissioner of Emergency Services and Public Protection;

(6) "Not guilty by reason of mental disease or defect" means a finding by a court or jury of not guilty by reason of mental disease or defect pursuant to section 53a-13 notwithstanding any pending appeal or habeas corpus proceeding arising from such finding;

(7) "Offender convicted of committing a crime with a deadly weapon" or "offender" means a person who has been convicted of an offense committed with a deadly weapon;

(8) "Offense committed with a deadly weapon" or "offense" means: (A) A violation of subsection (c) of section 2-1e, subsection (e) of section 29-28, subsections (a) to (e), inclusive, or (i) of section 29-33, section 29-34, subsection (a) of section 29-35, section 29-36, 29-36k, 29-37a or 29-37e, subsection (c) of section 29-37g, section 29-37j, subsection (b), (c) or (g) of section 53-202, section 53-202b, 53-202c, 53-202j, 53-202k, 53-202l, 53-202aa or 53-206b, subsection (b) of section 53a-8, section 53a-55a, 53a-56a, 53a-60a, 53a-60c, 53a-72b, 53a-92a, 53a-94a, 53a-102a, 53a-103a, 53a-211, 53a-212, 53a-216, 53a-217, 53a-217a, 53a-217b or 53a-217c, or a second or subsequent violation of section 53-202g; or (B) a violation of any section of the general statutes which constitutes a felony, as defined in section 53a-25, provided the court makes a finding that, at the time of the offense, the offender used a deadly weapon, or was armed with and threatened the use of or displayed or represented by words or conduct that the offender possessed a deadly weapon;

(9) "Registrant" means a person required to register under section 54-280a;

(10) "Registry" means a central record system in this state that is established pursuant to this section and receives, maintains and disseminates to law enforcement agencies information on persons convicted or found not guilty by reason of mental disease or defect of an offense committed with a deadly weapon; and

(11) "Release into the community" means, with respect to a conviction or a finding of not guilty by reason of mental disease or defect of an offense committed with a deadly weapon, (A) any release by a court after such conviction or finding of not guilty by reason of mental disease or defect, a sentence of probation or any other sentence under section 53a-28 that does not result in the offender's immediate placement in the custody of the Commissioner of Correction; (B) release from a correctional facility at the discretion of the Board of Pardons and Paroles, by the Department of Correction to a program authorized by section 18-100c or upon completion of the maximum term or terms of the offender's sentence or sentences, or to the supervision of the Court Support Services Division in accordance with the terms of the offender's sentence; or (C) temporary leave to an approved residence by the Psychiatric Security Review Board pursuant to section 17a-587, conditional release from a hospital for mental illness or a facility for persons with intellectual disability by the Psychiatric Security Review Board pursuant to section 17a-588 or release upon termination of commitment to the Psychiatric Security Review Board.

(b) The Department of Emergency Services and Public Protection shall, not later than January 1, 2014, establish and maintain a registry of all persons required to register under section 54-280a as offenders convicted of an offense committed with a deadly weapon. The department shall, in cooperation with the Office of the Chief Court Administrator, the Department of Correction and the Psychiatric Security Review Board, develop appropriate forms for use by agencies and individuals to report registration information, including changes of address. Upon receipt of registration information, the department shall enter the information into the registry and notify the local police department or state police troop having jurisdiction where the registrant resides or plans to reside. Upon receiving notification pursuant to section 54-280a that a registrant has changed his or her address, the department shall enter the information into the registry and notify the local police departments or state police troops having jurisdiction where the registrant previously resided and the jurisdiction where the registrant has relocated. The Commissioner of Emergency Services and Public Protection shall also ensure that the name and residence address of each registrant is available through the Connecticut on-line law enforcement communication teleprocessing system maintained by the department. If a registrant reports a residence in another state, the department may notify the state police agency of that state or such other agency in that state that maintains registry information, if known.

(c) The Department of Emergency Services and Public Protection may suspend the registration of any person registered under section 54-280a while such person is incarcerated, under civil commitment or residing outside this state. During the period that such registration is under suspension, the department may withdraw the registration information from access to law enforcement agencies. Upon the release of the registrant from incarceration or civil commitment or resumption of residency in this state by the registrant, the department shall reinstate the registration and redistribute the registration information in accordance with subsection (b) of this section. Suspension of registration shall not affect the date of expiration of the registration obligation of the registrant under section 54-280a.

(d) The Department of Emergency Services and Public Protection shall include in the registry the most recent photographic image of each registrant taken by the department, the Department of Correction, a law enforcement agency or the Court Support Services Division of the Judicial Department.

(e) Whenever the Commissioner of Emergency Services and Public Protection receives notice from a superior court pursuant to section 52-11 or a probate court pursuant to section 45a-99 that such court has ordered the change of name of a person, and the department determines that such person is listed in the registry, the department shall revise such person's registration information accordingly.

(f) The Commissioner of Emergency Services and Public Protection shall develop a protocol for the notification of other state agencies, the Judicial Department and local police departments whenever a person listed in the registry changes such person's name and notifies the commissioner of the new name pursuant to section 54-280a or whenever the commissioner determines pursuant to subsection (e) of this section that a person listed in the registry has changed such person's name.

(g) The information in the registry shall not be a public record or file for the purposes of section 1-200. Any information disclosed pursuant to this section or section 54-280a or 54-280b, shall not be further disclosed unless such disclosure is permitted under this section or section 54-280a or 54-280b.

Sec. 54-280a. Registration of person convicted of offense committed with a deadly weapon. Personal appearance requirement. Penalty.

(a) (1) Any person who has been convicted or found not guilty by reason of mental disease or defect of an offense committed with a deadly weapon and is released into the community on or after January 1, 2014, shall, within fourteen calendar days following such release or, if such person is in the custody of the Commissioner of Correction, at such time prior to release as the Commissioner of Correction shall direct, and whether or not such person's place of residence is in this state, register such person's name, identifying factors, criminal history record, residence address and electronic mail address with the Commissioner of Emergency Services and Public Protection, on such forms and in such locations as the Commissioner of Emergency Services and Public Protection shall direct, and shall maintain such registration for five years.

(2) Prior to accepting a plea of guilty or nolo contendere from a person with respect to an offense committed with a deadly weapon, the court shall (A) inform the person that the entry of a finding of guilty after acceptance of the plea will subject the person to the registration requirements of this section, and (B) determine that the person fully understands the consequences of the plea.

(3) If any person who is subject to registration under this section changes such person's name, such person shall, without undue delay, notify the Commissioner of Emergency Services and Public Protection in writing of the new name. If any person who is subject to registration under this section changes such person's address, such person shall, without undue delay, notify the Commissioner of Emergency Services and Public Protection in writing of the new address. During such period of registration, each registrant shall complete and return any forms mailed to such registrant to verify such registrant's residence address and shall submit to the retaking of a photographic image upon request of the Commissioner of Emergency Services and Public Protection.

(b) Any offender convicted of committing a crime with a deadly weapon who is required to register under this section shall, not later than twenty calendar days after each anniversary date of such initial registration, until the date such registration requirement expires under subdivision (1) of subsection (a) of this section, personally appear at the local police department or state police troop having jurisdiction where the registrant resides to verify and update, as appropriate, the contents of his or her registration. The local police department or state police troop, as the case may be, may defer such requirement to personally appear to a later date for good cause shown. Not later than thirty calendar days prior to such anniversary date, the Department of Emergency Services and Public Protection shall mail written notice of the personal appearance requirement of this subsection to the registrant and the local police department or state police troop having jurisdiction where the registrant resides. Not later than thirty calendar days after the anniversary date of each registrant, the local police department or state police troop having jurisdiction where the registrant resides shall notify the Commissioner of Emergency Services and Public Protection, on such form as the commissioner may prescribe, (1) whether the registrant complied with the personal appearance requirement of this subsection or whether such personal appearance requirement was deferred to a later date for good cause shown, and (2) if the personal appearance requirement was deferred to a later date for good cause shown, the local police department or state police troop shall indicate the later date established for such personal appearance and describe the good cause shown.

(c) Any person who is subject to registration under this section who violates any provisions of subsection (a) or (b) of this section, except a violation consisting of failure to notify the Commissioner of Emergency Services and Public Protection of a change of name or address, shall be guilty of a class D felony. Any person who is subject to registration under this section who fails to notify the Commissioner of Emergency Services and Public Protection of a change of name or address not later than five business days after such change of name or address shall be guilty of a class D felony.

Commentary

Sections 54-280 and 280a, effective January 1, 2014, are new, having been enacted as part of Public Act 13-3 in the wake of the Sandy Hook tragedy. Now, persons convicted of one or more of the offenses listed in Section 54-280 are required to register with the Commissioner of the Department of Emergency Services and Public Protection (DESPP), see Section 54-280b below, and to inform the Commissioner of any changes to either their names or addresses. See Section 45a-99, included in this publication, for further information concerning the reporting of a change of name. Persons convicted of offenses in other states are not required to register with the Commissioner of the Department of Emergency Services and Public Protection should they relocate to Connecticut. See Section 54-280 (2) ("Convicted" means that a person has a judgment entered in this state against such person by a court upon a plea of guilty, a plea of nolo contendere or a finding of guilty by a jury or the court ...) (emphasis supplied).

Sec. 54-280b. Registration information.

(a) The registration information for each registrant shall include:

(1) The offender's name, including any other name by which the offender has been legally known, and any aliases used by the offender;

(2) Identifying information, including a physical description of the offender;

(3) The current residence address of the offender;

(4) The date of conviction of the offense;

(5) A description of the offense; and

(6) If the offender was sentenced to a term of incarceration for such offense, a portion of which was not suspended, the date the offender was released from such incarceration.

(b) The offender shall sign and date the registration.

(c) At the time that the offender appears for the purpose of registering, the Department of Emergency Services and Public Protection shall photograph the offender and arrange for the fingerprinting of the offender and include such photograph and a complete set of fingerprints in the registry. If the offender is required to submit to the taking of a blood or other biological sample of sufficient quality for DNA (deoxyribonucleic acid) analysis pursuant to section 54-102g, and has not submitted to the taking of such sample, the commissioner shall also require such sample to be taken for analysis pursuant to section 54-102g.

(d) The Department of Emergency Services and Public Protection may require the offender to provide documentation to verify the contents of his or her registration.

CONNECTICUT PUBLIC ACTS

When Connecticut adopts new laws as Public Acts of the legislature, the legislation may delete or revise existing sections of the Connecticut General Statutes, or a Public Act may create an entirely new law. Legislation enacted by Public Acts does not immediately appear in the printed or on-line editions of the Connecticut General Statutes; it takes some time for new laws to be codified into the Statutes. As of the date of this edition of the Guide, the on-line version of the Connecticut General Statutes has been codified to include legislation through the 2016 Public Acts. Public Acts from 2018 and 2019 have not yet been codified.

Where Public Acts from 2020 through 2022 revised or deleted existing section of the Connecticut General Statutes, we have attempted to edit those changes into the statutes as reproduced on the preceding pages. New laws, however, although not codified into the Connecticut General Statutes, take effect either upon passage or at a stipulated date well before when the new laws can be codified. The following include Public Acts pertaining to or affecting firearms that were enacted in 2020, 2021, or 2022 and which may not yet have been codified:

Public Act No. 21-31
AN ACT CONCERNING ELECTRONIC DEFENSE WEAPONS.
Be it enacted by the Senate and House of Representatives in General Assembly convened:
Section 1. Section 29-38 of the general statutes is repealed and the following is substituted in lieu thereof (*Effective July 1, 2021*):

(a) Any person who knowingly has, in any vehicle owned, operated or occupied by such person, any weapon, any pistol or revolver for which a proper permit has not been issued as provided in section 29-28 or any machine gun which has not been registered as required by section 53-202, shall be guilty of a class D felony, and the presence of any such weapon, pistol or revolver, or machine gun in any vehicle shall be prima facie evidence of a violation of this section by the owner, operator and each occupant thereof. The word "weapon", as used in this section, means any BB. gun, any blackjack, any metal or brass knuckles, any police baton or nightstick, any dirk knife or switch knife, any knife having an automatic spring release device by which a blade is released from the handle, having a blade of over one and one-half inches in length, any stiletto, any knife the edged portion of the blade of which is four inches or more in length, any martial arts weapon or electronic defense weapon, as defined in section 53a-3, as amended by this act, or any other dangerous or deadly weapon or instrument.

(b) The provisions of this section shall not apply to: (1) Any officer charged with the preservation of the public peace while engaged in the pursuit of such officer's official duties; (2) any security guard having a baton or nightstick in a vehicle while engaged in the pursuit of such guard's official duties; (3) any person enrolled in and currently attending a martial arts school, with official verification of such enrollment and attendance, or any certified martial arts instructor, having any such martial arts weapon in a vehicle while traveling to or from such school or to or from an authorized event or competition; (4) any person having a BB. gun in a vehicle provided such weapon is unloaded and stored in the trunk of such vehicle or in a locked container other than the glove compartment or console;

(5) any person having a knife, the edged portion of the blade of which is four inches or more in length, in a vehicle if such person is (A) any member of the armed forces of the United States, as defined in section 27-103, or any reserve component thereof, or of the armed forces of the state, as defined in section 27-2, when on duty or going to or from duty, (B) any member of any military organization when on parade or when going to or from any place of assembly, (C) any person while transporting such knife as merchandise or for display at an authorized gun or knife show, (D) any person while lawfully removing such person's household goods or effects from one place to another, or from one residence to another, (E) any person while actually and peaceably engaged in carrying any such knife from such person's place of abode or business to a place or person where or by whom such knife is to be repaired, or while actually and peaceably returning to such person's place of abode or business with such knife after the same has been repaired, (F) any person holding a valid hunting, fishing or trapping license issued pursuant to chapter 490 or any saltwater fisherman while having such knife in a vehicle for lawful hunting, fishing or trapping activities, or (G) any person participating in an authorized historic reenactment; (6) any person having an electronic defense weapon, as defined in section 53a-3, as amended by this act, in a vehicle, who is twenty-one years of age or older and possesses a permit or certificate issued under the provisions of section 29-28, 29-36f, 29-37p or 29-38n; or [(6)] (7) any person having a dirk knife or police baton in a vehicle while lawfully moving such person's household goods or effects from one place to another, or from one residence to another.

Sec. 2. Section 53-206 of the general statutes is repealed and the following is substituted in lieu thereof (*Effective July 1, 2021*):

(a) Any person who carries upon his or her person any BB. gun, blackjack, metal or brass knuckles, or any dirk knife, or any switch knife, or any knife having an automatic spring release device by which a blade is released from the handle, having a blade of over one and one-half inches in length, or stiletto, or any knife the edged portion of the blade of which is four inches or more in length, any police baton or nightstick, or any martial arts weapon or electronic defense weapon, as defined in section 53a-3, as amended by this act, or any other dangerous or deadly weapon or instrument, shall be guilty of a class E felony. Whenever any person is found guilty of a violation of this section, any weapon or other instrument within the provisions of this section, found upon the body of such person, shall be forfeited to the municipality wherein such person was apprehended, notwithstanding any failure of the judgment of conviction to expressly impose such forfeiture.

(b) The provisions of this section shall not apply to (1) any officer charged with the preservation of the public peace while engaged in the pursuit of such officer's official duties; (2) the carrying of a baton or nightstick by a security guard while engaged in the pursuit of such guard's official duties; (3) the carrying of a knife, the edged portion of the blade of which is four inches or more in length, by (A) any member of the armed forces of the United States, as defined in section 27-103, or any reserve component thereof, or of the armed forces of the state, as defined in section 27-2, when on duty or going to or from duty, (B) any member of any military organization when on parade or when going to or from any place of assembly, (C) any person while transporting such knife as merchandise or for display at an authorized gun or knife show, (D) any person who is found with any such knife concealed upon one's person while lawfully removing such person's household goods or effects from one place to another, or from one residence to another, (E) any person while actually and peaceably engaged in carrying any such knife from such person's place of abode or business to a place or person where or by whom such knife is to be repaired, or while actually and peaceably returning to such person's place of abode or business with such knife after the same has been repaired, (F) any person holding a valid hunting, fishing or trapping license issued pursuant to chapter 490 or any saltwater fisherman carrying such knife for lawful hunting, fishing or trapping activities, or (G) any person while participating in an authorized historic reenactment; (4) the carrying by any person enrolled in or currently attending, or an instructor at, a martial arts school of a martial arts weapon while in a class or at an authorized event or competition or while transporting such weapon to or from such class, event or competition; (5) the carrying of a BB. gun by any person taking part in a supervised event or competition of the Boy Scouts of America or the Girl Scouts of America or in any other authorized event or competition while taking part in such event or competition or while transporting such weapon to or from such event or competition; (6) the carrying of an electronic defense weapon, as defined in section 53a-3, as amended by this act, by any person who is twenty-one years of age or older and possesses a permit or certificate issued under the provisions of section 29-28, 29-36f, 29-37p or 29-38n; and [(6)] (7) the carrying of a BB. gun by any person upon such person's own property or the property of another person provided such other person has authorized the carrying of such weapon on such property, and the transporting of such weapon to or from such property.

Sec. 3. (NEW) (*Effective July 1, 2021*) Any person who sells or transfers an electronic defense weapon, as defined in section 53a-3 of the general statutes, as amended by this act, to any person who is under twenty-one years of age or does not possess a permit or certificate issued under the provisions of section 29-28, 29-36f, 29-37p or 29-38n of the general statutes shall be guilty of a class D felony.

Sec. 4. Subdivision (20) of section 53a-3 of the general statutes is repealed and the following is substituted in lieu thereof (*Effective July 1, 2021*):

(20) "Electronic defense weapon" means a weapon which by electronic impulse or current is capable of immobilizing a person temporarily, [but is not capable of inflicting death or serious physical injury,] including a stun gun or other conductive energy device;

Commentary

New language added in subsections 1 and 2 makes it lawful for persons twenty-one years of age or older to carry electronic defense weapons (i.e. "stun guns") if the person has a permit to carry pistol or revolver, an eligibility certificate for pistol or revolver, a long gun certificate, or an ammunition eligibility certificate.

Public Act No. 21-67
AN ACT CONCERNING RISK PROTECTION ORDERS OR WARRANTS AND DISQUALIFIERS FOR FIREARM PERMITS AND ELIGIBILITY CERTIFICATES.

Be it enacted by the Senate and House of Representatives in General Assembly convened:

Section 1. Section 29-38c of the general statutes is repealed and the following is substituted in lieu thereof (*Effective June 1, 2022*):

(b) (1) Any family or household member or medical professional who has a good faith belief that a person poses a risk of imminent personal injury to himself or herself or to another person may make an application for a risk protection order investigation with the clerk of the court for any geographical area. The application and accompanying affidavit shall be made under oath and indicate: (A) The factual basis for the applicant's belief that such person poses a risk of imminent personal injury to himself or herself or to another person; (B) whether such person holds a permit under subsection (b) of section 29-28, as amended by this act, or an eligibility certificate issued under section 29-36f, as amended by this act, 29-37p, as amended by this act, or 29-38n or currently possesses one or more firearms or other deadly weapons or ammunition, if known; and (C) where any such firearm or other deadly weapon or ammunition is located, if known.

(2) Upon receipt of an application and affidavit pursuant to this subsection, if the court finds that there is a good faith belief that a person poses a risk of imminent personal injury to himself or herself or to another person, the court shall order a risk protection order investigation to determine if the person who is the subject of the application poses a risk of imminent personal injury to himself or herself or to another person. Upon issuance by the court of an order for investigation, the court shall: (A) Give notice to the Commissioner of Emergency Services and Public Protection of the issuance of the order for a risk protection order investigation; and (B) immediately give notice of the order and transmit the order and the application and affidavit on which the order is based to the law enforcement agency for the town in which the subject of the investigation resides. The court shall immediately enter into the National Instant Criminal Background Check System (NICS) a record indicating that the person who is the subject of the investigation is ineligible to purchase or otherwise receive a firearm.

(3) Upon receipt of an investigation order, the law enforcement agency shall immediately investigate whether the subject of the investigation poses a risk of imminent personal injury to himself or herself or to another person. If the law enforcement agency determines that there is probable cause to believe that the subject of the investigation poses a risk of imminent personal injury to himself or herself or to another person, such law enforcement agency shall seek a risk protection order, and when applicable, a warrant pursuant to subsection (a) of this section not later than twenty-four hours after receiving the investigation order, or, if the law enforcement agency needs additional time to complete the investigation, as soon thereafter as is practicable. If the law enforcement agency determines that there is no probable cause to believe that the subject of the investigation poses a risk of imminent personal injury to himself or herself or to another person, the law enforcement agency shall notify the court, the applicant, and the Commissioner of Emergency Services and Public Protection of such determination, in writing, not later than forty-eight hours after receiving the investigation order, if practicable, or, if the law enforcement agency needs additional time to complete the risk warrant investigation, as soon thereafter as is practicable. Upon receiving such notification that there was not a finding of probable cause, the court shall immediately remove or cancel any record entered into the National Instant Criminal Background Check System associated with such investigation for which there was no finding of probable cause.

Commentary

Section (b) is new, added by PA 21-67. This section expands the list of people who may apply for a risk protection investigation order to include any family or household member or medical professional. Previously such orders could be applied for only by two police officers, state's attorneys, or assistant state's attorneys.

The remainder of the act makes technical revisions to existing sections of the General Statutes. These revisions have been edited into the statutes in the preceding pages.

Connecticut Regulations

Sec. 29-36m-1. Scope and applicability.

These regulations shall apply to the sale, delivery, transfer or possession of any pistol or revolver, time limits for applying for certificates of possession for assault weapons and storage of weapons at correctional facilities.

(a) Restrictions after October 1, 1995. On and after October 1, 1995, no person may purchase or receive any pistol or revolver, except an antique pistol or revolver as defined in section 29-36m-2 of these regulations, unless such person:

(1) Holds a valid state permit to carry a pistol or revolver issued pursuant to subsection (b) of section 29-28 of the Connecticut General Statutes; or

(2) Holds a valid permit to sell at retail pistols or revolvers issued pursuant to subsection (a) of section 29-28 of the Connecticut General Statutes; or

(3) Holds a valid eligibility certificate for a pistol or revolver issued by the commissioner pursuant to section 29-36f of the Connecticut General Statutes; or

(4) Is a federal marshal, sheriff, parole officer or peace officer.

(b) General prohibitions.

(1) False statements and false information. No person shall make any false statement or give any false information in connection with any purchase, sale, delivery or other transfer of any pistol or revolver.

(2) Persons under twenty-one years. No person shall sell, barter, hire, lend, give, deliver or otherwise transfer to any person under the age of twenty-one (21) years any pistol or revolver.

Exceptions. A pistol or revolver may be temporarily transferred to any person only for the use by such person in target shooting or on a firing or shooting range, provided such use is otherwise permitted by law and is under the immediate supervision of a person eligible to possess a pistol or revolver.

Sec. 29-36m-2. Definitions.

As used in sections 29-36m-1 to 29-36m-22, inclusive:

(a) "Antique pistol or revolver" means any pistol or revolver which was manufactured in or before 1898 and any replica of such pistol or revolver provided such replica is not designed or redesigned for using rimfire or conventional centerfire fixed ammunition except rimfire or conventional centerfire fixed ammunition which is no longer manufactured in the United States and not readily available in the ordinary channel of commercial trade.

(b) "Commissioner" means the Commissioner of Emergency Services and Public Protection.

(c) "Convicted" means having a judgment of conviction entered by a court of competent jurisdiction.

(d) "Department" means the Department of Emergency Services and Public Protection.

(e) "Firing or shooting range" means any type of facility, indoor or outdoor, where firearms training, practice or competition can be conducted.

(f) "Immediate supervision" means supervision in which the supervisor is in the physical presence of, and has the continuous ability to direct, the individual being supervised.

(g) "Pistol or revolver" means any firearm having a barrel less than twelve inches in length.

(h) "Target shooting" means shooting at an inanimate object that usually has some type of physical reaction or scoring markings.

Sec. 29-36m-3. Applications for the sale, delivery or other transfer of a pistol or revolver.

(a) When application required. No person, firm or corporation shall sell, deliver or otherwise transfer any pistol or revolver except on written application.

Exemptions. The requirements of sections 29-36m-3 to 29-36m-6 of these regulations shall not apply to the following:

(1) Antique pistols or revolvers as defined in section 29-36m-2 of these regulations.

(2) The sale, delivery or other transfer of a pistol or revolver between:

(A) A federally licensed firearm manufacturer and a federally licensed firearm dealer; or

(B) A federally licensed firearm importer and a federally licensed firearm dealer; or

(C) Federally licensed firearm dealers.

(b) When sale, delivery or other transfer is prohibited. No person, firm or corporation shall sell, deliver or otherwise transfer any pistol or revolver to any person who:

(1) Has been convicted of a felony or a violation of subsection (c) of section 21a-279, section 53a-58, 53a-61, 53-61a, 53a-62, 53a-63, 53a-96, 53a-175, 53a-176, 53a-178, or 53a-181d of the Connecticut General Statutes; or

(2) Has been discharged from custody within the preceding twenty (20) years after having been found not guilty of a crime by reason of mental disease or defect pursuant to section 53a-13 of the Connecticut General Statutes; or

(3) Has been confined in a hospital for mental illness, as defined in section 17a-495 of the Connecticut General Statutes, within the preceding twelve (12) months by order of a probate court; or

(4) Knows that he is subject to a restraining or protective order issued by a court, after notice and an opportunity to be heard has been provided to such person, in a case involving the use, attempted use or threatened use of physical force against another person; or

(5) Is an alien illegally or unlawfully in the United States.

(c) Application.

(1) The application form for the sale, delivery or other transfer of a pistol or revolver shall be on the form prescribed by and obtained from the commissioner.

(2) The application for the sale, delivery or other transfer of a pistol or revolver shall be made in writing, under oath, and shall be completed legibly and in its entirety and in accordance with the directions on the form. Post office boxes shall not be an acceptable form of address.

(d) Manner of submission. The person, firm or corporation shall send, by first class mail on the day of receipt of such application, a copy of such application to the following:

(1) To the chief of police department of the municipality wherein the applicant resides or, where there is no chief of police, the first selectman or warden of such municipality; and

(2) To the commissioner.

(e) Retention period. The person, firm or corporation receiving the application shall retain such application for a minimum of five (5) years.

(f) Notification of possession prohibition. If either the municipal authority or the commissioner determines the existence of any reason that would prohibit the applicant from possession of a pistol or revolver, he shall send written notification to the person, firm or corporation to whom the application was made.

Sec. 29-36m-4. Waiting period for sale, delivery or other transfer of a pistol or revolver.

(a) No sale, delivery or other transfer of any pistol or revolver prior to October 1, 1995 shall be made until the expiration of two (2) weeks from the date of the mailing of the copies of the application in accordance with section 29-36m-3(d) of these regulations.

(b) The following persons shall be exempt from the two (2) week waiting period:

(1) The holder of a valid state permit to carry a pistol or revolver issued pursuant to subsection (b) of section 29-28 of the Connecticut General Statutes; or

(2) The holder of a valid permit to sell at retail pistols or revolvers issued pursuant to subsection (a) of section 29-28 of the Connecticut General Statutes; or

(3) The holder of a valid eligibility certificate for a pistol or revolver issued by the commissioner pursuant to section 29-36f of the Connecticut General Statutes; or

(4) Any federal marshal, sheriff, parole officer or peace officer.

(c) Prior to the sale, delivery or other transfer of a pistol or revolver to the holder of such permit or certificate, such person, firm or corporation shall verify with the issuing authority that the permit or certificate under which the exemption from the two (2) week waiting period is claimed is still valid and has not been suspended or revoked.

Sec. 29-36m-5. Manner of sale, delivery or other transfer of a pistol or revolver.

(a) Identification requirement. No sale, delivery or other transfer of any pistol or revolver shall be made unless the seller, deliverer or transferor either:

(1) Personally knows the purchaser, deliveree or transferee; or

(2) Is provided evidence of the identity of the purchaser, deliveree, or transferee in the form of one of the following:

(A) A valid motor vehicle operator's license; or

(B) An identity card issued pursuant to section 1-1h of the Connecticut General Statutes; or

(C) A valid passport.

(b) Packaging requirement. When any pistol or revolver is sold, delivered or otherwise transferred, it shall be:

(1) Enclosed in a package, the paper or wrapping of which is securely fastened;

(2) Unloaded; and

(3) Free of and not contain any gunpowder, or other explosive or any bullet, ball or shell.

Sec. 29-36m-6. Receipt for sale, delivery or other transfer.

(a) Signature required. At the time of sale, delivery or other transfer, a receipt for the pistol or revolver shall be signed by the purchaser, deliveree or other transferee.

(b) Contents of the receipt. The receipt shall contain the following information:

(1) Name, address and occupation of the purchaser, deliveree or transferee;

(2) The date of sale, delivery or other transfer;

(3) The caliber, make, model and manufacturer's number and a general description of the pistol or revolver;

(4) The purchaser, deliveree or transferee's identification number for one of the following:

(A) Permit to carry pistols or revolvers issued pursuant to subsection (b) of section 29-28 of the Connecticut General Statutes; or

(B) Permit to sell at retail pistols or revolvers issued pursuant to subsection (a) of section 29-28 of the Connecticut General Statutes; or

(C) Eligibility certificate for a pistol or revolver issued pursuant to section 29-36f of the Connecticut General Statutes; and

(5) The authorization number designated for the transfer by the department.

(c) Distribution of receipt. The seller, deliverer or other transferor of any pistol or revolver shall distribute copies of the receipt required by section 29-36m-6 of these regulations as follows:

(1) One (1) copy to the purchaser, deliveree or transferee; and

(2) One (1) copy by first class mail within forty-eight (48) hours of the sale, delivery or other transfer to the commissioner and the chief of police, or where there is no chief of

police, the warden of the borough or the first selectman of the town where the sale, delivery or other transfer took place.

Sec. 29-36m-7. Permits for retail sales of pistols or revolvers.

(a) When Permit required. No person who sells ten (10) or more pistols or revolvers in a calendar year or is a federally-licensed firearm dealer shall advertise, sell, deliver or offer or expose for sale or delivery, or have in his possession with intent to sell or deliver, any pistol or revolver without having a permit therefor.

(b) Application.

(1) The application for a permit for the retail sale of a pistol or revolver shall be on the form prescribed and obtained from the commissioner.

(2) The application for a permit for the retail sale of a pistol or revolver shall be made in writing, under oath, and shall be completed legibly and in its entirety and in accordance with the directions on the form. Post office boxes shall not be an acceptable form of address.

(3) The applicant shall provide the following with the completed application form:

(A) Demonstration that he is the holder of a valid eligibility certificate for a pistol or revolver issued pursuant to section 29-36f of the Connecticut General Statutes or a valid permit to carry a pistol or revolver issued pursuant to subsection (b) of section 29-28 of the Connecticut General Statutes; and

(B) Documentation sufficient to establish that local zoning requirements have been met for the location where the sale is to take place; and

Exception. Any person selling or exchanging a pistol or revolver for the enhancement of a personal collection or for a hobby or who sells all or part of his personal collection of pistols or revolvers shall be exempt from the requirements of section 29-36m-7(b)(3)(B) of these regulations.

(C) A permit fee in the amount of $100.00 for either an original permit or a renewal.

(c) Manner of submission. Applications for permits for retail sales of any pistol or revolver shall be submitted to one (1) of the following:

(1) The chief of police; or

(2) Where there is no chief of police, the warden of the borough or the first selectman of the town.

(d) Confidentiality of information. The name and address of a person issued a permit to sell at retail a pistol or revolver shall be confidential and shall not be disclosed except in the following instances:

(1) To law enforcement officials acting in the performance of their duties; or

(2) To the extent necessary to comply with a request made pursuant to section 29-33 of the Connecticut General Statutes for verification that the permit is still valid.

Sec. 29-36m-8. Permits for carrying a pistol or revolver.

(a) Who may apply. Persons applying for a permit to carry a pistol or revolver shall either:

(1) Have a bona fide residence or place of business within the jurisdiction of the issuing authority; or

(2) Be a bona fide resident of the United States having a permit or license to carry any firearm issued by the authority of any state or subdivision of the United States.

(b) Application.

(1) The application for a permit for carrying a pistol or revolver shall be on the form prescribed by and obtained from the commissioner.

(2) The application for a permit for carrying a pistol or revolver shall be made in writing, under oath, and shall be completed legibly and in its entirety and in accordance with the directions on the form. Post office boxes are not an acceptable form of address.

Exception. No Issuing Authority May Require Any Sworn Member Of The Department Of Emergency Services and Public Protection or an organized local police department to furnish his residence address in a permit application. Each such sworn member who has a permit to carry a pistol or revolver on May 26, 1992, shall be notified by the issuing authority of his right to revise his application to include his business or post office address in lieu of his residence address and shall be permitted to exercise such right to revise his application.

(3) The following shall be submitted with each completed application form:

(A) If applying for a local permit to carry a pistol or revolver, a complete set of fingerprints on forms specified and furnished by the commissioner or, if applying for a state permit to carry a pistol or revolver, the imprint of the right thumbprint on said forms. In either case, the fingerprints shall be taken by personnel at a municipal police department, a state police troop, or any resident state trooper's office.

(B) A color passport-type photograph, two (2″) inches wide by two (2″) inches high, showing a front view of the head and shoulders of the applicant with a plain, light background, taken within six (6) months prior to the date of the application. This photograph may be taken by personnel at a state police troop or the department of public safety, division of state police, special licensing and firearms unit.

(C) An affidavit signed by an instructor certified by the state, the National Rifle Association or the Department of Environmental Protection stating that the applicant successfully completed a safety or training course in the use of pistols and revolvers. Such statement shall specify that the instructor was so certified at the time he taught the course and shall include the full name of the applicant, and the date, location and duration of the course.

(D) A permit fee in the amount of $35.00 for either an original permit or a renewal.

(c) Manner of submission. Applications for local permits to carry a pistol or revolver shall be submitted to the chief of police or where there is no chief of police to the warden of the borough or the first selectman of the town. Applications for state permits to carry a pistol or revolver shall be submitted to the commissioner only after the applicant has obtained a local permit to carry a pistol or revolver.

(d) Confidentiality of information. The name and address of a person issued a permit to carry a pistol or revolver shall be confidential and shall not be disclosed except in the following instances:

(1) To law enforcement officials acting in the performance of their duties; or

(2) To the extent necessary to comply with a request made pursuant to section 29-33 of the Connecticut General Statutes for verification that the permit is still valid.

(e) Grounds for denial of permit. Each application shall be processed and reviewed in accordance with section 29-29 of the Connecticut General Statutes. No permit shall be issued if the applicant:

(1) Is determined to be an unsuitable person; or

(2) Intends to make an unlawful use of any pistol or revolver which he may be permitted to carry; or

(3) Has failed to successfully complete a course approved by the commissioner of public safety in the safety and use of pistols and revolvers including, but not limited to, a safety or training course in the use of pistols and revolvers available to the public offered by a law enforcement agency, a private or public educational institution or a firearms training school utilizing instructors certified by the National Rifle Association or the Department of Environmental Protection or a safety or training course in the use of pistols or revolvers conducted by an instructor certified by the state or the National Rifle Association; or

(4) Has been convicted of a felony or a violation of subsection (c) of section 21a-279, section 53a-58, 53a-61, 53-61a, 53a-62, 53a-63, 53a-96, 53a-175, 53a-176, 53a-178, or 53a-181d of the Connecticut General Statutes; or

(5) Has been discharged from custody within the preceding twenty (20) years after having been found not guilty of a crime by reason of mental disease or defect pursuant to section 53a-13 of the Connecticut General Statutes; or

(6) Has been confined in a hospital for mental illness, as defined in section 17a-495 of the Connecticut General Statutes, within the preceding twelve (12) months by order of a probate court; or

(7) Knows that he is subject to a restraining or protective order issued by a court, after notice and an opportunity to be heard has been provided to such person, in a case involving the use, attempted use or threatened use of physical force against another person; or

(8) Is an alien illegally or unlawfully in the United States.

(f) Issuance of permit. Each permit to carry any pistol or revolver shall be issued in triplicate. Copies of said permit shall be distributed as follows:

(1) In all cases, one (1) copy to the person to whom the permit is issued, and if a state permit, said copy shall be laminated and contain a full-face photograph of such permittee; and

(2) (A) If issued by the commissioner, one (1) copy to the local authority issuing the local permit and one to be retained by the commissioner; or

(B) If issued by the local authority, one (1) copy to the commissioner and one copy to be retained by the local authority.

Sec. 29-36m-9. Notification of address change.

Any person holding a permit to carry a pistol or revolver shall notify the issuing authority within two (2) business days of any change of his address. Such notification shall be in writing and shall state the permittee's old address and his new address.

Sec. 29-36m-10. Revocation of permit.

Any permit for the carrying of any pistol or revolver may be revoked by the issuing authority for cause.

(a) Conditions for mandatory revocation. Any permit for the carrying of any pistol or revolver shall be revoked upon the occurrence of any of the following:

(1) Upon conviction of the holder of such permit of a felony;

(2) Upon conviction of the holder of any of the following misdemeanors: violation of subsection (c) of section 21a-279, section 53a-58, 53a-61, 53-61a, 53a-62, 53a-63, 53a-96, 53a-175, 53a-176, 53a-178, or 53a-181d of the Connecticut General Statutes; or

(3) Upon the occurrence of any event which would have disqualified the holder from being issued the original permit or the renewal.

(b) Notification of revocation and surrender of permit.

(1) Upon revocation of any permit, the revoking authority shall notify the person whose permit is revoked in writing by first class mail return receipt requested. Within five (5) days of the receipt of such notification, the person whose permit is revoked shall turn the permit in to the issuing authority.

(2) Upon revocation of any permit by the commissioner, said commissioner shall notify the local authority in writing of such revocation.

(3) Upon revocation of any permit by the local authority, said local authority shall notify the commissioner in writing of such revocation.

Sec. 29-36m-11. Applications for eligibility certificates.

(a) Who may apply. Any person who is twenty-one (21) years of age or older may apply to the commissioner for an eligibility certificate for a pistol or revolver.

(b) Application procedure. The procedure for applying for an eligibility certificate shall be as follows:

(1) Application form. The applicant shall contact the department of public safety, division of state police, special licensing and firearms unit, to obtain the application for an eligibility certificate.

(2) Upon receipt of the request for an application for an eligibility certificate, the division of state police shall provide the applicant with the authorized department of public safety, division of state police, application form.

(3) The application for an eligibility certificate shall be made in writing, under oath, and shall be completed legibly and in its entirety and in accordance with the directions on the form. Post office boxes shall not be an acceptable form of address.

(4) The following shall be submitted with each completed application form:

(A) A complete set of fingerprints on forms specified and furnished by the commissioner, which fingerprints shall be taken by personnel at a municipal police department, a state police troop, or any resident state trooper's office.

(B) A color passport-type photograph, two inches (2″) wide by two inches (2″) high, showing a front view of the head and shoulders of the applicant with a plain, light background, taken within six (6) months prior to the date of the application. This photograph may be taken by personnel at a state police troop or the department of public safety, division of state police, special licensing and firearms unit.

(C) An affidavit signed by an instructor certified by the state, the National Rifle Association or the Department of Environmental Protection stating that the applicant successfully completed a safety or training course in the use of pistols and revolvers. Such statement shall specify that the instructor was so certified at the time he taught the course and shall include the full name of the applicant, and the date, location and duration of the course.

(D) A fee in the amount of $35.00 for either an original certificate or a renewal.

(c) Application review. Upon receipt of an application for an eligibility certificate, the Department of Public Safety, Division of State Police, Special Licensing and Firearms Unit, shall:

(1) Review the application for completeness;

(2) Complete national and state criminal history checks on the applicant; and

(3) Within sixty (60) days of the receipt of the national criminal history records check from the Federal Bureau of Investigation, either approve the application and issue the eligibility certificate or deny the application and notify the applicant in writing of the reason(s) for the denial of the application.

(d) Time for approval. With respect to all applications for eligibility certificates filed on or before July 1, 1995, and within ninety (90) days of the filing of an application for an eligibility certificate filed after July 1, 1995, the commissioner shall either:

(1) Approve the application and issue the eligibility certificate; or

(2) Issue a temporary eligibility certificate; or

(3) Deny the application and notify the applicant in writing of the reason(s) for denial.

(e) Grounds for denial of certificate. No eligibility certificate shall be issued if the applicant:

(1) Has failed to successfully complete a course approved by the Commissioner of Public Safety in the safety and use of pistols and revolvers including, but not limited to a safety or training course in the use of pistols and revolvers available to the public offered by a law enforcement agency, a private or public educational institution or a firearms training school utilizing instructors certified by the National Rifle Association or the Department of Environmental Protection or a safety or training course in the use of pistols or revolvers conducted by an instructor certified by the state or the National Rifle Association; or

(2) Has been convicted of a felony or a violation of subsection (c) of section 21a-279, section 53a-58, 53a-61, 53-61a, 53a-62, 53a-63, 53a-96, 53a-175, 53a-176, 53a-178, or 53a-181d of the Connecticut General Statutes; or

(3) Has been discharged from custody within the preceding twenty (20) years after having been found not guilty of a crime by reason of mental disease or defect pursuant to section 53a-13 of the Connecticut General Statutes; or

(4) Has been confined in a hospital for mental illness, as defined in section 17a-495 of the Connecticut General Statutes, within the preceding twelve (12) months by order of a probate court; or

(5) Knows that he is subject to a restraining or protective order issued by a court, after notice and an opportunity to be heard has been provided to such person, in a case involving the use, attempted use or threatened use of physical force against another person; or

(6) Is an alien illegally or unlawfully in the United States.

Sec. 29-36m-12. Temporary eligibility certificates.

Temporary eligibility certificates shall be valid until such time as the commissioner either approves or denies the application.

Sec. 29-36m-13. Notification of change of address.

A person holding an eligibility certificate shall notify the commissioner in writing within two (2) business days of any change of his address. The notification shall include his old address and his new address.

Sec. 29-36m-14. Expiration of certificate.

(a) The eligibility certificate shall expire five (5) years from the date of issuance. For renewals, the eligibility certificate shall expire five (5) years after the expiration date of the certificate being renewed. An eligibility certificate shall remain valid for a period of ninety (90) days from the date of expiration, except when such certificate has been revoked or for which revocation is pending.

(b) Notice of expiration of certificate. The commissioner shall send a notice of the expiration of an eligibility certificate to the certificate holder, by first class mail, at the address shown in accordance with the records of the commissioner, not less than ninety (90) days prior to the expiration of the certificate. Such notification shall be accompanied by an application form for the renewal of the certificate.

(c) Renewal applications. Applications for renewal shall be made not earlier than thirty-one (31) days prior, and not later than thirty-one (31) days after, the expiration of the certificate being renewed.

Sec. 29-36m-15. Revocation of eligibility certificate.

Any eligibility certificate shall be revoked by the commissioner upon the occurrence of any event which would have disqualified the holder from being issued the certificate. The commissioner shall notify the person whose eligibility certificate is being revoked in writing by first class mail return receipt requested and such person shall surrender such certificate to the commissioner within five (5) days of the receipt of the notification of revocation.

Sec. 29-36m-16. Transfer procedure upon ineligibility.

Within two (2) business days after the occurrence of any event that makes a person ineligible to possess a pistol or revolver, such person shall either:

(a) Deliver or surrender any and all pistol(s) and/or revolver(s) which he then possesses to a state police barracks (other than Troop W).

(1) The pistol(s) and/or revolver(s) shall be unloaded and enclosed in a package, the paper or wrapping of which shall be securely fastened in the same manner as is required for the sale, delivery or other transfer of a pistol or revolver set forth in section 29-36m-5(b) of these regulations.

(2) Upon receipt of the pistol(s) and/or revolver(s) at a state police barracks, the following shall occur:

(A) An incident number shall be drawn;

(B) DPS Form 293-C shall be completed and one (1) copy shall be provided to the ineligible person; and

(C) The pistol(s) and/or revolver(s) shall be properly secured and stored in the Troop evidence room.

(b) Transfer the pistol(s) and/or revolver(s) in accordance with sections 29-36m-3 to 29-36m-6, inclusive, of these regulations to any person eligible to possess a pistol or revolver.

Sec. 29-36m-17. Transfer after surrender or delivery.

At any time up to one (1) year after the surrender or delivery of a pistol or revolver to a state police barracks as provided for in section 29-36m-16 of these regulations, the ineligible person or his legal representative may transfer such pistols or revolvers to a person eligible to possess a pistol or revolver provided all of the following requirements are met:

(a) The ineligible person, or his legal representative, and the proposed transferee shall notify, in writing, by first class mail return receipt requested, the department of public safety, special licensing and firearms unit of the request for transfer of possession of such pistol(s) and/or revolver(s). Such notification shall identify the state police barracks where the pistol(s) and/or revolver(s) were surrendered or delivered.

(b) Within ten (10) days of the receipt of the written notification, the Department of Public Safety, Division of State Police, Special Licensing and Firearms Unit shall arrange for an appointment during the weekday business hours of 9:00 a.m. To 4:00 p.m. For the transfer of the pistol(s) and/or revolver(s).

(c) The transfer between the ineligible person and the proposed transferee shall be in accordance with sections 29-36m-3 to 29-36m-6, inclusive, of these regulations.

(d) Both the ineligible person, or his legal representative, and the proposed transferee shall appear at the location designated by the special licensing and firearms unit at the time of the scheduled appointment.

(e) The proposed transferee shall produce two (2) forms of valid photographic identification to the department of public safety, division of state police personnel and have obtained an authorization number from the department.

(f) A copy of the Sale, Delivery or Transfer form shall be made.

(g) All forms shall be checked for completeness and accuracy by Department of Public Safety Division of State Police personnel prior to the transfer.

Sec. 29-36m-18. Return of pistol or revolver after court order.

(a) Any person who, having become ineligible by reason of a restraining or protective order, is no longer subject to that order by reason of subsequent court order, may seek return of any pistol or revolver he, or his legal representative, surrendered or delivered to a state police barracks upon the occurrence of that ineligibility event.

(b) Such person shall bring to the Department of Public Safety, Division of State Police, Special Licensing and Firearms Unit, during the weekday hours of 9:00 a.m. To 4:00 p.m., a certified copy of the court order rescinding the restraining or protective order.

(c) Such certified copy of the court order shall be filed with the proper incident report.

(d) The pistol(s) and/or revolver(s) shall be returned after completion and notarization of the form for return of firearms.

Sec. 29-36m-19. Disposition of pistols and/or revolvers.

If, at the end of one (1) year from the date any pistol or revolver is surrendered or delivered to a state police barracks, such pistol or revolver is not transferred in accordance with section 29-36m-17 of these regulations or returned in accordance with section 29-36m-18 of these regulations, an investigating trooper at the state police barracks shall do the following:

(a) Send written notification, via certified mail return receipt requested, to the ineligible person at the last address shown for the ineligible person according to the records of the Department stating the date on which the pistol(s) and/or revolver(s) are to be disposed.

(b) Notify the individual designated by the Special Licensing and Firearms Unit of the Department of the date that the pistol(s) and/or revolver(s) may be picked up.

Sec. 29-36m-20. Time limit for application.

Any person who lawfully possesses an assault weapon prior to October 1, 1993, shall apply to the Department of Public Safety by October 1, 1994 for a certificate of possession in the manner provided for in the regulations adopted by the Department of Public Safety concerning applications for and the issuance of certificates of possession for assault weapons.

Exception. When a person lawfully possesses an assault weapon and is a member of the military or naval forces of this state or of the United States, the following shall apply:

(a) If such person is unable to apply for a certificate of possession by October 1, 1994 because he or she was on official duty outside of this state, such person shall apply for a certificate of possession within ninety (90) days of returning to the state.

(b) If such person has been transferred into the state after October 1, 1994, such person may apply to the Department of Public Safety for a certificate of possession within ninety (90) days of arriving in the state.

Sec. 29-36m-21. Right of appeal.

Any person aggrieved by (a) any refusal to issue or renew a permit to carry a pistol or revolver, a permit to sell at retail any pistol or revolver, an eligibility certificate for a pistol or revolver or a permit to carry a dangerous weapon; (b) any limitation or revocation of a permit or certificate issued under section 29-28, 29-36f or 53-206 of the Connecticut General Statutes and/or (c) a refusal or failure of any issuing authority to furnish a permit application form may appeal to the Board of Firearms Permit Examiners. Such appeal shall be taken within ninety (90) days after receipt of notice of the permit or certificate refusal, permit or certificate limitation or revocation, or refusal or failure to provide an application.

PART 2: FEDERAL STATUTES AND REGULATIONS

Federal Statutes

18 U.S.C. § 921. Definitions.

(a) As used in this chapter--

(1) The term "person" and the term "whoever" include any individual, corporation, company, association, firm, partnership, society, or joint stock company.

(2) The term "interstate or foreign commerce" includes commerce between any place in a State and any place outside of that State, or within any possession of the United States (not including the Canal Zone) or the District of Columbia, but such term does not include commerce between places within the same State but through any place outside of that State. The term "State" includes the District of Columbia, the Commonwealth of Puerto Rico, and the possessions of the United States (not including the Canal Zone).

(3) The term "firearm" means (A) any weapon (including a starter gun) which will or is designed to or may readily be converted to expel a projectile by the action of an explosive; (B) the frame or receiver of any such weapon; (C) any firearm muffler or firearm silencer; or (D) any destructive device. Such term does not include an antique firearm.

(4) The term "destructive device" means—

(A) any explosive, incendiary, or poison gas--

(i) bomb,

(ii) grenade,

(iii) rocket having a propellant charge of more than four ounces,

(iv) missile having an explosive or incendiary charge of more than one-quarter ounce,

(v) mine, or

(vi) device similar to any of the devices described in the preceding clauses;

(B) any type of weapon (other than a shotgun or a shotgun shell which the Attorney General finds is generally recognized as particularly suitable for sporting purposes) by whatever name known which will, or which may be readily converted to, expel a projectile by the action of an explosive or other propellant, and which has any barrel with a bore of more than one-half inch in diameter; and

(C) any combination of parts either designed or intended for use in converting any device into any destructive device described in subparagraph (A) or (B) and from which a destructive device may be readily assembled.

The term "destructive device" shall not include any device which is neither designed nor redesigned for use as a weapon; any device, although originally designed for use as a weapon, which is redesigned for use as a signaling, pyrotechnic, line throwing, safety, or similar device; surplus ordnance sold, loaned, or given by the Secretary of the Army pursuant to the provisions of section 4684(2), 4685, or 4686 of title 10; or any other device which the Attorney General finds is not likely to be used as a weapon, is an antique, or is a rifle which the owner intends to use solely for sporting, recreational or cultural purposes.

(5) The term "shotgun" means a weapon designed or redesigned, made or remade, and intended to be fired from the shoulder and designed or redesigned and made or remade to use the energy of an explosive to fire through a smooth bore either a number of ball shot or a single projectile for each single pull of the trigger.

(6) The term "short-barreled shotgun" means a shotgun having one or more barrels less than eighteen inches in length and any weapon made from a shotgun (whether by alteration, modification or otherwise) if such a weapon as modified has an overall length of less than twenty-six inches.

(7) The term "rifle" means a weapon designed or redesigned, made or remade, and intended to be fired from the shoulder and designed or redesigned and made or remade to use the energy of an explosive to fire only a single projectile through a rifled bore for each single pull of the trigger.

(8) The term "short-barreled rifle" means a rifle having one or more barrels less than sixteen inches in length and any weapon made from a rifle (whether by alteration, modification, or otherwise) if such weapon, as modified, has an overall length of less than twenty-six inches.

(9) The term "importer" means any person engaged in the business of importing or bringing firearms or ammunition into the United States for purposes of sale or distribution; and the term "licensed importer" means any such person licensed under the provisions of this chapter.

(10) The term "manufacturer" means any person engaged in the business of manufacturing firearms or ammunition for purposes of sale or distribution; and the term "licensed manufacturer" means any such person licensed under the provisions of this chapter.

(11) The term "dealer" means (A) any person engaged in the business of selling firearms at wholesale or retail, (B) any person engaged in the business of repairing firearms or of making or fitting special barrels, stocks, or trigger mechanisms to firearms, or (C) any person who is a pawnbroker. The term "licensed dealer" means any dealer who is licensed under the provisions of this chapter.

(12) The term "pawnbroker" means any person whose business or occupation includes the taking or receiving, by way of pledge or pawn, of any firearm as security for the payment or repayment of money.

(13) The term "collector" means any person who acquires, holds, or disposes of firearms as curios or relics, as the Attorney General shall by regulation define, and the term "licensed collector" means any such person licensed under the provisions of this chapter.

(14) The term "indictment" includes an indictment or information in any court under which a crime punishable by imprisonment for a term exceeding one year may be prosecuted.

(15) The term "fugitive from justice" means any person who has fled from any State to avoid prosecution for a crime or to avoid giving testimony in any criminal proceeding.

(16) The term "antique firearm" means--

(A) any firearm (including any firearm with a matchlock, flintlock, percussion cap, or similar type of ignition system) manufactured in or before 1898; or

(B) any replica of any firearm described in subparagraph (A) if such replica—

(i) is not designed or redesigned for using rimfire or conventional centerfire fixed ammunition, or

(ii) uses rimfire or conventional centerfire fixed ammunition which is no longer manufactured in the United States and which is not readily available in the ordinary channels of commercial trade; or

(C) any muzzle loading rifle, muzzle loading shotgun, or muzzle loading pistol, which is designed to use black powder, or a black powder substitute, and which cannot use fixed ammunition. For purposes of this subparagraph, the term "antique firearm" shall not include any weapon which incorporates a firearm frame or receiver, any firearm which is converted into a muzzle loading weapon, or any muzzle loading weapon which can be readily converted to fire fixed ammunition by replacing the barrel, bolt, breechblock, or any combination thereof.

(17)(A) The term "ammunition" means ammunition or cartridge cases, primers, bullets, or propellant powder designed for use in any firearm.

(B) The term "armor piercing ammunition" means--

(i) a projectile or projectile core which may be used in a handgun and which is constructed entirely (excluding the presence of traces of other substances) from one or a combination of tungsten alloys, steel, iron, brass, bronze, beryllium copper, or depleted uranium; or

(ii) a full jacketed projectile larger than .22 caliber designed and intended for use in a handgun and whose jacket has a weight of more than 25 percent of the total weight of the projectile.

(C) The term "armor piercing ammunition" does not include shotgun shot required by Federal or State environmental or game regulations for hunting purposes, a frangible projectile designed for target shooting, a projectile which the Attorney General finds is primarily intended to be used for sporting purposes, or any other projectile or projectile core which the Attorney General finds is intended to be used for industrial purposes, including a charge used in an oil and gas well perforating device.

(18) The term "Attorney General" means the Attorney General of the United States"

(19) The term "published ordinance" means a published law of any political subdivision of a State which the Attorney General determines to be relevant to the enforcement of this chapter and which is contained on a list compiled by the Attorney General, which list shall be published in the Federal Register, revised annually, and furnished to each licensee under this chapter.

(20) The term "crime punishable by imprisonment for a term exceeding one year" does not include--

(A) any Federal or State offenses pertaining to antitrust violations, unfair trade practices, restraints of trade, or other similar offenses relating to the regulation of business practices, or

(B) any State offense classified by the laws of the State as a misdemeanor and punishable by a term of imprisonment of two years or less.

What constitutes a conviction of such a crime shall be determined in accordance with the law of the jurisdiction in which the proceedings were held. Any conviction which has been expunged, or set aside or for which a person has been pardoned or has had civil rights restored shall not be considered a conviction for purposes of this chapter, unless such pardon, expungement, or restoration of civil rights expressly provides that the person may not ship, transport, possess, or receive firearms.

(21) The term "engaged in the business" means--

(A) as applied to a manufacturer of firearms, a person who devotes time, attention, and labor to manufacturing firearms as a regular course of trade or business with the principal objective of livelihood and profit through the sale or distribution of the firearms manufactured;

(B) as applied to a manufacturer of ammunition, a person who devotes time, attention, and labor to manufacturing ammunition as a regular course of trade or business with the principal objective of livelihood and profit through the sale or distribution of the ammunition manufactured;

(C) as applied to a dealer in firearms, as defined in section 921(a)(11)(A), a person who devotes time, attention, and labor to dealing in firearms as a regular course of trade or business to predominantly earn a profit through the repetitive purchase and resale of firearms, but such term shall not include a person who makes occasional sales, exchanges, or purchases of firearms for the enhancement of a personal collection or for a hobby, or who sells all or part of his personal collection of firearms;

(D) as applied to a dealer in firearms, as defined in section 921(a)(11)(B), a person who devotes time, attention, and labor to engaging in such activity as a regular course of trade or business with the principal objective of livelihood and profit, but such term shall not include a person who makes occasional repairs of firearms, or who occasionally fits special barrels, stocks, or trigger mechanisms to firearms;

(E) as applied to an importer of firearms, a person who devotes time, attention, and labor to importing firearms as a regular course of trade or business with the principal objective of livelihood and profit through the sale or distribution of the firearms imported; and

(F) as applied to an importer of ammunition, a person who devotes time, attention, and labor to importing ammunition as a regular course of trade or business with the principal objective of livelihood and profit through the sale or distribution of the ammunition imported.

(22) The term 'to predominantly earn a profit' means that the intent underlying the sale or disposition of firearms is predominantly one of obtaining pecuniary gain, as opposed to other intents, such as improving or liquidating a personal firearms collection: *Provided,* That proof of profit shall not be required as to a person who engages in the regular and repetitive purchase and disposition of firearms for criminal purposes or terrorism. For purposes of this paragraph, the term 'terrorism' means activity, directed against United States persons, which—

(A) is committed by an individual who is not a national or permanent resident alien of the United States;

(B) involves violent acts or acts dangerous to human life which would be a criminal violation if committed within the jurisdiction of the United States; and

(C) is intended—

(i) to intimidate or coerce a civilian population;

(ii) to influence the policy of a government by intimidation or coercion; or

(iii) to affect the conduct of a government by assassination or kidnapping.

(23) The term "with the principal objective of livelihood and profit" means that the intent underlying the sale or disposition of firearms is predominantly one of obtaining livelihood and pecuniary gain, as opposed to other intents, such as improving or liquidating a personal firearms collection: *Provided,* That proof of profit shall not be required as to a person who engages in the regular and repetitive purchase and disposition of firearms for criminal purposes or terrorism. For purposes of this paragraph, the term "terrorism" means activity, directed against United States persons, which--

(A) is committed by an individual who is not a national or permanent resident alien of the United States;

(B) involves violent acts or acts dangerous to human life which would be a criminal violation if committed within the jurisdiction of the United States; and

(C) is intended--

(i) to intimidate or coerce a civilian population;

(ii) to influence the policy of a government by intimidation or coercion; or

(iii) to affect the conduct of a government by assassination or kidnapping.

(24) The term "machinegun" has the meaning given such term in section 5845(b) of the National Firearms Act (26 U.S.C. 5845(b)).

(25) The terms "firearm silencer" and "firearm muffler" mean any device for silencing, muffling, or diminishing the report of a portable firearm, including any combination of parts, designed or redesigned, and intended for use in assembling or fabricating a firearm silencer or firearm muffler, and any part intended only for use in such assembly or fabrication.

(26) The term "school zone" means--

(A) in, or on the grounds of, a public, parochial or private school; or

(B) within a distance of 1,000 feet from the grounds of a public, parochial or private school.

(27) The term "school" means a school which provides elementary or secondary education, as determined under State law.

(28) The term "motor vehicle" has the meaning given such term in section 13102 of title 49, United States Code.

(29) The term "semiautomatic rifle" means any repeating rifle which utilizes a portion of the energy of a firing cartridge to extract the fired cartridge case and chamber the next round, and which requires a separate pull of the trigger to fire each cartridge.

(30) The term "handgun" means--

(A) a firearm which has a short stock and is designed to be held and fired by the use of a single hand; and

(B) any combination of parts from which a firearm described in subparagraph (A) can be assembled.

[(30), (31) Repealed. Pub.L. 103-322, Title XI, § 110105(2), Sept. 13, 1994, 108 Stat. 2000]

(32) The term "intimate partner" means, with respect to a person, the spouse of the person, a former spouse of the person, an individual who is a parent of a child of the person, and an individual who cohabitates or has cohabited with the person.

(33)(A) Except as provided in subparagraphs (B) and (C), the term "misdemeanor crime of domestic violence" means an offense that--

(i) is a misdemeanor under Federal, State, or Tribal law; and

(ii) has, as an element, the use or attempted use of physical force, or the threatened use of a deadly weapon, committed by a current or former spouse, parent, or guardian of the victim, by a person with whom the victim shares a child in common, by a person who is cohabiting with or has cohabited with the victim as a spouse, parent, or guardian, by a person similarly situated to a spouse, parent, or guardian of the victim, or by a person who has a current or recent former dating relationship with the victim.

(B)(i) A person shall not be considered to have been convicted of such an offense for purposes of this chapter, unless--

(I) the person was represented by counsel in the case, or knowingly and intelligently waived the right to counsel in the case; and

(II) in the case of a prosecution for an offense described in this paragraph for which a person was entitled to a jury trial in the jurisdiction in which the case was tried, either

(aa) the case was tried by a jury, or

(bb) the person knowingly and intelligently waived the right to have the case tried by a jury, by guilty plea or otherwise.

(ii) A person shall not be considered to have been convicted of such an offense for purposes of this chapter if the conviction has been expunged or set aside, or is an offense for which the person has been pardoned or has had civil rights restored (if the law of the applicable jurisdiction provides for the loss of civil rights under such an offense) unless the pardon, expungement, or restoration of civil rights expressly provides that the person may not ship, transport, possess, or receive firearms.

(C) A person shall not be considered to have been convicted of a misdemeanor crime of domestic violence against an individual in a dating relationship for purposes of this chapter if the conviction has been expunged or set aside, or is an offense for which the person has been pardoned or has had firearm rights restored unless the expungement, pardon, or restoration of rights expressly provides that the person may not ship, transport, possess, or receive firearms: Provided, That, in the case of a person who has not more than 1 conviction of a misdemeanor crime of domestic violence against an individual in a dating relationship, and is not otherwise prohibited under this chapter, the person shall not be disqualified from shipping, transport, possession, receipt, or purchase of a firearm under this chapter if 5 years have elapsed from the later of the judgment of conviction or the completion of the person's custodial or supervisory sentence, if any, and the person has not subsequently been convicted of another such offense, a misdemeanor under Federal, State, Tribal, or local law which has, as an element, the use or attempted use of physical force, or the threatened use of a deadly weapon, or any other offense that would disqualify the person under section 922(g). The national instant criminal background check system established under section 103 of the Brady Handgun Violence Prevention Act (34 U.S.C. 40901) shall be updated to reflect the status of the person. Restoration under this subparagraph is not available for a current or former spouse, parent, or guardian of the victim, a person with whom the victim shares a child in common, a person who is cohabiting with or has cohabited with the victim as a spouse, parent, or guardian, or a person similarly situated to a spouse, parent, or guardian of the victim.

(34) The term "secure gun storage or safety device" means--

(A) a device that, when installed on a firearm, is designed to prevent the firearm from being operated without first deactivating the device;

(B) a device incorporated into the design of the firearm that is designed to prevent the operation of the firearm by anyone not having access to the device; or

(C) a safe, gun safe, gun case, lock box, or other device that is designed to be or can be used to store a firearm and that is designed to be unlocked only by means of a key, a combination, or other similar means.

(35) The term "body armor" means any product sold or offered for sale, in interstate or foreign commerce, as personal protective body covering intended to protect against gunfire, regardless of whether the product is to be worn alone or is sold as a complement to another product or garment.

(36) The term "local law enforcement authority" means a bureau, office, department or other authority of a State or local government or Tribe that has jurisdiction to investigate a violation or potential violation of, or enforce, a State, local, or Tribal law.

(37)(A) The term "dating relationship" means a relationship between individuals who have or have recently had a continuing serious relationship of a romantic or intimate nature.

(B) Whether a relationship constitutes a dating relationship under subparagraph (A) shall be determined based on consideration of—

(i) the length of the relationship;
(ii) the nature of the relationship; and
(iii) the frequency and type of interaction between the individuals involved in the relationship.

(C) A casual acquaintanceship or ordinary fraternization in a business or social context does not constitute a dating relationship under subparagraph (A).

(b) For the purposes of this chapter, a member of the Armed Forces on active duty is a resident of the State in which his permanent duty station is located.

ANNOTATIONS:

U.S. v. Chovan, 735 F. 3d 1127 (9th Cir. 2013):

Application of provision prohibiting domestic violence misdemeanants from possessing firearms to defendant who had not committed domestic violence for 15 years was substantially related to government's important interest of preventing domestic gun violence, where defendant did not present evidence to directly contradict government's evidence that the rate of domestic violence recidivism is high and he did not directly prove that if a domestic abuser has not committed domestic violence for 15 years, that abuser is highly unlikely to do so again.

18 U.S.C. § 922. Unlawful acts.

(a) It shall be unlawful--

(1) for any person--

(A) except a licensed importer, licensed manufacturer, or licensed dealer, to engage in the business of importing, manufacturing, or dealing in firearms, or in the course of such business to ship, transport, or receive any firearm in interstate or foreign commerce; or

(B) except a licensed importer or licensed manufacturer, to engage in the business of importing or manufacturing ammunition, or in the course of such business, to ship, transport, or receive any ammunition in interstate or foreign commerce;

(2) for any importer, manufacturer, dealer, or collector licensed under the provisions of this chapter to ship or transport in interstate or foreign commerce any firearm to any person other than a licensed importer, licensed manufacturer, licensed dealer, or licensed collector, except that--

(A) this paragraph and subsection (b)(3) shall not be held to preclude a licensed importer, licensed manufacturer, licensed dealer, or licensed collector from returning a firearm or replacement firearm of the same kind and type to a person from whom it was received; and this paragraph shall not be held to preclude an individual from mailing a firearm owned in compliance with Federal, State, and local law to a licensed importer, licensed manufacturer, licensed dealer, or licensed collector;

(B) this paragraph shall not be held to preclude a licensed importer, licensed manufacturer, or licensed dealer from depositing a firearm for conveyance in the mails to any officer, employee, agent, or watchman who, pursuant to the provisions of section 1715 of this title, is eligible to receive through the mails pistols, revolvers, and other firearms capable of being concealed on the person, for use in connection with his official duty; and

(3) for any person, other than a licensed importer, licensed manufacturer, licensed dealer, or licensed collector to transport into or receive in the State where he resides (or if the person is a corporation or other business entity, the State where it maintains a place of business) any firearm purchased or otherwise obtained by such person outside that State, except that this paragraph (A) shall not preclude any person who lawfully acquires a firearm by bequest or intestate succession in a State other than his State of residence from transporting the firearm into or receiving it in that State, if it is lawful for such person to purchase or possess such firearm in that State, (B) shall not apply to the transportation or receipt of a firearm obtained in conformity with subsection (b)(3) of this section, and (C) shall not apply to the transportation of any firearm acquired in any State prior to the effective date of this chapter;

(4) for any person, other than a licensed importer, licensed manufacturer, licensed dealer, or licensed collector, to transport in interstate or foreign commerce any destructive device, machinegun (as defined in section 5845 of the Internal Revenue Code of 1986), short-barreled shotgun, or short-barreled rifle, except as specifically authorized by the Attorney General consistent with public safety and necessity;

(5) for any person (other than a licensed importer, licensed manufacturer, licensed dealer, or licensed collector) to transfer, sell, trade, give, transport, or deliver any firearm to any person (other than a licensed importer, licensed manufacturer, licensed dealer, or licensed collector) who the transferor knows or has reasonable cause to believe does not reside in (or if the person is a corporation or other business entity, does not maintain a place of business in) the State in which the transferor resides; except that this paragraph shall not apply to (A) the transfer, transportation, or delivery of a firearm made to carry out a bequest of a firearm to, or an acquisition by intestate succession of a firearm by, a person who is permitted to acquire or possess a firearm under the laws of the State of his residence, and (B) the loan or rental of a firearm to any person for temporary use for lawful sporting purposes;

(6) for any person in connection with the acquisition or attempted acquisition of any firearm or ammunition from a licensed importer, licensed manufacturer, licensed dealer, or licensed collector, knowingly to make any false or fictitious oral or written statement or to furnish or exhibit any false, fictitious, or misrepresented identification, intended or likely to deceive such importer, manufacturer, dealer, or collector with respect to any fact material to the lawfulness of the sale or other disposition of such firearm or ammunition under the provisions of this chapter;

(b) It shall be unlawful for any licensed importer, licensed manufacturer, licensed dealer, or licensed collector to sell or deliver--

(1) any firearm or ammunition to any individual who the licensee knows or has reasonable cause to believe is less than eighteen years of age, and, if the firearm, or ammunition is other than a shotgun or rifle, or ammunition for a shotgun or rifle, to any individual who the licensee knows or has reasonable cause to believe is less than twenty-one years of age;

(2) any firearm to any person in any State where the purchase or possession by such person of such firearm would be in violation of any State law or any published ordinance applicable at the place of sale, delivery or other disposition, unless the licensee knows or has reasonable cause to believe that the purchase or possession would not be in violation of such State law or such published ordinance;

(3) any firearm to any person who the licensee knows or has reasonable cause to believe does not reside in (or if the person is a corporation or other business entity, does not maintain a place of business in) the State in which the licensee's place of business is located, except that this paragraph (A) shall not apply to the sale or delivery of any rifle or shotgun to a resident of a State other than a State in which the licensee's place of business is located if the transferee meets in person with the transferor to accomplish the transfer, and the sale, delivery, and receipt fully comply with the legal conditions of sale in both such States (and any licensed manufacturer, importer or dealer shall be presumed, for purposes of this subparagraph, in the absence of evidence to the contrary, to have had actual knowledge of the State laws and published ordinances of both States), and (B) shall not apply to the loan or rental of a firearm to any person for temporary use for lawful sporting purposes;

(4) to any person any destructive device, machinegun (as defined in section 5845 of the Internal Revenue Code of 1986), short-barreled shotgun, or short-barreled rifle, except as specifically authorized by the Attorney General consistent with public safety and necessity; and

(5) any firearm or armor-piercing ammunition to any person unless the licensee notes in his records, required to be kept pursuant to section 923 of this chapter, the name, age, and place of residence of such person if the person is an individual, or the identity and principal and local places of business of such person if the person is a corporation or other business entity.

Paragraphs (1), (2), (3), and (4) of this subsection shall not apply to transactions between licensed importers, licensed manufacturers, licensed dealers, and licensed collectors. Paragraph (4) of this subsection shall not apply to a sale or delivery to any research organization designated by the Attorney General.

(c) In any case not otherwise prohibited by this chapter, a licensed importer, licensed manufacturer, or licensed dealer may sell a firearm to a person who does not appear in person at the licensee's business premises (other than another licensed importer, manufacturer, or dealer) only if--

(1) the transferee submits to the transferor a sworn statement in the following form:

"Subject to penalties provided by law, I swear that, in the case of any firearm other than a shotgun or a rifle, I am twenty-one years or more of age, or that, in the case of a shotgun or a rifle, I am eighteen years or more of age; that I am not prohibited by the provisions of chapter 44 of title 18, United States Code, from receiving a firearm in interstate or foreign commerce; and that my receipt of this firearm will not be in violation of any statute of the

State and published ordinance applicable to the locality in which I reside. Further, the true title, name, and address of the principal law enforcement officer of the locality to which the firearm will be delivered are

____

____

Signature _________________________ Date _____________"

And containing blank spaces for the attachment of a true copy of any permit or other information required pursuant to such statute or published ordinance;

(2) the transferor has, prior to the shipment or delivery of the firearm, forwarded by registered or certified mail (return receipt requested) a copy of the sworn statement, together with a description of the firearm, in a form prescribed by the Attorney General, to the chief law enforcement officer of the transferee's place of residence, and has received a return receipt evidencing delivery of the statement or has had the statement returned due to the refusal of the named addressee to accept such letter in accordance with United States Post Office Department regulations; and

(3) the transferor has delayed shipment or delivery for a period of at least seven days following receipt of the notification of the acceptance or refusal of delivery of the statement.

A copy of the sworn statement and a copy of the notification to the local law enforcement officer, together with evidence of receipt or rejection of that notification shall be retained by the licensee as a part of the records required to be kept under section 923(g).

(d) It shall be unlawful for any person to sell or otherwise dispose of any firearm or ammunition to any person knowing or having reasonable cause to believe that such person, including as a juvenile–

(1) is under indictment for, or has been convicted in any court of, a crime punishable by imprisonment for a term exceeding one year;

(2) is a fugitive from justice;

(3) is an unlawful user of or addicted to any controlled substance (as defined in section 102 of the Controlled Substances Act (21 U.S.C. 802));

(4) has been adjudicated as a mental defective or has been committed to any mental institution at 16 years of age or older;

(5) who, being an alien--

> (A) is illegally or unlawfully in the United States; or
>
> (B) except as provided in subsection (y)(2), has been admitted to the United States under a nonimmigrant visa (as that term is defined in section 101(a)(26) of the Immigration and Nationality Act (8 U.S.C. 1101(a)(26)));

(6) who has been discharged from the Armed Forces under dishonorable conditions;

(7) who, having been a citizen of the United States, has renounced his citizenship;

(8) is subject to a court order that restrains such person from harassing, stalking, or threatening an intimate partner of such person or child of such intimate partner or person, or engaging in other conduct that would place an intimate partner in reasonable fear of bodily injury to the partner or child, except that this paragraph shall only apply to a court order that--

(A) was issued after a hearing of which such person received actual notice, and at which such person had the opportunity to participate; and

(B)(i) includes a finding that such person represents a credible threat to the physical safety of such intimate partner or child; or (ii) by its terms explicitly prohibits the use, attempted use, or threatened use of physical force against such intimate partner or child that would reasonably be expected to cause bodily injury;

(9) has been convicted in any court of a misdemeanor crime of domestic violence;

(10) intends to sell or otherwise dispose of the firearm or ammunition in furtherance of a felony, a Federal crime of terrorism, or a drug trafficking offense (as such terms are defined in section 932(a)); or

(11) intends to sell or otherwise dispose of the firearm or ammunition to a person described in any of paragraphs (1) through (10).

This subsection shall not apply with respect to the sale or disposition of a firearm or ammunition to a licensed importer, licensed manufacturer, licensed dealer, or licensed collector who pursuant to subsection (b) of section 925 is not precluded from dealing in firearms or ammunition, or to a person who has been granted relief from disabilities pursuant to subsection (c) of section 925.

(e) It shall be unlawful for any person knowingly to deliver or cause to be delivered to any common or contract carrier for transportation or shipment in interstate or foreign commerce, to persons other than licensed importers, licensed manufacturers, licensed dealers, or licensed collectors, any package or other container in which there is any firearm or ammunition without written notice to the carrier that such firearm or ammunition is being transported or shipped; except that any passenger who owns or legally possesses a firearm or ammunition being transported aboard any common or contract carrier for movement with the passenger in interstate or foreign commerce may deliver said firearm or ammunition into the custody of the pilot, captain, conductor or operator of such common or contract carrier for the duration of the trip without violating any of the provisions of this chapter. No common or contract carrier shall require or cause any label, tag, or other written notice to be placed on the outside of any package, luggage, or other container that such package, luggage, or other container contains a firearm.

(f)(1) It shall be unlawful for any common or contract carrier to transport or deliver in interstate or foreign commerce any firearm or ammunition with knowledge or reasonable cause to believe that the shipment, transportation, or receipt thereof would be in violation of the provisions of this chapter.

(2) It shall be unlawful for any common or contract carrier to deliver in interstate or foreign commerce any firearm without obtaining written acknowledgement of receipt from the recipient of the package or other container in which there is a firearm.

(g) It shall be unlawful for any person--

(1) who has been convicted in any court of, a crime punishable by imprisonment for a term exceeding one year;

(2) who is a fugitive from justice;

(3) who is an unlawful user of or addicted to any controlled substance (as defined in section 102 of the Controlled Substances Act (21 U.S.C. 802));

(4) who has been adjudicated as a mental defective or who has been committed to a mental institution;

(5) who, being an alien--

(A) is illegally or unlawfully in the United States; or

(B) except as provided in subsection (y)(2), has been admitted to the United States under a nonimmigrant visa (as that term is defined in section 101(a)(26) of the Immigration and Nationality Act (8 U.S.C. 1101(a)(26)));

(6) who has been discharged from the Armed Forces under dishonorable conditions;

(7) who, having been a citizen of the United States, has renounced his citizenship;

(8) who is subject to a court order that--

(A) was issued after a hearing of which such person received actual notice, and at which such person had an opportunity to participate;

(B) restrains such person from harassing, stalking, or threatening an intimate partner of such person or child of such intimate partner or person, or engaging in other conduct that would place an intimate partner in reasonable fear of bodily injury to the partner or child; and

(C)(i) includes a finding that such person represents a credible threat to the physical safety of such intimate partner or child; or (ii) by its terms explicitly prohibits the use, attempted use, or threatened use of physical force against such intimate partner or child that would reasonably be expected to cause bodily injury; or

(9) who has been convicted in any court of a misdemeanor crime of domestic violence,

To ship or transport in interstate or foreign commerce, or possess in or affecting commerce, any firearm or ammunition; or to receive any firearm or ammunition which has been shipped or transported in interstate or foreign commerce.

(h) It shall be unlawful for any individual, who to that individual's knowledge and while being employed for any person described in any paragraph of subsection (g) of this section, in the course of such employment--

(1) to receive, possess, or transport any firearm or ammunition in or affecting interstate or foreign commerce; or

(2) to receive any firearm or ammunition which has been shipped or transported in interstate or foreign commerce.

(i) It shall be unlawful for any person to transport or ship in interstate or foreign commerce, any stolen firearm or stolen ammunition, knowing or having reasonable cause to believe that the firearm or ammunition was stolen.

(j) It shall be unlawful for any person to receive, possess, conceal, store, barter, sell, or dispose of any stolen firearm or stolen ammunition, or pledge or accept as security for a loan any stolen firearm or stolen ammunition, which is moving as, which is a part of, which constitutes, or which has been shipped or transported in, interstate or foreign commerce, either before or after it was stolen, knowing or having reasonable cause to believe that the firearm or ammunition was stolen.

(k) It shall be unlawful for any person knowingly to transport, ship, or receive, in interstate or foreign commerce, any firearm which has had the importer's or manufacturer's serial number removed, obliterated, or altered or to possess or receive any firearm which has had the importer's or manufacturer's serial number removed, obliterated, or altered and has, at any time, been shipped or transported in interstate or foreign commerce.

(l) Except as provided in section 925(d) of this chapter, it shall be unlawful for any person knowingly to import or bring into the United States or any possession thereof any firearm or ammunition; and it shall be unlawful for any person knowingly to receive any firearm or ammunition which has been imported or brought into the United States or any possession thereof in violation of the provisions of this chapter.

(m) It shall be unlawful for any licensed importer, licensed manufacturer, licensed dealer, or licensed collector knowingly to make any false entry in, to fail to make appropriate entry in, or to fail to properly maintain, any record which he is required to keep pursuant to section 923 of this chapter or regulations promulgated thereunder.

(n) It shall be unlawful for any person who is under indictment for a crime punishable by imprisonment for a term exceeding one year to ship or transport in interstate or foreign commerce any firearm or ammunition or receive any firearm or ammunition which has been shipped or transported in interstate or foreign commerce.

(o)(1) Except as provided in paragraph (2), it shall be unlawful for any person to transfer or possess a machinegun.

(2) This subsection does not apply with respect to--

(A) a transfer to or by, or possession by or under the authority of, the United States or any department or agency thereof or a State, or a department, agency, or political subdivision thereof; or

(B) any lawful transfer or lawful possession of a machinegun that was lawfully possessed before the date this subsection takes effect.

(p)(1) It shall be unlawful for any person to manufacture, import, sell, ship, deliver, possess, transfer, or receive any firearm--

(A) that, after removal of grips, stocks, and magazines, is not as detectable as the Security Exemplar, by walk-through metal detectors calibrated and operated to detect the Security Exemplar; or

(B) any major component of which, when subjected to inspection by the types of x-ray machines commonly used at airports, does not generate an image that accurately depicts the shape of the component. Barium sulfate or other compounds may be used in the fabrication of the component.

(2) For purposes of this subsection—

(A) the term "firearm" does not include the frame or receiver of any such weapon;

(B) the term "major component" means, with respect to a firearm, the barrel, the slide or cylinder, or the frame or receiver of the firearm; and

(C) the term "Security Exemplar" means an object, to be fabricated at the direction of the Attorney General, that is--

(i) constructed of, during the 12-month period beginning on the date of the enactment of this subsection, 3.7 ounces of material type 17-4 PH stainless steel in a shape resembling a handgun; and

(ii) suitable for testing and calibrating metal detectors:

Provided, however, That at the close of such 12-month period, and at appropriate times thereafter the Attorney General shall promulgate regulations to permit the manufacture, importation, sale, shipment, delivery, possession, transfer, or receipt of firearms previously prohibited under this subparagraph that are as detectable as a "Security Exemplar" which contains 3.7 ounces of material type 17-4 PH stainless steel, in a shape resembling a handgun, or such lesser amount as is detectable in view of advances in state-of-the-art developments in weapons detection technology.

(3) Under such rules and regulations as the Attorney General shall prescribe, this subsection shall not apply to the manufacture, possession, transfer, receipt, shipment, or delivery of a firearm by a licensed manufacturer or any person acting pursuant to a contract with a licensed manufacturer, for the purpose of examining and testing such firearm to determine whether paragraph (1) applies to such firearm. The Attorney General shall ensure that rules and regulations adopted pursuant to this paragraph do not impair the manufacture of prototype firearms or the development of new technology.

(4) The Attorney General shall permit the conditional importation of a firearm by a licensed importer or licensed manufacturer, for examination and testing to determine whether or not the unconditional importation of such firearm would violate this subsection.

(5) This subsection shall not apply to any firearm which—

(A) has been certified by the Secretary of Defense or the Director of Central Intelligence, after consultation with the Attorney General and the Administrator of the Federal Aviation Administration, as necessary for military or intelligence applications; and

(B) is manufactured for and sold exclusively to military or intelligence agencies of the United States.

(6) This subsection shall not apply with respect to any firearm manufactured in, imported into, or possessed in the United States before the date of the enactment of the Undetectable Firearms Act of 1988.

(q)(2)(A) It shall be unlawful for any individual knowingly to possess a firearm that has moved in or that otherwise affects interstate or foreign commerce at a place that the individual knows, or has reasonable cause to believe, is a school zone.

(B) Subparagraph (A) does not apply to the possession of a firearm--

(i) on private property not part of school grounds;

(ii) if the individual possessing the firearm is licensed to do so by the State in which the school zone is located or a political subdivision of the State, and the law of the State or political subdivision requires that, before an individual obtains such a license, the law enforcement authorities of the State or political subdivision verify that the individual is qualified under law to receive the license;

(iii) that is--

(I) not loaded; and

(II) in a locked container, or a locked firearms rack that is on a motor vehicle;

(iv) by an individual for use in a program approved by a school in the school zone;

(v) by an individual in accordance with a contract entered into between a school in the school zone and the individual or an employer of the individual;

(vi) by a law enforcement officer acting in his or her official capacity; or

(vii) that is unloaded and is possessed by an individual while traversing school premises for the purpose of gaining access to public or private lands open to hunting, if the entry on school premises is authorized by school authorities.

(3)(A) Except as provided in subparagraph (B), it shall be unlawful for any person, knowingly or with reckless disregard for the safety of another, to discharge or attempt to discharge a firearm that has moved in or that otherwise affects interstate or foreign commerce at a place that the person knows is a school zone.

(B) Subparagraph (A) does not apply to the discharge of a firearm--

(i) on private property not part of school grounds;

(ii) as part of a program approved by a school in the school zone, by an individual who is participating in the program;

(iii) by an individual in accordance with a contract entered into between a school in a school zone and the individual or an employer of the individual; or

(iv) by a law enforcement officer acting in his or her official capacity.

(4) Nothing in this subsection shall be construed as preempting or preventing a State or local government from enacting a statute establishing gun free school zones as provided in this subsection.

(r) It shall be unlawful for any person to assemble from imported parts any semiautomatic rifle or any shotgun which is identical to any rifle or shotgun prohibited from importation under section 925(d)(3) of this chapter as not being particularly suitable for or readily adaptable to sporting purposes except that this subsection shall not apply to--

(1) the assembly of any such rifle or shotgun for sale or distribution by a licensed manufacturer to the United States or any department or agency thereof or to any State or any department, agency, or political subdivision thereof; or

(2) the assembly of any such rifle or shotgun for the purposes of testing or experimentation authorized by the Attorney General.

(s)(1) Beginning on the date that is 90 days after the date of enactment of this subsection and ending on the day before the date that is 60 months after such date of enactment, it shall be unlawful for any licensed importer, licensed manufacturer, or licensed dealer to sell, deliver, or transfer a handgun (other than the return of a handgun to the person from whom it was received) to an individual who is not licensed under section 923, unless—

(A) after the most recent proposal of such transfer by the transferee--

(i) the transferor has--

(I) received from the transferee a statement of the transferee containing the information described in paragraph (3);

(II) verified the identity of the transferee by examining the identification document presented;

(III) within 1 day after the transferee furnishes the statement, provided notice of the contents of the statement to the chief law enforcement officer of the place of residence of the transferee; and

(IV) within 1 day after the transferee furnishes the statement, transmitted a copy of the statement to the chief law enforcement officer of the place of residence of the transferee; and

(ii)(I) 5 business days (meaning days on which State offices are open) have elapsed from the date the transferor furnished notice of the contents of the statement to the chief law enforcement officer, during which period the transferor has not received information from the chief law enforcement officer that receipt or possession of the handgun by the transferee would be in violation of Federal, State, or local law; or (II) the transferor has received notice from the chief law enforcement officer that the officer has no information indicating that receipt or possession of the handgun by the transferee would violate Federal, State, or local law;

(B) the transferee has presented to the transferor a written statement, issued by the chief law enforcement officer of the place of residence of the transferee during the 10-day period ending on the date of the most recent proposal of such transfer by the transferee, stating that the transferee requires access to a handgun because of a threat to the life of the transferee or of any member of the household of the transferee;

(C)(i) the transferee has presented to the transferor a permit that--

(I) allows the transferee to possess or acquire a handgun; and

(II) was issued not more than 5 years earlier by the State in which the transfer is to take place; and

(ii) the law of the State provides that such a permit is to be issued only after an authorized government official has verified that the information available to such official does not indicate that possession of a handgun by the transferee would be in violation of the law;

(D) the law of the State requires that, before any licensed importer, licensed manufacturer, or licensed dealer completes the transfer of a handgun to an individual who is not licensed under section 923, an authorized government official verify that the information available to such official does not indicate that possession of a handgun by the transferee would be in violation of law;

(E) the Attorney General has approved the transfer under section 5812 of the Internal Revenue Code of 1986; or

(F) on application of the transferor, the Attorney General has certified that compliance with subparagraph (A)(i)(III) is impracticable because--

(i) the ratio of the number of law enforcement officers of the State in which the transfer is to occur to the number of square miles of land area of the State does not exceed 0.0025;

(ii) the business premises of the transferor at which the transfer is to occur are extremely remote in relation to the chief law enforcement officer; and

(iii) there is an absence of telecommunications facilities in the geographical area in which the business premises are located.

(2) A chief law enforcement officer to whom a transferor has provided notice pursuant to paragraph (1)(A)(i)(III) shall make a reasonable effort to ascertain within 5 business days whether receipt or possession would be in violation of the law, including research in whatever State and local recordkeeping systems are available and in a national system designated by the Attorney General.

(3) The statement referred to in paragraph (1)(A)(i)(I) shall contain only--

(A) the name, address, and date of birth appearing on a valid identification document (as defined in section 1028(d)(1)) of the transferee containing a photograph of the transferee and a description of the identification used;

(B) a statement that the transferee--

(i) is not under indictment for, and has not been convicted in any court of, a crime punishable by imprisonment for a term exceeding 1 year, and has not been convicted in any court of a misdemeanor crime of domestic violence;

(ii) is not a fugitive from justice;

(iii) is not an unlawful user of or addicted to any controlled substance (as defined in section 102 of the Controlled Substances Act);

(iv) has not been adjudicated as a mental defective or been committed to a mental institution;

(v) is not an alien who--

(I) is illegally or unlawfully in the United States; or

(II) subject to subsection (y)(2), has been admitted to the United States under a nonimmigrant visa (as that term is defined in section 101(a)(26) of the Immigration and Nationality Act (8 U.S.C. 1101(a)(26)));

(vi) has not been discharged from the Armed Forces under dishonorable conditions; and

(vii) is not a person who, having been a citizen of the United States, has renounced such citizenship;

(C) the date the statement is made; and

(D) notice that the transferee intends to obtain a handgun from the transferor.

(4) Any transferor of a handgun who, after such transfer, receives a report from a chief law enforcement officer containing information that receipt or possession of the handgun by the transferee violates Federal, State, or local law shall, within 1 business day after receipt of such request, communicate any information related to the transfer that the transferor has about the transfer and the transferee to—

(A) the chief law enforcement officer of the place of business of the transferor; and

(B) the chief law enforcement officer of the place of residence of the transferee.

(5) Any transferor who receives information, not otherwise available to the public, in a report under this subsection shall not disclose such information except to the transferee, to law enforcement authorities, or pursuant to the direction of a court of law.

(6)(A) Any transferor who sells, delivers, or otherwise transfers a handgun to a transferee shall retain the copy of the statement of the transferee with respect to the handgun transaction, and shall retain evidence that the transferor has complied with subclauses (III) and (IV) of paragraph (1)(A)(i) with respect to the statement.

(B) Unless the chief law enforcement officer to whom a statement is transmitted under paragraph (1)(A)(i)(IV) determines that a transaction would violate Federal, State, or local law--

(i) the officer shall, within 20 business days after the date the transferee made the statement on the basis of which the notice was provided, destroy the statement, any record containing information derived from the statement, and any record created as a result of the notice required by paragraph (1)(A)(i)(III);

(ii) the information contained in the statement shall not be conveyed to any person except a person who has a need to know in order to carry out this subsection; and

(iii) the information contained in the statement shall not be used for any purpose other than to carry out this subsection.

(C) If a chief law enforcement officer determines that an individual is ineligible to receive a handgun and the individual requests the officer to provide the reason for such determination, the officer shall provide such reasons to the individual in writing within 20 business days after receipt of the request.

(7) A chief law enforcement officer or other person responsible for providing criminal history background information pursuant to this subsection shall not be liable in an action at law for damages—

(A) for failure to prevent the sale or transfer of a handgun to a person whose receipt or possession of the handgun is unlawful under this section; or

(B) for preventing such a sale or transfer to a person who may lawfully receive or possess a handgun.

(8) For purposes of this subsection, the term "chief law enforcement officer" means the chief of police, the sheriff, or an equivalent officer or the designee of any such individual.

(9) The Attorney General shall take necessary actions to ensure that the provisions of this subsection are published and disseminated to licensed dealers, law enforcement officials, and the public.

(t)(1) Beginning on the date that is 30 days after the Attorney General notifies licensees under section 103(d) of the Brady Handgun Violence Prevention Act that the national instant criminal background check system is established, a licensed importer, licensed manufacturer, or licensed dealer shall not transfer a firearm to any other person who is not licensed under this chapter, unless—

(A) before the completion of the transfer, the licensee contacts the national instant criminal background check system established under section 103 of that Act;

(B)(i) the system provides the licensee with a unique identification number; or

(ii) subject to subparagraph (C), 3 business days (meaning a day on which State offices are open) have elapsed since the licensee contacted the system, and the system has not notified the licensee that the receipt of a firearm by such other person would violate subsection (g) or (n) of this section;

(C) in the case of a person less than 21 years of age, in addition to all other requirements of this chapter—

(i) the system provides the licensee with a unique identification number;

(ii) 3 business days (meaning a day on which State offices are open) have elapsed since the licensee contacted the system, and the system has not notified the licensee that cause exists to further investigate a possibly disqualifying juvenile record under subsection (d); or

(iii) in the case of such a person with respect to whom the system notifies the licensee in accordance with clause (ii) that cause exists to further investigate a possibly disqualifying juvenile record under subsection (d), 10 business days (meaning a day on which State offices are open) have elapsed since the licensee contacted the system, and the system has not notified the licensee that—

(I) transferring the firearm to the other person would violate subsection (d) of this section; or

(II) receipt of a firearm by the other person would violate subsection (g) or (n) of this section, or State, local, or Tribal law; and

(D) the transferor has verified the identity of the transferee by examining a valid identification document (as defined in section 1028(d) of this title) of the transferee containing a photograph of the transferee.

(2) If transfer or receipt of a firearm would not violate subsection (d), (g), or (n) or State law, the system shall--

(A) assign a unique identification number to the transfer;

(B) provide the licensee with the number; and

(C) destroy all records of the system with respect to the call (other than the identifying number and the date the number was assigned) and all records of the system relating to the person or the transfer.

(3) Paragraph (1) shall not apply to a firearm transfer between a licensee and another person if-

(A)(i) such other person has presented to the licensee a permit that—

(I) allows such other person to possess or acquire a firearm; and

(II) was issued not more than 5 years earlier by the State in which the transfer is to take place; and

(ii) the law of the State provides that such a permit is to be issued only after an authorized government official has verified that the information available to such official does not indicate that possession of a firearm by such other person would be in violation of law;

(B) the Attorney General has approved the transfer under section 5812 of the Internal Revenue Code of 1986; or

(C) on application of the transferor, the Attorney General has certified that compliance with paragraph (1)(A) is impracticable because--

(i) the ratio of the number of law enforcement officers of the State in which the transfer is to occur to the number of square miles of land area of the State does not exceed 0.0025;

(ii) the business premises of the licensee at which the transfer is to occur are extremely remote in relation to the chief law enforcement officer (as defined in subsection (s)(8)); and

(iii) there is an absence of telecommunications facilities in the geographical area in which the business premises are located.

(4) If the national instant criminal background check system notifies the licensee that the information available to the system does not demonstrate that the transfer of a firearm to or receipt of a firearm by such other person would violate subsection (d), (g), or (n) (as applicable) or State law, and the licensee transfers a firearm to such other person, the licensee shall include in the record of the transfer the unique identification number provided by the system with respect to the transfer.

(5) If the licensee knowingly transfers a firearm to such other person and knowingly fails to comply with paragraph (1) of this subsection with respect to the transfer and, at the time such other person most recently proposed the transfer, the national instant criminal background check system was operating and information was available to the system demonstrating that receipt of a firearm by such other person would violate subsection (d), (g), or (n) (as applicable) of this section or State law, the Attorney General may, after notice and opportunity for a hearing, suspend for not more than 6 months or revoke any license issued to the licensee under section 923, and may impose on the licensee a civil fine of not more than $5,000.

(6) Neither a local government nor an employee of the Federal Government or of any State or local government, responsible for providing information to the national instant criminal background check system shall be liable in an action at law for damages—

(A) for failure to prevent the sale or transfer of a firearm to a person whose receipt or possession of the firearm is unlawful under this section; or

(B) for preventing such a sale or transfer to a person who may lawfully receive or possess a firearm.

(u) It shall be unlawful for a person to steal or unlawfully take or carry away from the person or the premises of a person who is licensed to engage in the business of importing, manufacturing, or dealing in firearms, any firearm in the licensee's business inventory that has been shipped or transported in interstate or foreign commerce.

[(v), (w) Repealed. Pub.L. 103-322, Title XI, § 110105(2), Sept. 13, 1994, 108 Stat. 2000]

(x)(1) It shall be unlawful for a person to sell, deliver, or otherwise transfer to a person who the transferor knows or has reasonable cause to believe is a juvenile--

(A) a handgun; or

(B) ammunition that is suitable for use only in a handgun.

(2) It shall be unlawful for any person who is a juvenile to knowingly possess--

(A) a handgun; or

(B) ammunition that is suitable for use only in a handgun.

(3) This subsection does not apply to--

(A) a temporary transfer of a handgun or ammunition to a juvenile or to the possession or use of a handgun or ammunition by a juvenile if the handgun and ammunition are possessed and used by the juvenile—

(i) in the course of employment, in the course of ranching or farming related to activities at the residence of the juvenile (or on property used for ranching or farming at which the juvenile, with the permission of the property owner or lessee, is performing activities related to the operation of the farm or ranch), target practice, hunting, or a course of instruction in the safe and lawful use of a handgun;

(ii) with the prior written consent of the juvenile's parent or guardian who is not prohibited by Federal, State, or local law from possessing a firearm, except—

(I) during transportation by the juvenile of an unloaded handgun in a locked container directly from the place of transfer to a place at which an activity described in clause (i) is to take place and transportation by the juvenile of that handgun, unloaded and in a locked container, directly from the place at which such an activity took place to the transferor; or

(II) with respect to ranching or farming activities as described in clause (i), a juvenile may possess and use a handgun or ammunition with the prior written approval of the juvenile's parent or legal guardian and at the direction of an adult who is not prohibited by Federal, State or local law from possessing a firearm;

(iii) the juvenile has the prior written consent in the juvenile's possession at all times when a handgun is in the possession of the juvenile; and

(iv) in accordance with State and local law;

(B) a juvenile who is a member of the Armed Forces of the United States or the National Guard who possesses or is armed with a handgun in the line of duty;

(C) a transfer by inheritance of title (but not possession) of a handgun or ammunition to a juvenile; or

(D) the possession of a handgun or ammunition by a juvenile taken in defense of the juvenile or other persons against an intruder into the residence of the juvenile or a residence in which the juvenile is an invited guest.

(4) A handgun or ammunition, the possession of which is transferred to a juvenile in circumstances in which the transferor is not in violation of this subsection shall not be subject to permanent confiscation by the Government if its possession by the juvenile subsequently becomes unlawful because of the conduct of the juvenile, but shall be returned to the lawful owner when such handgun or ammunition is no longer required by the Government for the purposes of investigation or prosecution.

(5) For purposes of this subsection, the term "juvenile" means a person who is less than 18 years of age.

(y) Provisions relating to aliens admitted under nonimmigrant visas--

(1) Definitions.--In this subsection--

(A) the term "alien" has the same meaning as in section 101(a)(3) of the Immigration and Nationality Act (8 U.S.C. 1101(a)(3)); and

(B) the term "nonimmigrant visa" has the same meaning as in section 101(a)(26) of the Immigration and Nationality Act (8 U.S.C. 1101(a)(26)).

(2) Exceptions.--Subsections (d)(5)(B), (g)(5)(B), and (s)(3)(B)(v)(II) do not apply to any alien who has been lawfully admitted to the United States under a nonimmigrant visa, if that alien is--

(A) admitted to the United States for lawful hunting or sporting purposes or is in possession of a hunting license or permit lawfully issued in the United States;

(B) an official representative of a foreign government who is--

(i) accredited to the United States Government or the Government's mission to an international organization having its headquarters in the United States; or

(ii) en route to or from another country to which that alien is accredited;

(C) an official of a foreign government or a distinguished foreign visitor who has been so designated by the Department of State; or

(D) a foreign law enforcement officer of a friendly foreign government entering the United States on official law enforcement business.

(3) Waiver--

(A) Conditions for waiver.--Any individual who has been admitted to the United States under a nonimmigrant visa may receive a waiver from the requirements of subsection (g)(5), if--

(i) the individual submits to the Attorney General a petition that meets the requirements of subparagraph (C); and

(ii) the Attorney General approves the petition.

(B) Petition.--Each petition under subparagraph (B) shall--

(i) demonstrate that the petitioner has resided in the United States for a continuous period of not less than 180 days before the date on which the petition is submitted under this paragraph; and

(ii) include a written statement from the embassy or consulate of the petitioner, authorizing the petitioner to acquire a firearm or ammunition and certifying that the alien would not, absent the application of subsection (g)(5)(B), otherwise be prohibited from such acquisition under subsection (g).

(C) Approval of petition.--The Attorney General shall approve a petition submitted in accordance with this paragraph, if the Attorney General determines that waiving the requirements of subsection (g)(5)(B) with respect to the petitioner--

(i) would be in the interests of justice; and

(ii) would not jeopardize the public safety.

(z) Secure gun storage or safety device.--

(1) In general.--Except as provided under paragraph (2), it shall be unlawful for any licensed importer, licensed manufacturer, or licensed dealer to sell, deliver, or transfer any handgun to any person other than any person licensed under this chapter, unless the transferee is provided with a secure gun storage or safety device (as defined in section 921(a)(34)) for that handgun.

(2) Exceptions.--Paragraph (1) shall not apply to--

(A)(i) the manufacture for, transfer to, or possession by, the United States, a department or agency of the United States, a State, or a department, agency, or political subdivision of a State, of a handgun; or

(ii) the transfer to, or possession by, a law enforcement officer employed by an entity referred to in clause (i) of a handgun for law enforcement purposes (whether on or off duty); or

(B) the transfer to, or possession by, a rail police officer employed by a rail carrier and certified or commissioned as a police officer under the laws of a State of a handgun for purposes of law enforcement (whether on or off duty);

(C) the transfer to any person of a handgun listed as a curio or relic by the Secretary pursuant to section 921(a)(13); or

(D) the transfer to any person of a handgun for which a secure gun storage or safety device is temporarily unavailable for the reasons described in the exceptions stated in section 923(e), if the licensed manufacturer, licensed importer, or licensed dealer delivers to the transferee within 10 calendar days from the date of the delivery of the handgun to the transferee a secure gun storage or safety device for the handgun.

(3) Liability for use.--

(A) In general.--Notwithstanding any other provision of law, a person who has lawful possession and control of a handgun, and who uses a secure gun storage or safety device with the handgun, shall be entitled to immunity from a qualified civil liability action.

(B) Prospective actions.--A qualified civil liability action may not be brought in any Federal or State court.

(C) Defined term.--As used in this paragraph, the term “qualified civil liability action”--

(i) means a civil action brought by any person against a person described in subparagraph (A) for damages resulting from the criminal or unlawful misuse of the handgun by a third party, if—

(I) the handgun was accessed by another person who did not have the permission or authorization of the person having lawful possession and control of the handgun to have access to it; and

(II) at the time access was gained by the person not so authorized, the handgun had been made inoperable by use of a secure gun storage or safety device; and

(ii) shall not include an action brought against the person having lawful possession and control of the handgun for negligent entrustment or negligence per se.

ANNOTATIONS:

United States v. Hayes, 555 U.S. 415, 129 S. Ct. 1079, 1084, 172 L. Ed. 2d 816 (2009):
Title 18 U.S.C.S. § 921(a)(33)(A) does not require a predicate-offense statute that includes, as a discrete element, the existence of a domestic relationship between offender and victim. Instead, in a prosecution under 18 U.S.C.S. § 922(g)(9), it suffices for the government to charge and prove a prior conviction that was, in fact, for an offense committed by the defendant against a spouse or other domestic victim.

Henderson v. United States, ___ U.S. ___, 135 S.Ct 1780 (2015):
Federal courts have equitable authority, even after a criminal proceeding has ended, to order a law enforcement agency to turn over property it has obtained during the case to the rightful owner or his designee, though Congress may cabin this power in various ways. Statutory provision making it unlawful for any person convicted of a felony to possess a firearm or ammunition prevents a court from exercising its equitable authority to instruct a law enforcement agency to return guns in its custody to a felon-owner, as that would place the felon-owner in violation of this provision. Statutory provision making it unlawful for any person convicted of a felony to possess a firearm or ammunition prevents a felon not only from holding his firearms himself, but also from maintaining control over those firearms in the hands of others. Statutory provision making it unlawful for any person convicted of a felony to possess a firearm or ammunition prevents a court from ordering the sale or transfer of a felon's firearms to someone willing to give the felon access to them or to accede to the felon's instructions about their use. This decision abrogated *United States v. Felici,* 208 F.3d 667 (2000).

Rehaif v. United States, ___ U.S. ___, 139 S. Ct. 2191 (2019)
A federal statute, 18 U.S.C. § 922(g), provides that "[i]t shall be unlawful" for certain individuals to possess firearms. The provision lists nine categories of individuals subject to the prohibition, including felons and aliens who are "illegally or unlawfully in the United States." *Ibid.* A separate provision, § 924(a)(2), adds that anyone who "*knowingly* violates" the first provision shall be fined or imprisoned for up to 10 years. (Emphasis added.)

The question here concerns the scope of the word "knowingly." Does it mean that the Government must prove that a defendant knew both that he engaged in the relevant conduct (that he possessed a firearm) and also that he fell within the relevant status (that he was a felon, an alien unlawfully in this country, or the like)? We hold that the word "knowingly" applies both to the defendant's conduct and to the defendant's status. To convict a defendant, the Government therefore must show that the defendant knew he possessed a firearm and also that he knew he had the relevant status when he possessed it.

The term "knowingly" in § 924(a)(2) modifies the verb "violates" and its direct object, which in this case is § 922(g). The proper interpretation of the statute thus turns on what it means for a defendant to know that he has "violate[d]" § 922(g). With some here-irrelevant omissions, § 922(g) makes possession of a firearm or ammunition unlawful when the following elements are satisfied: (1) a status element (in this case, "being an alien ... illegally or unlawfully in the United States"); (2) a possession element (to "possess"); (3) a jurisdictional element ("in or affecting commerce"); and (4) a firearm element (a "firearm or ammunition").

Commentary

This section is more commonly known as The Gun Control Act of 1968, 18 U.S.C. Chapter 44.

The NICS Improvement Amendments Act of 2007 (NIAA), Pub. L. 110-180, was signed into law by the President on January 8, 2008. The NIAA amends the Brady Handgun Violence Prevention Act of 1993 ("the Brady Act") (Pub. L. 103-159), under which the Attorney General established the National Instant Criminal Background Check System (NICS). The Brady Act requires Federal Firearms Licensees (ffls) to contact the NICS before transferring a firearm to an unlicensed person for information on whether the proposed transferee is prohibited from receiving or possessing a firearm under state or federal law. The NIAA was a bipartisan effort to strengthen the NICS by increasing the quantity and quality of relevant records accessible to the system.

Use of medical marijuana for medicinal purposes and its applicability to the sale, transfer or possession of firearms under federal law. *A number of states, Connecticut among them, have passed legislation allowing under state law the use or possession of marijuana for medicinal purposes. Federal law, 18 U.S. C. § 922(g)(3), prohibits any person who is an unlawful user of or addicted to any controlled substance (as defined in section 102 of the Controlled Substances Act (21 U.S.C. 802)) from shipping, transporting, receiving or possessing firearms or ammunition. Marijuana is listed in the Controlled Substances Act as a Schedule I controlled substance, and there are no exceptions in Federal law for marijuana purportedly used for medicinal purposes, even if such use is sanctioned by State law. Further, Federal law, 18 U.S. C. § 922(d)(3), makes it unlawful for any person to sell or otherwise dispose of any firearm or ammunition to any person knowing or having reasonable cause to believe that such person is an unlawful user of or addicted to a controlled substance. As provided by 27 C.F.R. § 478.11, 'an inference of current use may be drawn from evidence of a recent use or possession of a controlled substance or a pattern of use or possession that reasonably covers the present time. Therefore, any person who uses or is addicted to marijuana, regardless of whether his or her State has passed legislation authorizing marijuana use for medicinal purposes, is an unlawful user of or addicted to a controlled substance, and is prohibited by Federal law from possessing firearms or ammunition. Such persons should answer "yes" to question 11.e. On ATF Form 4473 (August 2008), Firearms Transaction Record, and licensed dealers may not transfer firearms or ammunition to them. Further, if a dealer is aware that the potential transferee is in possession of a certificate authorizing the possession and use of marijuana under State law, then such dealer has reasonable cause to believe that the person is an unlawful user of a controlled substance. As such, a dealer may not transfer firearms or ammunition to the person, even if the person answered "no" to question 11.e. On ATF Form 4473. See https://www.atf.gov/files/press/releases/2011/09/ 092611-atf-open-letter-to-all-ffls-marijuana-for-medicinal-purposes.pdf.*

18 U.S.C. § 923. Licensing.

(a) No person shall engage in the business of importing, manufacturing, or dealing in firearms, or importing or manufacturing ammunition, until he has filed an application with and received a license to do so from the Attorney General. The application shall be in such form and contain only that information necessary to determine eligibility for licensing as the Attorney General shall by regulation prescribe and shall include a photograph and fingerprints of the applicant. Each applicant shall pay a fee for obtaining such a license, a separate fee being required for each place in which the applicant is to do business, as follows:

(1) If the applicant is a manufacturer-

(A) of destructive devices, ammunition for destructive devices or armor piercing ammunition, a fee of $1,000 per year;

(B) of firearms other than destructive devices, a fee of $50 per year; or

(C) of ammunition for firearms, other than ammunition for destructive devices or armor piercing ammunition, a fee of $10 per year.

(2) If the applicant is an importer-

(A) of destructive devices, ammunition for destructive devices or armor piercing ammunition, a fee of $1,000 per year; or

(B) of firearms other than destructive devices or ammunition for firearms other than destructive devices, or ammunition other than armor piercing ammunition, a fee of $50 per year.

(3) If the applicant is a dealer-

(A) in destructive devices or ammunition for destructive devices, a fee of $1,000 per year; or

(B) who is not a dealer in destructive devices, a fee of $200 for 3 years, except that the fee for renewal of a valid license shall be $90 for 3 years.

(b) Any person desiring to be licensed as a collector shall file an application for such license with the Attorney General. The application shall be in such form and contain only that information necessary to determine eligibility as the Attorney General shall by regulation prescribe. The fee for such license shall be $10 per year. Any license granted under this subsection shall only apply to transactions in curios and relics.

(c) Upon the filing of a proper application and payment of the prescribed fee, the Attorney General shall issue to a qualified applicant the appropriate license which, subject to the provisions of this chapter and other applicable provisions of law, shall entitle the licensee to transport, ship, and receive firearms and ammunition covered by such license in interstate or foreign commerce during the period stated in the license. Nothing in this chapter shall be construed to prohibit a licensed manufacturer, importer, or dealer from maintaining and disposing of a personal collection of firearms, subject only to such restrictions as apply in this chapter to dispositions by a person other than a licensed manufacturer, importer, or dealer. If any firearm is so disposed of by a licensee within one year after its transfer from his business inventory into such licensee's personal collection or if such disposition or any other acquisition is made for the purpose of willfully evading the restrictions placed upon licensees by this chapter, then such firearm shall be deemed part of such licensee's business inventory, except that any licensed manufacturer, importer, or dealer who has maintained a firearm as part of a personal collection for one year and who sells or otherwise disposes of such firearm shall record the description of the firearm in a bound volume, containing the name and place of residence and date of birth of the transferee if the transferee is an individual, or the identity and principal and local places of business of the transferee if the transferee is a corporation or other business entity: *Provided*, That no other recordkeeping shall be required.

(d)(1) Any application submitted under subsection (a) or (b) of this section shall be approved if—

(A) the applicant is twenty-one years of age or over;

(B) the applicant (including, in the case of a corporation, partnership, or association, any individual possessing, directly or indirectly, the power to direct or cause the direction of the management and policies of the corporation, partnership, or association) is not prohibited from transporting, shipping, or receiving firearms or ammunition in interstate or foreign commerce under section 922(g) and (n) of this chapter;

(C) the applicant has not willfully violated any of the provisions of this chapter or regulations issued thereunder;

(D) the applicant has not willfully failed to disclose any material information required, or has not made any false statement as to any material fact, in connection with his application;

(E) the applicant has in a State (i) premises from which he conducts business subject to license under this chapter or from which he intends to conduct such business within a reasonable period of time, or (ii) in the case of a collector, premises from which he conducts his collecting subject to license under this chapter or from which he intends to conduct such collecting within a reasonable period of time;

(F) the applicant certifies that—

(i) the business to be conducted under the license is not prohibited by State or local law in the place where the licensed premise is located;

(ii)(I) within 30 days after the application is approved the business will comply with the requirements of State and local law applicable to the conduct of the business; and (II) the business will not be conducted under the license until the requirements of State and local law applicable to the business have been met; and

(iii) that the applicant has sent or delivered a form to be prescribed by the Attorney General, to the chief law enforcement officer of the locality in which the premises are located, which indicates that the applicant intends to apply for a Federal firearms license; and

(G) in the case of an application to be licensed as a dealer, the applicant certifies that secure gun storage or safety devices will be available at any place in which firearms are sold under the license to persons who are not licensees (subject to the exception that in any case in which a secure gun storage or safety device is temporarily unavailable because of theft, casualty loss, consumer sales, backorders from a manufacturer, or any other similar reason beyond the control of the licensee, the dealer shall not be considered to be in violation of the requirement under this subparagraph to make available such a device).

(2) The Attorney General must approve or deny an application for a license within the 60-day period beginning on the date it is received. If the Attorney General fails to act within such period, the applicant may file an action under section 1361 of title 28 to compel the Attorney General to act. If the Attorney General approves an applicant's application, such applicant shall be issued a license upon the payment of the prescribed fee.

(e) The Attorney General may, after notice and opportunity for hearing, revoke any license issued under this section if the holder of such license has willfully violated any provision of this chapter or any rule or regulation prescribed by the Attorney General under this chapter or fails to have secure gun storage or safety devices available at any place in which firearms are sold under the license to persons who are not licensees (except that in any case in which a secure gun storage or safety device is temporarily unavailable because of theft, casualty loss, consumer sales, backorders from a manufacturer, or any other similar reason beyond the control of the licensee, the dealer shall not be considered to be in violation of the requirement to make available such a device). The Attorney General may, after notice and opportunity for hearing, revoke the license of a dealer who willfully transfers armor piercing ammunition. The Attorney General's action under this subsection may be reviewed only as provided in subsection (f) of this section.

(f)(1) Any person whose application for a license is denied and any holder of a license which is revoked shall receive a written notice from the Attorney General stating specifically the grounds upon which the application was denied or upon which the license was revoked. Any notice of a revocation of a license shall be given to the holder of such license before the effective date of the revocation.

(2) If the Attorney General denies an application for, or revokes, a license, he shall, upon request by the aggrieved party, promptly hold a hearing to review his denial or revocation. In the case of a revocation of a license, the Attorney General shall upon the request of the holder of the license stay the effective date of the revocation. A hearing held under this paragraph shall be held at a location convenient to the aggrieved party.

(3) If after a hearing held under paragraph (2) the Attorney General decides not to reverse his decision to deny an application or revoke a license, the Attorney General shall give notice of his decision to the aggrieved party. The aggrieved party may at any time within sixty days after the date notice was given under this paragraph file a petition with the United States district court for the district in which he resides or has his principal place of business for a de novo judicial review of such denial or revocation. In a proceeding conducted under this subsection, the court may consider any evidence submitted by the parties to the proceeding whether or not such evidence was considered at the hearing held under paragraph (2). If the court decides that the Attorney General was not authorized to deny the application or to revoke the license, the court shall order the Attorney General to take such action as may be necessary to comply with the judgment of the court.

(4) If criminal proceedings are instituted against a licensee alleging any violation of this chapter or of rules or regulations prescribed under this chapter, and the licensee is acquitted of such charges, or such proceedings are terminated, other than upon motion of the Government before trial upon such charges, the Attorney General shall be absolutely barred from denying or revoking any license granted under this chapter where such denial or revocation is based in whole or in part on the facts which form the basis of such criminal charges. No proceedings for the revocation of a license shall be instituted by the Attorney General more than one year after the filing of the indictment or information.

(g)(1)(A) Each licensed importer, licensed manufacturer, and licensed dealer shall maintain such records of importation, production, shipment, receipt, sale, or other disposition of firearms at his place of business for such period, and in such form, as the

Attorney General may by regulations prescribe. Such importers, manufacturers, and dealers shall not be required to submit to the Attorney General reports and information with respect to such records and the contents thereof, except as expressly required by this section. The Attorney General, when he has reasonable cause to believe a violation of this chapter has occurred and that evidence thereof may be found on such premises, may, upon demonstrating such cause before a Federal magistrate judge and securing from such magistrate judge a warrant authorizing entry, enter during business hours the premises (including places of storage) of any licensed firearms importer, licensed manufacturer, licensed dealer, licensed collector, or any licensed importer or manufacturer of ammunition, for the purpose of inspecting or examining—

(i) any records or documents required to be kept by such licensed importer, licensed manufacturer, licensed dealer, or licensed collector under this chapter or rules or regulations under this chapter, and

(ii) any firearms or ammunition kept or stored by such licensed importer, licensed manufacturer, licensed dealer, or licensed collector, at such premises.

(B) The Attorney General may inspect or examine the inventory and records of a licensed importer, licensed manufacturer, or licensed dealer without such reasonable cause or warrant--

(i) in the course of a reasonable inquiry during the course of a criminal investigation of a person or persons other than the licensee;

(ii) for ensuring compliance with the record keeping requirements of this chapter--

(I) not more than once during any 12-month period; or

(II) at any time with respect to records relating to a firearm involved in a criminal investigation that is traced to the licensee; or

(iii) when such inspection or examination may be required for determining the disposition of one or more particular firearms in the course of a bona fide criminal investigation.

(C) The Attorney General may inspect the inventory and records of a licensed collector without such reasonable cause or warrant--

(i) for ensuring compliance with the record keeping requirements of this chapter not more than once during any twelve-month period; or

(ii) when such inspection or examination may be required for determining the disposition of one or more particular firearms in the course of a bona fide criminal investigation.

(D) At the election of a licensed collector, the annual inspection of records and inventory permitted under this paragraph shall be performed at the office of the Attorney General designated for such inspections which is located in closest proximity to the premises where the inventory and records of such licensed collector are maintained. The inspection and examination authorized by this paragraph shall not be construed as authorizing the Attorney General to seize any records or other documents other than those records or documents constituting material evidence of a violation of law. If the Attorney General seizes such records or documents, copies shall be provided the licensee within a reasonable time. The Attorney General may make available to any Federal, State, or local law enforcement agency any information which he may obtain by reason of this chapter with respect to the identification of persons prohibited from purchasing or receiving firearms or ammunition who have purchased or received firearms or ammunition, together with a description of such firearms or ammunition, and he may provide information to the extent such information may be contained in the records required to be maintained by this chapter, when so requested by any Federal, State, or local law enforcement agency.

(2) Each licensed collector shall maintain in a bound volume the nature of which the Attorney General may by regulations prescribe, records of the receipt, sale, or other disposition of firearms. Such records shall include the name and address of any person to whom the collector sells or otherwise disposes of a firearm. Such collector shall not be required to submit to the Attorney General reports and information with respect to such records and the contents thereof, except as expressly required by this section.

(3)(A) Each licensee shall prepare a report of multiple sales or other dispositions whenever the licensee sells or otherwise disposes of, at one time or during any five consecutive business days, two or more pistols, or revolvers, or any combination of pistols and revolvers totaling two or more, to an unlicensed person. The report shall be prepared on a form specified by the Attorney General and forwarded to the office specified thereon and to the department of State police or State law enforcement agency of the State or local law enforcement agency of the local jurisdiction in which the sale or other disposition took place, not later than the close of business on the day that the multiple sale or other disposition occurs.

(B) Except in the case of forms and contents thereof regarding a purchaser who is prohibited by subsection (g) or (n) of section 922 of this title from receipt of a firearm, the department of State police or State law enforcement agency or local law enforcement agency of the local jurisdiction shall not disclose any such form or the contents thereof to any person or entity, and shall destroy each such form and any record of the contents thereof no more than 20 days from the date such form is received. No later than the date that is 6 months after the effective date of this subparagraph, and at the end of each 6-month period thereafter, the department of State police or State law enforcement agency or local law enforcement agency of the local jurisdiction shall certify to the Attorney General of the United States that no disclosure contrary to this subparagraph has been made and that all forms and any record of the contents thereof have been destroyed as provided in this subparagraph.

(4) Where a firearms or ammunition business is discontinued and succeeded by a new licensee, the records required to be kept by this chapter shall appropriately reflect such facts and shall be delivered to the successor. Where discontinuance of the business is absolute, such records shall be delivered within thirty days after the business discontinuance to the Attorney General. However, where State law or local ordinance requires the delivery of records to other responsible authority, the Attorney General may arrange for the delivery of such records to such other responsible authority.

(5)(A) Each licensee shall, when required by letter issued by the Attorney General, and until notified to the contrary in writing by the Attorney General, submit on a form specified by the Attorney General, for periods and at the times specified in such letter, all record information required to be kept by this chapter or such lesser record information as the Attorney General in such letter may specify.

(B) The Attorney General may authorize such record information to be submitted in a manner other than that prescribed in subparagraph (A) of this paragraph when it is shown by a licensee that an alternate method of reporting is reasonably necessary and will not unduly hinder the effective administration of this chapter. A licensee may use an alternate method of reporting if the licensee describes the proposed alternate method of reporting and the need therefor in a letter application submitted to the Attorney General, and the Attorney General approves such alternate method of reporting.

(6) Each licensee shall report the theft or loss of a firearm from the licensee's inventory or collection, within 48 hours after the theft or loss is discovered, to the Attorney General and to the appropriate local authorities.

(7) Each licensee shall respond immediately to, and in no event later than 24 hours after the receipt of, a request by the Attorney General for information contained in the records required to be kept by this chapter as may be required for determining the disposition of 1 or more firearms in the course of a bona fide criminal investigation. The requested information shall be provided orally or in writing, as the Attorney General may require. The Attorney General shall implement a system whereby the licensee can positively identify and establish that an individual requesting information via telephone is employed by and authorized by the agency to request such information.

(h) Licenses issued under the provisions of subsection (c) of this section shall be kept posted and kept available for inspection on the premises covered by the license.

(i) Licensed importers and licensed manufacturers shall identify by means of a serial number engraved or cast on the receiver or frame of the weapon, in such manner as the Attorney General shall by regulations prescribe, each firearm imported or manufactured by such importer or manufacturer.

(j) A licensed importer, licensed manufacturer, or licensed dealer may, under rules or regulations prescribed by the Attorney General, conduct business temporarily at a location other than the location specified on the license if such temporary location is the location for a gun show or event sponsored by any national, State, or local organization, or any affiliate of any such organization devoted to the collection, competitive use, or other sporting use of firearms in the community, and such location is in the State which is specified on the license. Records of receipt and disposition of firearms transactions conducted at such temporary location shall include the location of the sale or other disposition and shall be entered in the permanent records of the licensee and retained on the location specified on the license. Nothing in this subsection shall authorize any licensee to conduct business in or from any motorized or towed vehicle. Notwithstanding the provisions of subsection (a) of this section, a separate fee shall not be required of a licensee with respect to business conducted under this subsection. Any inspection or examination of inventory or records under this chapter by the Attorney General at such temporary location shall be limited to inventory consisting of, or records relating to, firearms held or disposed at such temporary location. Nothing in this subsection shall be construed to authorize the Attorney General to inspect or examine the inventory or records of a licensed importer, licensed manufacturer, or licensed dealer at any location other than the location specified on the license. Nothing in this subsection shall be construed to diminish in any manner any right to display, sell, or otherwise dispose of firearms or ammunition, which is in effect before the date of the enactment of the Firearms Owners' Protection Act, including the right of a licensee to conduct "curios or relics" firearms transfers and business away from their business premises with another licensee without regard as to whether the location of where the business is conducted is located in the State specified on the license of either licensee.

(k) Licensed importers and licensed manufacturers shall mark all armor piercing projectiles and packages containing such projectiles for distribution in the manner prescribed by the Attorney General by regulation. The Attorney General shall furnish information to each dealer licensed under this chapter defining which projectiles are considered armor piercing ammunition as defined in section 921(a)(17)(B).

(l) The Attorney General shall notify the chief law enforcement officer in the appropriate State and local jurisdictions of the names and addresses of all persons in the State to whom a firearms license is issued.

18 U.S.C. § 924 Penalties.

(a)(1) Except as otherwise provided in this subsection, subsection (b), (c), (f), or (p) of this section, or in section 929, whoever--

(A) knowingly makes any false statement or representation with respect to the information required by this chapter to be kept in the records of a person licensed under this chapter or in applying for any license or exemption or relief from disability under the provisions of this chapter;

(B) knowingly violates subsection (a)(4), (f), (k), or (q) of section 922;

(C) knowingly imports or brings into the United States or any possession thereof any firearm or ammunition in violation of section 922(l); or

(D) willfully violates any other provision of this chapter,

Shall be fined under this title, imprisoned not more than five years, or both.

(2) Whoever knowingly violates subsection (a)(6), (h), (i), (j), or (o) of section 922 shall be fined as provided in this title, imprisoned not more than 10 years, or both.

(3) Any licensed dealer, licensed importer, licensed manufacturer, or licensed collector who knowingly--

(A) makes any false statement or representation with respect to the information required by the provisions of this chapter to be kept in the records of a person licensed under this chapter, or

(B) violates subsection (m) of section 922,

Shall be fined under this title, imprisoned not more than one year, or both.

(4) Whoever violates section 922(q) shall be fined under this title, imprisoned for not more than 5 years, or both. Notwithstanding any other provision of law, the term of imprisonment imposed under this paragraph shall not run concurrently with any other term of imprisonment imposed under any other provision of law. Except for the authorization of

a term of imprisonment of not more than 5 years made in this paragraph, for the purpose of any other law a violation of section 922(q) shall be deemed to be a misdemeanor.

(5) Whoever knowingly violates subsection (s) or (t) of section 922 shall be fined under this title, imprisoned for not more than 1 year, or both.

(6)(A)(i) A juvenile who violates section 922(x) shall be fined under this title, imprisoned not more than 1 year, or both, except that a juvenile described in clause (ii) shall be sentenced to probation on appropriate conditions and shall not be incarcerated unless the juvenile fails to comply with a condition of probation.

(ii) A juvenile is described in this clause if--

(I) the offense of which the juvenile is charged is possession of a handgun or ammunition in violation of section 922(x)(2); and

(II) the juvenile has not been convicted in any court of an offense (including an offense under section 922(x) or a similar State law, but not including any other offense consisting of conduct that if engaged in by an adult would not constitute an offense) or adjudicated as a juvenile delinquent for conduct that if engaged in by an adult would constitute an offense.

(B) A person other than a juvenile who knowingly violates section 922(x)--

(i) shall be fined under this title, imprisoned not more than 1 year, or both; and

(ii) if the person sold, delivered, or otherwise transferred a handgun or ammunition to a juvenile knowing or having reasonable cause to know that the juvenile intended to carry or otherwise possess or discharge or otherwise use the handgun or ammunition in the commission of a crime of violence, shall be fined under this title, imprisoned not more than 10 years, or both.

(7) Whoever knowingly violates section 931 shall be fined under this title, imprisoned not more than 3 years, or both.

(8) Whoever knowingly violates subsection (d) or (g) of section 922 shall be fined under this title, imprisoned for not more than 15 years, or both.

(b) Whoever, with intent to commit therewith an offense punishable by imprisonment for a term exceeding one year, or with knowledge or reasonable cause to believe that an offense punishable by imprisonment for a term exceeding one year is to be committed therewith, ships, transports, or receives a firearm or any ammunition in interstate or foreign commerce shall be fined under this title, or imprisoned not more than ten years, or both.

(c)(1)(A) Except to the extent that a greater minimum sentence is otherwise provided by this subsection or by any other provision of law, any person who, during and in relation to any crime of violence or drug trafficking crime (including a crime of violence or drug trafficking crime that provides for an enhanced punishment if committed by the use of a deadly or dangerous weapon or device) for which the person may be prosecuted in a court of the United States, uses or carries a firearm, or who, in furtherance of any such crime, possesses a firearm, shall, in addition to the punishment provided for such crime of violence or drug trafficking crime--

(i) be sentenced to a term of imprisonment of not less than 5 years;

(ii) if the firearm is brandished, be sentenced to a term of imprisonment of not less than 7 years; and

(iii) if the firearm is discharged, be sentenced to a term of imprisonment of not less than 10 years.

(B) If the firearm possessed by a person convicted of a violation of this subsection--

(i) is a short-barreled rifle, short-barreled shotgun, or semiautomatic assault weapon, the person shall be sentenced to a term of imprisonment of not less than 10 years; or

(ii) is a machinegun or a destructive device, or is equipped with a firearm silencer or firearm muffler, the person shall be sentenced to a term of imprisonment of not less than 30 years.

(C) In the case of a second or subsequent conviction under this subsection, the person shall--

(i) be sentenced to a term of imprisonment of not less than 25 years; and

(ii) if the firearm involved is a machinegun or a destructive device, or is equipped with a firearm silencer or firearm muffler, be sentenced to imprisonment for life.

(D) Notwithstanding any other provision of law--

(i) a court shall not place on probation any person convicted of a violation of this subsection; and

(ii) no term of imprisonment imposed on a person under this subsection shall run concurrently with any other term of imprisonment imposed on the person, including any term of imprisonment imposed for the crime of violence or drug trafficking crime during which the firearm was used, carried, or possessed.

(2) For purposes of this subsection, the term "drug trafficking crime" means any felony punishable under the Controlled Substances Act (21 U.S.C. 801 et seq.), the Controlled Substances Import and Export Act (21 U.S.C. 951 et seq.), or chapter 705 of title 46.

(3) For purposes of this subsection the term "crime of violence" means an offense that is a felony and--

(A) has as an element the use, attempted use, or threatened use of physical force against the person or property of another, or

(B) that by its nature, involves a substantial risk that physical force against the person or property of another may be used in the course of committing the offense.

(4) For purposes of this subsection, the term "brandish" means, with respect to a firearm, to display all or part of the firearm, or otherwise make the presence of the firearm known to another person, in order to intimidate that person, regardless of whether the firearm is directly visible to that person.

(5) Except to the extent that a greater minimum sentence is otherwise provided under this subsection, or by any other provision of law, any person who, during and in relation to any crime of violence or drug trafficking crime (including a crime of violence or drug trafficking crime that provides for an enhanced punishment if committed by the use of a deadly or dangerous weapon or device) for which the person may be prosecuted in a court

of the United States, uses or carries armor piercing ammunition, or who, in furtherance of any such crime, possesses armor piercing ammunition, shall, in addition to the punishment provided for such crime of violence or drug trafficking crime or conviction under this section--

(A) be sentenced to a term of imprisonment of not less than 15 years; and

(B) if death results from the use of such ammunition--

(i) if the killing is murder (as defined in section 1111), be punished by death or sentenced to a term of imprisonment for any term of years or for life; and

(ii) if the killing is manslaughter (as defined in section 1112), be punished as provided in section 1112.

(d)(1) Any firearm or ammunition involved in or used in any knowing violation of subsection (a)(4), (a)(6), (f), (g), (h), (i), (j), or (k) of section 922, or knowing importation or bringing into the United States or any possession thereof any firearm or ammunition in violation of section 922(l), or knowing violation of section 924, 932, 0r 933, or willful violation of any other provision of this chapter or any rule or regulation promulgated thereunder, or any violation of any other criminal law of the United States, or any firearm or ammunition intended to be used in any offense referred to in paragraph (3) of this subsection, where such intent is demonstrated by clear and convincing evidence, shall be subject to seizure and forfeiture, and all provisions of the Internal Revenue Code of 1986 relating to the seizure, forfeiture, and disposition of firearms, as defined in section 5845(a) of that Code, shall, so far as applicable, extend to seizures and forfeitures under the provisions of this chapter: Provided, That upon acquittal of the owner or possessor, or dismissal of the charges against him other than upon motion of the Government prior to trial, or lapse of or court termination of the restraining order to which he is subject, the seized or relinquished firearms or ammunition shall be returned forthwith to the owner or possessor or to a person delegated by the owner or possessor unless the return of the firearms or ammunition would place the owner or possessor or his delegate in violation of law. Any action or proceeding for the forfeiture of firearms or ammunition shall be commenced within one hundred and twenty days of such seizure.

(2)(A) In any action or proceeding for the return of firearms or ammunition seized under the provisions of this chapter, the court shall allow the prevailing party, other than the United States, a reasonable attorney's fee, and the United States shall be liable therefor.

(B) In any other action or proceeding under the provisions of this chapter, the court, when it finds that such action was without foundation, or was initiated vexatiously, frivolously, or in bad faith, shall allow the prevailing party, other than the United States, a reasonable attorney's fee, and the United States shall be liable therefor.

(C) Only those firearms or quantities of ammunition particularly named and individually identified as involved in or used in any violation of the provisions of this chapter or any rule or regulation issued thereunder, or any other criminal law of the United States or as intended to be used in any offense referred to in paragraph (3) of this subsection, where such intent is demonstrated by clear and convincing evidence, shall be subject to seizure, forfeiture, and disposition.

(D) The United States shall be liable for attorneys' fees under this paragraph only to the extent provided in advance by appropriation Acts.

(3) The offenses referred to in paragraphs (1) and (2)(C) of this subsection are--

(A) any crime of violence, as that term is defined in section 924(c)(3) of this title;

(B) any offense punishable under the Controlled Substances Act (21 U.S.C. 801 et seq.) Or the Controlled Substances Import and Export Act (21 U.S.C. 951 et seq.);

(C) any offense described in section 922(a)(1), 922(a)(3), 922(a)(5), or 922(b)(3) of this title, where the firearm or ammunition intended to be used in any such offense is involved in a pattern of activities which includes a violation of any offense described in section 922(a)(1), 922(a)(3), 922(a)(5), or 922(b)(3) of this title;

(D) any offense described in section 922(d) of this title where the firearm or ammunition is intended to be used in such offense by the transferor of such firearm or ammunition;

(E) any offense described in section 922(i), 922(j), 922(l), 922(n), or 924(b) of this title;

(F) any offense which may be prosecuted in a court of the United States which involves the exportation of firearms or ammunition; and

(G) any offense under section 932 or 933.

(e)(1) In the case of a person who violates section 922(g) of this title and has three previous convictions by any court referred to in section 922(g)(1) of this title for a violent felony or a serious drug offense, or both, committed on occasions different from one another, such person shall be fined under this title and imprisoned not less than fifteen years, and, notwithstanding any other provision of law, the court shall not suspend the sentence of, or grant a probationary sentence to, such person with respect to the conviction under section 922(g).

(2) As used in this subsection--

(A) the term "serious drug offense" means--

(i) an offense under the Controlled Substances Act (21 U.S.C. 801 et seq.), the Controlled Substances Import and Export Act (21 U.S.C. 951 et seq.), or chapter 705 of title 46, for which a maximum term of imprisonment of ten years or more is prescribed by law; or

(ii) an offense under State law, involving manufacturing, distributing, or possessing with intent to manufacture or distribute, a controlled substance (as defined in section 102 of the Controlled Substances Act (21 U.S.C. 802)), for which a maximum term of imprisonment of ten years or more is prescribed by law;

(B) the term "violent felony" means any crime punishable by imprisonment for a term exceeding one year, or any act of juvenile delinquency involving the use or carrying of a firearm, knife, or destructive device that would be punishable by imprisonment for such term if committed by an adult, that--

(i) has as an element the use, attempted use, or threatened use of physical force against the person of another; or

(ii) is burglary, arson, or extortion, involves use of explosives, or otherwise involves conduct that presents a serious potential risk of physical injury to another; and

(C) the term "conviction" includes a finding that a person has committed an act of juvenile delinquency involving a violent felony.

(f) In the case of a person who knowingly violates section 922(p), such person shall be fined under this title, or imprisoned not more than 5 years, or both.

(g) Whoever, with the intent to engage in conduct which--

(1) constitutes an offense listed in section 1961(1),

(2) is punishable under the Controlled Substances Act (21 U.S.C. 801 et seq.), the Controlled Substances Import and Export Act (21 U.S.C. 951 et seq.), or chapter 705 of title 46,

(3) violates any State law relating to any controlled substance (as defined in section 102(6) of the Controlled Substances Act (21 U.S.C. 802(6))), or

(4) constitutes a crime of violence (as defined in subsection (c)(3)),

Travels from any State or foreign country into any other State and acquires, transfers, or attempts to acquire or transfer, a firearm in such other State in furtherance of such purpose, shall be imprisoned not more than 10 years, fined in accordance with this title, or both.

(h) Whoever knowingly receives or transfers a firearm or ammunition, or attempts or conspires to do so, knowing or having reasonable cause to believe that such firearm or ammunition will be used to commit a felony, a Federal crime of terrorism, or a drug trafficking crime (as such terms are defined in section 932(a)), or a crime under the Arms Export Control Act (22 U.S.C. 2751 et seq.), the Export Control Reform Act of 2018 (50 U.S.C. 4801 et seq.), the International Emergency Economic Powers Act (50 U.S.C. 1701 et seq.), or the Foreign Narcotics Kingpin Designation Act (21 U.S.C. 1901 et seq.), shall be fined under this title, imprisoned for not more than 15 years, or both,

(i)(1) A person who knowingly violates section 922(u) shall be fined under this title, imprisoned not more than 10 years, or both.

(2) Nothing contained in this subsection shall be construed as indicating an intent on the part of Congress to occupy the field in which provisions of this subsection operate to the exclusion of State laws on the same subject matter, nor shall any provision of this subsection be construed as invalidating any provision of State law unless such provision is inconsistent with any of the purposes of this subsection.

(j) A person who, in the course of a violation of subsection (c), causes the death of a person through the use of a firearm, shall--

(1) if the killing is a murder (as defined in section 1111), be punished by death or by imprisonment for any term of years or for life; and

(2) if the killing is manslaughter (as defined in section 1112), be punished as provided in that section.

(k)(1) A person who smuggles or knowingly brings into the United States a firearm or ammunition, or attempts or conspires to do so, with intent to engage in or to promote conduct that—

(A) is punishable under the Controlled Substances Import and Export Act (21 U.S.C. 951 et seq.), or chapter 705 of title 46; or

(B) constitutes a felony, a Federal crime of terrorism, or a drug trafficking crime (as such terms are defined in section 932(a)), shall be fined under this title, imprisoned for not more than 15 years, or both.

(2) A person who smuggles or knowingly takes out of the United States a firearm or ammunition, or attempts or conspires to do so, with intent to engage in or to promote conduct that—

(A) would be punishable under the Controlled Substances Import and Export Act (21 U.S.C. 951 et seq.), or chapter 705 of title 46, if the conduct had occurred within the United States; or

(B) would constitute a felony or a Federal crime of terrorism (as such terms are defined in section 932(a)) for which the person may be prosecuted in a court of the United States, if the conduct had occurred within the United States, shall be fined under this title, imprisoned for not more than 15 years, or both

(l) A person who steals any firearm which is moving as, or is a part of, or which has moved in, interstate or foreign commerce shall be imprisoned for not more than 10 years, fined under this title, or both.

(m) A person who steals any firearm from a licensed importer, licensed manufacturer, licensed dealer, or licensed collector shall be fined under this title, imprisoned not more than 10 years, or both.

(n) A person who, with the intent to engage in conduct that constitutes a violation of section 922(a)(1)(A), travels from any State or foreign country into any other State and acquires, or attempts to acquire, a firearm in such other State in furtherance of such purpose shall be imprisoned for not more than 10 years.

(o) A person who conspires to commit an offense under subsection (c) shall be imprisoned for not more than 20 years, fined under this title, or both; and if the firearm is a machinegun or destructive device, or is equipped with a firearm silencer or muffler, shall be imprisoned for any term of years or life.

(p) Penalties relating to secure gun storage or safety device.--

(1) In general.--

(A) Suspension or revocation of license; civil penalties.--With respect to each violation of section 922(z)(1) by a licensed manufacturer, licensed importer, or licensed dealer, the Secretary may, after notice and opportunity for hearing--

(i) suspend for not more than 6 months, or revoke, the license issued to the licensee under this chapter that was used to conduct the firearms transfer; or

(ii) subject the licensee to a civil penalty in an amount equal to not more than $2,500.

(B) Review.--An action of the Secretary under this paragraph may be reviewed only as provided under section 923(f).

(2) Administrative remedies.--The suspension or revocation of a license or the imposition of a civil penalty under paragraph (1) shall not preclude any administrative remedy that is otherwise available to the Secretary.

18 U.S.C. § 926a. Interstate transportation of firearms.

Notwithstanding any other provision of any law or any rule or regulation of a State or any political subdivision thereof, any person who is not otherwise prohibited by this chapter from transporting, shipping, or receiving a firearm shall be entitled to transport a firearm for any lawful purpose from any place where he may lawfully possess and carry such firearm to any other place where he may lawfully possess and carry such firearm if, during such transportation the firearm is unloaded, and neither the firearm nor any ammunition being transported is readily accessible or is directly accessible from the passenger compartment of such transporting vehicle: *Provided,* That in the case of a vehicle without a compartment separate from the driver's compartment the firearm or ammunition shall be contained in a locked container other than the glove compartment or console.

ANNOTATIONS:

Association of New Jersey Rifle and Pistol Clubs Inc. V. Port Authority of New York and New Jersey, 730 F.3d 252 (3rd Cir. 2013):

Statute permitting interstate transportation of firearms protected transportation of firearm only in vehicle; statute did not contemplate non-vehicular transportation of firearms.

Torraco v. Port Authority of New York and New Jersey, 615 F.3d 129 (2d Cir. 2010):

Provision of Firearms Owners' Protection Act (FOPA) generally allowing person not otherwise prohibited from transporting, shipping, or receiving firearm to transport firearm for lawful purpose from "any place where he may lawfully possess and carry such firearm to any other place where he may lawfully possess and carry such firearm" without incurring criminal liability under local gun laws was so vague and amorphous that its enforcement would strain judicial competence, and therefore § 1983 did not provide damages remedy for alleged violation of statute. Police Officers are not required to know gun laws of all 50 states, and if officer has probable cause to arrest, and is reasonably cautious in determining that requirements of FOPA are not met, then officer is not liable for false arrest or violation of § 1983.

Revell v. Port Authority of New York & New Jersey, 598 F. 3d 128 (3rd Cir. 2010):

In upholding a dismissal of 42 U.S.C. § 1983 claims, the court found that the plaintiff could not avail himself of Title 18 USC 926A protection since § 926A clearly requires the traveler to part ways with his weapon and ammunition during travel such that any firearm and ammunition is not readily accessible during travel.

Coalition of New Jersey Sportsmen v. Florio, 744 F. Supp. 602 (D.N.J. 1990):

Federal statute permitting transportation of firearms from one state in which they are legal, through another state in which they are illegal, to a third state in which they are legal, provided firearms were transported in prescribed safe manner, did not preempt state statute regulating possession of weapons.

Matter of Two Seized Firearms, 127 N.J. 84, 602 A.2d 728 (N.J. 1992):

Federal statute which assures gun owners freedom to travel from state to state with weapons legally possessed in state of residence did not preclude forfeiture in New Jersey of loaded handgun found in glove compartment of Florida motorist's van and a loaded handgun kept underneath and behind the driver's seat; both handguns were "readily accessible" and loaded.

Law Enforcement Officers Safety Act (LEOSA)

18 U.S.C. § 926b. Carrying of concealed firearms by qualified law enforcement officers.

(a) Notwithstanding any other provision of the law of any State or any political subdivision thereof, an individual who is a qualified law enforcement officer and who is carrying the identification required by subsection (d) may carry a concealed firearm that has been shipped or transported in interstate or foreign commerce, subject to subsection (b).

(b) This section shall not be construed to supersede or limit the laws of any State that--

(1) permit private persons or entities to prohibit or restrict the possession of concealed firearms on their property; or

(2) prohibit or restrict the possession of firearms on any State or local government property, installation, building, base, or park.

(c) As used in this section, the term "qualified law enforcement officer" means an employee of a governmental agency who--

(1) is authorized by law to engage in or supervise the prevention, detection, investigation, or prosecution of, or the incarceration of any person for, any violation of law, and has statutory powers of arrest;

(2) is authorized by the agency to carry a firearm;

(3) is not the subject of any disciplinary action by the agency which could result in suspension or loss of police powers;

(4) meets standards, if any, established by the agency which require the employee to regularly qualify in the use of a firearm;

(5) is not under the influence of alcohol or another intoxicating or hallucinatory drug or substance; and

(6) is not prohibited by Federal law from receiving a firearm.

(d) The identification required by this subsection is the photographic identification issued by the governmental agency for which the individual is employed as a law enforcement officer.

(e) As used in this section, the term "firearm"--

(1) except as provided in this subsection, has the same meaning as in section 921 of this title;

(2) includes ammunition not expressly prohibited by Federal law or subject to the provisions of the National Firearms Act; and

(3) does not include--

(A) any machinegun (as defined in section 5845 of the National Firearms Act);

(B) any firearm silencer (as defined in section 921 of this title); and

(C) any destructive device (as defined in section 921 of this title).

(f) For the purposes of this section, a law enforcement officer of the Amtrak Police Department, a law enforcement officer of the Federal Reserve, or a law enforcement or police officer of the executive branch of the Federal Government qualifies as an employee of a governmental agency who is authorized by law to engage in or supervise the prevention, detection, investigation, or prosecution of, or the incarceration of any person for, any violation of law, and has statutory powers of arrest or apprehension under section 807(b) of title 10, United States Code (article 7 (b) of the Uniform Code of Military Justice).

18 U.S.C. § 926c. Carrying of concealed firearms by qualified retired law enforcement officers.

(a) Notwithstanding any other provision of the law of any State or any political subdivision thereof, an individual who is a qualified retired law enforcement officer and who is carrying the identification required by subsection (d) may carry a concealed firearm that has been shipped or transported in interstate or foreign commerce, subject to subsection (b).

(b) This section shall not be construed to supersede or limit the laws of any State that--

(1) permit private persons or entities to prohibit or restrict the possession of concealed firearms on their property; or

(2) prohibit or restrict the possession of firearms on any State or local government property, installation, building, base, or park.

(c) As used in this section, the term "qualified retired law enforcement officer" means an individual who--

(1) separated from service in good standing from service with a public agency as a law enforcement officer;

(2) before such separation, was authorized by law to engage in or supervise the prevention, detection, investigation, or prosecution of, or the incarceration of any person for, any violation of law, and had statutory powers of arrest or apprehension under section 807(b) of title 10, United States Code (article 7(b) of the Uniform Code of Military Justice);

(3)(A) before such separation, served as a law enforcement officer for an aggregate of 10 years or more; or (B) separated from service with such agency, after completing any applicable probationary period of such service, due to a service-connected disability, as determined by such agency;

(4) during the most recent 12-month period, has met, at the expense of the individual, the standards for qualification in firearms training for active law enforcement officers, as determined by the former agency of the individual, the State in which the individual resides or, if the State has not established such standards, either a law enforcement agency within the State in which the individual resides or the standards used by a certified firearms instructor that is qualified to conduct a firearms qualification test for active duty officers within that State;

(5)(A) has not been officially found by a qualified medical professional employed by the agency to be unqualified for reasons relating to mental health and as a result of this finding will not be issued the photographic identification as described in subsection (d)(1); or (B) has not entered into an agreement with the agency from which the individual is separating from service in which that individual acknowledges he or she is not qualified under this section for reasons relating to mental health and for those reasons will not receive or accept the photographic identification as described in subsection (d)(1);

(6) is not under the influence of alcohol or another intoxicating or hallucinatory drug or substance; and

(7) is not prohibited by Federal law from receiving a firearm.

(d) The identification required by this subsection is--

(1) a photographic identification issued by the agency from which the individual separated from service as a law enforcement officer that identifies the person as having been employed as a police officer or law enforcement officer and indicates that the individual has, not less recently than one year before the date the individual is carrying the concealed firearm, been tested or otherwise found by the agency to meet the active duty standards for qualification in firearms training as established by the agency to carry a firearm of the same type as the concealed firearm; or

(2)(A) a photographic identification issued by the agency from which the individual separated from service as a law enforcement officer that identifies the person as having been employed as a police officer or law enforcement officer; and (B) a certification issued by the State in which the individual resides or by a certified firearms instructor that is qualified to conduct a firearms qualification test for active duty officers within that State that indicates that the individual has, not less than 1 year before the date the individual is carrying the concealed firearm, been tested or otherwise found by the State or a certified firearms instructor that is qualified to conduct a firearms qualification test for active duty officers within that State to have met--

(I) the active duty standards for qualification in firearms training, as established by the State, to carry a firearm of the same type as the concealed firearm; or

(II) if the State has not established such standards, standards set by any law enforcement agency within that State to carry a firearm of the same type as the concealed firearm.

(e) As used in this section--

(1) the term "firearm"--

(A) except as provided in this paragraph, has the same meaning as in section 921 of this title;

(B) includes ammunition not expressly prohibited by Federal law or subject to the provisions of the National Firearms Act; and

(C) does not include--

(i) any machinegun (as defined in section 5845 of the National Firearms Act);
(ii) any firearm silencer (as defined in section 921 of this title); and
(iii) any destructive device (as defined in section 921 of this title); and

(2) the term "service with a public agency as a law enforcement officer" includes service as a law enforcement officer of the Amtrak Police Department, service as a law enforcement officer of the Federal Reserve, or service as a law enforcement or police officer of the executive branch of the Federal Government.

ANNOTATIONS:

Johnson v. N.Y. State Dept. Of Corr. Services, 709 F. Supp. 2d 178 (N.D.N.Y. 2010):
Congress did not expressly intend to create private cause of action under Law Enforcement Officers Safety Act (LEOSA), precluding retired corrections officers' action against state agencies for declarative and injunctive relief under LEOSA provision permitting retired officers to carry concealed weapons in interstate commerce; any rights expressly conferred by LEOSA were contingent upon retired officer's possession of identification, but nothing in LEOSA bestowed either explicit right to obtain that identification or federal remedy for state agency's failure to issue such identification.

Commentary

The Law Enforcement Officers Safety Improvements Act of 2010, Public Law No: 111-272 (2010), made significant changes to the scope of this statute. Formerly, only retired police officers who served for at least fifteen years were eligible for LEOSA's benefits. The definition of "qualified retired law enforcement officer" was expanded in 2010 to include individuals, although not formally retired under the commonly understood meaning of that term, who separated in good standing from service with a public agency as a law enforcement officer and, before such separation, (1) were authorized by law to engage in or supervise the prevention, detection, investigation, or prosecution of, or the incarceration of any person for, any violation of law, (2) had statutory powers of arrest and, (3) served as a law enforcement officer for an aggregate of 10 years or more; or separated from service with such agency, after completing any applicable probationary period of such service, due to a service-connected disability, as determined by such agency.

In order to meet the strict statutory standards, qualified retired law enforcement officers must carry photographic identification, consistent with LEOSA requirements, issued by the agency from which the individual separated from service as a law enforcement officer, indicating that the officer has been tested or otherwise found by the agency to meet the active duty standards for qualification in firearms training as established by the agency to carry a firearm of the same type as the concealed firearm. The statute does not define the meaning of the term "type." The legislative history establishes, however, that law enforcement agencies possess the authority to enforce some limitation on the type of firearm to be carried. As such, qualification does not permit qualified retired law enforcement officers to simply carry any weapon they choose. The extent of a law enforcement agency's ability to restrict the type of weapon a qualified retired law enforcement officer is authorized to carry is, however, unclear. However, restriction of LEOSA qualification to a specific firearm, as opposed to a "type" of firearm, is not consistent with the statute. It is not unreasonable to restrict the "type" requirement to distinctions between semi-automatic pistols and revolvers. However, nothing in the law prevents an officer from qualifying with both. Weapons carried pursuant to the authority of LEOSA must be carried concealed.

Connecticut has not established statewide proficiency standards with a firearm applicable to all law enforcement officers. As a result, qualified retired law enforcement officers must meet the active duty standards for qualification in firearms training to carry a firearm of the same type as the concealed firearm they intend to carry as established by the agency from which they retired. Different agencies have established different standards. Qualified retired law enforcement officers must meet the standards of the agency from which the individual separated from service as a law enforcement officer.

Certification of firearms proficiency is valid under LEOSA for one year. Qualified retired law enforcement officers must, therefore, be recertified on a yearly basis. The privileges afforded by LEOSA automatically expire upon expiration of the one year period. Retired law enforcement officers who continue to carry firearms after their LEOSA certification has expired must meet the standards applicable to the jurisdiction in which they are located.

The LEOSA-qualified person does not generally require a state-issued permit for carrying concealed firearms. LEOSA overrides state and local permitting laws, but not other federal laws, e.g., the federal Gun-Free School Zone Act of 1995 which prohibits carrying a firearm within 1000 feet of any elementary or secondary school or federal laws and agency policies that restrict the carrying of concealed firearms in certain federal buildings and lands. LEOSA also does not override state laws which restrict the locations at which permitted firearms may lawfully be carried, such as in state parks or buildings, or in private premises in which the owner has posted notice that firearms are not permitted.

Finally, it should be noted that The Law Enforcement Officers Safety Act of 2004, and the Law Enforcement Officers Safety Act Improvements Act of 2010, provide no authority for anyone to act in the capacity of a law enforcement official.

18 U.S.C. § 930. Possession of firearms and dangerous weapons in Federal facilities.

(a) Except as provided in subsection (d), whoever knowingly possesses or causes to be present a firearm or other dangerous weapon in a Federal facility (other than a Federal court facility), or attempts to do so, shall be fined under this title or imprisoned not more than 1 year, or both.

...

(d) Subsection (a) shall not apply to-- (1) the lawful performance of official duties by an officer, agent, or employee of the United States, a State, or a political subdivision thereof, who is authorized by law to engage in or supervise the prevention, detection, investigation, or prosecution of any violation of law; (2) the possession of a firearm or other dangerous weapon by a Federal official or a member of the Armed Forces if such possession is authorized by law; or (3) the lawful carrying of firearms or other dangerous weapons in a Federal facility incident to hunting or other lawful purposes. (e) (1) Except as provided in paragraph (2), whoever knowingly possesses or causes to be present a firearm or other dangerous weapon in a Federal court facility, or attempts to do so, shall be fined under this title, imprisoned not more than 2 years, or both. (2) Paragraph (1) shall not apply to conduct which is described in paragraph (1) or (2) of subsection (d).

18 U.S.C. § 932. Straw purchasing of firearms.

(a) Definitions.—For purposes of this section—

(1) the term "drug trafficking crime"—

(A) has the meaning given that term in section 924(c)(2); and

(B) includes a felony punishable under the law of a State for which the conduct constituting the offense would constitute a felony punishable under the Controlled Substances Act (21 U.S.C. 801 et seq.), the Controlled Substances Import and Export Act (21 U.S.C. 951 et seq.), or chapter 705 of title 46;

(2) the term "Federal crime of terrorism" has the meaning given that term in section 2332b(g)(5); and

(3) the term "felony" means any offense under Federal or State law punishable by imprisonment for a term exceeding 1 year.

(b) Violation.—It shall be unlawful for any person to knowingly purchase, or conspire to purchase, any firearm in or otherwise affecting interstate or foreign commerce for, on behalf of, or at the request or demand of any other person, knowing or having reasonable cause to believe that such other person—

(1) meets the criteria of 1 or more paragraphs of section 922(d);

(2) intends to use, carry, possess, or sell or otherwise dispose of the firearm in furtherance of a felony, a Federal crime of terrorism, or a drug trafficking crime; or

(3) intends to sell or otherwise dispose of the firearm to a person described in paragraph (1) or (2).

(c) Penalty.—

(1) In general.—

Except as provided in paragraph (2), any person who violates subsection (b) shall be fined under this title, imprisoned for not more than 15 years, or both.

(2) Use in felonies, crimes of terrorism, or drug trafficking crimes.—

If a violation of subsection (b) is committed knowing or with reasonable cause to believe that any firearm involved will be used to commit a felony, a Federal crime of terrorism, or a drug trafficking crime, the person shall be sentenced to a term of imprisonment of not more than 25 years.

18 U.S.C. § 933. Trafficking in firearms

(a) IN GENERAL.—It shall be unlawful for any person to—

(1) ship, transport, transfer, cause to be transported, or otherwise dispose of any firearm to another person in or otherwise affecting interstate or foreign commerce, if such person knows or has reasonable cause to believe that the use, carrying, or possession of a firearm by the recipient would constitute a felony (as defined in section 932(a));

(2) receive from another person any firearm in or otherwise affecting interstate or foreign commerce, if the recipient knows or has reasonable cause to believe that such receipt would constitute a felony; or

(3) attempt or conspire to commit the conduct described in paragraph (1) or (2).

(b) PENALTY.—Any person who violates subsection (a) shall be fined under this title, imprisoned for not more than 15 years, or both.

18 U.S.C. § 934. Forfeiture and fines

(a) FORFEITURE.—

(1) IN GENERAL.—Any person convicted of a violation of section 932 or 933 shall forfeit to the United States, irrespective of any provision of State law—

(A) any property constituting, or derived from, any proceeds the person obtained, directly or indirectly, as the result of such violation; and

(B) any of the person's property used, or intended to be used, in any manner or part, to commit, or to facilitate the commission of, such violation, except that for any forfeiture of any firearm or ammunition pursuant to this section, section 924(d) shall apply.

(2) IMPOSITION.—The court, in imposing sentence on a person convicted of a violation of section 932 or 933, shall order, in addition to any other sentence imposed pursuant to section 932 or 933, that the person forfeit to the United States all property described in paragraph (1).

(b) FINES.—A defendant who derives profits or other proceeds from an offense under section 932 or 933 may be fined not more than the greater of—

(1) the fine otherwise authorized by this part; or

(2) the amount equal to twice the gross profits or other proceeds of the offense under section 932 or 933.

26 U.S.C. § 5802. Registration of importers, manufacturers, and dealers.

On first engaging in business and thereafter on or before the first day of July of each year, each importer, manufacturer, and dealer in firearms shall register with the Secretary in each internal revenue district in which such business is to be carried on, his name, including any trade name, and the address of each location in the district where he will conduct such business. An individual required to register under this section shall include a photograph and fingerprints of the individual with the initial application. Where there is a change during the taxable year in the location of, or the trade name used in, such business, the importer, manufacturer, or dealer shall file an application with the Secretary to amend his registration. Firearms operations of an importer, manufacturer, or dealer may not be commenced at the new location or under a new trade name prior to approval by the Secretary of the application.

26 U.S.C. § 5812. Transfers

(a) Application.--A firearm shall not be transferred unless (1) the transferor of the firearm has filed with the Secretary a written application, in duplicate, for the transfer and registration of the firearm to the transferee on the application form prescribed by the Secretary; (2) any tax payable on the transfer is paid as evidenced by the proper stamp affixed to the original application form; (3) the transferee is identified in the application form in such manner as the Secretary may by regulations prescribe, except that, if such person is an individual, the identification must include his fingerprints and his photograph; (4) the transferor of the firearm is identified in the application form in such manner as the Secretary may by regulations prescribe; (5) the firearm is identified in the application form in such manner as the Secretary may by regulations prescribe; and (6) the application form shows that the Secretary has approved the transfer and the registration of the firearm to the transferee. Applications shall be denied if the transfer, receipt, or possession of the firearm would place the transferee in violation of law.

(b) Transfer of possession.--The transferee of a firearm shall not take possession of the firearm unless the Secretary has approved the transfer and registration of the firearm to the transferee as required by subsection (a) of this section.

26 U.S.C. § 5822. Making.

No person shall make a firearm unless he has (a) filed with the Secretary a written application, in duplicate, to make and register the firearm on the form prescribed by the Secretary; (b) paid any tax payable on the making and such payment is evidenced by the proper stamp affixed to the original application form; (c) identified the firearm to be made in the application form in such manner as the Secretary may by regulations prescribe; (d) identified himself in the application form in such manner as the Secretary may by regulations prescribe, except that, if such person is an individual, the identification must include his fingerprints and his photograph; and (e) obtained the approval of the Secretary to make and register the firearm and the application form shows such approval. Applications shall be denied if the making or possession of the firearm would place the person making the firearm in violation of law.

26 U.S.C § 5841. Registration of firearms.

(a) Central registry.--The Secretary shall maintain a central registry of all firearms in the United States which are not in the possession or under the control of the United States. This registry shall be known as the National Firearms Registration and Transfer Record. The registry shall include--

(1) identification of the firearm;

(2) date of registration; and

(3) identification and address of person entitled to possession of the firearm.

(b) By whom registered.--Each manufacturer, importer, and maker shall register each firearm he manufactures, imports, or makes. Each firearm transferred shall be registered to the transferee by the transferor.

(c) How registered.--Each manufacturer shall notify the Secretary of the manufacture of a firearm in such manner as may by regulations be prescribed and such notification shall effect the registration of the firearm required by this section. Each importer, maker, and transferor of a firearm shall, prior to importing, making, or transferring a firearm, obtain authorization in such manner as required by this chapter or regulations issued thereunder to import, make, or transfer the firearm, and such authorization shall effect the registration of the firearm required by this section.

(d) Firearms registered on effective date of this Act.--A person shown as possessing a firearm by the records maintained by the Secretary pursuant to the National Firearms Act in force on the day immediately prior to the effective date of the National Firearms Act of 1968 shall be considered to have registered under this section the firearms in his possession which are disclosed by that record as being in his possession.

(e) Proof of registration.--A person possessing a firearm registered as required by this section shall retain proof of registration which shall be made available to the Secretary upon request.

ANNOTATIONS:

United States v. Thompson/Center Arms Company, 504 U.S. 505 (1992):

The definition of "make" includes not only "putting together," but also "manufacturing ... Or otherwise producing a firearm." Congress understood "making" to cover more than final assembly - some disassembled aggregation of parts must be included. Since the narrowest example of a combination of parts that might be included is a set of parts that could be used to make nothing but a short-barreled rifle, the aggregation of such a set of parts must fall within the definition of "making" such a rifle.

Definition of "machinegun" found in Gun Control Act, to include any combination of parts from which machinegun could be assembled, and definition of "silencer" under Firearm Owners' Protection Act, to include any combination of parts which could be used for assembling or fabricating silencer, did not establish that Congress, by not including similar reference to component parts in defining "firearm" for purposes of statute imposing tax on making of firearm did not intend for components to be included within definition.

Commentary

The rules concerning how and when one reconfigures a pistol to a rifle through the addition of barrels, stocks, and other parts, and from a rifle to a pistol when one reconfigures the weapon by removal of those components has been the subject of much confusion and misunderstanding. Specifically, ATF was asked to determine whether such a pistol, once returned to a pistol configuration from a rifle, becomes a "weapon made from a rifle" as defined under the National Firearms Act (NFA). In order to clarify their interpretation of the relevant law and regulations, in order to ensure that gun owners and dealers would be better able to understand their legal obligations, the U.S.

Department of Justice, Bureau of Alcohol, Tobacco, Firearms and Explosives (BATFE) published its Ruling 2011-4 (July 25, 2011) which provides as follows:

> *Held,* a firearm, as defined by the National Firearms Act (NFA), 26 U.S.C. 5845(a)(3), is made when unassembled parts are placed in close proximity in such a way that they:
>
> (a) Serve no useful purpose other than to make a rifle having a barrel or barrels of less than 16 inches in length (e.g., a receiver, an attachable shoulder stock, and barrel of less than 16 inches in length); or
>
> (b) Convert a complete weapon into such an NFA firearm, including –
>
> (1) A pistol and attachable shoulder stock; and
>
> (2) A rifle with a barrel of 16 inches or more in length, and an attachable barrel of less than 16 inches in length.
>
> Such weapons must be registered and are subject to all requirements of the NFA.
>
> *Held further,* a firearm, as defined by 26 U.S.C. 5845(a)(3) and (a)(4), is not made when parts in a kit that were originally designed to be configured as both a pistol and a rifle are assembled or re-assembled in a configuration not regulated under the NFA (e.g., as a pistol, or a rifle with a barrel of 16 inches or more in length).
>
> *Held further,* a firearm, as defined by 26 U.S.C. 5845(a)(3) and (a)(4), is not made when a pistol is attached to a part or parts designed to convert the pistol into a rifle with a barrel of 16 inches or more in length, and the parts are later unassembled in a configuration not regulated under the NFA (e.g., as a pistol).
>
> *Held further,* a firearm, as defined by 26 U.S.C. 5845(a)(4), is made when a handgun or other weapon with an overall length of less than 26 inches, or a barrel or barrels of less than 16 inches in length, is assembled or produced from a weapon originally assembled or produced only as a rifle. Such weapons must be registered and are subject to all requirements of the NFA.
>
> To the extent this ruling may be inconsistent with any prior letter rulings, they are hereby superseded.

Therefore, so long as a parts kit or collection of parts is not used to make a firearm regulated under the NFA (e.g., a short-barreled rifle or "any other weapon" as defined by 26 U.S.C. 5845(e)), no NFA firearm is made when the same parts are assembled or re-assembled in a configuration not regulated under the NFA (e.g., a pistol, or a rifle with a barrel of 16 inches or more in length). Merely assembling and disassembling such a rifle does not result in the making of a new weapon; rather, it is the same rifle in a knockdown condition (i.e., complete as to all component parts). Likewise, because it is the same weapon when reconfigured as a pistol, no "weapon made from a rifle" subject to the NFA has been made.

Nonetheless, if a handgun or other weapon with an overall length of less than 26 inches, or a barrel or barrels of less than 16 inches in length is assembled or otherwise produced from a weapon originally assembled or produced only as a rifle, such a weapon is a "weapon made from a rifle" as defined by 26 U.S.C. 5845(a)(4). Such a weapon would not be a "pistol" because the weapon was not originally designed, made, and intended to fire a projectile by one hand. Id., ATF Ruling 2011-4, available online at https://www.atf.gov/files/regulations-rulings/rulings/atf-rulings/atf-ruling-2011-4.pdf.

Similarly, the BATFE has long held that by installing a vertical fore grip on a handgun, the handgun is no longer designed to be held and fired by the use of a single hand. Therefore, if individuals install a vertical fore grip on a handgun, they are "making" a firearm requiring registration with ATF's NFA branch. Making an unregistered "All Other Weapons" (AOW) is punishable by a fine and ten (10) years imprisonment. See "Adding a Vertical Fore Grip to A Handgun, U.S. Department of Justice, Bureau of Alcohol, Tobacco, Firearms and Explosives Memorandum dated May 4, 2006 (Washington, D.C.), available online at https://www.atf.gov/press/releases/2006/04/041006-openletter-nfa-adding-vertical-fore-grip.html.

To lawfully add a vertical fore grip to a handgun, a person must make an appropriate application on ATF Form 1, "Application to Make and Register a Firearm." The applicant must submit the completed form, along with a fingerprint card bearing the applicant's fingerprints; a photograph; and $200.00. The application will be reviewed by the NFA Branch. If the applicant is not prohibited from possessing a firearm under Federal, State, or local law, and possession of an "AOW" is not prohibited in the applicant's State of residence, the form will be approved. Only then may the person add a vertical fore grip to the designated handgun. See Title 26 U.S.C. §§ 5821-5822.

26 U.S.C. § 5842. Identification of firearms

(a) Identification of firearms other than destructive devices.--Each manufacturer and importer and anyone making a firearm shall identify each firearm, other than a destructive device, manufactured, imported, or made by a serial number which may not be readily removed, obliterated, or altered, the name of the manufacturer, importer, or maker, and such other identification as the Secretary may by regulations prescribe.

(b) Firearms without serial number.--Any person who possesses a firearm, other than a destructive device, which does not bear the serial number and other information required by subsection (a) of this section shall identify the firearm with a serial number assigned by the Secretary and any other information the Secretary may by regulations prescribe.

(c) Identification of destructive device.--Any firearm classified as a destructive device shall be identified in such manner as the Secretary may by regulations prescribe.

26 U.S.C. § 5843. Records and returns.

Importers, manufacturers, and dealers shall keep such records of, and render such returns in relation to, the importation, manufacture, making, receipt, and sale, or other disposition, of firearms as the Secretary may by regulations prescribe.

26 U.S.C. § 5844. Importation.

No firearm shall be imported or brought into the United States or any territory under its control or jurisdiction unless the importer establishes, under regulations as may be prescribed by the Secretary, that the firearm to be imported or brought in is--

(1) being imported or brought in for the use of the United States or any department, independent establishment, or agency thereof or any State or possession or any political subdivision thereof; or

(2) being imported or brought in for scientific or research purposes; or

(3) being imported or brought in solely for testing or use as a model by a registered manufacturer or solely for use as a sample by a registered importer or registered dealer;

Except that, the Secretary may permit the conditional importation or bringing in of a firearm for examination and testing in connection with classifying the firearm.

26 U.S.C. § 5845. Definitions.

For the purpose of this chapter—

(a) Firearm.--The term "firearm" means (1) a shotgun having a barrel or barrels of less than 18 inches in length; (2) a weapon made from a shotgun if such weapon as modified has an overall length of less than 26 inches or a barrel or barrels of less than 18 inches in length; (3) a rifle having a barrel or barrels of less than 16 inches in length; (4) a weapon made from a rifle if such weapon as modified has an overall length of less than 26 inches or a barrel or barrels of less than 16 inches in length; (5) any other weapon, as defined in subsection (e); (6) a machinegun; (7) any silencer (as defined in section 921 of Title 18, United States Code); and (8) a destructive device. The term "firearm" shall not include an antique firearm or any device (other than a machinegun or destructive device) which, although designed as a weapon, the Secretary finds by reason of the date of its manufacture, value, design, and other characteristics is primarily a collector's item and is not likely to be used as a weapon.

(b) Machinegun.--The term "machinegun" means any weapon which shoots, is designed to shoot, or can be readily restored to shoot, automatically more than one shot, without manual reloading, by a single function of the trigger. The term shall also include the frame or receiver of any such weapon, any part designed and intended solely and exclusively, or combination of parts designed and intended, for use in converting a weapon into a machinegun, and any combination of parts from which a machinegun can be assembled if such parts are in the possession or under the control of a person.

(c) Rifle.--The term "rifle" means a weapon designed or redesigned, made or remade, and intended to be fired from the shoulder and designed or redesigned and made or remade to use the energy of the explosive in a fixed cartridge to fire only a single projectile through a rifled bore for each single pull of the trigger, and shall include any such weapon which may be readily restored to fire a fixed cartridge.

(d) Shotgun.--The term "shotgun" means a weapon designed or redesigned, made or remade, and intended to be fired from the shoulder and designed or redesigned and made or remade to use the energy of the explosive in a fixed shotgun shell to fire through a smooth bore either a number of projectiles (ball shot) or a single projectile for each pull of the trigger, and shall include any such weapon which may be readily restored to fire a fixed shotgun shell.

(e) Any other weapon.--The term "any other weapon" means any weapon or device capable of being concealed on the person from which a shot can be discharged through the energy of an explosive, a pistol or revolver having a barrel with a smooth bore designed or redesigned to fire a fixed shotgun shell, weapons with combination shotgun and rifle barrels 12 inches or more, less than 18 inches in length, from which only a single discharge can be made from either barrel without manual reloading, and shall include any such weapon which may be readily restored to fire. Such term shall not include a pistol or a revolver having a rifled bore, or rifled bores, or weapons designed, made, or intended to be fired from the shoulder and not capable of firing fixed ammunition.

(f) Destructive device.--The term "destructive device" means (1) any explosive, incendiary, or poison gas (A) bomb, (B) grenade, (C) rocket having a propellant charge of more than four ounces, (D) missile having an explosive or incendiary charge of more than one-quarter ounce, (E) mine, or (F) similar device; (2) any type of weapon by whatever name known which will, or which may be readily converted to, expel a projectile by the action of an explosive or other propellant, the barrel or barrels of which have a bore of more than one-half inch in diameter, except a shotgun or shotgun shell which the Secretary finds is generally recognized as particularly suitable for sporting purposes; and (3) any combination of parts either designed or intended for use in converting any device into a destructive device as defined in subparagraphs (1) and (2) and from which a destructive device may be readily assembled. The term "destructive device" shall not include any device which is neither designed nor redesigned for use as a weapon; any device, although originally designed for use as a weapon, which is redesigned for use as a signaling, pyrotechnic, line throwing, safety, or similar device; surplus ordnance sold, loaned, or given by the Secretary of the Army pursuant to the provisions of section 4684(2), 4685, or 4686 of Title 10 of the United States Code; or any other device which the Secretary finds is not likely to be used as a weapon, or is an antique or is a rifle which the owner intends to use solely for sporting purposes.

(g) Antique firearm.--The term "antique firearm" means any firearm not designed or redesigned for using rim fire or conventional center fire ignition with fixed ammunition and manufactured in or before 1898 (including any matchlock, flintlock, percussion cap, or similar type of ignition system or replica thereof, whether actually manufactured before or after the year 1898) and also any firearm using fixed ammunition manufactured in or before 1898, for which ammunition is no longer manufactured in the United States and is not readily available in the ordinary channels of commercial trade.

(h) Unserviceable firearm.--The term "unserviceable firearm" means a firearm which is incapable of discharging a shot by means of an explosive and incapable of being readily restored to a firing condition.

(i) Make.--The term "make", and the various derivatives of such word, shall include manufacturing (other than by one qualified to engage in such business under this chapter), putting together, altering, any combination of these, or otherwise producing a firearm.

(j) Transfer.--The term "transfer" and the various derivatives of such word, shall include selling, assigning, pledging, leasing, loaning, giving away, or otherwise disposing of.

(k) Dealer.--The term "dealer" means any person, not a manufacturer or importer, engaged in the business of selling, renting, leasing, or loaning firearms and shall include pawnbrokers who accept firearms as collateral for loans.

(l) Importer.--The term "importer" means any person who is engaged in the business of importing or bringing firearms into the United States.

(m) Manufacturer.--The term "manufacturer" means any person who is engaged in the business of manufacturing firearms.

26 U.S.C. § 5849. Citation of chapter.

This chapter may be cited as the "National Firearms Act" and any reference in any other provision of law to the "National Firearms Act" shall be held to refer to the provisions of this chapter.

26 U.S.C. § 5861. Prohibited acts.

It shall be unlawful for any person--

(a) to engage in business as a manufacturer or importer of, or dealer in, firearms without having paid the special (occupational) tax required by section 5801 for his business or having registered as required by section 5802; or

(b) to receive or possess a firearm transferred to him in violation of the provisions of this chapter; or

(c) to receive or possess a firearm made in violation of the provisions of this chapter; or

(d) to receive or possess a firearm which is not registered to him in the National Firearms Registration and Transfer Record; or

(e) to transfer a firearm in violation of the provisions of this chapter; or

(f) to make a firearm in violation of the provisions of this chapter; or

(g) to obliterate, remove, change, or alter the serial number or other identification of a firearm required by this chapter; or

(h) to receive or possess a firearm having the serial number or other identification required by this chapter obliterated, removed, changed, or altered; or

(i) to receive or possess a firearm which is not identified by a serial number as required by this chapter; or

(j) to transport, deliver, or receive any firearm in interstate commerce which has not been registered as required by this chapter; or

(k) to receive or possess a firearm which has been imported or brought into the United States in violation of section 5844; or

(l) to make, or cause the making of, a false entry on any application, return, or record required by this chapter, knowing such entry to be false.

ANNOTATIONS:

U.S. v. Lim, 444 F.3d 910 (7th Cir. 2006), *certiorari denied,* 127 S.Ct. 239, 549 U.S. 908, 166 L.Ed.2d 189:

Provision of National Firearms Act, prohibiting the possession of an unregistered firearm, was legitimate exercise of Congress's taxation power; other provisions of the Act required payment of transfer tax and registration of the firearm by the transferor, and attaching criminal consequences to possession of unregistered firearm was rational way of discouraging the transfer of untaxed firearms, and aiding the enforcement of the transfer tax.

U.S. v. Wright, 117 F.3d 1265 (11th Cir. 1997), *certiorari denied,* 118 S.Ct. 584, 522 U.S. 1007, 139 L.Ed.2d 422, *opinion vacated in part on rehearing,* 133 F.3d 1412, *certiorari denied,* 119 S.Ct. 217, 525 U.S. 894, 142 L.Ed.2d 178:

Statutes criminalizing possession of machineguns and possession of unregistered destructive devices did not violate defendant's right to bear arms under Second Amendment, notwithstanding defendant's membership in state's unorganized militia, absent showing of reasonable relationship between such possession and preservation or efficiency of well-regulated militia that was actively maintained by state and used for common defense.

U.S. v. Warin, 530 F.2d 103 (6th Cir. 1976), *certiorari denied,* 96 S.Ct. 3168, 426 U.S. 948, 49 L.Ed.2d 1185:

Requirement of this section that no one may possess a submachine gun which is not registered to him in the National Firearms Registration and Transfer Record is a reasonable regulation for the maintenance of public order.

U.S. v. Williams, 446 F.2d 486 (5th Cir. 1971):

This section and § 5871 of this title proscribing offense of and penalty for possession of an unregistered firearm are not violative of right to bear arms as guaranteed by Second Amendment.

26 U.S.C. § 5871. Penalties.

Any person who violates or fails to comply with any provision of this chapter shall, upon conviction, be fined not more than $10,000, or be imprisoned not more than ten years, or both.

26 U.S.C. § 5872. Forfeitures.

(a) Laws applicable.--Any firearm involved in any violation of the provisions of this chapter shall be subject to seizure and forfeiture, and (except as provided in subsection (b)) all the provisions of internal revenue laws relating to searches, seizures, and forfeitures of unstamped articles are extended to and made to apply to the articles taxed under this chapter, and the persons to whom this chapter applies.

(b) Disposal.--In the case of the forfeiture of any firearm by reason of a violation of this chapter, no notice of public sale shall be required; no such firearm shall be sold at public sale; if such firearm is forfeited for a violation of this chapter and there is no remission or mitigation of forfeiture thereof, it shall be delivered by the Secretary to the Administrator of General Services, General Services Administration, who may order such firearm destroyed or may sell it to any State, or possession, or political subdivision thereof, or at the request of the Secretary, may authorize its retention for official use of the Treasury Department, or may transfer it without charge to any executive department or independent establishment of the Government for use by it.

28 U.S.C. § 534. Acquisition, preservation, and exchange of identification records and information; appointment of officials.

(a) The Attorney General shall—

(1) acquire, collect, classify, and preserve identification, criminal identification, crime, and other records;

(2) acquire, collect, classify, and preserve any information which would assist in the identification of any deceased individual who has not been identified after the discovery of such deceased individual;

(3) acquire, collect, classify, and preserve any information which would assist in the location of any missing person (including an unemancipated person as defined by the laws of the place of residence of such person) and provide confirmation as to any entry for such a person to the parent, legal guardian, or next of kin of that person (and the Attorney General may acquire, collect, classify, and preserve such information from such parent, guardian, or next of kin);

(4) exchange such records and information with, and for the official use of, authorized officials of the Federal Government, including the United States Sentencing Commission, the States, including State sentencing commissions, Indian tribes, cities, and penal and other institutions; and

(5) provide a person licensed as an importer, manufacturer, or dealer of firearms under chapter 44 of title 18 with information necessary to verify whether firearms offered for sale to such licensees have been stolen.

(b) The exchange of records and information authorized by subsection (a)(4) of this section is subject to cancellation if dissemination is made outside the receiving departments or related agencies, except for dissemination authorized under subsection (a)(5) of this section.

(c) The Attorney General may appoint officials to perform the functions authorized by this section.

(d) Indian Law Enforcement Agencies.—

(1) In general.—The Attorney General shall permit tribal and Bureau of Indian Affairs law enforcement agencies—

(A) to access and enter information into Federal criminal information databases; and

(B) to obtain information from the databases.

(2) Tribal Access Program.—

(A) In general.—

The Attorney General shall establish a program, to be known as the "Tribal Access Program", to enhance the ability of tribal governments and their authorized agencies to access, enter information into, and obtain information from national criminal information databases under this section.

(B) Authorization of appropriations.—

There is authorized to be appropriated to carry out the Tribal Access Program under subparagraph (A) $6,000,000 for each of fiscal years 2023 through 2027, to remain available until expended.

(3) Information sharing.—

To the extent otherwise permitted by law, any report issued as a result of the analysis of information entered into national criminal information databases or obtained from Federal criminal databases shall be shared with each Indian tribe of jurisdiction, including Indian tribes located in the State of Maine.

(e) For purposes of this section, the term "other institutions" includes—

(1) railroad police departments which perform the administration of criminal justice and have arrest powers pursuant to a State statute, which allocate a substantial part of their annual budget to the administration of criminal justice, and which meet training requirements established by law or ordinance for law enforcement officers; and

(2) police departments of private colleges or universities which perform the administration of criminal justice and have arrest powers pursuant to a State statute, which allocate a substantial part of their annual budget to the administration of criminal justice, and which meet training requirements established by law or ordinance for law enforcement officers.

(f)(1) Information from national crime information databases consisting of identification records, criminal history records, protection orders, and wanted person records may be disseminated to civil or criminal courts for use in domestic violence or stalking cases. Nothing in this subsection shall be construed to permit access to such records for any other purpose.

(2) Federal, tribal, and State criminal justice agencies authorized to enter information into criminal information databases may include—

(A) arrests, convictions, and arrest warrants for stalking or domestic violence or for violations of protection orders for the protection of parties from stalking or domestic violence; and

(B) protection orders for the protection of persons from stalking or domestic violence, provided such orders are subject to periodic verification.

(3) As used in this subsection—

(A) the term "national crime information databases" means the National Crime Information Center and its incorporated criminal history databases, including the Interstate Identification Index; and

(B) the term "protection order" includes—

(i) any injunction, restraining order, or any other order issued by a civil or criminal court for the purpose of preventing violent or threatening acts or harassment against, sexual violence or contact or communication with or physical proximity to, another person, including any temporary or final orders issued by civil or criminal courts whether obtained by filing an independent action or as a pendente lite order in another proceeding so long as any civil order was issued in response to a complaint, petition, or motion filed by or on behalf of a person seeking protection; and

(ii) any support, child custody or visitation provisions, orders, remedies, or relief issued as part of a protection order, restraining order, or stay away injunction pursuant to State, tribal, territorial, or local law authorizing the issuance of protection orders, restraining orders, or injunctions for the protection of victims of domestic violence, dating violence, sexual assault, or stalking.

Federal Regulations

Title 27, Code of Federal Regulations, Chapter 1, Subchapter C

27 C.F.R. § 53.11. Meaning of terms.

When used in this part and in forms prescribed under this part, where not otherwise distinctly expressed or manifestly incompatible with the intent thereof, terms shall have the meanings ascribed in this section. Words in the plural form shall include the singular, and vice versa, and words importing the masculine gender shall include the feminine. The terms "includes" and "including" do not exclude other things not enumerated which are in the same general class or are otherwise within the scope thereof.

Appropriate TTB officer. An officer or employee of the Alcohol and Tobacco Tax and Trade Bureau (TTB) authorized to perform any functions relating to the administration or enforcement of this part by TTB Order 1135.53, Delegation of the Administrator's Authorities in 27 CFR Part 53, Manufacturers Excise Taxes--Firearms and Ammunition . . . .

Firearms. Any portable weapons, such as rifles, carbines, machine guns, shotguns, or fowling pieces, from which a shot, bullet, or other projectile may be discharged by an explosive.

Importer. Any person who brings a taxable article into the United States from a source outside the United States, or who withdraws such an article from a customs bonded warehouse for sale or use in the United States. If the nominal importer of a taxable article is not its beneficial owner (for example, the nominal importer is a customs broker engaged by the beneficial owner), the beneficial owner is the "importer" of the article for purposes of chapter 32 of the Code and is liable for tax on his sale or use of the article in the United States. See section 4219 of the Code and 27 CFR 53.121 for the circumstances under which sales by persons other than the manufacturer or importer are subject to the manufacturers excise tax.

Knockdown condition. A taxable article that is unassembled but complete as to all component parts.

Manufacturer. Includes any person who produces a taxable article from scrap, salvage, or junk material, or from new or raw material, by processing, manipulating, or changing the form of an article or by combining or assembling two or more articles. The term also includes a "producer" and an "importer." Under certain circumstances, as where a person manufactures or produces a taxable article for another person who furnishes materials under an agreement whereby the person who furnished the materials retains title thereto and to the finished article, the person for whom the taxable article is manufactured or produced, and not the person who actually manufactures or produces it, will be considered the manufacturer.

A manufacturer who sells a taxable article in a knockdown condition is liable for the tax as a manufacturer. Whether the person who buys such component parts or accessories and assembles a taxable article from them will be liable for tax as a manufacturer of a taxable article will depend on the relative amount of labor, material, and overhead required to assemble the completed article and on whether the article is assembled for business or personal use.

Person. An individual, trust, estate, partnership, association, company, or corporation. When used in connection with penalties, seizures, and forfeitures, the term includes an officer or employee of a partnership, who as an officer, employee or member, is under a duty to perform the act in respect of which the violation occurs.

Pistols. Small projectile firearms which have a short one-hand stock or butt at an angle to the line of bore and a short barrel or barrels, and which are designed, made, and intended to be aimed and fired from one hand. The term does not include gadget devices, guns altered or converted to resemble pistols, or small portable guns erroneously referred to as pistols, as, for example, Nazi belt buckle pistols, glove pistols, or one-hand stock guns firing fixed shotgun or fixed rifle ammunition . . . .

Purchaser. Includes a lessee where the lessor is also the manufacturer of the article.

Revolvers. Small projectile firearms of the pistol type, having a breech-loading chambered cylinder so arranged that the cocking of the hammer or movement of the trigger rotates it and brings the next cartridge in line with the barrel for firing.

Sale. An agreement whereby the seller transfers the property (that is, the title or the substantial incidents of ownership in goods) to the buyer for a consideration called the price, which may consist of money, services, or other things . . . .

Shells and cartridges. Include any article consisting of a projectile, explosive, and container that is designed, assembled, and ready for use without further manufacture in firearms, pistols or revolvers. A person who reloads used shell or cartridge casings is a manufacturer of shells or cartridges within the meaning of section 4181 if such reloaded shells or cartridges are sold by the reloader. However, the reloader is not a manufacturer of shells or cartridges if, in return for a fee and expenses, he reloads casings of shells or cartridges submitted by a customer and returns the reloaded shells or cartridges with the identical casings provided by the customer to that customer. Under such circumstances, the customer would be the manufacturer of the shells or cartridges and may be liable for tax on the sale of articles. See section 4218 of the Code and § 53.112 . . . .

Title 27, Code of Federal Regulations, Chapter 2, Subchapter B, Part 478.

Subpart A – Definitions.

27 C.F.R. § 478.11. Meaning of terms.

When used in this part and in forms prescribed under this part, where not otherwise distinctly expressed or manifestly incompatible with the intent thereof, terms shall have the meanings ascribed in this section. Words in the plural form shall include the singular, and vice versa, and words importing the masculine gender shall include the feminine. The terms "includes" and "including" do not exclude other things not enumerated which are in the same general class or are otherwise within the scope thereof.

Act. 18 U.S.C. Chapter 44.

Adjudicated as a mental defective. (a) A determination by a court, board, commission, or other lawful authority that a person, as a result of marked subnormal intelligence, or mental illness, incompetency, condition, or disease:

(1) Is a danger to himself or to others; or

(2) Lacks the mental capacity to contract or manage his own affairs.

(b) The term shall include—

(1) A finding of insanity by a court in a criminal case; and

(2) Those persons found incompetent to stand trial or found not guilty by reason of lack of mental responsibility pursuant to articles 50a and 72b of the Uniform Code of Military Justice, 10 U.S.C. 850a, 876b.

Alien. Any person not a citizen or national of the United States.

Alien illegally or unlawfully in the United States. Aliens who are unlawfully in the United States are not in valid immigrant, nonimmigrant or parole status. The term includes any alien—

(a) Who unlawfully entered the United States without inspection and authorization by an immigration officer and who has not been paroled into the United States under section 212(d)(5) of the Immigration and Nationality Act (INA);

(b) Who is a nonimmigrant and whose authorized period of stay has expired or who has violated the terms of the nonimmigrant category in which he or she was admitted;

(c) Paroled under INA section 212(d)(5) whose authorized period of parole has expired or whose parole status has been terminated; or

(d) Under an order of deportation, exclusion, or removal, or under an order to depart the United States voluntarily, whether or not he or she has left the United States.

Ammunition. Ammunition or cartridge cases, primers, bullets, or propellent powder designed for use in any firearm other than an antique firearm. The term shall not include (a) any shotgun shot or pellet not designed for use as the single, complete projectile load for one shotgun hull or casing, nor (b) any unloaded, non-metallic shotgun hull or casing not having a primer.

Antique firearm. (a) Any firearm (including any firearm with a matchlock, flintlock, percussion cap, or similar type of ignition system) manufactured in or before 1898; and (b) any replica of any firearm described in paragraph (a) of this definition if such replica (1) is not designed or redesigned for using rimfire or conventional centerfire fixed ammunition, or (2) uses rimfire or conventional centerfire fixed ammunition which is no longer manufactured in the United States and which is not readily available in the ordinary channels of commercial trade.

Armor piercing ammunition. Projectiles or projectile cores which may be used in a handgun and which are constructed entirely (excluding the presence of traces of other substances) from one or a combination of tungsten alloys, steel, iron, brass, bronze, beryllium copper, or depleted uranium; or full jacketed projectiles larger than .22 caliber designed and intended for use in a handgun and whose jacket has a weight of more than 25 percent of the total weight of the projectile. The term does not include shotgun shot required by Federal or State environmental or game regulations for hunting purposes, frangible projectiles designed for target shooting, projectiles which the Director finds are primarily intended to be used for sporting purposes, or any other projectiles or projectile cores which the Director finds are intended to be used for industrial purposes, including charges used in oil and gas well perforating devices.

Collector. Any person who acquires, holds, or disposes of firearms as curios or relics.

Collection premises. The premises described on the license of a collector as the location at which he maintains his collection of curios and relics.

Committed to a mental institution. A formal commitment of a person to a mental institution by a court, board, commission, or other lawful authority. The term includes a commitment to a mental institution involuntarily. The term includes commitment for mental defectiveness or mental illness. It also includes commitments for other reasons, such as for drug use. The term does not include a person in a mental institution for observation or a voluntary admission to a mental institution.

Controlled substance. A drug or other substance, or immediate precursor, as defined in section 102 of the Controlled Substances Act, 21 U.S.C. 802. The term includes, but is not limited to, marijuana, depressants, stimulants, and narcotic drugs. The term does not include distilled spirits, wine, malt beverages, or tobacco, as those terms are defined or used in Subtitle E of the Internal Revenue Code of 1986, as amended.

Crime punishable by imprisonment for a term exceeding 1 year. Any Federal, State or foreign offense for which the maximum penalty, whether or not imposed, is capital punishment or imprisonment in excess of 1 year. The term shall not include (a) any Federal or State offenses pertaining to antitrust violations, unfair trade practices, restraints of trade, or other similar offenses relating to the regulation of business practices or (b) any State offense classified by the laws of the State as a misdemeanor and punishable by a term of imprisonment of 2 years or less. What constitutes a conviction of such a crime shall be determined in accordance with the law of the jurisdiction in which the proceedings were held. Any conviction which has been expunged or set aside or for which a person has been pardoned or has had civil rights restored shall not be considered a conviction for the purposes of the Act or this part, unless such pardon, expunction, or restoration of civil rights expressly provides that the person may not ship, transport, possess, or receive firearms, or unless the person is prohibited by the law of the jurisdiction in which the proceedings were held from receiving or possessing any firearms.

Curios or relics. Firearms which are of special interest to collectors by reason of some quality other than is associated with firearms intended for sporting use or as offensive or defensive weapons. To be recognized as curios or relics, firearms must fall within one of the following categories:

(a) Firearms which were manufactured at least 50 years prior to the current date, but not including replicas thereof;

(b) Firearms which are certified by the curator of a municipal, State, or Federal museum which exhibits firearms to be curios or relics of museum interest; and

(c) Any other firearms which derive a substantial part of their monetary value from the fact that they are novel, rare, bizarre, or because of their association with some historical figure, period, or event. Proof of qualification of a particular firearm under this category may be established by evidence of present value and evidence that like firearms are not available except as collector's items, or that the value of like firearms available in ordinary commercial channels is substantially less.

Dealer. Any person engaged in the business of selling firearms at wholesale or retail; any person engaged in the business of repairing firearms or of making or fitting special barrels, stocks, or trigger mechanisms to firearms; or any person who is a pawnbroker. The term shall include any person who engages in such business or occupation on a part-time basis.

Destructive device. (a) Any explosive, incendiary, or poison gas (1) bomb, (2) grenade, (3) rocket having a propellant charge of more than 4 ounces, (4) missile having an explosive or incendiary charge of more than one-quarter ounce, (5) mine, or (6) device similar to any of the devices described in the preceding paragraphs of this definition; (b) any type of weapon (other than a shotgun or a shotgun shell which the Director finds is generally recognized as particularly suitable for sporting purposes) by whatever name known which will, or which may be readily converted to, expel a projectile by the action of an explosive or other propellant, and which has any barrel with a bore of more than one-half inch in diameter; and (c) any combination of parts either designed or intended for use in converting any device into any destructive device described in paragraph (a) or (b) of this section and from which a destructive device may be readily assembled. The term shall not include any device which is neither designed nor redesigned for use as a weapon; any device, although originally designed for use as a weapon, which is redesigned for use as a signaling, pyrotechnic, line throwing, safety, or similar device; surplus ordnance sold, loaned, or given by the Secretary of the Army pursuant to the provisions of section 4684(2), 4685, or 4686 of title 10, United States Code; or any other device which the Director finds is not likely to be used as a weapon, is an antique, or is a rifle which the owner intends to use solely for sporting, recreational, or cultural purposes.

Director. The Director, Bureau of Alcohol, Tobacco and Firearms, the Department of the Treasury, Washington, DC.

Discharged under dishonorable conditions. Separation from the U.S. Armed Forces resulting from a dishonorable discharge or dismissal adjudged by a general court-martial. The term does not include any separation from the Armed Forces resulting from any other discharge, e.g., a bad conduct discharge.

Engaged in the business—

(a) Manufacturer of firearms. A person who devotes time, attention, and labor to manufacturing firearms as a regular course of trade or business with the principal objective of livelihood and profit through the sale or distribution of the firearms manufactured;

(b) Manufacturer of ammunition. A person who devotes time, attention, and labor to manufacturing ammunition as a regular course of trade or business with the principal objective of livelihood and profit through the sale or distribution of the ammunition manufactured;

(c) Dealer in firearms other than a gunsmith or a pawnbroker. A person who devotes time, attention, and labor to dealing in firearms as a regular course of trade or business with the principal objective of livelihood and profit through the repetitive purchase and resale of firearms, but such a term shall not include a person who makes occasional sales, exchanges, or purchases of firearms for the enhancement of a personal collection or for a hobby, or who sells all or part of his personal collection of firearms;

(d) Gunsmith. A person who devotes time, attention, and labor to engaging in such activity as a regular course of trade or business with the principal objective of livelihood and profit, but such a term shall not include a person who makes occasional repairs of firearms or who occasionally fits special barrels, stocks, or trigger mechanisms to firearms;

(e) Importer of firearms. A person who devotes time, attention, and labor to importing firearms as a regular course of trade or business with the principal objective of livelihood and profit through the sale or distribution of the firearms imported; and,

(f) Importer of ammunition. A person who devotes time, attention, and labor to importing ammunition as a regular course of trade or business with the principal objective of livelihood and profit through the sale or distribution of the ammunition imported.

Executed under penalties of perjury. Signed with the prescribed declaration under the penalties of perjury as provided on or with respect to the return form, or other document or, where no form of declaration is prescribed, with the declaration:

"I declare under the penalties of perjury that this--(insert type of document, such as, statement, application, request, certificate), including the documents submitted in support thereof, has been examined by me and, to the best of my knowledge and belief, is true, correct, and complete."

Federal Firearms Act. 15 U.S.C. Chapter 18.

Firearm. Any weapon, including a starter gun, which will or is designed to or may readily be converted to expel a projectile by the action of an explosive; the frame or receiver of any such weapon; any firearm muffler or firearm silencer; or any destructive device; but the term shall not include an antique firearm. In the case of a licensed collector, the term shall mean only curios and relics.

Firearm frame or receiver. That part of a firearm which provides housing for the hammer, bolt or breechblock, and firing mechanism, and which is usually threaded at its forward portion to receive the barrel.

Firearm muffler or firearm silencer. Any device for silencing, muffling, or diminishing the report of a portable firearm, including any combination of parts, designed or redesigned, and intended for use in assembling or fabricating a firearm silencer or firearm muffler, and any part intended only for use in such assembly or fabrication.

Fugitive from justice. Any person who has fled from any State to avoid prosecution for a felony or a misdemeanor; or any person who leaves the State to avoid giving testimony in any criminal proceeding. The term also includes any person who knows that misdemeanor or felony charges are pending against such person and who leaves the State of prosecution.

Handgun. (a) Any firearm which has a short stock and is designed to be held and fired by the use of a single hand; and

(b) Any combination of parts from which a firearm described in paragraph (a) can be assembled.

Hunting license or permit lawfully issued in the United States. A license or permit issued by a State for hunting which is valid and unexpired.

Identification document. A document containing the name, residence address, date of birth, and photograph of the holder and which was made or issued by or under the authority of the United States Government, a State, political subdivision of a State, a foreign government, political subdivision of a foreign government, an international governmental or an international quasi- governmental organization which, when completed with information concerning a particular individual, is of a type intended or commonly accepted for the purpose of identification of individuals.

Indictment. Includes an indictment or information in any court, under which a crime punishable by imprisonment for a term exceeding 1 year (as defined in this section) may be prosecuted, or in military cases to any offense punishable by imprisonment for a term exceeding 1 year which has been referred to a general court-martial. An information is a formal accusation of a crime, differing from an indictment in that it is made by a prosecuting attorney and not a grand jury.

Interstate or foreign commerce. Includes commerce between any place in a State and any place outside of that State, or within any possession of the United States (not including the Canal Zone) or the District of Columbia. The term shall not include commerce between places within the same State but through any place outside of that State.

Intimate partner. With respect to a person, the spouse of the person, a former spouse of the person, an individual who is a parent of a child of the person, and an individual who cohabitates or has cohabitated with the person.

Large capacity ammunition feeding device. A magazine, belt, drum, feed strip, or similar device for a firearm manufactured after September 13, 1994, that has a capacity of, or that can be readily restored or converted to accept, more than 10 rounds of ammunition. The term does not include an attached tubular device designed to accept, and capable of operating only with, .22 caliber rimfire ammunition, or a fixed device for a manually operated firearm, or a fixed device for a firearm listed in 18 U.S.C. 922, appendix A.

Licensed collector. A collector of curios and relics only and licensed under the provisions of this part.

Licensed dealer. A dealer licensed under the provisions of this part.

Licensed importer. An importer licensed under the provisions of this part.

Licensed manufacturer. A manufacturer licensed under the provisions of this part.

Machine gun. Any weapon which shoots, is designed to shoot, or can be readily restored to shoot, automatically more than one shot, without manual reloading, by a single function of the trigger. The term shall also include the frame or receiver of any such weapon, any part designed and intended solely and exclusively, or combination of parts designed and intended, for use in converting a weapon into a machine gun, and any combination of parts from which a machine gun can be assembled if such parts are in the possession or under the control of a person.

Manufacturer. Any person engaged in the business of manufacturing firearms or ammunition. The term shall include any person who engages in such business on a part-time basis.

Mental institution. Includes mental health facilities, mental hospitals, sanitariums, psychiatric facilities, and other facilities that provide diagnoses by licensed professionals of mental retardation or mental illness, including a psychiatric ward in a general hospital.

Misdemeanor crime of domestic violence. (a) Is a Federal, State or local offense that:

(1) Is a misdemeanor under Federal or State law or, in States which do not classify offenses as misdemeanors, is an offense punishable by imprisonment for a term of one year or less, and includes offenses that are punishable only by a fine. (This is true whether or not the State statute specifically defines the offense as a "misdemeanor" or as a "misdemeanor crime of domestic violence." The term includes all such misdemeanor convictions in Indian Courts established pursuant to 25 CFR part 11.);

(2) Has, as an element, the use or attempted use of physical force (e.g., assault and battery), or the threatened use of a deadly weapon; and

(3) Was committed by a current or former spouse, parent, or guardian of the victim, by a person with whom the victim shares a child in common, by a person who is cohabiting with or has cohabited with the victim as a spouse, parent, or guardian, (e.g., the equivalent of a "common law" marriage even if such relationship is not recognized under the law), or a person similarly situated to a spouse, parent, or guardian of the victim (e.g., two persons who are residing at the same location in an intimate relationship with the intent to make that place their home would be similarly situated to a spouse)

(b) A person shall not be considered to have been convicted of such an offense for purposes of this part unless:

(1) The person is considered to have been convicted by the jurisdiction in which the proceedings were held.

(2) The person was represented by counsel in the case, or knowingly and intelligently waived the right to counsel in the case; and

(3) In the case of a prosecution for which a person was entitled to a jury trial in the jurisdiction in which the case was tried, either

(i) The case was tried by a jury, or

(ii) The person knowingly and intelligently waived the right to have the case tried by a jury, by guilty plea or otherwise.

(c) A person shall not be considered to have been convicted of such an offense for purposes of this part if the conviction has been expunged or set aside, or is an offense for which the person has been pardoned or has had civil rights restored (if the law of the jurisdiction in which the proceedings were held provides for the loss of civil rights upon conviction for such an offense) unless the pardon, expunction, or restoration of civil rights expressly provides that the person may not ship, transport, possess, or receive firearms, and the person is not otherwise prohibited by the law of the jurisdiction in which the proceedings were held from receiving or possessing any firearms.

National Firearms Act. 26 U.S.C. Chapter 53.

NICS. The National Instant Criminal Background Check System established by the Attorney General pursuant to 18 U.S.C. 922(t).

Nonimmigrant alien. An alien in the United States in a nonimmigrant classification as defined by section 101(a)(15) of the Immigration and Nationality Act (8 U.S.C. 1101(a)(15)).

Nonimmigrant visa. A visa properly issued to an alien as an eligible nonimmigrant by a competent officer as provided in the Immigration and Nationality Act, 8 U.S.C. 1101 et seq.

Pawnbroker. Any person whose business or occupation includes the taking or receiving, by way of pledge or pawn, of any firearm as security for the payment or repayment of money. The term shall include any person who engages in such business on a part-time basis.

Permanently inoperable. A firearm which is incapable of discharging a shot by means of an explosive and incapable of being readily restored to a firing condition. An acceptable method of rendering most firearms permanently inoperable is to fusion weld the chamber closed and fusion weld the barrel solidly to the frame. Certain unusual firearms require other methods to render the firearm permanently inoperable. Contact ATF for instructions.

Person. Any individual, corporation, company, association, firm, partnership, society, or joint stock company.

Pistol. A weapon originally designed, made, and intended to fire a projectile (bullet) from one or more barrels when held in one hand, and having (a) a chamber(s) as an integral part(s) of, or permanently aligned with, the bore(s); and (b) a short stock designed to be gripped by one hand and at an angle to and extending below the line of the bore(s).

Published ordinance. A published law of any political subdivision of a State which the Director determines to be relevant to the enforcement of this part and which is contained on a list compiled by the Director, which list is incorporated by reference in the Federal Register, revised annually, and furnished to licensees under this part.

Renounced U.S. citizenship. (a) A person has renounced his U.S. citizenship if the person, having been a citizen of the United States, has renounced citizenship either—

(1) Before a diplomatic or consular officer of the United States in a foreign state pursuant to 8 U.S.C. 1481(a)(5); or

(2) Before an officer designated by the Attorney General when the United States is in a state of war pursuant to 8 U.S.C. 1481(a)(6).

(b) The term shall not include any renunciation of citizenship that has been reversed as a result of administrative or judicial appeal.

Revolver. A projectile weapon, of the pistol type, having a breechloading chambered cylinder so arranged that the cocking of the hammer or movement of the trigger rotates it and brings the next cartridge in line with the barrel for firing.

Rifle. A weapon designed or redesigned, made or remade, and intended to be fired from the shoulder, and designed or redesigned and made or remade to use the energy of the explosive in a fixed metallic cartridge to fire only a single projectile through a rifled bore for each single pull of the trigger.

Semiautomatic assault weapon. (a) Any of the firearms, or copies or duplicates of the firearms in any caliber, known as:

(1) Norinco, Mitchell, and Poly Technologies Avtomat Kalashnikovs (all models),

(2) Action Arms Israeli Military Industries UZI and Galil,

(3) Beretta Ar70 (SC–70),

(4) Colt AR–15,

(5) Fabrique National FN/FAL, FN/LAR, and FNC,

(6) SWD M–10, M–11, M–11/9, and M–12,

(7) Steyr AUG,

(8) INTRATEC TEC–9, TEC–DC9 and TEC–22, and

(9) Revolving cylinder shotguns, such as (or similar to) the Street Sweeper and Striker 12;

(b) A semiautomatic rifle that has an ability to accept a detachable magazine and has at least 2 of--

(1) A folding or telescoping stock,

(2) A pistol grip that protrudes conspicuously beneath the action of the weapon,

(3) A bayonet mount,

(4) A flash suppressor or threaded barrel designed to accommodate a flash suppressor, and

(5) A grenade launcher;

(c) A semiautomatic pistol that has an ability to accept a detachable magazine and has at least 2 of--

(1) An ammunition magazine that attaches to the pistol outside of the pistol grip,

(2) A threaded barrel capable of accepting a barrel extender, flash suppressor, forward handgrip, or silencer,

(3) A shroud that is attached to, or partially or completely encircles, the barrel and that permits the shooter to hold the firearm with the nontrigger hand without being burned,

(4) A manufactured weight of 50 ounces or more when the pistol is unloaded, and

(5) A semiautomatic version of an automatic firearm; and

(d) A semiautomatic shotgun that has at least 2 of--

(1) A folding or telescoping stock,

(2) A pistol grip that protrudes conspicuously beneath the action of the weapon,

(3) A fixed magazine capacity in excess of 5 rounds, and

(4) An ability to accept a detachable magazine.

Semiautomatic pistol. Any repeating pistol which utilizes a portion of the energy of a firing cartridge to extract the fired cartridge case and chamber the next round, and which requires a separate pull of the trigger to fire each cartridge.

Semiautomatic rifle. Any repeating rifle which utilizes a portion of the energy of a firing cartridge to extract the fired cartridge case and chamber the next round, and which requires a separate pull of the trigger to fire each cartridge.

Semiautomatic shotgun. Any repeating shotgun which utilizes a portion of the energy of a firing cartridge to extract the fired cartridge case and chamber the next round, and which requires a separate pull of the trigger to fire each cartridge.

Short-barreled rifle. A rifle having one or more barrels less than 16 inches in length, and any weapon made from a rifle, whether by alteration, modification, or otherwise, if such weapon, as modified, has an overall length of less than 26 inches.

Short-barreled shotgun. A shotgun having one or more barrels less than 18 inches in length, and any weapon made from a shotgun, whether by alteration, modification, or otherwise, if such weapon as modified has an overall length of less than 26 inches.

Shotgun. A weapon designed or redesigned, made or remade, and intended to be fired from the shoulder, and designed or redesigned and made or remade to use the energy of the explosive in a fixed shotgun shell to fire through a smooth bore either a number of ball shot or a single projectile for each single pull of the trigger.

State of residence. The State in which an individual resides. An individual resides in a State if he or she is present in a State with the intention of making a home in that State. If an individual is on active duty as a member of the Armed Forces, the individual's State of residence is the State in which his or her permanent duty station is located, as stated in 18 U.S.C. 921(b).

Unlawful user of or addicted to any controlled substance. A person who uses a controlled substance and has lost the power of self-control with reference to the use of controlled substance; and any person who is a current user of a controlled substance in a manner other than as prescribed by a licensed physician. Such use is not limited to the use of drugs on a particular day, or within a matter of days or weeks before, but rather that the unlawful use has occurred recently enough to indicate that the individual is actively engaged in such conduct. A person may be an unlawful current user of a controlled substance even though the substance is not being used at the precise time the person seeks to acquire a firearm or receives or possesses a firearm. An inference of current use may be drawn from evidence of a recent use or possession of a controlled substance or a pattern of use or possession that reasonably covers the present time, e.g., a conviction for use or possession of a controlled substance within the past year; multiple arrests for such offenses within the past 5 years if the most recent arrest occurred within the past year; or persons found through a drug test to use a controlled substance unlawfully, provided that the test was administered within the past year. For a current or former member of the Armed Forces, an inference of current use may be drawn from recent disciplinary or other administrative action based on confirmed drug use, e.g., court-martial conviction, nonjudicial punishment, or an administrative discharge based on drug use or drug rehabilitation failure.

Unserviceable firearm. A firearm which is incapable of discharging a shot by means of an explosive and is incapable of being readily restored to a firing condition.

Subpart C – Administrative and Miscellaneous Provisions.

27 C.F.R. § 478.32. Prohibited shipment, transportation, possession, or receipt of firearms and ammunition by certain persons.

(a) No person may ship or transport any firearm or ammunition in interstate or foreign commerce, or receive any firearm or ammunition which has been shipped or transported in interstate or foreign commerce, or possess any firearm or ammunition in or affecting commerce, who:

(1) Has been convicted in any court of a crime punishable by imprisonment for a term exceeding 1 year,

(2) Is a fugitive from justice,

(3) Is an unlawful user of or addicted to any controlled substance (as defined in section 102 of the Controlled Substances Act, 21 U.S.C. 802),

(4) Has been adjudicated as a mental defective or has been committed to a mental institution,

(5) Being an alien--

(i) Is illegally or unlawfully in the United States; or

(ii) Except as provided in paragraph (f) of this section, has been admitted to the United States under a nonimmigrant visa: Provided, That the provisions of this paragraph (a)(5)(ii) do not apply to any alien who has been lawfully admitted to the United States under a nonimmigrant visa, if that alien is--

(A) Admitted to the United States for lawful hunting or sporting purposes or is in possession of a hunting license or permit lawfully issued in the United States;

(B) An official representative of a foreign government who is either accredited to the United States Government or the Government's mission to an international organization having its headquarters in the United States or is en route to or from another country to which that alien is accredited. This exception only applies if the firearm or ammunition is shipped, transported, possessed, or received in the representative's official capacity;

(C) An official of a foreign government or a distinguished foreign visitor who has been so designated by the Department of State. This exception only applies if the firearm or ammunition is shipped, transported, possessed, or received in the official's or visitor's official capacity, except if the visitor is a private individual who does not have an official capacity; or

(D) A foreign law enforcement officer of a friendly foreign government entering the United States on official law enforcement business,

(6) Has been discharged from the Armed Forces under dishonorable conditions,

(7) Having been a citizen of the United States, has renounced citizenship,

(8) Is subject to a court order that--

(i) Was issued after a hearing of which such person received actual notice, and at which such person had an opportunity to participate;

(ii) Restrains such person from harassing, stalking, or threatening an intimate partner of such person or child of such intimate partner or person, or engaging in other conduct that would place an intimate partner in reasonable fear of bodily injury to the partner or child; and

(iii)(A) Includes a finding that such person represents a credible threat to the physical safety of such intimate partner or child; or

(B) By its terms explicitly prohibits the use, attempted use, or threatened use of physical force against such intimate partner or child that would reasonably be expected to cause bodily injury, or

(9) Has been convicted of a misdemeanor crime of domestic violence.

(b) No person who is under indictment for a crime punishable by imprisonment for a term exceeding one year may ship or transport any firearm or ammunition in interstate or foreign commerce or receive any firearm or ammunition which has been shipped or transported in interstate or foreign commerce.

(c) Any individual, who to that individual's knowledge and while being employed by any person described in paragraph (a) of this section, may not in the course of such employment receive, possess, or transport any firearm or ammunition in commerce or affecting commerce or receive any firearm or ammunition which has been shipped or transported in interstate or foreign commerce.

(d) No person may sell or otherwise dispose of any firearm or ammunition to any person knowing or having reasonable cause to believe that such person:

(1) Is under indictment for, or has been convicted in any court of, a crime punishable by imprisonment for a term exceeding 1 year,

(2) Is a fugitive from justice,

(3) Is an unlawful user of or addicted to any controlled substance (as defined in section 102 of the Controlled Substances Act, 21 U.S.C. 802),

(4) Has been adjudicated as a mental defective or has been committed to a mental institution,

(5) Being an alien--

(i) Is illegally or unlawfully in the United States; or

(ii) Except as provided in paragraph (f) of this section, has been admitted to the United States under a nonimmigrant visa: Provided, That the provisions of this paragraph (d)(5)(ii) do not apply to any alien who has been lawfully admitted to the United States under a nonimmigrant visa, if that alien is--

(A) Admitted to the United States for lawful hunting or sporting purposes or is in possession of a hunting license or permit lawfully issued in the United States;

(B) An official representative of a foreign government who is either accredited to the United States Government or the Government's mission to an international organization having its headquarters in the United States or en route to or from another country to which that alien is accredited. This exception only applies if the firearm or ammunition is shipped, transported, possessed, or received in the representative's official capacity;

(C) An official of a foreign government or a distinguished foreign visitor who has been so designated by the Department of State. This exception only applies if the firearm or ammunition is shipped, transported, possessed, or received in the official's or visitor's official capacity, except if the visitor is a private individual who does not have an official capacity; or

(D) A foreign law enforcement officer of a friendly foreign government entering the United States on official law enforcement business,

(6) Has been discharged from the Armed Forces under dishonorable conditions,

(7) Having been a citizen of the United States, has renounced citizenship,

(8) Is subject to a court order that restrains such person from harassing, stalking, or threatening an intimate partner of such person or child of such intimate partner or person, or engaging in other conduct that would place an intimate partner in reasonable fear of bodily injury to the partner or child: Provided, That the provisions of this paragraph shall only apply to a court order that--

(i) Was issued after a hearing of which such person received actual notice, and at which such person had the opportunity to participate; and

(ii)(A) Includes a finding that such person represents a credible threat to the physical safety of such intimate partner or child; or

(B) By its terms explicitly prohibits the use, attempted use, or threatened use of physical force against such intimate partner or child that would reasonably be expected to cause bodily injury, or

(9) Has been convicted of a misdemeanor crime of domestic violence.

(e) The actual notice required by paragraphs (a)(8)(i) and (d)(8)(i) of this section is notice expressly and actually given, and brought home to the party directly, including service of process personally served on the party and service by mail. Actual notice also includes proof of facts and circumstances that raise the inference that the party received notice including, but not limited to, proof that notice was left at the party's dwelling house or usual place of abode with some person of suitable age and discretion residing therein; or proof that the party signed a return receipt for a hearing notice which had been mailed to the party. It does not include notice published in a newspaper.

(f) Pursuant to 18 U.S.C. 922(y)(3), any individual who has been admitted to the United States under a nonimmigrant visa may receive a waiver from the prohibition contained in paragraph (a)(5)(ii) of this section if the Attorney General approves a petition for the waiver.

27 C.F.R. § 478.33a. Theft of firearms.

No person shall steal or unlawfully take or carry away from the person or the premises of a person who is licensed to engage in the business of importing, manufacturing, or dealing in firearms, any firearm in the licensee's business inventory that has been shipped or transported in interstate or foreign commerce.

27 C.F.R. § 478.34. Removed, obliterated, or altered serial number.

No person shall knowingly transport, ship, or receive in interstate or foreign commerce any firearm which has had the importer's or manufacturer's serial number removed, obliterated, or altered, or possess or receive any firearm which has had the importer's or manufacturer's serial number removed, obliterated, or altered and has, at any time, been shipped or transported in interstate or foreign commerce.

27 C.F.R. § 478.36. Transfer or possession of machine guns.

No person shall transfer or possess a machine gun except:

(a) A transfer to or by, or possession by or under the authority of, the United States, or any department or agency thereof, or a State, or a department, agency, or political subdivision thereof. (See Part 479 of this chapter); or

(b) Any lawful transfer or lawful possession of a machine gun that was lawfully possessed before May 19, 1986 (See Part 479 of this chapter).

27 C.F.R. § 478.37. Manufacture, importation and sale of armor piercing ammunition.

No person shall manufacture or import, and no manufacturer or importer shall sell or deliver, armor piercing ammunition, except:

(a) The manufacture or importation, or the sale or delivery by any manufacturer or importer, of armor piercing ammunition for the use of the United States or any department or agency thereof or any State or any department, agency or political subdivision thereof;

(b) The manufacture, or the sale or delivery by a manufacturer or importer, of armor piercing ammunition for the purpose of exportation; or

(c) The sale or delivery by a manufacturer or importer of armor piercing ammunition for the purposes of testing or experimentation as authorized by the Director under the provisions of § 478.149.

27 C.F.R. § 478.38. Transportation of firearms.

Notwithstanding any other provision of any law or any rule or regulation of a State or any political subdivision thereof, any person who is not otherwise prohibited by this chapter from transporting, shipping, or receiving a firearm shall be entitled to transport a firearm for any lawful purpose from any place where such person may lawfully possess and carry such firearm to any other place where such person may lawfully possess and carry such firearm if, during such transportation the firearm is unloaded, and neither the firearm nor any ammunition being transported is readily accessible or is directly accessible from the passenger compartment of such transporting vehicle: Provided, That in the case of a vehicle without a compartment separate from the driver's compartment the firearm or ammunition shall be contained in a locked container other than the glove compartment or console.

27 C.F.R. § 478.39. Assembly of semiautomatic rifles or shotguns.

(a) No person shall assemble a semiautomatic rifle or any shotgun using more than 10 of the imported parts listed in paragraph (c) of this section if the assembled firearm is prohibited from importation under section 925(d)(3) as not being particularly suitable for or readily adaptable to sporting purposes.

(b) The provisions of this section shall not apply to:

(1) The assembly of such rifle or shotgun for sale or distribution by a licensed manufacturer to the United States or any department or agency thereof or to any State or any department, agency, or political subdivision thereof; or

(2) The assembly of such rifle or shotgun for the purposes of testing or experimentation authorized by the Director under the provisions of § 478.151; or

(3) The repair of any rifle or shotgun which had been imported into or assembled in the United States prior to November 30, 1990, or the replacement of any part of such firearm.

(c) For purposes of this section, the term imported parts are:

(1) Frames, receivers, receiver castings, forgings or stampings

(2) Barrels

(3) Barrel extensions

(4) Mounting blocks (trunions)

(5) Muzzle attachments

(6) Bolts

(7) Bolt carriers

(8) Operating rods

(9) Gas pistons

(10) Trigger housings

(11) Triggers

(12) Hammers

(13) Sears

(14) Disconnectors

(15) Buttstocks

(16) Pistol grips

(17) Forearms, handguards

(18) Magazine bodies

(19) Followers

(20) Floorplates

27 C.F.R. § 478.39a. Reporting theft or loss of firearms.

Each licensee shall report the theft or loss of a firearm from the licensee's inventory (including any firearm which has been transferred from the licensee's inventory to a personal collection and held as a personal firearm for at least 1 year), or from the collection of a licensed collector, within 48 hours after the theft or loss is discovered. Licensees shall report thefts or losses by telephoning 1–888–930–9275 (nationwide toll free number) and by preparing ATF Form 3310.11, Federal Firearms Licensee Theft/Loss Report, in accordance with the instructions on the form. The original of the report shall be forwarded to the office specified thereon, and Copy 1 shall be retained by the licensee as part of the licensee's permanent records. Theft or loss of any firearm shall also be reported to the appropriate local authorities.

27 C.F.R. § 478.40. Manufacture, transfer, and possession of semiautomatic assault weapons.

(a) Prohibition. No person shall manufacture, transfer, or possess a semiautomatic assault weapon.

(b) Exceptions. The provisions of paragraph (a) of this section shall not apply to

(1) The possession or transfer of any semiautomatic assault weapon otherwise lawfully possessed in the United States under Federal law on September 13, 1994;

(2) Any of the firearms, or replicas or duplicates of the firearms, specified in 18 U.S.C. 922, appendix A, as such firearms existed on October 1, 1993;

(3) Any firearm that—

(i) Is manually operated by bolt, pump, lever, or slide action;

(ii) Has been rendered permanently inoperable; or

(iii) Is an antique firearm;

(4) Any semiautomatic rifle that cannot accept a detachable magazine that holds more than 5 rounds of ammunition;

(5) Any semiautomatic shotgun that cannot hold more than 5 rounds of ammunition in a fixed or detachable magazine;

(6) The manufacture for, transfer to, or possession by the United States or a department or agency of the United States or a State or a department, agency, or political subdivision of a State, or a transfer to or possession by a law enforcement officer employed by such an entity for purposes of law enforcement;

(7) The transfer to a licensee under title I of the Atomic Energy Act of 1954 (42 U.S.C. 2011 et seq.) For purposes of establishing and maintaining an on-site physical protection system and security organization required by Federal law, or possession by an employee or contractor of such licensee on-site for such purposes or off-site for purposes of licensee-authorized training or transportation of nuclear materials;

(8) The possession, by an individual who is retired from service with a law enforcement agency and is not otherwise prohibited from receiving a firearm, of a semiautomatic assault weapon transferred to the individual by the agency upon such retirement;

(9) The manufacture, transfer, or possession of a semiautomatic assault weapon by a licensed manufacturer or licensed importer for the purposes of testing or experimentation as authorized by the Director under the provisions of § 478.153; or

(10) The manufacture, transfer, or possession of a semiautomatic assault weapon by a licensed manufacturer, licensed importer, or licensed dealer for the purpose of exportation in compliance with the Arms Export Control Act (22 U.S.C. 2778).

(c) Manufacture and dealing in semiautomatic assault weapons. Subject to compliance with the provisions of this part, licensed manufacturers and licensed dealers in semiautomatic assault weapons may manufacture and deal in such weapons manufactured after September 13, 1994: Provided, The licensee obtains evidence that the weapons will be disposed of in accordance with paragraph (b) of this section. Examples of acceptable evidence include the following:

(1) Contracts between the manufacturer and dealers stating that the weapons may only be sold to law enforcement agencies, law enforcement officers, or other purchasers specified in paragraph (b) of this section;

(2) Copies of purchase orders submitted to the manufacturer or dealer by law enforcement agencies or other purchasers specified in paragraph (b) of this section;

(3) Copies of letters submitted to the manufacturer or dealer by government agencies, law enforcement officers, or other purchasers specified in paragraph (b) of this section expressing an interest in purchasing the semiautomatic assault weapons;

(4) Letters from dealers to the manufacturer stating that sales will only be made to law enforcement agencies, law enforcement officers, or other purchasers specified in paragraph (b) of this section; and

(5) Letters from law enforcement officers purchasing in accordance with paragraph (b)(6) of this section and § 478.132.

27 C.F.R. § 478.40a. Transfer and possession of large capacity ammunition feeding devices.

(a) Prohibition. No person shall transfer or possess a large capacity ammunition feeding device.

(b) Exceptions. The provisions of paragraph (a) of this section shall not apply to:

(1) The possession or transfer of any large capacity ammunition feeding device otherwise lawfully possessed on September 13, 1994;

(2) The manufacture for, transfer to, or possession by the United States or a department or agency of the United States or a State or a department, agency, or political subdivision of a State, or a transfer to or possession by a law enforcement officer employed by such an entity for purposes of law enforcement;

(3) The transfer to a licensee under title I of the Atomic Energy Act of 1954 for purposes of establishing and maintaining an on-site physical protection system and security organization required by Federal law, or possession by an employee or contractor of such licensee on-site for such purposes or off-site for purposes of licensee-authorized training or transportation of nuclear materials;

(4) The possession, by an individual who is retired from service with a law enforcement agency and is not otherwise prohibited from receiving ammunition, of a large capacity ammunition feeding device transferred to the individual by the agency upon such retirement;

(5) The manufacture, transfer, or possession of any large capacity ammunition feeding device by a manufacturer or importer for the purposes of testing or experimentation in accordance with § 478.153; or

(6) The manufacture, transfer, or possession of any large capacity ammunition feeding device by a manufacturer or importer for the purpose of exportation in accordance with the Arms Export Control Act (22 U.S.C. 2778).

(c) Importation, manufacture, and dealing in large capacity ammunition feeding devices. Possession and transfer of large capacity ammunition feeding devices by persons who manufacture, import, or deal in such devices will be presumed to be lawful if such persons maintain evidence establishing that the devices are possessed and transferred for sale to purchasers specified in paragraph (b) of this section. Examples of acceptable evidence include the following:

(1) Contracts between persons who import or manufacture such devices and persons who deal in such devices stating that the devices may only be sold to law enforcement agencies or other purchasers specified in paragraph (b) of this section;

(2) Copies of purchase orders submitted to persons who manufacture, import, or deal in such devices by law enforcement agencies or other purchasers specified in paragraph (b) of this section;

(3) Copies of letters submitted to persons who manufacture, import, or deal in such devices by government agencies or other purchasers specified in paragraph (b) of this section expressing an interest in purchasing the devices;

(4) Letters from persons who deal in such devices to persons who import or manufacture such devices stating that sales will only be made to law enforcement agencies or other purchasers specified in paragraph (b) of this section; and

(5) Letters from law enforcement officers purchasing in accordance with paragraph (b)(2) of this section and § 478.132.

Subpart D – Licenses.

27 C.F.R. § 478.41. General.

(a) Each person intending to engage in business as an importer or manufacturer of firearms or ammunition, or a dealer in firearms shall, before commencing such business, obtain the license required by this subpart for the business to be operated. Each person who desires to obtain a license as a collector of curios or relics may obtain such a license under the provisions of this subpart.

(b) Each person intending to engage in business as a firearms or ammunition importer or manufacturer, or dealer in firearms shall file an application, with the required fee (see § 478.42), with ATF in accordance with the instructions on the form (see § 478.44), and, pursuant to § 478.47, receive the license required for such business from the Chief, Federal Firearms Licensing Center. Except as provided in § 478.50, a license must be obtained for each business and each place at which the applicant is to do business. A license as an importer or manufacturer of firearms or ammunition, or a dealer in firearms shall, subject to the provisions of the Act and other applicable provisions of law, entitle the licensee to transport, ship, and receive firearms and ammunition covered by such license in interstate or foreign commerce and to engage in the business specified by the license, at the location described on the license, and for the period stated on the license. However, it shall not be necessary for a licensed importer or a licensed manufacturer to also obtain a dealer's license in order to engage in business on the licensed premises as a dealer in the same type of firearms authorized by the license to be imported or manufactured. Payment of the license fee as an importer or manufacturer of destructive devices, ammunition for destructive devices or armor piercing ammunition or as a dealer in destructive devices includes the privilege of importing or manufacturing firearms other than destructive devices and ammunition for other than destructive devices or ammunition other than armor piercing ammunition, or dealing in firearms other than destructive devices, as the case may be, by such a licensee at the licensed premises.

(c) Each person seeking the privileges of a collector licensed under this part shall file an application, with the required fee (see § 478.42), with ATF in accordance with the instructions on the form (see § 478.44), and pursuant to § 478.47, receive from the Chief, Federal Firearms Licensing Center, the license covering the collection of curious and relics.

A separate license may be obtained for each collection premises, and such license shall, subject to the provisions of the Act and other applicable provisions of law, entitle the licensee to transport, ship, receive, and acquire curios and relics in interstate or foreign commerce, and to make disposition of curios and relics in interstate or foreign commerce, to any other person licensed under the provisions of this part, for the period stated on the license.

(d) The collector license provided by this part shall apply only to transactions related to a collector's activity in acquiring, holding or disposing of curios and relics. A collector's license does not authorize the collector to engage in a business required to be licensed under the Act or this part. Therefore, if the acquisitions and dispositions of curios and relics by a collector bring the collector within the definition of a manufacturer, importer, or dealer under this part, he shall qualify as such. (See also § 478.93 of this part.)

27 C.F.R. § 478.50. Locations covered by license.

The license covers the class of business or the activity specified in the license at the address specified therein. A separate license must be obtained for each location at which a firearms or ammunition business or activity requiring a license under this part is conducted except:

(a) No license is required to cover a separate warehouse used by the licensee solely for storage of firearms or ammunition if the records required by this part are maintained at the licensed premises served by such warehouse;

(b) A licensed collector may acquire curios and relics at any location, and dispose of curios or relics to any licensee or to other persons who are residents of the State where the collector's license is held and the disposition is made;

(c) A licensee may conduct business at a gun show pursuant to the provision of § 478.100; or

(d) A licensed importer, manufacturer, or dealer may engage in the business of dealing in curio or relic firearms with another licensee at any location pursuant to the provisions of § 478.100.

27 C.F.R. § 478.57. Discontinuance of business.

(a) Where a firearm or ammunition business is either discontinued or succeeded by a new owner, the owner of the business discontinued or succeeded shall within 30 days thereof furnish to the Chief, Federal Firearms Licensing Center notification of the discontinuance or succession. (See also § 478.127.)

(b) Since section 922(v), Title 18, U.S.C., makes it unlawful to transfer or possess a semiautomatic assault weapon, except as provided in the law, any licensed manufacturer, licensed importer, or licensed dealer intending to discontinue business shall, prior to going out of business, transfer in compliance with the provisions of this part any semiautomatic assault weapon manufactured or imported after September 13, 1994, to a person specified in § 478.40(b), or, subject to the provisions of §§ 478.40(c) and 478.132, a licensed manufacturer, a licensed importer, or a licensed dealer.

(c) Since section 922(w), Title 18, U.S.C., makes it unlawful to transfer or possess a large capacity ammunition feeding device, except as provided in the law, any person who manufactures, imports, or deals in such devices and who intends to discontinue business shall, prior to going out of business, transfer in compliance with the provisions of this part any large capacity ammunition feeding device manufactured after September 13, 1994, to a person specified in § 478.40a(b), or, subject to the provisions of §§ 478.40a(c) and 478.132, a person who manufactures, imports, or deals in such devices.

27 C.F.R. § 478.58. State or other law.

A license issued under this part confers no right or privilege to conduct business or activity contrary to State or other law. The holder of such a license is not by reason of the rights and privileges granted by that license immune from punishment for operating a firearm or ammunition business or activity in violation of the provisions of any State or other law. Similarly, compliance with the provisions of any State or other law affords no immunity under Federal law or regulations.

Subpart F – Conduct of Business.

27 C.F.R. § 478.93. Authorized operations by a licensed collector.

The license issued to a collector of curios or relics under the provisions of this part shall cover only transactions by the licensed collector in curios and relics. The collector's license is of no force or effect and a licensed collector is of the same status under the Act and this part as a nonlicensee with respect to (a) any acquisition or disposition of firearms other than curios or relics, or any transportation, shipment, or receipt of firearms other than curios or relics in interstate or foreign commerce, and (b) any transaction with a nonlicensee involving any firearm other than a curio or relic. (See also § 478.50.) A collectors license is not necessary to receive or dispose of ammunition, and a licensed collector is not precluded by law from receiving or disposing of armor piercing ammunition. However, a licensed collector may not dispose of any ammunition to a person prohibited from receiving or possessing ammunition (see § 478.99(c)). Any licensed collector who disposes of armor piercing ammunition must record the disposition as required by § 478.125(a) and (b).

27 C.F.R. § 478.94. Sales or deliveries between licensees.

A licensed importer, licensed manufacturer, or licensed dealer selling or otherwise disposing of firearms, and a licensed collector selling or otherwise disposing of curios or relics, to another licensee shall verify the identity and licensed status of the transferee prior to making the transaction. Verification shall be established by the transferee furnishing to the transferor a certified copy of the transferee's license and by such other means as the transferor deems necessary: *Provided*, That it shall not be required (a) for a transferee who has furnished a certified copy of its license to a transferor to again furnish such certified copy to that transferor during the term of the transferee's current license, (b) for a licensee to furnish a certified copy of its license to another licensee if a firearm is being returned either directly or through another licensee to such licensee and (c) for licensees of multilicensed business organizations to furnish certified copies of their licenses to other licensed locations operated by such organization: *Provided further*, That a multilicensed business organization may furnish to a transferor, in lieu of a certified copy of each license, a list, certified to be true, correct and complete, containing the name, address, license number, and the date of license expiration of each licensed location operated by such organization, and the transferor may sell or otherwise dispose of firearms as provided by this section to any licensee appearing on such list without requiring a certified copy of a license therefrom. A transferor licensee who has the certified information required by this section may sell or dispose of firearms to a licensee for not more than 45 days following the expiration date of the transferee's license.

27 C.F.R. § 478.96. Out-of-State and mail order sales.

(a) The provisions of this section shall apply when a firearm is purchased by or delivered to a person not otherwise prohibited by the Act from purchasing or receiving it.

(b) A licensed importer, licensed manufacturer, or licensed dealer may sell a firearm that is not subject to the provisions of § 478.102(a) to a nonlicensee who does not appear in person at the licensee's business premises if the nonlicensee is a resident of the same State in which the licensee's business premises are located, and the nonlicensee furnishes to the licensee the firearms transaction record, Form 4473, required by § 478.124. The nonlicensee shall attach to such record a true copy of any permit or other information required pursuant to any statute of the State and published ordinance applicable to the locality in which he resides. The licensee shall prior to shipment or delivery of the firearm, forward by registered or certified mail (return receipt requested) a copy of the record, Form 4473, to the chief law enforcement officer named on such record, and delay shipment or delivery of the firearm for a period of at least 7 days following receipt by the licensee of the return receipt evidencing delivery of the copy of the record to such chief law enforcement officer, or the return of the copy of the record to him due to the refusal of such chief law enforcement officer to accept same in accordance with U.S. Postal Service regulations. The original Form 4473, and evidence of receipt or rejection of delivery of the copy of the Form 4473 sent to the chief law enforcement officer shall be retained by the licensee as a part of the records required of him to be kept under the provisions of subpart H of this part.

(c)(1) A licensed importer, licensed manufacturer, or licensed dealer may sell or deliver a rifle or shotgun, and a licensed collector may sell or deliver a rifle or shotgun that is a curio or relic to a nonlicensed resident of a State other than the State in which the licensee's place of business is located if--

(i) The purchaser meets with the licensee in person at the licensee's premises to accomplish the transfer, sale, and delivery of the rifle or shotgun;

(ii) The licensed importer, licensed manufacturer, or licensed dealer complies with the provisions of § 478.102;

(iii) The purchaser furnishes to the licensed importer, licensed manufacturer, or licensed dealer the firearms transaction record, Form 4473, required by § 478.124; and

(iv) The sale, delivery, and receipt of the rifle or shotgun fully comply with the legal conditions of sale in both such States.

(2) For purposes of paragraph (c) of this section, any licensed manufacturer, licensed importer, or licensed dealer is presumed, in the absence of evidence to the contrary, to have had actual knowledge of the State laws and published ordinances of both such States.

27 C.F.R. § 478.97. Loan or rental of firearms.

(a) A licensee may lend or rent a firearm to any person for temporary use off the premises of the licensee for lawful sporting purposes: Provided, That the delivery of the firearm to such person is not prohibited by § 478.99(b) or § 478.99(c), the licensee complies with the requirements of § 478.102, and the licensee records such loan or rental in the records required to be kept by him under Subpart H of this part.

(b) A club, association, or similar organization temporarily furnishing firearms (whether by loan, rental, or otherwise) to participants in a skeet, trap, target, or similar shooting activity for use at the time and place such activity is held does not, unattended by other circumstances, cause such club, association, or similar organization to be engaged in the business of a dealer in firearms or as engaging in firearms transactions. Therefore, licensing and recordkeeping requirements contained in this part pertaining to firearms transactions would not apply to this temporary furnishing of firearms for use on premises on which such an activity is conducted.

27 C.F.R. § 478.98. Sales or deliveries of destructive devices and certain firearms.

The sale or delivery by a licensee of any destructive device, machine gun, short-barreled shotgun, or short-barreled rifle, to any person other than another licensee who is licensed under this part to deal in such device or firearm, is prohibited unless the person to receive such device or firearm furnishes to the licensee a sworn statement setting forth

(a) The reasons why there is a reasonable necessity for such person to purchase or otherwise acquire the device or weapon; and

(b) That such person's receipt or possession of the device or weapon would be consistent with public safety. Such sworn statement shall be made on the application to transfer and register the firearm required by Part 479 of this chapter. The sale or delivery of the device or weapon shall not be made until the application for transfer is approved by the Director and returned to the licensee (transferor) as provided in Part 479 of this chapter.

27 C.F.R. § 478.99. Certain prohibited sales or deliveries.

(a) Interstate sales or deliveries. A licensed importer, licensed manufacturer, licensed dealer, or licensed collector shall not sell or deliver any firearm to any person not licensed under this part and who the licensee knows or has reasonable cause to believe does not reside in (or if a corporation or other business entity, does not maintain a place of business in) the State in which the licensee's place of business or activity is located: *Provided*, That the foregoing provisions of this paragraph (1) shall not apply to the sale or delivery of a rifle or shotgun (curio or relic, in the case of a licensed collector) to a resident of a State other than the State in which the licensee's place of business or collection premises is located if the requirements of § 478.96(c) are fully met, and (2) shall not apply to the loan or rental of a firearm to any person for temporary use for lawful sporting purposes (see § 478.97).

(b) Sales or deliveries to underaged persons. A licensed importer, licensed manufacturer, licensed dealer, or licensed collector shall not sell or deliver (1) any firearm or ammunition to any individual who the importer, manufacturer, dealer, or collector knows or has reasonable cause to believe is less than 18 years of age, and, if the firearm, or ammunition, is other than a shotgun or rifle, or ammunition for a shotgun or rifle, to any individual who the importer, manufacturer, dealer, or collector knows or has reasonable cause to believe is less than 21 years of age, or (2) any firearm to any person in any State where the purchase or possession by such person of such firearm would be in violation of any State law or any published ordinance applicable at the place of sale, delivery, or other disposition, unless the importer, manufacturer, dealer, or collector knows or has reasonable cause to believe that the purchase or possession would not be in violation of such State law or such published ordinance.

(c) Sales or deliveries to prohibited categories of persons. A licensed manufacturer, licensed importer, licensed dealer, or licensed collector shall not sell or otherwise dispose of any firearm or ammunition to any person knowing or having reasonable cause to believe that such person:

(1) Is, except as provided by § 478.143, under indictment for, or, except as provided by § 478.144, has been convicted in any court of a crime punishable by imprisonment for a term exceeding 1 year;

(2) Is a fugitive from justice;

(3) Is an unlawful user of or addicted to any controlled substance (as defined in section 102 of the Controlled Substance Act, 21 U.S.C. 802);

(4) Has been adjudicated as a mental defective or has been committed to any mental institution;

(5) Is an alien illegally or unlawfully in the United States or, except as provided in § 478.32(f), is an alien who has been admitted to the United States under a nonimmigrant visa: Provided, That the provisions of this paragraph (c)(5) do not apply to any alien who has been lawfully admitted to the United States under a nonimmigrant visa if that alien is—

(i) Admitted to the United States for lawful hunting or sporting purposes or is in possession of a hunting license or permit lawfully issued in the United States;

(ii) An official representative of a foreign government who is either accredited to the United States Government or the Government's mission to an international organization having its headquarters in the United States or en route to or from another country to which that alien is accredited. This exception only applies if the firearm or ammunition is shipped, transported, possessed, or received in the representative's official capacity;

(iii) An official of a foreign government or a distinguished foreign visitor who has been so designated by the Department of State. This exception only applies if the firearm or ammunition is shipped, transported, possessed, or received in the official's or visitor's official capacity, except if the visitor is a private individual who does not have an official capacity; or

(iv) A foreign law enforcement officer of a friendly foreign government entering the United States on official law enforcement business;

(6) Has been discharged from the Armed Forces under dishonorable conditions;

(7) Who, having been a citizen of the United States, has renounced citizenship;

(8) Is subject to a court order that restrains such person from harassing, stalking, or threatening an intimate partner of such person or child of such intimate partner or person, or engaging in other conduct that would place an intimate partner in reasonable fear of bodily injury to the partner or child, except that this paragraph shall only apply to a court order that—

(i) Was issued after a hearing of which such person received actual notice, and at which such person had the opportunity to participate; and

(ii)(A) Includes a finding that such person represents a credible threat to the physical safety of such intimate partner or child; or

(B) By its terms explicitly prohibits the use, attempted use, or threatened use of physical force against such intimate partner or child that would reasonably be expected to cause bodily injury, or

(9) Has been convicted of a misdemeanor crime of domestic violence.

(d) Manufacture, importation, and sale of armor piercing ammunition by licensed importers and licensed manufacturers. A licensed importer or licensed manufacturer shall not import or manufacture armor piercing ammunition or sell or deliver such ammunition, except:

(1) For use of the United States or any department or agency thereof or any State or any department, agency, or political subdivision thereof;

(2) For the purpose of exportation; or

(3) For the purpose of testing or experimentation authorized by the Director under the provisions of § 478.149.

(e) Transfer of armor piercing ammunition by licensed dealers. A licensed dealer shall not willfully transfer armor piercing ammunition: Provided, That armor piercing ammunition received and maintained by the licensed dealer as business inventory prior to August 28, 1986, may be transferred to any department or agency of the United States or any State or political subdivision thereof if a record of such ammunition is maintained in the form and manner prescribed by § 478.125(c). Any licensed dealer who violates this paragraph is subject to license revocation. See subpart E of this part. For purposes of this paragraph, the Director shall furnish each licensed dealer information defining which projectiles are considered armor piercing. Such information may not be all-inclusive for purposes of the prohibition on manufacture, importation, or sale or delivery by a manufacturer or importer of such ammunition or 18 U.S.C. 929 relating to criminal misuse of such ammunition.

27 C.F.R. § 478.100. Conduct of business away from licensed premises.

(a)(1) A licensee may conduct business temporarily at a gun show or event as defined in paragraph (b) if the gun show or event is located in the same State specified on the license: *Provided*, That such business shall not be conducted from any motorized or towed vehicle. The premises of the gun show or event at which the licensee conducts business shall be considered part of the licensed premises. Accordingly, no separate fee or license is required for the gun show or event locations. However, licensees shall comply with the provisions of § 478.91 relating to posting of licenses (or a copy thereof) while conducting business at the gun show or event.

(2) A licensed importer, manufacturer, or dealer may engage in the business of dealing in curio or relic firearms with another licensee at any location.

(b) A gun show or an event is a function sponsored by any national, State, or local organization, devoted to the collection, competitive use, or other sporting use of firearms, or an organization or association that sponsors functions devoted to the collection, competitive use, or other sporting use of firearms in the community.

(c) Licensees conducting business at locations other than the premises specified on their license under the provisions of paragraph (a) of this section shall maintain firearms records in the form and manner prescribed by subpart H of this part. In addition, records of firearms transactions conducted at such locations shall include the location of the sale or other disposition, be entered in the acquisition and disposition records of the licensee, and retained on the premises specified on the license.

27 C.F.R. § 478.101. Record of transactions.

Every licensee shall maintain firearms and armor piercing ammunition records in such form and manner as is prescribed by subpart H of this part.

Subpart G – Importation.

27 C.F.R. § 478.111. General.

(a) Section 922(a)(3) of the Act makes it unlawful, with certain exceptions not pertinent here, for any person other than a licensee to transport into or receive in the State where the person resides any firearm purchased or otherwise obtained by the person outside of that State. However, section 925(a)(4) provides a limited exception for the transportation, shipment, receipt or importation of certain firearms and ammunition by certain members of the United States Armed Forces. Section 922(1) of the Act makes it unlawful for any person knowingly to import or bring into the United States or any possession thereof any firearm or ammunition except as provided by section 925(d) of the Act, which section provides standards for importing or bringing firearms or ammunition into the United States. Section 925(d) also provides standards for importing or bringing firearm barrels into the United States. Accordingly, no firearm, firearm barrel, or ammunition may be imported or brought into the United States except as provided by this part.

(b) Where a firearm, firearm barrel, or ammunition is imported and the authorization for importation required by this subpart has not been obtained by the person importing same, such person shall:

(1) Store, at the person's expense, such firearm, firearm barrel, or ammunition at a facility designated by U.S Customs or the Director of Industry Operations to await the issuance of the required authorization or other disposition; or

(2) Abandon such firearm, firearm barrel, or ammunition to the U.S. Government; or

(3) Export such firearm, firearm barrel, or ammunition.

(c) Any inquiry relative to the provisions or procedures under this subpart, other than that pertaining to the payment of customs duties or the release from Customs custody of firearms, firearm barrels, or ammunition authorized by the Director to be imported, shall be directed to the Director of Industry Operations for reply.

27 C.F.R. § 478.114. Importation by members of the U.S. Armed Forces.

(a) The Director may issue a permit authorizing the importation of a firearm or ammunition into the United States to the place of residence of any military member of the U.S. Armed Forces who is on active duty outside the United States, or who has been on active duty outside the United States within the 60–day period immediately preceding the intended importation: Provided, That such firearm or ammunition is generally recognized as particularly suitable for or readily adaptable to sporting purposes and is intended for the personal use of such member.

Commentary

Details concerning the application process, along with other related administrative provisions can be viewed online at the Government Printing Office website, located at http://www.gpo.gov/fdsys/granule/CFR-2012-title27-vol3/CFR-2012-title27-vol3-sec478-114.

27 C.F.R. § 478.118. Importation of certain firearms classified as curios or relics.

Notwithstanding any other provision of this part, a licensed importer may import all rifles and shotguns classified by the Director as curios or relics, and all handguns classified by the Director as curios or relics that are determined to be generally recognized as particularly suitable for or readily adaptable to sporting purposes. The importation of such curio or relic firearms must be in accordance with the applicable importation provisions of this part and the importation provisions of 27 CFR part 447. Curios or relics which fall within the definition of "firearm" under 26 U.S.C. 5845(a) must also meet the importation provisions of 27 CFR part 479 before they may be imported.

27 C.F.R. § 478.119. Importation of ammunition feeding devices.

(a) No ammunition feeding device shall be imported or brought into the United States unless the Director has authorized the importation of such device.

(b) For purposes of this section, an "ammunition feeding device" is a magazine, belt, drum, feed strip, or similar device for a firearm that has a capacity of, or that can be readily restored or converted to accept, more than 10 rounds of ammunition. The term does not include an attached tubular device designed to accept, and capable of operating only with, .22 caliber rimfire ammunition, or a fixed device for a manually operated firearm, or a fixed device for a firearm listed in 18 U.S.C. 922, appendix A.

Commentary

Detailed procedures concerning the process of obtaining authorization to import ammunition feeding devices can be obtained online at the Government Printing Office website at http://www.gpo.gov/fdsys/granule/CFR-2010-title27-vol3/CFR-2010-title27-vol3-sec478-119/content-detail.html.

Subpart H – Records.

27 C.F.R. § 478.121. General.

(a) The records pertaining to firearms transactions prescribed by this part shall be retained on the licensed premises in the manner prescribed by this subpart and for the length of time prescribed by § 478.129. The records pertaining to ammunition prescribed by this part shall be retained on the licensed premises in the manner prescribed by § 478.125.

(b) ATF officers may, for the purposes and under the conditions prescribed in § 478.23, enter the premises of any licensed importer, licensed manufacturer, licensed dealer, or licensed collector for the purpose of examining or inspecting any record or document required by or obtained under this part. Section 923(g) of the Act requires licensed importers, licensed manufacturers, licensed dealers, and licensed collectors to make such records available for such examination or inspection during business hours or, in the case of licensed collectors, hours of operation, as provided in § 478.23.

(c) Each licensed importer, licensed manufacturer, licensed dealer, and licensed collector shall maintain such records of importation, production, shipment, receipt, sale, or other disposition, whether temporary or permanent, of firearms and such records of the disposition of ammunition as the regulations contained in this part prescribe. Section 922(m) of the Act makes it unlawful for any licensed importer, licensed manufacturer, licensed dealer, or licensed collector knowingly to make any false entry in, to fail to make appropriate entry in, or to fail to properly maintain any such record.

(d) For recordkeeping requirements for sales by licensees at gun shows see § 478.100(c).

Commentary

Detailed procedures concerning recordkeeping requirements can be obtained online at the Government Printing Office website at http://www.gpo.gov/fdsys/granule/CFR-2012-title27-vol3/CFR-2012-title27-vol3-sec478-121/content-detail.html.

27 C.F.R. § 478.134. Sale of firearms to law enforcement officers.

(a) Law enforcement officers purchasing firearms for official use who provide the licensee with a certification on agency letterhead, signed by a person in authority within the agency (other than the officer purchasing the firearm), stating that the officer will use the firearm in official duties and that a records check reveals that the purchasing officer has no convictions for misdemeanor crimes of domestic violence are not required to complete Form 4473 or Form 5300.35. The law enforcement officer purchasing the firearm may purchase a firearm from a licensee in another State, regardless of where the officer resides or where the agency is located.

(b)(1) The following individuals are considered to have sufficient authority to certify that law enforcement officers purchasing firearms will use the firearms in the performance of official duties:

(i) In a city or county police department, the director of public safety or the chief or commissioner of police.

(ii) In a sheriff's office, the sheriff.

(iii) In a State police or highway patrol department, the superintendent or the supervisor in charge of the office to which the State officer or employee is assigned.

(iv) In Federal law enforcement offices, the supervisor in charge of the office to which the Federal officer or employee is assigned.

(2) An individual signing on behalf of the person in authority is acceptable, provided there is a proper delegation of authority.

(c) Licensees are not required to prepare a Form 4473 or Form 5300.35 covering sales of firearm made in accordance with paragraph (a) of this section to law enforcement officers for official use. However, disposition to the officer must be entered into the licensee's permanent records, and the certification letter must be retained in the licensee's files.

Subpart I – Exemptions, Seizures and Forfeitures.

27 C.F.R. § 478.142. Effect of pardons and expunctions of convictions.

(a) A pardon granted by the President of the United States regarding a Federal conviction for a crime punishable by imprisonment for a term exceeding 1 year shall remove any disability which otherwise would be imposed by the provisions of this part with respect to that conviction.

(b) A pardon granted by the Governor of a State or other State pardoning authority or by the pardoning authority of a foreign jurisdiction with respect to a conviction, or any expunction, reversal, setting aside of a conviction, or other proceeding rendering a conviction nugatory, or a restoration of civil rights shall remove any disability which otherwise would be imposed by the provisions of this part with respect to the conviction, unless:

(1) The pardon, expunction, setting aside, or other proceeding rendering a conviction nugatory, or restoration of civil rights expressly provides that the person may not ship, transport, possess or receive firearms; or

(2) The pardon, expunction, setting aside, or other proceeding rendering a conviction nugatory, or restoration of civil rights did not fully restore the rights of the person to possess or receive firearms under the law of the jurisdiction where the conviction occurred.

27 C.F.R. § 478.144. Relief from disabilities under the Act.

(a) Any person may make application for relief from the disabilities under section 922 (g) and (n) of the Act (see § 478.32).

> **Commentary**
>
> *Detailed procedures concerning relief from disabilities can be obtained online at the Government Printing Office website at http://www.gpo.gov/fdsys/granule/CFR-2012-title27-vol3/CFR-2012-title27-vol3-sec478-144/content-detail.html.*

27 C.F.R. § 478.152. Seizure and forfeiture.

(a) Any firearm or ammunition involved in or used in any knowing violation of subsections (a)(4), (a)(6), (f), (g), (h), (i), (j), or (k) of section 922 of the Act, or knowing importation or bringing into the United States or any possession thereof any firearm or ammunition in violation of section 922(l) of the Act, or knowing violation of section 924 of the Act, or willful violation of any other provision of the Act or of this part, or any violation of any other criminal law of the United States, or any firearm or ammunition intended to be used in any offense referred to in paragraph (c) of this section, where such intent is demonstrated by clear and convincing evidence, shall be subject to seizure and forfeiture, and all provisions of the Internal Revenue Code of 1986 relating to the seizure, forfeiture, and disposition of firearms, as defined in section 5845(a) of that Code, shall, so far as applicable, extend to seizures and forfeitures under the provisions of the Act: Provided, That upon acquittal of the owner or possessor, or dismissal of the charges against such person other than upon motion of the Government prior to trial, or lapse of or court termination of the restraining order to which he is subject, the seized or relinquished firearms or ammunition shall be returned forthwith to the owner or possessor or to a person delegated by the owner or possessor unless the return of the firearms or ammunition would place the owner or possessor or the delegate of the owner or possessor in violation of law. Any action or proceeding for the forfeiture of firearms or ammunition shall be commenced within 120 days of such seizure.

(b) Only those firearms or quantities of ammunition particularly named and individually identified as involved in or used in any violation of the provisions of the Act or this part, or any other criminal law of the United States or as intended to be used in any offense referred to in paragraph (c) of this section, where such intent is demonstrated by clear and convincing evidence, shall be subject to seizure, forfeiture and disposition.

(c) The offenses referred to in paragraphs (a) and (b) of this section for which firearms and ammunition intended to be used in such offenses are subject to seizure and forfeiture are:

(1) Any crime of violence, as that term is defined in section 924(c)(3) of the Act;

(2) Any offense punishable under the Controlled Substances Act (21 U.S.C. 801 et seq.) Or the Controlled Substances Import and Export Act (21 U.S.C. 951 et seq.);

(3) Any offense described in section 922(a)(1), 922(a)(3), 922(a)(5), or 922(b)(3) of the Act, where the firearm or ammunition intended to be used in such offense is involved in a pattern of activities which includes a violation of any offense described in section 922(a)(1), 922(a)(3), 922(a)(5), or 922(b)(3) of the Act;

(4) Any offense described in section 922(d) of the Act where the firearm or ammunition is intended to be used in such offense by the transferor of such firearm or ammunition;

(5) Any offense described in section 922(i), 922(j), 922(l), 922(n), or 924(b) of the Act; and

(6) Any offense which may be prosecuted in a court of the United States which involves the exportation of firearms or ammunition.

Title 27, Code of Federal Regulations, Chapter 2, Subchapter B, Part 479.

Subpart A – Scope of Regulations.

27 C.F.R. § 479.1. General.
This part contains the procedural and substantive requirements relative to the importation, manufacture, making, exportation, identification and registration of, and the dealing in, machine guns, destructive devices and certain other firearms under the provisions of the National Firearms Act (26 U.S.C. Chapter 53).

Subpart B – Definitions.

27 C.F.R. § 479.11. Meaning of terms.
When used in this part and in forms prescribed under this part, where not otherwise distinctly expressed or manifestly incompatible with the intent thereof, terms shall have the meanings ascribed in this section. Words in the plural form shall include the singular, and vice versa, and words importing the masculine gender shall include the feminine. The terms "includes" and "including" do not exclude other things not enumerated which are in the same general class or are otherwise within the scope thereof.

Antique firearm. Any firearm not designed or redesigned for using rim fire or conventional center fire ignition with fixed ammunition and manufactured in or before 1898 (including any matchlock, flintlock, percussion cap, or similar type of ignition system or replica thereof, whether actually manufactured before or after the year 1898) and also any firearm using fixed ammunition manufactured in or before 1898, for which ammunition is no longer manufactured in the United States and is not readily available in the ordinary channels of commercial trade.

Any other weapon. Any weapon or device capable of being concealed on the person from which a shot can be discharged through the energy of an explosive, a pistol or revolver having a barrel with a smooth bore designed or redesigned to fire a fixed shotgun shell, weapons with combination shotgun and rifle barrels 12 inches or more, less than 18 inches in length, from which only a single discharge can be made from either barrel without manual reloading, and shall include any such weapon which may be readily restored to fire. Such term shall not include a pistol or a revolver having a rifled bore, or rifled bores, or weapons designed, made, or intended to be fired from the shoulder and not capable of firing fixed ammunition.

Destructive device. (a) Any explosive, incendiary, or poison gas (1) bomb, (2) grenade, (3) rocket having a propellant charge of more than 4 ounces, (4) missile having an explosive or incendiary charge of more than one-quarter ounce, (5) mine, or (6) similar device; (b) any type of weapon by whatever name known which will, or which may be readily converted to, expel a projectile by the action of an explosive or other propellant, the barrel or barrels of which have a bore of more than one-half inch in diameter, except a shotgun or shotgun shell which the Director finds is generally recognized as particularly suitable for sporting purposes; and (c) any combination of parts either designed or intended for use in converting any device into a destructive device as described in paragraphs (a) and (b) of this definition and from which a destructive device may be readily assembled. The term shall not include any device which is neither designed or redesigned for use as a weapon; any device, although originally designed for use as a weapon, which is redesigned for use as a signaling, pyrotechnic, line throwing, safety, or similar device; surplus ordnance sold, loaned, or given by the Secretary of the Army under 10 U.S.C. 4684(2), 4685, or 4686, or any device which the Director finds is not likely to be used as a weapon, or is an antique or is a rifle which the owner intends to use solely for sporting purposes.

Executed under penalties of perjury. Signed with the prescribed declaration under the penalties of perjury as provided on or with respect to the return, form, or other document or, where no form of declaration is prescribed, with the declaration:

"I declare under the penalties of perjury that this--(insert type of document, such as, statement, application, request, certificate), including the documents submitted in support thereof, has been examined by me and, to the best of my knowledge and belief, is true, correct, and complete."

Exportation. The severance of goods from the mass of things belonging to this country with the intention of uniting them to the mass of things belonging to some foreign country.

Exporter. Any person who exports firearms from the United States.

Firearm. (a) A shotgun having a barrel or barrels of less than 18 inches in length; (b) a weapon made from a shotgun if such weapon as modified has an overall length of less than 26 inches or a barrel or barrels of less than 18 inches in length; (c) a rifle having a barrel or barrels of less than 16 inches in length; (d) a weapon made from a rifle if such weapon as modified has an overall length of less than 26 inches or a barrel or barrels of less than 16 inches in length; (e) any other weapon, as defined in this subpart; (f) a machine gun; (g) a muffler or a silencer for any firearm whether or not such firearm is included within this definition; and (h) a destructive device. The term shall not include an antique firearm or any device (other than a machine gun or destructive device) which, although designed as a weapon, the Director finds by reason of the date of its manufacture, value, design, and other characteristics is primarily a collector's item and is not likely to be used as a weapon. For purposes of this definition, the length of the barrel having an integral chamber(s) on a shotgun or rifle shall be determined by measuring the distance between the muzzle and the face of the bolt, breech, or breech block when closed and when the shotgun or rifle is cocked. The overall length of a weapon made from a shotgun or rifle is the distance between the extreme ends of the weapon measured along a line parallel to the center line of the bore.

Fixed ammunition. That self-contained unit consisting of the case, primer, propellant charge, and projectile or projectiles.

Frame or receiver. That part of a firearm which provides housing for the hammer, bolt or breechblock and firing mechanism, and which is usually threaded at its forward portion to receive the barrel.

Importation. The bringing of a firearm within the limits of the United States or any territory under its control or jurisdiction, from a place outside thereof (whether such place be a foreign country or territory subject to the jurisdiction of the United States), with intent to unlade. Except that, bringing a firearm from a foreign country or a territory subject to the jurisdiction of the United States into a foreign trade zone for storage pending shipment to a foreign country or subsequent importation into this country, under Title 26 of the United States Code, and this part, shall not be deemed importation.

Importer. Any person who is engaged in the business of importing or bringing firearms into the United States.

Machine gun. Any weapon which shoots, is designed to shoot, or can be readily restored to shoot, automatically more than one shot, without manual reloading, by a single function of the trigger. The term shall also include the frame or receiver of any such weapon, any part designed and intended solely and exclusively, or combination of parts designed and intended, for use in converting a weapon into a machine gun, and any combination of parts from which a machine gun can be assembled if such parts are in the possession or under the control of a person.

Make. This term and the various derivatives thereof shall include manufacturing (other than by one qualified to engage in such business under this part), putting together, altering, any combination of these, or otherwise producing a firearm.

Manual reloading. The inserting of a cartridge or shell into the chamber of a firearm either with the hands or by means of a mechanical device controlled and energized by the hands.

Manufacturer. Any person who is engaged in the business of manufacturing firearms.

Muffler or silencer. Any device for silencing, muffling, or diminishing the report of a portable firearm, including any combination of parts, designed or redesigned, and intended for the use in assembling or fabricating a firearm silencer or firearm muffler, and any part intended only for use in such assembly or fabrication.

Person. A partnership, company, association, trust, estate, or corporation, as well as a natural person.

Pistol. A weapon originally designed, made, and intended to fire a projectile (bullet) from one or more barrels when held in one hand, and having (a) a chamber(s) as an integral part(s) of, or permanently aligned with, the bore(s); and (b) a short stock designed to be gripped by one hand and at an angle to and extending below the line of the bore(s).

Revolver. A projectile weapon, of the pistol type, having a breechloading chambered cylinder so arranged that the cocking of the hammer or movement of the trigger rotates it and brings the next cartridge in line with the barrel for firing.

Rifle. A weapon designed or redesigned, made or remade, and intended to be fired from the shoulder and designed or redesigned and made or remade to use the energy of the explosive in a fixed cartridge to fire only a single projectile through a rifled bore for each single pull of the trigger, and shall include any such weapon which may be readily restored to fire a fixed cartridge.

Shotgun. A weapon designed or redesigned, made or remade, and intended to be fired from the shoulder and designed or redesigned and made or remade to use the energy of the explosive in a fixed shotgun shell to fire through a smooth bore either a number of projectiles (ball shot) or a single projectile for each pull of the trigger, and shall include any such weapon which may be readily restored to fire a fixed shotgun shell.

Transfer. This term and the various derivatives thereof shall include selling, assigning, pledging, leasing, loaning, giving away, or otherwise disposing of.

Unserviceable firearm. A firearm which is incapable of discharging a shot by means of an explosive and incapable of being readily restored to a firing condition.

Subpart C – Administrative and Miscellaneous Provisions.

27 C.F.R. § 479.22. Right of entry and examination.

Any ATF officer or employee of the Bureau of Alcohol, Tobacco and Firearms duly authorized to perform any function relating to the administration or enforcement of this part may enter during business hours the premises (including places of storage) of any importer or manufacturer of or dealer in firearms, to examine any books, papers, or records required to be kept pursuant to this part, and any firearms kept by such importer, manufacturer or dealer on such premises, and may require the production of any books, papers, or records necessary to determine any liability for tax under 26 U.S.C. Chapter 53, or the observance of 26 U.S.C. Chapter 53, and this part.

27 C.F.R. § 479.25. Collector's items.

The Director shall determine in accordance with 26 U.S.C. 5845(a), whether a firearm or device, which although originally designed as a weapon, is by reason of the date of its manufacture, value, design, and other characteristics primarily a collector's item and is not likely to be used as a weapon. A person who desires to obtain a determination under that provision of law shall follow the procedures prescribed in § 479.24 relating to destructive device determinations, and shall include information as to date of manufacture, value, design and other characteristics which would sustain a finding that the firearm or device is primarily a collector's item and is not likely to be used as a weapon.

Subpart G – Registration and identification of Firearms.

27 C.F.R. § 479.105. Transfer and possession of machine guns.

(a) General. As provided by 26 U.S.C. 5812 and 26 U.S.C. 5822, an application to make or transfer a firearm shall be denied if the making, transfer, receipt, or possession of the firearm would place the maker or transferee in violation of law. Section 922(o), Title 18, U.S.C., makes it unlawful for any person to transfer or possess a machine gun, except a transfer to or by, or possession by or under the authority of, the United States or any department or agency thereof or a State, or a department, agency, or political subdivision thereof; or any lawful transfer or lawful possession of a machine gun that was lawfully possessed before May 19, 1986. Therefore, notwithstanding any other provision of this part, no application to make, transfer, or import a machine gun will be approved except as provided by this section.

(b) Machine guns lawfully possessed prior to May 19, 1986. A machine gun possessed in compliance with the provisions of this part prior to May 19, 1986, may continue to be lawfully possessed by the person to whom the machine gun is registered and may, upon compliance with the provisions of this part, be lawfully transferred to and possessed by the transferee.

(c) Importation and manufacture. Subject to compliance with the provisions of this part, importers and manufacturers qualified under this part may import and manufacture machine guns on or after May 19, 1986, for sale or distribution to any department or agency of the United States or any State or political subdivision thereof, or for use by dealers qualified under this part as sales samples as provided in paragraph (d) of this section. The registration of such machine guns under this part and their subsequent transfer shall be conditioned upon and restricted to the sale or distribution of such weapons for the official use of Federal, State or local governmental entities. Subject to compliance with the provisions of this part, manufacturers qualified under this part may manufacture machine guns on or after May 19, 1986, for exportation in compliance with the Arms Export Control Act (22 U.S.C. 2778) and regulations prescribed thereunder by the Department of State.

(d) Dealer sales samples. Subject to compliance with the provisions of this part, applications to transfer and register a machine gun manufactured or imported on or after May 19, 1986, to dealers qualified under this part will be approved if it is established by specific information the expected governmental customers who would require a demonstration of the weapon, information as to the availability of the machine gun to fill subsequent orders, and letters from governmental entities expressing a need for a particular model or interest in seeing a demonstration of a particular weapon. Applications to transfer more than one machine gun of a particular model to a dealer must also establish the dealer's need for the quantity of samples sought to be transferred.

(e) The making of machine guns on or after May 19, 1986. Subject to compliance with the provisions of this part, applications to make and register machine guns on or after May 19, 1986, for the benefit of a Federal, State or local governmental entity (e.g., an invention for possible future use of a governmental entity or the making of a weapon in connection with research and development on behalf of such an entity) will be approved if it is established by specific information that the machine gun is particularly suitable for use by Federal, State or local governmental entities and that the making of the weapon is at the request and on behalf of such an entity.

(f) Discontinuance of business. Since section 922(o), Title 18, U.S.C., makes it unlawful to transfer or possess a machine gun except as provided in the law, any qualified manufacturer, importer, or dealer intending to discontinue business shall, prior to going out of business, transfer in compliance with the provisions of this part any machine gun manufactured or imported after May 19, 1986, to a Federal, State or local governmental entity, qualified manufacturer, qualified importer, or, subject to the provisions of paragraph (d) of this section, dealer qualified to possess such, machine gun.

Subpart J – Stolen or Lost Firearms or Documents.

27 C.F.R. § 479.141. Stolen or lost firearms.

Whenever any registered firearm is stolen or lost, the person losing possession thereof will, immediately upon discovery of such theft or loss, make a report to the Director showing the following: (a) Name and address of the person in whose name the firearm is registered, (b) kind of firearm, (c) serial number, (d) model, (e) caliber, (f) manufacturer of the firearm, (g) date and place of theft or loss, and (h) complete statement of facts and circumstances surrounding such theft or loss.

27 C.F.R. § 479.142. Stolen or lost documents.

When any Forms 1, 2, 3, 4, 5, 6A, or 10 (Firearms) evidencing possession of a firearm is stolen, lost, or destroyed, the person losing possession will immediately upon discovery of the theft, loss, or destruction report the matter to the Director. The report will show in detail the circumstances of the theft, loss, or destruction and will include all known facts which may serve to identify the document. Upon receipt of the report, the Director will make such investigation as appears appropriate and may issue a duplicate document upon such conditions as the circumstances warrant.

Subpart N – Penalties and Forfeitures.

27 C.F.R. § 479.181. Penalties.

Any person who violates or fails to comply with the requirements of 26 U.S.C. Chapter 53 shall, upon conviction, be subject to the penalties imposed under 26 U.S.C. 5871.

27 C.F.R. § 479.182. Forfeitures.

Any firearm involved in any violation of the provisions of 26 U.S.C. Chapter 53, shall be subject to seizure, and forfeiture under the internal revenue laws: Provided, however, That the disposition of forfeited firearms shall be in conformance with the requirements of 26 U.S.C. 5872. In addition, any vessel, vehicle or aircraft used to transport, carry, convey or conceal or possess any firearm with respect to which there has been committed any violation of any provision of 26 U.S.C. Chapter 53, or the regulations in this part issued pursuant thereto, shall be subject to seizure and forfeiture under the Customs laws, as provided by the act of August 9, 1939 (49 U.S.C. App., Chapter 11).

Title 38, Code of Federal Regulations, Chapter I, Part 1, Subgroup 6, Section 1.218

38 CFR § 1.218 - Security and law enforcement at VA facilities

(a)Authority and rules of conduct. Pursuant to 38 U.S.C. 901, the following rules and regulations apply at all property under the charge and control of VA (and not under the charge and control of the General Services Administration) and to all persons entering in or on such property. The head of the facility is charged with the responsibility for the enforcement of these rules and regulations and shall cause these rules and regulations to be posted in a conspicuous place on the property.

(1)Closing property to public. The head of the facility, or designee, shall establish visiting hours for the convenience of the public and shall establish specific hours for the transaction of business with the public. The property shall be closed to the public during other than the hours so established. In emergency situations, the property shall be closed to the public when reasonably necessary to ensure the orderly conduct of Government business. The decision to close a property during an emergency shall be made by the head of the facility or designee. The head of the facility or designee shall have authority to designate areas within a facility as closed to the public.

(2)Recording presence. Admission to property during periods when such property is closed to the public will be limited to persons authorized by the head of the facility or designee. Such persons may be required to sign a register and/or display identification documents when requested to do so by VA police, or other authorized individual. No person, without authorization, shall enter upon or remain on such property while the property is closed. Failure to leave such premises by unauthorized persons shall constitute an offense under this paragraph.

...

(13)Weapons and explosives. No person while on property shall carry firearms, other dangerous or deadly weapons, or explosives, either openly or concealed, except for official purposes.

(b)Schedule of offenses and penalties. Conduct in violation of the rules and regulations set forth in paragraph (a) of this section subjects an offender to arrest and removal from the premises. Whomever shall be found guilty of violating these rules and regulations while on any property under the charge and control of VA is subject to a fine as stated in the schedule set forth herein or, if appropriate, the payment of fixed sum in lieu of appearance (forfeiture of collateral) as may be provided for in rules of the United States District Court. Violations included in the schedule of offenses and penalties may also subject an offender to a term of imprisonment of not more than six months, as may be determined appropriate by a magistrate or judge of the United States District Court:

...

(37) Possession of firearms, carried either openly or concealed, whether loaded or unloaded (except by Federal or State law enforcement officers on official business, $500.

(38) Introduction or possession of explosives, or explosive devices which fire a projectile, ammunition, or combustibles, $500.

(39) Possession of knives which exceed a blade length of 3 inches; switchblade knives; any of the variety of hatchets, clubs and hand-held weapons; or brass knuckles, $300.

(40) The unauthorized possession of any of the variety of incapacitating liquid or gas-emitting weapons, $200.

Commentary:

It is important to be aware of the distinction between 18 U.S. Code § 930, which applies to federal facilities in general, and 38 C.F.R. § 1.218, which applies specifically to facilities under the control of the Veterans Administration rather than under the General Services

Administration. 18 U.S.C. § 930 specifically defines "federal facility" as a building in which federal employees are regularly present for work, and it prohibits the carrying or possession of firearms or dangerous weapons "in" federal facilities. Thus, 18 U.S.C. prohibits possession and carry inside federal buildings, but does not address outdoor areas such as parking lots. However, 38 C.F.R. § 1.218 applies to all real property controlled by the Veterans Administration. Therefore, it applies to parking lots as well as to the interiors of buildings.

It should be noted that the Veterans Administration hospital in West Haven has signs posted at all entrances to the property stating that firearms and weapons are prohibited on the property under the purview of 18 U.S. Code § 930. While this is incorrect and misleading, it does not appear to invalidate the provisions of 38 C.F.R. § 1.218.

Title 39, Code of Federal Regulations, Chapter I, Subchapter D, Part 232

39 CFR § 232.1 - Conduct on postal property

(a)Applicability. This section applies to all real property under the charge and control of the Postal Service, to all tenant agencies, and to all persons entering in or on such property. This section shall be posted and kept posted at a conspicuous place on all such property. This section shall not apply to –

(i) Any portions of real property, owned or leased by the Postal Service, that are leased or subleased by the Postal Service to private tenants for their exclusive use;

(ii) With respect to sections 232.1(h)(1) and 232.1(o), sidewalks along the street frontage of postal property falling within the property lines of the Postal Service that are not physically distinguishable from adjacent municipal or other public sidewalks, and any paved areas adjacent to such sidewalks that are not physically distinguishable from such sidewalks.

(b)Inspection, recording presence.

(1) Purses, briefcases, and other containers brought into, while on, or being removed from the property are subject to inspection. However, items brought directly to a postal facility's customer mailing acceptance area and deposited in the mail are not subject to inspection, except as provided by section 274 of the Administrative Support Manual. A person arrested for violation of this section may be searched incident to that arrest.

(2) Vehicles and their contents brought into, while on, or being removed from restricted nonpublic areas are subject to inspection. A prominently displayed sign shall advise in advance that vehicles and their contents are subject to inspection when entering the restricted nonpublic area, while in the confines of the area, or when leaving the area. Persons entering these areas who object and refuse to consent to the inspection of the vehicle, its contents, or both, may be denied entry; after entering the area without objection, consent shall be implied. A full search of a person and any vehicle driven or occupied by the person may accompany an arrest.

(3) Except as otherwise ordered, properties must be closed to the public after normal business hours. Properties also may be closed to the public in emergency situations and at such other times as may be necessary for the orderly conduct of business. Admission to properties during periods when such properties are closed to the public may be limited to

authorized individuals who may be required to sign the register and display identification documents when requested by security force personnel or other authorized individuals.

...

(l)Weapons and explosives. Notwithstanding the provisions of any other law, rule or regulation, no person while on postal property may carry firearms, other dangerous or deadly weapons, or explosives, either openly or concealed, or store the same on postal property, except for official purposes.

> ***Commentary***
>
> *It is important to be aware of the distinction between 18 U.S. Code § 930, which applies to federal facilities in general, and 39 C.F.R. 232.1, which applies specifically to United States Postal Service facilities. 18 U.S.C. § 930 specifically defines "federal facility" as a building in which federal employees are regularly present for work, and it prohibits the carrying or possession of firearms or dangerous weapons "in" federal facilities. Thus, 18 U.S.C. prohibits possession and carry inside federal buildings, but does not address outdoor areas such as parking lots. However, 39 C.F.R. 323.1 applies to all real property owned or leased by the Postal Service. Therefore, it applies to parking lots as well as to the interiors of buildings.*
>
> *This was tested in the case of* Bonidy et al v. U.S. Postal Service et al, 10th U.S. Circuit Court of Appeals, No. 13-1374.*The 10th U.S. Circuit Court of Appeals ruled that the Postal Service prohibition against firearms on Postal Service property is not unconstitutional.*

Title 49, Code of Federal Regulations, Part 1540, Subpart B

49 C.F.R. § 1540.111 – Carriage of weapons, explosives, and incendiaries by individuals.

(a) *On an individual's person or accessible property—prohibitions.* Except as provided in paragraph (b) of this section, an individual may not have a weapon, explosive, or incendiary, on or about the individual's person or accessible property—

(1) When performance has begun of the inspection of the individual's person or accessible property before entering a sterile area, or before boarding an aircraft for which screening is conducted under §1544.201 or §1546.201 of this chapter;

(2) When the individual is entering or in a sterile area; or

(3) When the individual is attempting to board or onboard an aircraft for which screening is conducted under §§1544.201, 1546.201, or 1562.23 of this chapter.

(b) *On an individual's person or accessible property—permitted carriage of a weapon.* Paragraph (a) of this section does not apply as to carriage of firearms and other weapons if the individual is one of the following:

(1) Law enforcement personnel required to carry a firearm or other weapons while in the performance of law enforcement duty at the airport.

(2) An individual authorized to carry a weapon in accordance with §§1544.219, 1544.221, 1544.223, 1546.211, or subpart B of part 1562 of this chapter.

(3) An individual authorized to carry a weapon in a sterile area under a security program.

(c) *In checked baggage.* A passenger may not transport or offer for transport in checked baggage or in baggage carried in an inaccessible cargo hold under §1562.23 of this chapter:

(1) Any loaded firearm(s).

(2) Any unloaded firearm(s) unless—

(i) The passenger declares to the aircraft operator, either orally or in writing, before checking the baggage, that the passenger has a firearm in his or her bag and that it is unloaded;

(ii) The firearm is unloaded;

(iii) The firearm is carried in a hard-sided container; and

(iv) The container in which it is carried is locked, and only the passenger retains the key or combination.

(3) Any unauthorized explosive or incendiary.

(d) *Ammunition.* This section does not prohibit the carriage of ammunition in checked baggage or in the same container as a firearm. Title 49 CFR part 175 provides additional requirements governing carriage of ammunition on aircraft.

BRADY HANDGUN VIOLENCE PREVENTION ACT OF 1993

...

SEC. 103. NATIONAL INSTANT CRIMINAL BACKGROUND CHECK SYSTEM.

(a) DETERMINATION OF TIMETABLES.—Not later than 6 months after the date of enactment of this Act, the Attorney General shall—

(1) determine the type of computer hardware and software that will be used to operate the national instant criminal background check system and the means by which State criminal records systems and the telephone or electronic device of licensees will communicate with the national system;

(2) investigate the criminal records system of each State and determine for each State a timetable by which the State should be able to provide criminal records on an on-line capacity basis to the national system; and

(3) notify each State of the determinations made pursuant to paragraphs (1) and (2).

(b) ESTABLISHMENT OF SYSTEM.—(1) IN GENERAL—Not later than 60 months after the date of the enactment of this Act, the Attorney General shall establish a national instant criminal background check system that any licensee may contact, by telephone or by other electronic means in addition to the telephone, for information, to be supplied immediately, on whether receipt of a firearm by a prospective transferee would violate section 922 of title 18, United States Code, or State law.

(2) VOLUNTARY BACKGROUND CHECKS.—

(A) IN GENERAL.—Not later than 90 days after the date of enactment of this paragraph, the Attorney General shall promulgate regulations allowing licensees to use the national instant criminal background check system established under this section for purposes of voluntarily conducting an employment background check relating to a current or prospective employee. The Attorney General may not collect a fee for an employment background check under this subparagraph.

(B) NOTICE.—Before conducting an employment background check relating to a current or prospective employee under subparagraph (A), a licensee shall—

(i) provide written notice to the current or prospective employee that the licensee intends to conduct the background check; and

(ii) obtain consent to conduct the background check from the current or prospective employee in writing.

(C) EXEMPTION.—An employment background check conducted by a licensee under subparagraph (A) shall not be governed by the Fair Credit Reporting Act (15 U.S.C. 1681 et seq.).

(D) APPEAL.—Any individual who is the subject of an employment background check conducted by a licensee under subparagraph (A) the result of which indicates that the individual is prohibited from possessing a firearm or ammunition pursuant to subsection (g) or (n) of section 922 of title 18, United States Code, may appeal the results of the background check in the same manner and to the same extent as if the individual had been the subject of a background check relating to the transfer of a firearm.

(c) EXPEDITED ACTION BY THE ATTORNEY GENERAL.—The Attorney General shall expedite—

(1) the upgrading and indexing of State criminal history records in the Federal criminal records system maintained by the Federal Bureau of Investigation;

(2) the development of hardware and software systems to link State criminal history check systems into the national instant criminal background check system established by the Attorney General pursuant to this section; and

(3) the current revitalization initiatives by the Federal Bureau of Investigation for technologically advanced fingerprint and criminal records identification.

(d) NOTIFICATION OF LICENSEES.—On establishment of the system under this section, the Attorney General shall notify each licensee and the chief law enforcement officer of each State of the existence and purpose of the system and the means to be used to contact the system.

(e) ADMINISTRATIVE PROVISIONS.—

(1) AUTHORITY TO OBTAIN OFFICIAL INFORMATION.—Notwithstanding any other law, the Attorney General may secure directly from any department or agency of the United States such information on persons for whom receipt of a firearm would violate subsection (g) or (n) of section 922 of title 18, United States Code or State law, as is necessary to enable the system to operate in accordance with this section. On request of the Attorney General, the head of such department or agency shall furnish such information to the system.

(2) OTHER AUTHORITY.—-The Attorney General shall develop such computer software, design and obtain such telecommunications and computer hardware, and employ such personnel, as are necessary to establish and operate the system in accordance with this section.

(f) WRITTEN REASONS PROVIDED ON REQUEST.—If the national instant criminal background check system determines that an individual is ineligible to receive a firearm and the individual requests the system to provide the reasons for the determination, the system shall provide such reasons to the individual, in writing, within 5 business days after the date of the request.

(g) CORRECTION OF ERRONEOUS SYSTEM INFORMATION.—If the system established under this section informs an individual contacting the system that receipt of a firearm by a prospective transferee would violate subsection (g) or (n) of section 922 of title 18, United States Code or State law, the prospective transferee may request the Attorney General to provide the prospective transferee with the reasons therefor. Upon receipt of such a request, the Attorney General shall immediately comply with the request. The prospective transferee may submit to the Attorney General information to correct, clarify, or supplement records of the system with respect to the prospective transferee. After receipt of such information, the Attorney General shall immediately consider the information, investigate the matter further, and correct all erroneous Federal records relating to the prospective transferee and give notice of the error to any Federal department or agency or any State that was the source of such erroneous records.

(h) REGULATIONS.— After 90 days' notice to the public and an opportunity for hearing by interested parties, the Attorney General shall prescribe regulations to ensure the privacy and security of the information of the system established under this section.

(i) PROHIBITION RELATING To ESTABLISHMENT OF REGISTRATION SYSTEMS WITH RESPECT TO FIREARMS.—No department, agency, officer, or employee of the United States may—

(1) require that any record or portion thereof generated by the system established under this section be recorded at or transferred to a facility owned, managed, or controlled by the United States or any State or political subdivision thereof; or

(2) use the system established under this section to establish any system for the registration of firearms, firearm owners, or firearm transactions or dispositions, except with respect to persons, prohibited by section 922 (g) or (n) of title 18, United States Code or State law, from receiving a firearm,

(j) DEFINITIONS.— As used in this section:

(1) LICENSEE.— The term "licensee" means a licensed importer (as defined in section 921(aX9) of title 18, United States Code), a licensed manufacturer (as defined in section 921(aX10) of that title), or a licensed dealer (as defined in section 921(aXll) of that title).

(2) OTHER TERMS.—The terms "firearm", "handgun", "licensed importer", "licensed manufacturer", and licensed dealer" have the meanings stated in section 921(a) of title 18, United States Code, as amended by subsection (a)(2).

(k) AUTHORIZATION OF APPROPRIATIONS.—There are authorized to be appropriated, which may be appropriated from the Violent Crime Reduction Trust Fund established by section 1115 of title 31, United States Code, such sums as are necessary to enable the Attorney General to carry out this section.

(l) REQUIREMENTS RELATING TO BACKGROUND CHECKS FOR PERSONS UNDER AGE 21.—If a licensee contacts the system established under this section regarding a proposed transfer of a firearm to a person less than 21 years of age in accordance with subsection (t) of section 922 of title 18, United States Code, the system shall—

(1) immediately contact—

(A) the criminal history repository or juvenile justice information system, as appropriate, of the State in which the person resides for the purpose of determining whether the person has a possibly disqualifying juvenile record under subsection (d) of such section 922;

(B) the appropriate State custodian of mental health adjudication records in the State in which the person resides to determine whether the person has a possibly disqualifying juvenile record under subsection (d) of such section 922; and[1]

---

[1] Pursuant to Title II, section (a)(3) of the Bipartisan Safer Communities Act, the changes made to the Brady Handgun Control Act by paragraphs (1)(B) and (2) are automatically repealed effective September 30, 2032, and the provisions of law amended by those paragraphs are restored as if those paragraphs had not been amended.

(C) a local law enforcement agency of the jurisdiction in which the person resides for the purpose of determining whether the person has a possibly disqualifying juvenile record under subsection (d) of such section 922;

(2) as soon as possible, but in no case more than 3 business days, after the licensee contacts the system, notify the licensee whether cause exists to further investigate a possibly disqualifying juvenile record under subsection (d) of such section 922; and[2]

(3) if there is cause for further investigation, as soon as possible, but in no case more than 10 business days, after the licensee contacts the system, notify the licensee whether—

(A) transfer of a firearm to the person would violate subsection (d) of such section 922; or

(B) receipt of a firearm by the person would violate subsection (g) or (n) of such section 922, or State, local, or Tribal law.

...

Commentary

The Brady Handgun Violence Prevention Act of 1993 included a number of provisions that were not of a type that were suitable for codification as either federal statutes (under the United States Code) or regulations (under the Code of Federal Regulations). The Bipartisan Safer Communities Act of 2022 (Public Law 117–159) included a number of revisions to the uncodified portions of the Brady Handgun Control Act, particularly Section 103 pertaining to the National Instant Criminal Background Check System (NICS). Section 103 of the Brady Handgun Control Act, as amended, is reproduced above to make the revised language available.

---

[2] Ibid.

INDEX OF WORDS AND PHRASES

APPENDIX A

INDEX TO SELECTED FEDERAL FIREARMS OFFENSES

Offense Section	**Description**	**Statutory Maximum**
18 U.S.C. § 922(a)(1)	Willful engagement in firearms business without a license (cf. 26 U.S.C. § 5861(a))	5 years (§ 924(a)(1)(D))
18 U.S.C. § 922(a)(2)	Willful shipment or transport of firearm to unlicensed recipient	5 years (§ 924(a)(1)(D))
18 U.S.C. § 922(a)(3)	Willful receipt of firearm from out of state by unlicensed person	5 years (§ 924(a)(1)(D))
18 U.S.C. § 922(a)(4)	Knowing interstate transport of certain weapons by unlicensed person	5 years (§ 924(a)(1)(B))
18 U.S.C. § 922(a)(5)	Willful transfer, sale, or transport of weapon by unlicensed person to another unlicensed, out-of-state person	5 years (§ 924(a)(1)(D))
18 U.S.C. § 922(a)(6)	Knowing making of false statement in connection with purchase of firearm (cf. § 924(a)(1)(A), 26 U.S.C. § 5861(*l*))	10 years (§ 924(a)(2))
18 U.S.C. § 922(a)(7)	Willful manufacture or importation of armor-piercing ammunition	5 years (§ 924(a)(1)(D))
18 U.S.C. § 922(a)(8)	Willful sale or delivery of armor-piercing ammunition	5 years (§ 924(a)(1)(D))
18 U.S.C. § 922(b)(1)	Willful sale by licensee to juvenile (cf. § 922(x)(1))	5 years (§ 924(a)(1)(D))
18 U.S.C. § 922(b)(2)	Willful sale by license to person in violation of state law	5 years (§ 924(a)(1)(D))
18 U.S.C. § 922(b)(3)	Willful sale by licensee to out-of-state recipient	5 years (§ 924(a)(1)(D))
18 U.S.C. § 922(b)(4)	Willful sale by licensee of certain prohibited weapons	5 years (§ 924(a)(1)(D))
18 U.S.C. § 922(b)(5)	Willful sale by licensee without proper record-keeping	5 years (§ 924(a)(1)(D))
18 U.S.C. § 922(d)	Knowing sale to prohibited person	10 years (§ 924(a)(2))
18 U.S.C. § 922(e)	Willful delivery of firearm to common carrier without written notice	5 years (§ 924(a)(1)(D))
18 U.S.C. § 922(g)	Knowing possession of firearm by prohibited person	10 years (§ 924(a)(2))
18 U.S.C. § 922(i)	Knowing shipment or transport of stolen firearm	10 years (§ 924(a)(2))
18 U.S.C. § 922(j)	Knowing possession, etc., of stolen firearm (cf. 26 U.S.C. § 5861 922(u), § 924(*l*), (m))	10 years (§ 924(a)(2))
18 U.S.C. § 922(k)	Knowing possession, receipt, shipment, or transport of firearm with altered or	5 years (§ 924(a)(1)(B))

	obliterated serial number (cf. 26 U.S.C. § 5861(g), (h), (i))	
18 U.S.C. § 922(*l*)	Knowing importation or receipt of firearms (cf. 26 U.S.C. § 5861(k))	5 years (§ 924(a)(1)(C))
18 U.S.C. § 922(m)	Knowing falsification of records by licensee (cf. 26 U.S.C. § 5861(*l*))	1 year (§ 924(a)(3))
18 U.S.C. § 922(n)	Knowing shipment, transport, or receipt of firearm by person under felony indictment	5 years (§ 924(a)(1)(D))
18 U.S.C. § 922(o)	Knowing possession of machine gun	10 years (§ 924(a)(2))
18 U.S.C. § 922(p)	Knowing manufacture, importation, sale, shipment, or possession of firearms designed to avoid detection	5 years (§ 924(f))
18 U.S.C. § 922(q)(2), (3)	Knowing possession or knowing or reckless discharge of firearm in school zone	5 years *consecutive* (§ 924(a)(4))
18 U.S.C. § 922(r)	Knowing assembly of shotgun or semiautomatic rifle from imported parts	5 years (§ 924(a)(1)(B))
18 U.S.C. § 922(s)	Knowing sale or transfer of handgun without background check	1 year (§ 924(a)(5))
18 U.S.C. § 922(t)(1)	Transfer if firearm by licensee without contacting NICS	5 years (§ 924(a)(1)(D))
18 U.S.C. § 922(u)	Steal or unlawfully remove any firearm from licensee's inventory	5 years (§ 924(a)(1)(D))
18 U.S.C. § 922(x)(1)	Knowingly sell, deliver, or transfer a handgun or handgun ammunition to a juvenile	5 years (§ 924(a)(1)(D))
18 U.S.C. § 922(x)(2)	Knowingly possess a handgun or handgun ammunition by a juvenile	5 years (§ 924(a)(1)(D))
26 U.S.C. § 5861(g)	Obliteration, alteration or removal of serial number (cf. 18 U.S.C. § 922(k))	10 years (§ 5871)
26 U.S.C. § 5861(h)	Receipt or possession of firearm with obliterated, removed, or altered serial number (cf. 18 U.S.C. § 922(k))	10 years (§ 5871)
26 U.S.C. § 5861(i)	Receipt or possession of firearm unidentified by serial number (cf. 18 U.S.C. § 922(k))	10 years (§ 5871)
26 U.S.C. § 5861(j)	Transport, delivery, or receipt of unregistered firearm	10 years (§ 5871)
26 U.S.C. § 5861(k)	Receipt or possession of unlawfully imported firearm (cf. 18 U.S.C. § 922(*l*))	10 years (§ 5871)
26 U.S.C. § 5861(*l*)	Knowingly making false entry on application or record (cf. 18 U.S.C. §§ 922(m), 924(a)(1)(A), 924(a)(3))	10 years (§ 5871)

Selected Offenses Involving Use

18 U.S.C. § 36
18 U.S.C. § 111
18 U.S.C. § 112
18 U.S.C. § 924©
18 U.S.C. § 2113(d)
18 U.S.C. § 2114

Selected Offenses Involving Manufacture

18 U.S.C. § 922(a)(7)
18 U.S.C. § 922(p)
18 U.S.C. § 922®
18 U.S.C. § 922(v)
26 U.S.C. § 5861(f)

Selected Offenses Involving Sale, Transfer

18 U.S.C. § 922(a)(5), (8)
18 U.S.C. § 922(b)(1), (2), (3), (4), (5)
18 U.S.C. § 922(d)
18 U.S.C. § 922(j)
18 U.S.C. § 922(s), (t)
18 U.S.C. § 922(x)
18 U.S.C. § 924(h)
26 U.S.C. § 5861(e)

Selected Offenses Involving Shipping, Transport

18 U.S.C. § 922(a)(2), (3), (4), (5)
18 U.S.C. § 922(i)
18 U.S.C. § 922(k)
18 U.S.C. § 922(n)
18 U.S.C. § 922(p)
18 U.S.C. § 922(b)
26 U.S.C. § 5861(j)

Selected offenses Involving Possession, Receipt

18 U.S.C. § 922(a)(3)
18 U.S.C. § 922(g)
18 U.S.C. § 922(j)
18 U.S.C. § 922(k)
18 U.S.C. § 922(*l*)
18 U.S.C. § 922(n)
18 U.S.C. § 922(o)
18 U.S.C. § 922(p)
18 U.S.C. § 922(q)
18 U.S.C. § 922(v)
18 U.S.C. § 924(b), (c)
26 U.S.C. § 5861(b), (c), (d), (h), (i), (j), (k)

Guideline Enhancements for Firearms, Dangerous Weapons

U.S.S.G. § 2A2.2(b)(2)	Aggravated Assault
U.S.S.G. § 2A2.3(a)(1)	Minor Assault
U.S.S.G. § 2A2.4(b)(1)	Obstructing or impeding officers
U.S.S.G. § 2A3.1(b)(1)	Criminal sexual abuse
U.S.S.G. § 2A4.1(b)(3)	Kidnapping
U.S.S.G. § 2A6.2(b)(1)	Stalking or domestic violence
U.S.S.G. § 2B1.1(c)(1)	Theft
U.S.S.G. § 2B2.1(b)(3)	Burglary
U.S.S.G. § 2B2.1(b)(4)	Burglary
U.S.S.G. § 2B2.3(b)(2)	Trespass
U.S.S.G. § 2B3.1(b)(2)	Robbery
U.S.S.G. § 2B3.2(b)(3)	Extortion
U.S.S.G. § 2B5.1(b)(3)	Counterfeiting
U.S.S.G. § 2D1.1(b)(1)	Drugs
U.S.S.G. § 2D1.11(b)(1)	Listed chemicals
U.S.S.G. § 2E2.1(b)(1)	Extortionate credit
U.S.S.G. § 2F1.1(b)(6)	Fraud
U.S.S.G. § 2H4.1(b)(2)	Peonage, involuntary servitude
U.S.S.G. § 2L1.1(b)(4)	Alien smuggling
U.S.S.G. § 2P1.2(a)(1)	Prison contraband
U.S.S.G. § 5K2.6	Weapons
U.S.S.G. § 5K2.17	High-capacity semiautomatic firearms

APPENDIX B

STATE OF CONNECTICUT
BOARD OF FIREARMS PERMIT EXAMINERS
FINAL DECISION
DECLARATORY RULING ON PETITION CONCERNING APPLICATIONS

I. INTRODUCTION

On September 28, 2009, the Board of Firearms Permit Examiners received a petition for declaratory ruling from Jack Goldberg (hereafter "Petitioner") requesting a ruling on sixteen separate issues. At a meeting of the Board on October 8, 2009 the Board voted to issue a declaratory ruling in response to Question 3, to the extent that this question comes within the Board's jurisdiction. With respect to the petitioner's other questions, as phrased Questions 1, 2, 4, 5, 6, 7, 8, 9, 10, 11, 12, 13, 14, 15, and 16 did not express questions which fall within the Board's statutory jurisdiction to issue a declaratory ruling under Conn. Gen. Stat. §4-176(a). Accordingly, the Board has declined to issue a declaratory ruling with respect to those questions.

II. FACTS

The Board agreed to issue a declaratory ruling on the following issue: "With respect to a permit to carry a pistol or revolver, is a person unsuitable if he does not supply to the issuing authority upon demand any additional information beyond that required by the standard state application form?"

The Petitioner's request is a pure issue of law which does not require the presentation of evidence. The Board is aware, however, of the practice in some jurisdictions of requiring additional material to be submitted with the original application which are not specified in the statute such as letters of reference, medical releases, detailed resumes, and credit histories.

III. PARTIES

PETITIONER:
Mr. Jack Goldberg
530 Maple Street
Wethersfield, Connecticut

RESPONDANTS:
John A. Danaher, III
Commissioner, Department of Public Safety
1111 Country Club Road
Middletown, CT 06457

Office of the Governor
State Capitol
210 Capitol Avenue
Hartford, CT 06106

PARTIES (Continued):

Kevin Kane
Chief State's Attorney
300 Corporate Place
Rocky Hill, CT 06067

Stephen R. Sarnoski
Assistant Attorney General
Mackenzie Hall
110 Sherman Street
Hartford, CT 06105-2294

Thomas Flaherty,
Executive Director
Police Officer Standards &
Training Council
285 Preston A venue
Meriden, CT 06450

Honorable Barbara M.
Quinn
Chief Court Administrator
231 Capitol A venue
Hartford, CT 06106

Leonard T. Benedetto
160 Otis Street
Stratford, CT 06615

Mr. Scott Wilson
8 Summer Street
New London, CT 06320

First Selectman Robert
Burbank
Town of Andover
17 School Road
Andover, CT 06232

First Selectman Derrylyn
Gorski
Town of Bethany
40 Peck Road
Bethany, CT 06525

First Selectman William
Ballinger
Town of Fitchville
1 River Road
Fitchville, CT 06334

First Selectman Kathleen
Zabel
Town of Burlington
200 Spielman Highway
Burlington, CT 06013

First Selectman Linda
Riley Hodge
Town of Colchester
127 Norwich Avenue
Colchester, CT 06415

First Selectman Gordon
Ridgway
Town of Cornwall
26 Pine Street
Cornwall, CT 06753

First Selectman James
Hayden
Town of East Granby
9 Center Street
East Granby, CT 06026

First Selectman Richard
Woodward
Town of Eastford
P.O. Box 98
Eastford, CT 06242-0098

First Selectman Richard
Matters
Town of North Franklin
7 Meeting House Hill
Road
North Franklin, CT 06254

First Selectman Tony
Bondi
Town of Haddam
30 Field Park Drive
Haddam, CT 06438

First Selectman Ralph
Fletcher
Town of Ashford
5 Town Hall Road
Ashford, CT 06278-1530

First Selectman Jeffrey
Hamel
Town of Bethlehem
P.O. Box 160
Bethlehem, CT 06751

First Selectman William
Stuart
Town of Bridgewater
44 Main Street South
Bridgewater, CT 06752

First Selectman Robert
Dubos
Town of Chaplin
P.O. Box 286
Chaplin, CT 06235

First Selectman Thomas
mckeon
Town of Colebrook
P.O. Box 5
Colebrook, CT 06021

First Selectman Richard
Smith
Town of Deep River
174 Main Street
Deep River, CT 06417

First Selectman Mark Walter
Town of East Haddam
7 Main Street, PO Box K
East Haddam, CT 06423

First Selectman Michael Stupinski
Town of Ellington
PO Box 187
Ellington, CT 06029

First Selectman Robert Valentine
Town of Goshen
42 North Street, Box 187
Goshen, CT 06756

First Selectman Maurice Bisson
Town of Hampton
P.O. Box 143
Hampton, CT 06247

First Selectman Susan Cable
Town of Beacon Falls
10 Maple A venue
Beacon Falls, CT 06403

Town Manager Louie Chapman
Town of Bloomfield
800 Bloomfield A venue
Bloomfield, CT 06002

First Selectman Roger Engle
Town of Brooklyn
4 Wolf Den Rd.
PO Box 356
Brooklyn, CT 06234

First Selectman Thomas Marsh
Town of Chester
203 Middlesex A venue
Chester, CT 06412-0218

First Selectman Donald Cianci
Town of Columbia
Route 87
Columbia, CT 06237

First Selectman Laura Francis
Town of Durham
30 Town House Road
Durham, CT 06422

First Selectman Paul Formica
Town of Niantic
108 Pennsylvania Ave I
Niantic, CT 06357

First Selectman Philip Miller
Town of Essex
29 West A venue
Essex, CT 06426

First Selectman Philip Anthony
Town of Jewett City
28 Main Street
Jewett City, CT 06351

First Selectman Wade Cole
Town of East Hartland
22 South Road
East Hartland, CT 06027

First Selectman Frank Chiaramonte
Town of Harwinton
100 Bentley Drive
Harwinton, CT 06791

Chairman of Town Council Janice Thurlow
Town of Danielson
P.O. Box 6000
Danielson, CT 06239-6000

Mayor Fred Allyn
Town of Ledyard
7 41 Colonel Ledyard Highway
Ledyard, CT 06339

First Selectman Ralph Eno
Town of Lyme
480 Hamburg Road
Lyme, CT 06371

First Selectman Jon Brayshaw
Town of Middlefield
393 Jackson Hill Road
Middlefield, CT 06455

First Selectman Jolm Hodge
Town of New Fairfield
RT. 39, 4 Brush Hill Road
New Fairfield, CT 06812

First Selectman Nicholas Mullane
Town of North Stonington
40 Main Street
North Stonington, CT 06359

First Selectman Susan Bransfield
Town of Portland
P.O. Box 71
Portland, CT 06480

First Selectman Barbara Henry
Town of Roxbury
P.O. Box 203
Roxbury, CT 06783

First Selectman Malcolm Brown
Town of Sharon
P.O. Box 385
Sharon, CT 06069

Town Manager Jared Clark
Town of Hebron
15 Gilead Street
Hebron, CT 06248

Town Manager Bruce Beneway
Town of Danielson
PO Box 6000
Danielson, CT 06239

First Selectman Thomas Sparkman
Town of Lisbon
2 Newent Road
Lisbon, CT 06351

Town Manager Matthew Hart
Town of Mansfield
4 So. Eagleville Road
Mansfield, CT 06268

Mayor Joseph Jaskiewicz
Town of Uncasville
310 Norwich-New London Turnpike
Uncasville, CT 06382

First Selectman Earl Russell Macinnes
Town of New Hartford
530 Main Street, P.O. Box 316
New Hartford, CT 06057

First Selectman Mary Ann Drayton Rogers
Town of Oxford
486 Oxford Road
Oxford, CT 06483

First Selectman Robert Congdon
Town of Preston
389 Route 2
Preston, CT 06365

First Selectman Curtis Rand
Town of Salisbury
P.O. Box 548
Salisbury, CT 06068

First Selectman Andrea 0 Connor
Town of Sherman
Rt. 39 South I PO Box 39
Sherman, CT 06784

First Selectman Ruth Epstein
Town of Kent
P.O. Box 678
Kent, CT 06757

First Selectman Richard Cabral
Town of Killingworth
323 Route 81
Killingworth, CT 06417

First Selectman Leo Paul
Town of Litchfield
74 West Street
Litchfield, CT 06759

First Selectman William Black
Town of Marlborough
PO Box 29
Marlborough, CT 06447

First Selectman Karen Paradis
Town of Morris
3 East Street, P.O. Box 66
Morris, CT 06763

First Selectman Douglas Humes
Town of Canaan
100 Pease Street Box 876
Canaan, CT 06018

First Selectman James Rivers
Town of Pomfret Center
5 Haven Road, Route 44
Pomfret Center, CT 06259

Mayor Robert Chatfield
Town of Prospect
36 Center Street
Prospect, CT 06712

First Selectman Clark Steams
Town of Scotland
P.O. Box 288
Scotland, CT 06462

First Selectman David Pinney
Town of Somers
600 Main Street, P.O. Box 308
Somers, CT 06071

First Selectman H. William Davis
Town of Southbury
501 Main Street
Southbury, CT 06488

First Selectman Russell Gray
Town of Oneco
P.O. Box 157
Oneco, CT 06373 0157

Town Manager Steven Werbner
Town of Tolland
21 Tolland Green
Tolland, CT 06084

First Selectman Jack Travers
Town of Warren
7 Sackett Hill Road
Warren, CT 06754

First Selectman Michael Eldredge
Town of Willington
40 Old Farms Road
Willington, CT 06279

First Selectman Paul Hinckley
Town of Woodbury
P.O. Box 369
Woodbury, CT 06798-0369

Chief Mark Rinaldo
Town of Avon
60 West Main Street
Avon, CT 06001

Acting Chief Jeff Blatter
Town of Bloomfield
785 Park Avenue
Bloomfield, CT 06002

Chief John divenere
Town of Bristol
131 North Main Street
Bristol, CT 06010

Chief Michael Cruess
Town of Cheshire
500 Highland Avenue
Cheshire, CT 06410

First Selectman Catherine Osten
Town of Baltic
1 Main Street, P .0. Box 677
Baltic, CT 06330

First Selectman Larry Groh
Town of N. Grosvenordale
815 Riverside Drive
P.O. Box 899
N. Grosvenordale, CT 06255-0899

First Selectman Thomas Fitzgerald
Town of Union
1024 Buckley Highway
Union, CT 06076

First Selectman Mark Lyon
Town of Washington Depot
2 Bryan Plaza, P.O. Box 383
Washington Depot, CT 06794

First Selectman Kenneth Fracasso
Town of Winsted
338 Main Street
Winsted, CT 06098

First Selectman Allan Walker
Town of Woodstock
415 Route 169
Woodstock, CT 06281-3039

Chief Paul Fitzgerald
Town of Berlin
240 Kensington Road
Berlin, CT 06037-9990

Chief John decarlo
Town of Branford
33 Laurel Street
Branford, CT 06405

Chief Robin Montgomery
Town of Brookfield
63 Silvermine Road
Brookfield, CT 06804

Chief Joseph Faughnan
Town of Clinton
170 East Main Street
Clinton, CT 06413

First Selectman Michael Krol
Town of Stafford Springs
1 Main Street
Stafford Springs, CT 06076

Chairman of Town Council Frederick Daniels
Town of Tolland
21 Tolland Green
Tolland, CT 06084

First Selectman Gilbert Grimm
Town of Voluntown
P.O. Box 96
Voluntown, CT 06384-0096

First Selectman Noel Bishop
Town of Westbrook
866 Boston Post Road
Westbrook, CT 06498

First Selectman Jean desmet
Town of Willimantic
979 Main Street
Willimantic, CT 06226

Chief Kevin Hale
Town of Ansonia
2 Elm Street
Ansonia, CT 06401

Chief Jeffrey Finch
Town of Bethel
P.O. Box 142
Bethel, CT 06801

Acting Chief Joseph Gaudett
Town of Bridgeport
300 Congress Street
Bridgeport, CT 06604

Interim Chief Lori Coppinger
Town of Canton
45 River Road
Canton, CT 06019

Chief Mark Palmer
Town of Coventry
1585 Main Street
Coventry, CT 06238

Chief Anthony J. Salvatore
Town of Cromwell
5 West Street
Cromwell, CT 06416

Chief Alan D. Baker
Town of Danbury
375 Main Street
Danbury, CT 06810

Chief Duanne J. Lovello
Town of Darien
25 Hecker Avenue
Darien, CT 06820

Chief Gene Mascolo
Town of Derby
125 Water Street
Derby, CT 06418

Chief Matthew A. Reimondo
Town of East Hampton
20 East High Street
East Hampton, CT 06424

Chief Mark J. Sirois
Town of East Hartford
31 School Street
East Hartford, CT 06108

Chief Leonard L. Gallo
Town of East Haven
471 North High Street
P.O. Box 544,
East Haven, CT 06512

Chief Edward J. Demarco, Jr.
Town of East Windsor
25 School St.
East Windsor, CT 06088

Chief John F. Solomon
Town of Easton
P.O. Box 7
Easton, CT 06612

Chief Carl J. Sferrazza
Chief
Town of Enfield
293 Elm Street
Enfield, CT 06082

David J. Peck
Town of Fairfield
100 Reef Road
Fairfield, CT 06430

Chief Paul Melanson
Town of Farmington
319 Ne\v Britain Avenue
Farmington, CT 06085

Chief Thomas Sweeney
Town of Glastonbury
P.O. Box 535
Glastonbury, CT 06033

Chief David Watkins
Town of Granby
15 North Granby Road
Granby, CT 06035

Chief Dave Ridberg
Town of Greenwich
11 Bruce Place
Greenwich, CT 06836-1404

Chief Bruno Giulini
Town of Groton City
295 Meridian Street
Groton City, CT 06340

Chief John C. Drumm
Town of Groton Long Point
P.O. Box 3738
Groton Long Point, CT 06340

Chief Kelly Fogg
Town of Groton
68 Groton Long Point Road
8208 Groton Town, CT 06340

Chief Thomas Terribile
Town of Guilford
400 Church Street
Guilford, CT 06437-

Chief Thomas J. Wydra
Town of Hamden
2900 Dixwell Avenue
Hamden, CT 06518

Chief Daryl K. Roberts
City of Hartford
50 Jennings Road
Hartford, CT 06120

Acting Chief Robert F. Nolan
Town of Madison
9 Campus Drive
Madison, CT 06443

Chief Marc Montminy
Town of Manchester
P.O. Box 191
Manchester, CT 06045-0191

Chief Jeffrey Cossette
Town of Meriden
50 West Main Street
Meriden, CT 06451

Chief Richard Guisti
Town of Middlebury
200 Southford Rd.
Middlebury, CT 06762

Acting Chief Patrick mcmahon
Town of Middletown
222 Main Street
Middletown, CT 06457

Chief Keith Mello
Town of Milford
430 Boston Post Road
Milford, CT 06460

Chief John L. Salvatore
Town of Monroe
7 Fan Hill Road
Monroe, CT 06468

Chief Christopher Edson
Town of Naugatuck
211 Spring Street
Naugatuck, CT 06770

Chief William Gagliardi
Town of New Britain
125 Columbus Boulevard
New Britain, CT 06051

Chief Edward Nadriezny
Town of New Canaan
174 South Ave
New Canaan, CT 06840

Chief James Lewis
City of New Haven
1 Union Avenue
New Haven, CT 06519

Chief Margaret Ackley
City of New London
5 Governor Winthrop Boulevard
New London, CT 06320

Chief Colin D. Mccormack
Town of New Milford
P.O. Box 419
New Milford, CT 06776

Chief Richard Mulhall
Town of Newington
131 Cedar Street
Newington, CT 06111

Chief Michael Kehoe
Town of Newtown
3 Main Street
Newtown, CT 06470

Chief Matthew L. Canelli
Town of North Branford
P.O. Box 287
North Branford, CT 06471-0287

Chief James dicarlo
Town of North Haven
8 Linsley Street
North Haven, CT 06473

Chief Harry Rilling
Town of Norwalk
One Monroe Street
Norwalk, CT 06854

Chief Louis Fusaro
Town of Norwich
70 Thames Street
Norwich, CT 06360

Chief Michael Spera
Town of Old Saybrook
225 Main Street
P.O. Box 301
Old Saybrook, CT 06475

Chief Robert Gagne
Town of Orange
P.O. Box 617
Orange, CT 06477-0617

Chief Robert Hoffman
Town of Plainfield
210 Norwich Road
Plainfield, CT 06374

Chief Daniel J. Coppinger
Town of Plainville
1 Central Square
Plainville, CT 06062

Chief Karen Krasicky
Town of Plymouth
P.O. Box 34
Plymouth, CT 06786

Chief Rick Hayes
Town of Putnam
189 Church Street
Putnam, CT 06260

Chief Douglas Fuchs
Town of Redding
96 Hill Road
Redding, CT 06260

Chief John Roche
Town of Ridgefield
76 East Ridge Road
Ridgefield, CT 06877

Chief Michael Custer
Town of Rocky Hill
699 Old Main Street
Rocky Hill, CT 06067

Chief Michael E. Metzler
Town of Seymour
11 Franklin Street
Seymour, CT 06483

Chief John Hurliman
Town of Shelton
85 Wheeler Street
Shelton, CT 06484

Chief Peter N. Ingvertsen
Town of Simsbury
933 Hopmeadow Street
Simsbury, CT 06070

Chief John Daly
Town of Southington
69 Lazy Lane
Southington, CT 06489

Chief Gary K. Tyler
Town of South Windsor
151 Sand Hill Road
South Windsor, CT 06074

Chief Brent B. Larrabee
Town of Stamford
805 Bedford Street
Stamford, CT 06901

Chief Darren Stewart
Town of Stonington
173 South Board Street
Stonington, CT 06379

Chief John J. Buturla
Town of Stratford
900 Longbrook Avenue
Stratford, CT 06497

Chief Michael Manzi
Town of Suffield
911 Mountain Road
Suffield, CT 06078

Chief Eugene F. Torrence
Town of Thomaston
PO Box 158, Main Street
Thomaston, CT 06787

Chief Michael Maniago
Town of Torrington
576 Main Street
Torrington, CT 06790

Chief Thomas Kiely
Town of Trumbull
158 Edison Road
Trumbull, CT 06611

Chief James Kenny
Town of Vernon
725 Hartford Turnpike
Vernon, CT 06066

Chief Douglas Dortenzio
Town of Wallingford
135 North Main Street
Wallingford, CT 06492-3709

Chief Michael Gugliotti
Town of Waterbury
255 East Main Street
Waterbury, CT 06702

Chief Murray Pendleton
Town of Waterford
41 Avery Lane
Waterford, CT 06385

Chief John Gavallas
Town of Watertown
195 French Street
Watertown, CT 06795

Chief James Strillacci
Town of West Hartford
103 Raymond Road
West Hartford, CT 06107

Chief Ronald Quagliani
Town of West Haven
200 Saw Mill Rd.
West Haven, CT 06516

Chief John Troxell
Town of Weston
P.O. Box 1182
Weston, CT 06883

Chief Alfred Fiore
Town of Westport
50 Jesup Road
Westport, CT 06880

Chief James Cetran
Town of Wethersfield
250 Silas Deane Highway
Wethersfield, CT 06109

Chief Lisa Maruzo-Bolduc
Town of Willimantic
22 Meadow Street
P.O. Box 5
Willimantic, CT 06226

Chief Michael Lombardo
Town of Wilton
240 Danbury Road
Wilton, CT 06897

Chief Nicholas Guerreiro
Town of Winsted
338 Main Street
Winsted, CT 06098

Chief Kevin C. Searles
Town of Windsor
340 Bloomfield Avenue
Windsor, CT 06095-2796

Chief John T. Suchocki, Jr.
Town of Windsor Locks
4 Volunteer Drive
Windsor Locks, CT 06096

Chief Neil O'Leary
Town of Wolcott
225 Nichols Road
Wolcott, CT 06716

Chief Eugene F. Marcucci
Town of Woodbridge
4 Meeting House Lane
Woodbridge, CT

ANALYSIS OF THE ISSUES PRESENTED BY THE PETITION

A. SCOPE OF OUR ANALYSIS

The Petitioner's question was not precise as to when in the "process" additional information might be required. We therefore take this opportunity to address the information an applicant must provide at various stages of the permit process in order for the issuing authority to make a reliable determination of an applicant's eligibility and suitability for a permit to carry pistols and revolvers outside his place of business or residence.

Accordingly, we address what is required of an applicant upon submission of his application, and what additional information may be requested during the course of the issuing authority's investigation.

B. SUBMISSION OF ORIGINAL APPLICATION

Connecticut has a two-tiered process for the issuing of pistol permits. An applicant makes an initial application to the police chief or where there is no police chief, the first selectman of the town, who are by law required to conduct an investigation concerning his eligibility for a permit and whether he is a "suitable" person to be issued a permit.

Connecticut General Statutes § 29-28(b) provides that

Upon the application of any person having a bona fide residence or place of business within the jurisdiction of [an issuing] ... Authority[1], [the issuing authority] may issue a temporary state permit to such person to carry a pistol or revolver within the state, provided such authority shall find that such applicant intends to make no use of any pistol or revolver which such applicant may be permitted to carry under such permit other than a lawful use and that such person is a suitable person to receive such permit.

[1] An issuing authority is a chief of police where there is an organized police department, or the warden or first selectman of a town where there is no police department. Conn. Gen. Stat. § 29-28.

Upon receipt of a temporary state permit, the commissioner of public safety may issue or deny a permanent state permit. Conn. Gen. Stat. § 28-29a(b).

The Board of Firearms Permit Examiners hears appeals from denials and revocations of pistol permits by issuing authorities. Any person aggrieved by the issuing authority's decision may appeal to the Board. The Board conducts a de novo review of the issuing authority's decision. Unless the Board finds that a denial by the issuing authority was for 'just and proper cause", the Board "shall order such permit or certificate to be issued ...." Conn. Gen. Stat. § 29-32b(b).

The statutes prescribe the manner in which an application is to be processed by the issuing authority. Section 29-28a(a) provides that "[r]equests for temporary state permits under section 29-28 shall be submitted ... On application forms prescribed by the Commissioner of Public Safety." That section further states that "Upon written request by any person for a temporary state permit not on a prescribed application form, or upon request by any person for such application form, the local authority shall supply such forms."

In addition to the application on the form prescribed by the commissioner, the applicant must submit: (1) proof of completion of a course approved by the commissioner in safety and use of pistols and revolvers; Conn. Gen. Stat. § 29-28(b)(1); (2) proof that the applicant is not an alien illegally or unlawfully in the United States; Conn. Gen. Stat. § 29-28(b)(9); (3) proof that he is not less than twenty-one years of age; Conn. Gen. Stat. § 29-28(b)(10); (4) fingerprints for a criminal record check Conn. Gen. Stat. § 29-29(a) and (b); and (5) the fees prescribed by law; Conn. Gen. Stat. § 29-30.

The issuing authority then conducts an investigation to determine whether the applicant is "suitable" within the time frame prescribed by the statute. Conn. Gen. Stat. § 29-28(d). The Board is aware that some police chiefs or first selectmen require applicants to submit additional materials with their application which are not specified in the statute. Specifically, several towns require one or more "letters of reference" to be submitted with the application. Such letters are of little utility in the initial suitability determination inasmuch as they are solicited directly by the applicant from persons presumably friendly to him. Other towns require submission of documents and information far in excess of the statutory requirements, such as credit checks, medical releases, and detailed personal resumes. A careful analysis of the applicable law by this Board reveals no authorization for such requirements contained in the statutes.

Indeed, nothing in the statute authorizes an issuing authority to add to the requirements of the statute or to the form prescribed by the Commissioner of Public Safety at the time a person submits an application for a permit to carry pistols and revolvers. This is clear from the comprehensive list of matters recited in Conn. Gen. Stat. § 29-28(b) which would foreclose eligibility and the detailed and precise manner in which the General Assembly chose to address the nature of the application in Conn. Gen. Stat. § 29-28a(a). This is also clear in light of the Attorney General's 1968 opinion in a closely analogous context, wherein that official advised his Board that:

If the legislature had intended that each municipal police department devise an appropriate application form for the carrying of handgun, it would not have expressly provided that the application forms be prescribed by the Commissioner of State Police. The clear and obvious intent of the General Assembly was to provide a uniform application for statewide use by issuing authorities. The authority to prescribe such a form having been granted to the Commissioner of State Police, a municipal police department may not alter, change or add to the prescribed form no matter how laudable the intent or motive for doing so.

Report of the Attorney General, pp. 141-142. July 9, 1968 (Emphasis added).

"In exercising its judgment as to whether facts fall within the ambit of the term 'just cause,' the board must find that the facts constitute a 'reasonable ground' for the adverse action as opposed to a 'frivolous or incompetent ground'." *Cassella v. Civil Service Commission,* 202 Conn. 28, 37, 519 A.2d 67 (1987). In light of the strong legislative policy favoring "a uniform application for state-wide use by issuing authorities", it is the determination of the Board that the statute does not permit an issuing authority to require submission of additional material at the time an applicant files his application on a form prescribed by the commissioner together with the required statutory fees and proof of (a) completion of a course approved by the commissioner in Safety and use of pistols and revolvers, (b) that the applicant is not an alien illegally or unlawfully in the United States, (c) that he is not less than twenty-one years of age, and (d) fingerprints for a criminal record check. Refusal to submit additional material with the initial application, such as letters of reference, does not, ipso facto, render the applicant unsuitable. Further, such failure to submit this additional material does not relieve an issuing authority of its statutory duty to conduct an investigation into the applicant's suitability and to process the application within the statutory time frame. Accordingly, an applicant's failure to submit these additional materials with the initial application would not constitute "just and proper cause" for denial.

C. REQUESTS FOR ADDITIONAL INFORMATION DURING THE INVESTIGATION

An issuing authority is not a mere rubber stamp. The statutes contemplate a bona fide investigation of an applicant's suitability. The determination of an applicant's suitability by the issuing authority and, if required, by the Board, is necessarily constrained by "General Statutes §§ 29-28 through 29-38 [which] clearly indicate a legislative intent to protect the safety of the general public from individuals whose conduct has shown them to be lacking the essential character or temperament to be entrusted with a weapon." *Dwyer v. Farrell,* 193 Conn. 7, 12-13 (1984). Although Connecticut's firearms licensing laws do not specifically define the terms "suitable" and "unsuitable," the decision in *Smith's Appeal from County Commissioners,* 65 Conn. 135 (1894) affords an appropriate definition:

A person is "suitable" who by reason of his character,-his reputation in the community, his previous conduct as a licensee-is shown to be suited or adapted to the orderly conduct of a business which the law regards as so dangerous to public welfare that its transaction by any other than a carefully selected person duly licensed is made a criminal offense.

While Conn. Gen. Stat. § 29-28(b) provides a list of mandatory disqualifications, the issuing authority and the Board possess discretionary authority to consider other conduct that establishes cause for a finding that the applicant is not a suitable person to carry firearms. *Crane v. Chairman, Board of Firearms Permit Examiners, Unreported Decision,* (Conn. Super., Aug. 25, 1999) (No. CV 980068024S), (Dyer, J).

It therefore follows logically that the issuing authority may require an applicant to provide additional information concerning eligibility or suitability once an issue arises during the course of the investigation carried out in furtherance of the applicant's initial application.

The Superior Court addressed this issue in *Basilicato v. State,* 46 Conn.Supp. 550, 760 A.2d 155 (1999), *affirmed per curiam* 60 Conn. App. 503, 760 A.2d 140 (2000). In that case, the applicant applied to the chief of police of the Town of West Haven pursuant to General Statutes § 29-28 for a pistol permit. In that application, he made mention of the fact that he had been treated for mental or emotional problems and that he had lost time from work resulting from stress, and that he had been disabled from working since October 1, 1991, because of the condition. On May 30, 1996, the officer conducting the investigation of the applicant's suitability requested that the applicant obtain from his stress management counselor a letter indicating that she saw "no problems with the possessing or carrying of a handgun." The plaintiff declined to comply with that request, and the chief of police declined to issue the permit. On appeal to the Board, we determined that the police chief appropriately withheld the permit on the basis of the applicant's failure to furnish him with the requested information. The Board found that the consideration of an applicant's mental and emotional stability is relevant to determine suitability to possess a pistol permit. Our decision was affirmed on appeal to the Superior Court. The Appellate Court affirmed the judgment of the trial court.

Common sense and the interest of public safety affirm that the issuing authority is not confined to issues of mental health in requesting additional information to resolve specific issues uncovered by the investigation or revealed in the application. This Board has consistently refused to issue permits when appellants have submitted incomplete or inaccurate applications because we ourselves rely on the issuing authority's investigation in carrying out our statutory mandate. It is certainly appropriate for issuing authorities to investigate issues concerning an applicant's mental health status, criminal history, pattern of domestic violence, drug or alcohol abuse, extremist conduct, reckless, negligent, or irresponsible conduct, poor judgment, dishonesty, bad character, association with known criminals or disruptive persons, or any other issue which tends to undermine confidence in an applicant's potential for safely carrying firearms outside the confines of his home or business.

Once such issues have been uncovered, either on the face of the application or statutorily required submissions or in the course of the issuing authority's investigation, the issuing authority may require the applicant to submit such information, documents, or other material sufficient to resolve the question of eligibility or suitability.

The statute does not prescribe the form or the time frame in which such additional submissions must be made and the Board declines to do so. Most issues will certainly be resolved informally. We can foresee issues arising at the moment the application is filed based on an applicant's answers to the questions on the required form. The issuing authority may not refuse the application at this point, but may immediately request more specific information at that time. We decline to exalt form over substance in a process which should be flexible enough to accommodate both the public and private interests involved.

When such issues arise and the issuing authority seeks further specific information, failure to provide such information may, by itself, be sufficient to deem an applicant unsuitable;

however such a determination must be made on a case by case basis from all of the facts and circumstances of the case.

IV. CONCLUSION

Unanimously adopted by the Board this 14th day of January, 2010.
BY THE BOARD

/s/
JOSEPH T. CORRADINO
Chairman

/s/
T. WILLIAM KNAPP
Secretary of the Board

ARTHUR C. CARR
M. PETER KUCK
KENNETH V. TRAMADEO
KYLE E. OVERTURF
Members of the Board

COPYRIGHT DISCLAIMER

The question has been raised whether or not the materials created by Assistant Attorney General Stephen Sarnoski are subject to copyright, and whether or not Mr, Sarnoski can grant permission to reproduce his Commentaries and Annotations from the 2015 edition of the *Connecticut Firearms Law Reference Guide.* To answer this question, the author turned to section 51-216a of the Connecticut General Statutes, which says:

> **Sec. 51-216a. (Formerly Sec. 51-16). Commission on Official Legal Publications. Publications. Copyrights.** (a) The Commission on Official Legal Publications shall be an agency of the Judicial Branch and shall be composed of the Chief Justice of the Supreme Court, who shall be chairperson, ex officio; the Chief Court Administrator, ex officio; a judge or former judge of the Supreme Court and a state referee, both of whom shall be appointed by the Chief Justice; the Reporter of Judicial Decisions; and one other employee of the Judicial Branch appointed by the Chief Justice.
>
> (b) The commission shall acquire, publish, distribute and maintain for the benefit of the state a sufficient supply of the official legal publications, which shall consist of: (1) The Connecticut Reports consisting of the reports of cases determined by the Supreme Court as prepared for publication by the Reporter of Judicial Decisions, (2) reports of cases determined by the Appellate Court as prepared for publication by the Reporter of Judicial Decisions, (3) the Connecticut Law Journal, (4) the Connecticut Practice Book and cumulative supplements thereto, and (5) such additional publications pertaining to the state Judicial Branch, the Supreme Court, the Appellate Court, the Superior Court and the practice of law as may be assigned to the commission. The commission may publish, maintain and distribute the official legal publications in available alternative formats. An alternative format includes an electronic format and may be the sole method for the publication, maintenance and distribution of all official legal publications and all archived official legal publications.
>
> (c) The commission shall publish in the Connecticut Law Journal except as they may be incorporated into any revision of the Connecticut Practice Book: (1) Rules adopted by the judges of the Supreme Court, including, but not limited to, the rules adopted by the Supreme Court for the courts of probate, (2) the rules of the Appellate Court, and (3) the rules of the Superior Court.
>
> (d) The commission may publish in the Connecticut Law Journal, or prepare for separate publication and publish, such other documents and information as in its opinion are proper or of sufficient importance to warrant publication.
>
> (e) The commission may establish an electronic bulletin board to provide information to members of the public upon such terms as it deems to be in the best interest of the state.
>
> (f) The commission shall, to the extent it finds it desirable to do so, cause official legal publications to be copyrighted in the name of the Secretary of the State for the benefit of the people of the state.
>
> (g) If printed, all official legal publications published by the commission pursuant to this section shall be printed on paper that meets or exceeds the American National Standards Institute standards for permanent paper, unless such paper is not available.

Previous editions of the *Connecticut Firearms Law Reference Guide* were not produced, printed, or distributed by or through the Commission on Official Legal Publications, nor were they copyrighted by the Commission on Official Legal Publications in the name of the Secretary of the State. It is the editor's and publisher's belief, therefore, that the materials contained in previous editions of the Connecticut Firearms Law Reference Guide are in the public domain, and that Mr. Sarnoski has authority to grant permission (as he has done on two separate occasions) for these materials to be reproduced.

Made in the USA
Monee, IL
04 November 2026

67385774R10164